THIS
IMPERMANENT
EARTH

GEORGIA REVIEW BOOKS

EDITED BY Gerald Maa

THIS IMPERMANENT EARTH

ENVIRONMENTAL
WRITING FROM
The Georgia Review

EDITED BY
Douglas Carlson
AND Soham Patel

THE UNIVERSITY OF
GEORGIA PRESS
ATHENS

© 2021 by the University of Georgia Press
Athens, Georgia 30602
www.ugapress.org
All rights reserved
Designed by Kaelin Chappell Broaddus
Set in 9.5/13.5 Dolly Pro Regular by Kaelin Chappell Broaddus

Most University of Georgia Press titles are
available from popular e-book vendors.

Printed digitally

Library of Congress Control Number: 2021937741

ISBN 9780820360263 (hardback)
ISBN 9780820360270 (paperback)
ISBN 9780820360287 (ebook)

Contents

PART TWO
2000–2017
DOUGLAS
CARLSON
119

THIS
IMPERMANENT
EARTH

DOUGLAS CARLSON

Introduction

John Muir set the course for a century of writing about the environment in *My First Summer in the Sierra* (1911): "When we try to pick out anything by itself, we find it hitched to everything else in the Universe." This awe over the complex and nuanced interconnection within the natural world would soon evolve into accepting the fact that humans are "hitched" as well and then into despairing that we are the species that poses the gravest threat to the more-than-human world and to ourselves.

A half-century after Muir, Rachel Carson also acknowledged the importance of what came to be called the Web of Life when she published the essay "Help Your Child to Wonder" in *Woman's Home Companion* (July 1956). Concurrently, she was researching, writing, and subsequently defending *Silent Spring*, her indictment of indiscriminate pesticide use and the profit-based worldview that engendered such use. Thus environmental writing's "human problem": our presence in the environment as the species most likely to destroy it. Capping two centuries of poor environmental choices and one year after the 2015 Paris Agreement to reduce global heating, Americans elected a government that deliberately set out to eviscerate any regulations established to mitigate climate disaster, instead choosing to exacerbate it to gain wealth and power. Small wonder that the progress of environmental nonfiction in the United States is partly informed by a growing awareness of the damage the American Dream inevitably inflicts on the natural world. Such writing, however, was slow to enter mainstream American literature.

Traditional American nature writing has its sources in New England, where a genteel and quiet subspecies of nonfiction emerged from American Romanticism. Place-based essays by Sarah Fenimore Cooper and Henry David Thoreau, for example, celebrated the natural beauty and satisfying order the authors found in the wilder spaces near their homes while recognizing the growing harm of industrialization. Then, after being partially lost in the national acrimony of

Reconstruction and deliberately buried by the makers of the country's Gilded Age, environmental issues centering on diminished natural beauty gradually regained visibility near the start of the twentieth century through a public conflict that grew out of a recognition of the disastrous results of national greed. That conflict pitted utilitarian conservationists such as Theodore Roosevelt and Gifford Pinchot against preservationists like John Muir and Mary Austin. At the base of the disagreement was not whether endangered land should be rescued but rather to what use the protected land should be put. Generally speaking, Roosevelt's stance—via Pinchot—was anthropocentric: land was to be managed for its best return. Muir wanted his land untouched. Problematic labels aside, however, the end result was a National Parks and Forest system that helped, for the moment, to save the American landscape.

During this time of American romanticism, an intellectual air at home and abroad, charged with new information and ideas, demanded a reappraisal of self-identification. While an innate distrust of the upper class reinforced a popular longing for the pastoral, intellectual forces were at work to disrupt the psychological equilibrium of not only millionaires but also ordinary people. For example, Charles Darwin's *On the Origin of Species* (1859) and Charles Lyell's *Geological Evidences of the Antiquity of Man* (1863) brought mostly unwelcome clarity to a culture well pleased with its material gains and technological advances. Many Americans were discomfited by the idea that they were not made in their god's image on the sixth day of an event a few thousand years prior. And then, as the new century advanced, the once-firm self-image identified with American industrial and business identity was eroded further by Einstein on time and Freud on personality. All knowledge seemed to be in doubt, and in their attempts to situate humans in the more-than-human world, environmental writers were able to draw on this newfound humility.

As with Darwin and Einstein, more recent groundbreakers' impacts will be measured over time more by the general public's understanding and perception of their work than by the work itself. Darwin threatened modern humans' primacy; Freud made them question their own will. Likewise, the nature-writing vanguard had its interpreters. While such nature writers as Joseph Wood Krutch, Loren Eisely, and Aldo Leopold laid the intellectual framework for the environmental ethics to come and Eugene Odum framed the science of ecology, two writers closer to the popular taste—Roger Tory Peterson and Rachel Carson—built connections between natural history and the popular culture of the time.

Peterson, a naturalist by avocation and an artist out of the Art Students League and the National Academy of Design, wrote and painted *A Field Guide to the Birds* (1934), a book whose popularity has persisted across five editions. More important, however, was his concept of the practical field guide. Previously, formal study of the natural world embodied white privilege: academics and wealthy hobbyists. Peterson's *Guide* and its dozens of progeny—his guides to butterflies, wildflowers, seashells, medicinal plants and herbs, venomous animals and poisonous plants—democratized information. In effect, Peterson and the other guide authors gave Americans a personal language to use when they considered the environment. The premise is simple: it is much easier to care about something enough to save it when you know its name.

Rachel Carson was working during the mid-twentieth century as a marine biologist for the Bureau of Fisheries, supplementing her income with writing projects that turned eventually into three highly successful books: *Under the Sea Wind* (1941); *The Sea around Us* (1951), which won the National Book Award in 1952; and *The Edge of the Sea* (1955). These are books of often lyrical prose celebrating the natural beauty of the ocean and praising the elegance of its ecological systems. But it was her awareness of the global accumulation of poisons that prompted her to write *Silent Spring* in 1961 and to defend it against well-organized and -financed attacks from both business and political sectors.

In 1954, the United States tested a hydrogen bomb over Bikini Atoll. The resulting fallout eventually killed more than a dozen fishermen outside the safety zone and sickened others. In 1959, a small sampling of cranberries that had caused tumors in rats accidentally entered the marketplace causing a national uproar. In the intervening five years, public health began to be measured against a larger-than-previous definition of environment, and people started to become concerned over the entirety of their physical living conditions: a causal relationship between smoking and cancer was established; the government entered into controversies over aerial pesticide poisoning; and in St. Louis the cancer-causing isotope strontium-90 was found in dangerous levels in a large sampling of children's teeth, which prompted similar studies and results worldwide that initiated talks about a nuclear test ban treaty. Americans no longer trusted their food, their air, or their government; it was the perfect time for Carson's campaign against the wanton use of pesticides and other chemicals. And on a broader cultural scale, knowledge joined necessity to spark an environmental activism supported by evidence from within ecological systems.

During this time of growing general environmental awareness, however, *The Georgia Review*'s pages, much like those of most literary journals at that time, revealed little reaction to these changes in how popular culture was beginning to perceive the environment. A pattern of American reading emerged at mid-century that favored such European writers as Kafka and Mann and Americans McCullers, Mailer, and Greene. Writing was introspective and character driven: anthropocentric. In Georgia, the *Review*'s editors and nonfiction authors saw the outdoor world primarily in the agrarian and regional way in which its readers saw it. Such titles as "Fishing in Georgia" (Spring 1948), "Pimientos in Georgia" (Spring 1949), "Georgia and the Grape" (Fall 1949), and "Pests of Georgia's Fruits" (Summer 1951) typify the range of interest in the nonhuman world held by what became the best-known intellectual movement of the mid-twentieth-century South: the Southern Agrarians. *The Georgia Review*'s ties with the Agrarian movement were actual as well as elective; founding editor John Donald Wade contributed a piece to the Agrarian manifesto, *Here I Stand*. Agrarian conservationism was farm and leisure oriented: keep the soil productive if possible, hate urban expansion and urban greed, kill wildlife for sport and food. Humans maintained their "dominion over the fishes of the sea, the fowls of the air." The magazine would remain, as Wade put it in 1947, "turning on subjects of special interest to Georgians, and all, as nearly as feasible, written by Georgians or people associated with Georgia."

Gradually, however, the *Review* would pull away from strict regionalism under the four university-based editors who followed Wade. The last of this quartet, Edward Krickel, published *The Georgia Review*'s initial significant move toward environmental awareness with Jerome Bump's "Hopkins, the Humanities, and the Environment" (Summer 1974), a forward-looking study of Gerard Manley Hopkins's poem "Pied Beauty" and related works. Bump calls for literature and the humanities to do the job of contextualizing environmental issues beyond "a linear symbol system, much less simplistic dualisms." Although Bump's entire essay is outside the purview of this collection—it moves quickly beyond environmental issues to focus on Hopkins's oeuvre—an excerpt, which follows this introduction, deserves inclusion for the clarifying work it does in establishing an intellectual basis for the selections that follow.

By the time *The Georgia Review* published its first work of environmental nonfiction, James Kilgo's "Actual Field Conditions" (Summer 1987), popular thinking and trends had unfolded in other venues and on other platforms to enable a robust and growing tradition of essays that attempted to define the relationship between the human and the nonhuman worlds. In the United States, environmental activists borrowed from the energy of the larger antiwar and civil rights movements of the 1960s. Important books carried on Rachel Carson's two-part approach to the natural world: a sense of wonder and beauty combined with an abhorrence of what public policy and private enterprise were doing to the landscape. Edward Abbey's *Desert Solitaire* (1968) comes to mind, as does his teacher Wallace Stegner's 1960 *Wilderness Letter* and *The Quiet Crisis* (1963). The first half of the next decade proved remarkable for its environmental advances: the first Earth Day in 1970 foreshadowed the establishment of the Environmental Protection Agency, the Clean Water Act, the Endangered Species Act, and the

National Environmental Protection Act—a law enacted specifically to protect the rights of natural objects from the federal government. But as promising as the 1970s were, the 1980s were an environmental disaster. Ronald Reagan ("You know, a tree is a tree, how many do you have to look at?") and his interior secretary James Watt ("My responsibility is to follow the Scriptures, which call upon us to occupy the land until Jesus returns. . . . We will mine more, drill more, cut more timber") mounted an attempt to monetize the natural world that was unmatched until the Trump administration.

Meanwhile under Stanley Lindberg, who became the *Review*'s editor in 1977, the magazine began to seek cross-disciplinary nonfiction, which opened the way for the essays in this collection. Present during all these years until his retirement in 2019 and editor in chief for most of them, Stephen Corey didn't intend the magazine to aspire to be *Orion* or *Sierra* but wanted to create another space and some new audiences for writing that had become vital. This collection, then, begins at the confluence of Lindberg and Corey's new *Georgia Review* and the rapid expansion of nature writing. The forms range widely—from natural history to cultural critique, memoir to exposé, conservation ethic to social justice—as do the modes—from traditional assaying to lyric or narrative. And as this collection will show, the breadth of both topic and point of view found in environmental writing would broaden as the twenty-first century began. What began in Roosevelt's day as a longing for a return to earlier, less materialistic times has gradually come to be an examination of elemental causes and conditions. The core of this writing, however, continues to be authors in conversation with an essential, existential task: interpreting the dynamic interdependence of human beings and the natural world, trying to find a way for people to coexist with the earth.

Three environmental-writing features helped to shape *This Impermanent Earth*. When I guest-edited the Spring 1993 issue, the authors we solicited responded with essays within the nature writing tradition—an admixture of culture, natural history, and examination of universal issues. In Spring 2009, Stephen and I edited "Culture and the Environment—A Conversation in Five Essays," which featured invited responses to Scott Russell Sanders's essay "Simplicity and Sanity." The significant editorial undertaking of that issue placed *The Georgia Review* firmly among those journals with a commitment to environmental issues. Stephen and I, with Soham Patel, who joined the staff in 2018, collaborated on an environmental writing feature (Fall 2018) titled "I Am What Is Around Me: Opening Up the Environmental Dialogue." The "opening up" enabled work that joined environmental writing in conversation with issues of social justice and human rights. Finally, with the support of new editor Gerald Maa, Soham and I have assembled a section of solicited works that represent the possibilities and potential for work that resists labels and frames questions in new and complex ways.

Soham and I have offered commentaries preceding each of the sections, but I take responsibility for any missteps or omissions in the book's curation. Space restrictions demanded difficult choices within a literature whose edges continue to expand and shift, an evolution that, we hope, provides a cohesive narrative for the varied work we present here.

PART ONE
1987–2000

SOHAM
PATEL

Environmental writing had a wide readership by the late twentieth century as popular culture began to read it more earnestly and as writers and storytellers began to see how their work required a rigorous attention to the factual terms of their backyards. Around the world, writers such as the Indian environmentalist Vandana Shiva were actively participating in the battle to protect the ecosystem. An important figure in ecofeminism, Shiva embodies the spirit of eco-writing in this period. Her writing often considers how ecological science and ancestral wisdom teaches humans about this planet. In 1993, the Right Livelihood Award Foundation awarded Shiva, the author of more than twenty-five books on the environment, the Alternative Nobel Peace Prize for her interdisciplinary research on science, technology, and environmental policy.

Meanwhile, environmental writers from U.S. mainstream majority culture, especially in the late 1980s and early 1990s, concerned themselves with stewardship, relinquishment, conquering, and conservation. The call to simplicity, however, so often the focus in early environmental writing, while admirable, undermines class struggle within the nation's capitalist structure and too often takes for granted the fact that poor people and people of color in the United States are disproportionately affected by environmental destruction and bad environmental policy. Louise Erdrich's brief piece in the 1993 issue of *The Georgia Review* offers a refreshing perspective from the homogeneous ethos of environmental writing in the magazine up until her inclusion. Erdrich's inquiry into the agency of a being other than herself encourages observation and imitation of the nonhuman participators on the planet with us—in short, she pleads with us to be more like the skunk, to "putter, destinationless, in a serene belligerence—past hunters, past death overhead, past all the death all around."

The essays in this section share restless curiosity as their core, though they come to their investigations from wildly different corners of the natural world. One such case, James Kilgo's "Actual Field Conditions," featured in *The Georgia Review*'s Summer 1987 issue, reflects on birdwatching as a community practice during sojourns Kilgo made studying and illustrating wading bird populations in South Georgia with ornithologists he had befriended. Kilgo urges readers to imagine the mythological view of birds in poetry ("Keats's nightingale, Shelley's skylark, Hopkins' kestrel, and Yeats's swans") and to have the language and knowledge of avian ritual. The wading birds under study in the South Georgia rookery Kilgo frequents are "colonial nesters," "intruders," including one cattle egret "that had made its way across the Atlantic from Africa at the end of the nineteenth century and has since worked its way north to our continent." The North American continent in question, according to Kilgo, is of course lived on by human societies who have, like the birds, taken over sites formerly lived on by others. Scientific ornithological studies after the act of record keeping, of course, then tend toward conservation, then protection, environmental control, and sometimes political policy. Not only do the birds need to not be neglected by the human societies who share their habitats but also the humans, situated in a position to help the birds survive in a dire environment, need to take an active role.

In contrast Kilgo's focus on an aspect of the natural world around us, Robert Finch's essay "Being at Two with Nature" critiques and documents the American canon of nature writing as a practice and way of life. This essay is a reminder that although scientists and poets are radically different in profession, their work requires a similar rigor. "Nature is the source from which our consciousness and identity have sprung," he writes, "—and which still informs them, whether we recognize it or not." Nature writers live outside a lot of conventional structures of critique, which also situate them uniquely to open the world to readers who aren't paying attention to their immediacy. "Being at Two with Nature" questions the moral obligation placed on humans, as privileged species, to protect nonhumans while attempting to parse apart any real difference, if any, between nature writing and environmental writing.

In Spring 1993 *The Georgia Review* published a special issue, *Focus on Nature Writing*, which included essays by Douglas Carlson, Barry Lopez, Jane Brox, Louise Erdrich, Sydney Lea, and Brenden Galvin. As if in answer to Finch's critique, the featured writers drew from many modes: storytelling (recollecting), historical and scientific research, analysis and criticism, and in Galvin's case, building a case for making an ecopoetic paradigm shift within the discourse of nature writing through a careful study of poets like Robert Lowell. In "The Contemporary Poet and the Natural World" (not included in this book), Galvin claims to be "aware of how art serves its maker before it serves any idea or any other person," but he also knows "poetry has to deal with what's outside the mind and body"; thus "knowledge can't be divorced from the natural world." Galvin's essay also aims to complicate binary thinking that would reduce any kind of nature writing simply to "green propaganda" through his methods of exploration.

As Louise Erdrich writes in her 1993 essay "Skunk Dreams," "I may be a woman who has dreamed herself a skunk, or a skunk still dreaming that she is a woman." In such a claim, Erdrich demonstrates how subjectivity is not distinct from place or source. The writers in this section immerse themselves in the natural world as a way of learning more about themselves as part of nature and as practitioners whose act of perception is informed by careful attention. They draw from the traditions of nature writing, memoir, scientific writing, and the lyric to remind us that we are not disinterested or distanced parties in relation to ecological disaster but rather participants and recipients.

JEROME BUMP

From "Hopkins, the Humanities, and the Environment"

The emergence of ecology, Gestalt psychology, and the theories of relativity and indeterminacy in modern physics and quantum theory has revealed that the primary cause of the accelerating destruction of our natural environment is our habitual confusion of certain mental models with reality. In our love affair with technology we forget that multi-dimensional reality cannot always be translated into a linear symbol system, much less simplistic dualisms. Preoccupied with specialization and minute analysis, we have often taken for granted such categorical oppositions as man vs. nature, cause vs. effect, matter vs. energy, organism vs. behavior, and so on. The trouble is that by looking only at the opposite poles of such dualisms we ignore everything in the middle, and fail to recognize the dependency of each pole on the other. Moreover, unable to conceive of opposites as aspects of the same thing, we have no word for the larger unit which contains both opposites. Take the man vs. nature dualism, for instance. The search for a word for the greater whole which includes both man and nature has been intensified by the sudden increase in our capacity to destroy our world since World War II, dramatized by nuclear explosions and the extinction of various species. The result has been the sudden popularity of the term "ecology." Unfortunately, like "God" and other terms used to bridge the gap between the poles of dualisms, "ecology" is often a vague, catch-all concept, and has now been used by so many people to mean so many things that it has already joined our lexicon of polite, meaningless words.

Nevertheless, a conception of the unity of the whole is still badly needed; the idea of an "ecosystem" remains indispensable—a special equilibrium achieved not by the levelling of individual variety but by promoting it, a harmonious unity of contained conflicts, a special interlocking of the self-seeking actions of individual organisms and the communal well-being upon which they are dependent. And the goal of the ecological movement remains as challenging and revolutionary as ever: to replace the dissection of reality, the basic preoccupation of

Western thought in the last few centuries, with an attempt to comprehend multifarious effects simultaneously, to cope intellectually with the complex unity of things, ultimately an attempt to make the ecological concepts of synthesis and homeostasis as dominant in the next century as analysis and progress have been in the last two centuries.

Many in the avant-garde of this new intellectual movement have perceived the necessity of replacing the man-nature dualism with the idea of man as a participating member in the whole community of living species, the subject-object dualism with the idea of mutual interdependency of organism and environment, and the cause vs. effect dualism with the ideas of relativity and mutual implication. Some are also beginning to consider the possibility of rejecting altogether our basic concept of man as isolated brain, with all its corollary dualisms of mind vs. body, thought vs. feeling, adult vs. child, and civilized vs. primitive, and resurrecting the idea of the whole man that the humanities have cultivated for so long. Interdisciplinary thinkers in a variety of fields are re-evaluating the child's vision of unity with nature, the tribal man's sense of the unbroken solidarity of life and his ability to identify with other creatures, the personal sense of historical continuity and the necessity for conservation fostered by the Chinese family system, the Greek medical concept of the harmony of the body, and the possibility of a biological basis for intuition. In the humanities, now that we have begun to see what Albert Schweitzer meant when he said that the great fault of all Western ethics is that they have dealt only with the relations between man and man, we can begin to see some of the dangers inherent in the narcissistic preoccupation with the individual-in-isolation which has increasingly dominated Western art in the last two centuries.

Obviously, as ecology develops as a synthetic discipline, science's counterpart to art, the inclusion of the humanities becomes more necessary. The humanities must also play a greater role in the conservation movement and the solution of immediate environmental crises. As two officers of the Smithsonian, S. Dillon Ripley and Helmut K. Buechener, put it, "the natural scientist will probably have less influence on the evolution of a conceptual environment relevant to today's ecological crisis than the humanist. Man's conceptual environment, not science, will determine, the future of humanity. The humanist has the responsibility of developing our understanding of values with relevance to the central ecological problem of our times."

To meet this responsibility, whether in education, mass media, or environmental research, we must, first, develop a historical perspective. Though historical continuity is the basic philosophy of conservation, ecologists and environmental engineers as well as humanists often lack not only a sense of the genetics of basic ecological ideas but even a sense of the history of past attempts to solve particular problems. Notice, for instance, how the designers of urban freeways have only magnified the worst errors of the railroad builders of the nineteenth century. In general, few have realized that many of the basic ideas of ecology may be traced to Malthus, Lyell, and Darwin, and that the battle for legislation against industrial pollution was begun in England over a century ago. England, for instance, passed a national law against the pollution of rivers almost twenty years before river pollution ever became a serious problem in America.

Moreover, few conservationists realize that the conservation ethic derives from nineteenth-century Romanticism, or that there were many nineteenth-century defenders of the environment in the arts. Some writers on environmental issues mention Dickens' *Hard Times*, of course, and sometimes Ruskin, but I have yet to find anybody who is even aware of the contributions of, say, Gerard Manley Hopkins. Obviously, if his attempt to develop our understanding of ecological values is to be successful, the humanist as well as the scientist must learn how to avoid the mistakes and build on the successes of his predecessors. There is much we can learn today from the efforts of nineteenth-century artists to create a sensitivity to their environment how their efforts assisted the struggles for pollution, conservation, and restoration legislation, to what extent their moral suasion was a replacement for it, where they succeeded, and why they failed.

Because our language controls so much of our response to the world around us, literature is particularly important. Creative literature can make us conscious of the arbitrary limits of language and stretch them to encompass more of experienced reality; it can expose our categorical dualisms as fictions which we have taken literally and replace them with new fictions more congruent with a larger reality. Because poetry, for instance, is such a rich source of relatively small models which represent unity in variety without oversimplifying complexity or levelling individuality, it can be useful in interdisciplinary environmental science. In Paul Ehrenfeld's textbook, *Biological Conservation*, for example, on one page a titration curve for acetic acid is employed to demonstrate the buffer effect, and on the opposite page a thirteen-line poem from Vonnegut's *Cat's Cradle* is quoted to illustrate "Hidden Relationships and Unforeseen Ramifications." This is but one recognition of the fact that in many ways poets have anticipated environmental scientists and have expressed their ideas in more concrete, enduring, and persuasive language. This is particularly true of those few poets who, motivated by what would now be known as "ecological awareness," continually experimented with various literary structures to communicate it.

JAMES KILGO

Actual Field Conditions

As creatures of song and flight, birds suggest
so powerfully the impulses of the mind and
spirit that Adam himself must have made the
connection. Even in ancient mythology and fairy
tale, according to Marie Louise von Franz, birds
stand for "a nearly bodiless entity, an inhabitant
of the air, of the wind sphere, which has always
been associated with the human psyche." Poets
have persisted in the mythological view. Keats's
nightingale, Shelley's skylark, Hopkins' kestrel,
and Yeats's swans all correspond to something
in our nature that refuses to accept mortality
and dreams of the freedom of flying. The major
weakness in this way of seeing, as any ornithologist
will quickly tell you, is its failure to recognize the
behavior of birds under actual field conditions.

When I was a boy there were men in my hometown who were respected for their
knowledge of birds. They were not bird lovers in the usual sense of that term but
farmers and foresters who spoke without self-consciousness about such things
as declines in the redheaded woodpecker population or the rare occurrence in
our area of a painted bunting. I assumed that these were matters of general interest, and I never thought it unusual when my parents called to my attention some
bird that caught their eye.

Once, when we were fishing on the creek below our house, my father suddenly gripped me by the shoulder and whispered, "Look!" He put his hand on the
back of my head and aimed my gaze toward a ferny spot on the far bank. There,
flitting about among the sun-splotched leaves, was a small yellow bird I had

never seen before. "That's a prothonotary warbler," he said. The conjunction of that improbable name with the brilliant flame color of its breast seemed marvelous to me.

The first bird I remember identifying on my own was a black and white warbler. I was ten or eleven years old, sitting one morning on a log near the creek when I spied it in the low canopy overhead. Although I was familiar with the species from an illustration by Louis Agassiz Fuertes in a set of cards I had ordered from Arm and Hammer Soda, I was not prepared for the precision of zebra striping on a bird so tiny. I ran all the way home, excited by a wild conviction that something had been settled.

What had been settled, I understood much later, was my experience of that particular species. The sight of the bird required a response—I had to *do* something about it. A camera would have worked—even a gun, I'm afraid, because I wanted to *have* the bird—but the name alone was enough. Armed only with that, I applied it, ratified the act of seeing, and appropriated the black and white warbler.

Perhaps the obvious way of seizing and holding such moments of delight, especially for one who is able to draw, is by painting the bird. For some reason, that possibility did not occur to me until I was grown. By the time it did, I had devoted several years to avid birding, naming every new species I could find until my fascination with birds was reduced to a mere game of listing, in which the checking off of a species amounts almost to a cancellation of it. As if that weren't bad enough, the game became for me a competition with other such binocular-visioned people.

Then one day on the beach of Sapelo, a barrier island off the coast of Georgia, something happened that changed my way of looking at birds. I was participating in a Christmas bird count with a small group of experienced birders and ornithologists. On Saturday night one of them reported having seen what he thought was a stilt sandpiper on the south end of the beach. Because that species occurs rarely on the South Atlantic coast, most of us needed it for our lists, so early the next morning the whole crowd piled into a couple of vehicles and headed down the strand.

We must have presented quite a spectacle as we climbed from the jeeps—a brigade of birders, wrapped in heavy coats and armed with binoculars, some even with a 'scope and tripod, tramping down an empty winter beach to "get" a sandpiper. According to Roger Tory Peterson's description, the bird is almost indistinguishable at that time of year from dowitchers and lesser yellowlegs. Even the man who had reported seeing it had had trouble confirming identification because it was part of a mixed flock of small shorebirds.

The sun stood before us upon the water, its reflection blazing on the wet sand where the waves reached and retreated, and a cold salt wind was glowing off the ocean. I began to doubt that I would have the patience to sort out a stilt sandpiper from a large flock of sand-colored shorebirds, and I was bothered as well by the legitimacy of my recording it if someone else identified it first.

On the point at the end of the beach hundreds of birds were racing along the edge of the surf; hundreds more lay dozing in the dry sand, their feathers ruffled by the steady wind; and a few big, solitary willets stood here and there like unhappy schoolteachers watching children at recess. I took one look through my binoculars into the glare and realized that I didn't care enough about a stilt sandpiper to bother.

Looking for something to pick up—driftwood, bottle, or shell—I left the crowd and climbed the high dunes. On the other side, between me and the marsh, lay a long, shallow lagoon. It appeared to be connected to the sound at high tide, but now with the ebb it was an isolated pool. A flock of large birds, all of a kind, was wading in it, stretching, preening, and feeding. They were a species I had seen before—marbled godwits—but I grabbed my binoculars anyway and focused on one bird. From that angle the light upon its mottled brown plumage was ideal; I could even detect the flesh-colored base of its recurved bill. Then I lowered the glasses in favor of the whole choreography. There must be fifty of them, I thought, and I marveled at their obedience to the common will that moved them all in one direction, comprehending a dozen little sideshows of casual interaction. I delighted in the repetition of muted color and graceful form, reflected fifty times in blue water.

Suddenly, by a shared impulse the godwits rose crying from the pool and wheeled in an arc above me, their cinnamon wings flashing in the sun. I watched them fly south toward St. Simons, hearing their cries after I could no longer distinguish the flock in the shimmering air.

With the dying away of their cries I sat down on the dune. The other bird watchers were scattered on the beach below me, still focused on the flock of sandpipers, but I was not ready yet to rejoin them. For I had seen godwits rising in the sun—a glory of godwits crying down upon the marshes—and I felt strangely abandoned. I wanted to grab hold of that moment with both hands, before it faded away with the birds, and keep it; and I wanted to tell my friends on the beach about it so they could see it too. If only I could paint it all, I thought—the strong winter light and the birds' insistent cries. I could at least try, I decided, and I would, would paint it in watercolor, bathed in that light, and those who saw it would feel something of the loneliness I had felt.

Not long after the Christmas count on Sapelo I saw the illustrations by Robert Verity Clem for *The Shorebirds of North America*. They represented exactly the kind of thing I wanted to do. For the next year I studied them as well as the work of Fuertes and George Miksch Sutton, sketched hundreds of birds in the field, and often picked up road-kills to learn anatomy and plumage patterns. It was not mere illustration that I sought but a representation of the *experience of seeing* a particular bird in its habitat, as I had seen the black and white warbler that day on the creek or those godwits rising above me in the sun.

The ornithologist who introduced me to the behavior of birds under actual field conditions was a South Georgia farmer named Calvin Hardy, one of the group on the Christmas count. When I met him on the dock, waiting for the boat to Sapelo, I could see right away that he was different from the rest of us. Big and sturdy, as though cut to a larger pattern than most men, he gave the impression that if something broke he could fix it.

I was not surprised to hear that Calvin was a farmer and a forester. In fact, he reminded me of those men whose interest in birds I had noticed when growing up. Before the weekend was over I learned, partly by talking to him but mostly from a mutual friend, that he was also an airplane pilot and a carpenter of better-than-average skill; that he had published papers on herpetology, mammalogy, and ornithology; that he photographed wildflowers, and collected stamps, coins, antique turpentining equipment, and local folklore; and that he lived in an old railroad depot he had moved two miles from its original site after cutting it in half with a chainsaw.

Somehow Calvin and I discovered quickly that each of us had stories the other wanted to hear, so we spent the late night hours of that weekend drinking coffee and talking. By the time we left the island Sunday afternoon, I knew that he, like me, was one of those people who has to do something about birds. Painting, I had just realized, was the thing I would do; Calvin's was science. At that time he was working on the nesting habits of herons and egrets. "Come on down to South Georgia in June," he said, "and we'll go into a rookery."

Most wading birds are colonial nesters. The colony is called a rookery, or by some a heronry. In South Georgia the birds often select lime sink ponds as nesting sites. As long as a colony remains undisturbed the birds will return to it year after year until they eventually fill the capacity of the place; an established rookery may contain six different species of wading birds and as many as two thousand nests. Calvin had been going into the rookeries in his part of the state for several years, mainly for the purpose of determining and monitoring flucuations in the populations of the predominant species—the little blue heron and the cattle egret, the latter an exotic that had made its way across the Atlantic from Africa at the end of the nineteenth century and has since worked its way north to our continent. Though the intruder does not compete for food with native species, Calvin suspected that it was taking over sites formerly held by the little blues.

In May he called to remind me of the invitation. The nesting season would be at its peak in a few weeks, he said; we might find as many as five or six species. I needed no encouragement. The rookery would afford a rare opportunity to photograph and sketch the wading birds in their own bedroom. I could hardly wait.

The morning was already hot when we climbed from the truck and started across a brushy field. Ahead of us stood the woods, quietly shimmering through the heat waves as though nothing remarkable were happening within its shadow. But presently we began to detect a commotion, a murmur of flaps and squawks. As we drew nearer, the trees before us seemed to bloom with white birds. Herons were ascending, reluctantly it appeared, to hover above the canopy, legs a-dangle, and complain at our intrusion. Still nearer, we caught a vague whiff of organic effluvium that grew stronger as we approached the trees.

Beneath the canopy we paused at the edge of what appeared to be not water but a pale-green floor; through it rose a thin forest of tupelo gum, red maple, pond cypress, and pine. The flapping activity of the adult birds receded before us to the far reaches of the rookery, and for a moment I could neither see nor hear young birds. After the clamor that had greeted us, the silence seemed unnatural. I thought of alligators, prehistoric submarines cruising noiselessly beneath the green floor, and I felt some reluctance to enter the rookery. Calvin had not mentioned gators to me, but since we were entering their habitat I thought I might ask.

"I wouldn't worry about them," he said. Then he smiled, "But if you do get tangled up with one, remember now that his belly is the soft part."

His smile was no sure sign that he was kidding—he smiled most of the time—so I checked a bit furtively to see that my Randall skinning knife was still securely fastened on my hip. Then I followed him in.

A thick mat of vegetation, streaked and splashed with chalky excrement, lay upon the surface of the pond. Beneath this the water was a warm chowder. Ten yards out we were waist-deep in it, pushing the surface before us like a buckling rug and releasing smells that engulfed us as we moved.

Calvin was already busy recording data with a pad and a mechanical counter as he moved confidently through the trees. I was dropping behind, still a little conscious of my legs but mainly marveling at the nests—frail platforms, four or five to a tree sometimes, lying in the forks of branches six to eight feet above the water. Looking up from underneath I could see the sky through them, and many of them held clutches of three eggs. By climbing onto the roots of a tree and holding on to the trunk I was able to look into several nests. The eggs were of the palest blue-green, as large as golf balls and oval in form. What astonished me most was the capacity of such slight nests to support their weight.

Many of the nests contained newly hatched chicks, nestled in damp clumps (sometimes around an addled egg), and looking back at me with yellow reptilian eyes. From the number of fledglings standing about on the edges of nests and neighboring branches, I figured that these birds, in their ravenous determination to receive food before their siblings, quickly developed the strong legs that enabled them to climb out of their flimsy quarters. Once out, however, they remained in the immediate vicinity, jostling each other in clumsy sidestep as they awaited the return of their parents with food. Most of the birds we saw were in this stage of development: ineffectual sentinels protesting our presence by gaping and squawking and, in their excitement, sometimes regurgitating or defecating as we passed by or paused to take pictures of them.

Most birds in the fledgling stage are ungainly—hence the tale of the ugly duckling—but few species present a greater contrast between the immature stages and the adult than wading birds. Crowned with ludicrous patches of hairy down, these tailless white creatures seemed badly put together—too much neck, too much leg, and none of it under control. They looked to be in constant danger of toppling from the branches, and occasionally a bird would indeed lose its balance. We saw one hanging upside down, wings fallen open so that the light shone through the membranes, and clutching its perch with the toes of one desperate foot.

I wondered how long the bird could last in that position and how long a gator would take to find it once it had let go. Calvin said he doubted that alligator predation was a significant factor in the mortality of immature birds, though he was sure that the reptiles took an occasional victim as they scavenged the rookery. Just then he pointed out a young bird crawling from the thick gravy at the base of a tree and clambering laboriously up its trunk, using beak, claws, and even wings like some prehistoric creature moving from the amphibian stage through the reptilian to the avian in one heroic action. But I was not moved to admiration. In its mindless determination to survive, the creature seemed hideous to me—but I was hot and filthy, and I had already seen too many birds, too many eggs.

On our way out of the rookery Calvin spied a pair of anhinga chicks perched in their nest about ten feet up and had me stand on his shoulders to photograph them. Their buff down looked as thick as the nap on a baby harp seal, and I had to restrain an impulse to stroke them. After snapping several pictures I lowered the camera to Calvin and embraced the tree to shinny down the trunk. As I glanced over my shoulder at the green surface beneath me, I felt suddenly that I was suspended above the primal generative slime itself, composite of earth, air, fire, and water, secreted from the earth by what Annie Dillard has called "the pressure of fecundity." I clung to the tree, appalled by the terrific energy that digested sticks, eggs, leaves, excrement, even baby birds, and bubbled up a scum of duckweed, releasing in the process a blast of heat and odor. God knows, I thought, what it might produce if it had the time.

"You need some help?" Calvin asked. The question restored my equilibrium. This was after all only a rookery. So I climbed down and followed in his wake toward dry land. As we approached the edge, the adult herons and egrets with a clapping and beating of wings began to reclaim the area we had deserted, young birds commenced to clamor again for food, and the rookery resumed its normal business. Give them a wooded lime-sink pond, I thought, and they will do the rest—these ethereal white creatures—by dropping sticks and laying eggs and regurgitating a mash of protein and defecating thousands of times a day. And the result? New egrets, hundreds of them emerging from the rank miasma to glide like angels upon fields of summer hay or to float upon their individual images in quiet ponds.

Near the edge of the rookery a white egret rose up from a low nest ahead of us and flapped off through the trees. Calvin sensed it was something different, but he resisted a conclusion. In the nest we found a wet, new chick and two eggs, one cracking even as we looked at it. "Snowy egret," he guessed, but the scientist in him required confirmation so we hid and waited for the parent to return.

The most elegant of American wading birds, the snowy is a predominantly coastal species, and we were over a hundred miles inland. Calvin suspected that this might be a nesting record for the interior of the state—he had never found snowies in a rookery before. I shared a little of his excitement, but my thoughts were of a different nature. As wading birds go, the stumpy little cattle egrets we had been observing occupy he lower end of the aesthetic yardstick. Somehow, it seemed to me, that fact had something to do with the evidence we had just seen of the birds' appetite for breeding. I had no trouble envisioning a field of cattle egrets shamelessly engaged in the business of reproduction, but the image of snowy egrets copulating had never before occurred to me.

When the adult returned to the nest we spotted instantly the bright yellow toes on black feet that confirmed Calvin's impression. Grasping a thin branch, the egret seemed to reverse the direction of its wing beats in a frantic effort to balance itself. I couldn't tell which parent this was, but the bird's white flurry in that shadowed place startled me into a vision of a gorgeous male, nuptial plumes a-quiver as he climbed the back of a crouching female and held her neck in his beak.

I didn't give much thought to painting that night. As we sat in front of his house, watching purple martins in the heavy twilight, Calvin interpreted the statistics we had gathered, and his eyes sparkled as he recalled various details of our trip. But my skull was filled with a green stew that sloshed when I lay down to sleep, and my imagination struggled with wet wings to climb out of it. If I were praying to the same God who charged egrets with the procreative urge, I didn't see how I could expect much of an audience.

The next morning Calvin took me up in his Taylorcraft, a flying machine of uncertain vintage that reminded me more of a kite than a airplane. He thought he had discovered the general location of a new rookery in the next county and wanted to see if he could verify it from the air. About ten miles west of town, at fifteen hundred feet, he pointed out a cool green spot on the ground that looked exactly like a mint, dropped down onto the patchwork of fields and woods. "Recognize that?" he asked. White specks, brilliant particles against the dark ground were converging upon the spot and radiating from it in slow, deliberate flights. I felt as though I were looking down through clear water at something going on in another world. The effects of the day before were already beginning to diminish; nothing about the mint-green spot prompted memory of the rookery's reek and clamor. I began to understand the lofty point of view. It was easy up here to ignore rookeries, even to deny the fall of baby birds, and I saw that there might be some chance for the imagination in the clean, cold, blue air.

Then came the hawks. They appeared at first as a dark shape out in front of us. We didn't recognize it immediately, the thing not in flight but falling, and hurtling not away but toward us. Then, for a single instant, we saw clearly two birds in clasped union; for that frozen moment they seemed suspended in the force of their own energy. Almost into the prop, they split apart, one blown past the windshield, the other peeling away below. If I had been standing up, my knees would have buckled.

"What was that?" I shouted above the engine.

"Red-tails, weren't they?"

"I mean, what were they doing?"

"What did it look like?"

"You mean they really do it in the air like that?"

"What do you think?" he asked.

But I couldn't answer. I was so exhilarated by that incredible intersection, thinking was out of the question.

On the ground again, I remembered Walt Whitman's poem about the free fall of copulating eagles: "a swirling mass tight grappling, / In tumbling turning clustering loops, straight downward falling." A single, graphic image of what he calls their dalliance, it risks no statement of meaning, evidently because Whitman thought the image was message enough. I agree with his judgment, but I had made closer contact with the birds I saw. Their attractive force clapped me to them. And though the roar of the plane had interrupted their long tumble and blasted them apart, I continued to fall with them, convinced that the whole green earth below was one damned rookery, its power as strong as gravity.

ROBERT FINCH

Being at Two with Nature

On Cape Cod, where I live, most people still enter their houses through the back door. This is a holdover from the old days when the front door, the formal entrance, was used only rarely—usually by the minister, the sheriff, or the undertaker. These figures were greeted with ceremony and good china, but they were kept in the front parlor and were not expected to stay long. The inhabitants, on the other hand, tended naturally to use the rear entrance, up a dirt path lined with dogs and chickens and the day's wash.

In this respect, at least, the field of nature writing is something like the traditional Cape Cod house. Most of what I would call nature writing is done not by scientists or formally trained naturalists, or even by writers with substantial scientific backgrounds, but by writers who slip in through the back door of the humanities. There have been notable exceptions, of course—Aldo Leopold, Rachel Carson, Loren Eiseley, René Dubos, E.O. Wilson, for example—who had established credentials in the natural sciences before being recognized as literary figures. But most of us are novelists, poets, artists, journalists, actors, philosophers, theologians. We tend to get our grounding in natural history on our own or secondhand, leading somewhat parasitical lives by associating with, and appropriating material and ideas from, professional scientists and naturalists.

My own case is fairly typical. I grew up along the glass-littered, oil-sheened banks of the Passaic River in industrial New Jersey. Until I was twenty-five years old I could not tell a maple from an oak (or imagine why anyone would care to know). I did read *Walden* in high school, not as a "nature book" but, like most adolescents, as a blueprint for making my own life memorable and extraordinary.

In college I took only one elective science course: an introductory class in ecology (this in the days when only scientists used the word *ecology*) taught by the late George C. Clarke, a wonderful old-school marine biologist long associated with the Woods Hole Oceanographic Institute. From that course I remember only two facts, both about wind: that in parts of Texas on a windy day it is possible for a man to expectorate for half a mile; and that the highest wind velocity ever recorded was on Mt. Washington in New Hampshire during the hurricane of 1938, when the anemometer reached a wind velocity of 213 mph—and then was blown off the mountain.

In graduate school I took one other natural-history course, this time in ornithology. I had an instructor who was doing his doctoral dissertation on the feeding habits of vultures in the Caribbean. One day he passed out a reprint of an article he had written on his research methods. It described how he had trapped the birds, massaged their crops to force them to throw up, and then carefully analyzed the vomit—which showed a predominance of coconut, followed by the remains of rodents, insects, and some other vegetable matter. I remember thinking, as an English graduate student, that his methods and results were not all that different from those we were being taught to employ in our own discipline.

These minimal formal experiences with the biological sciences may have had something to do with my eventual gravitation into nature writing, but I doubt it. Instead I seem to have backed into the field through a general love of literature, a desire to be a writer, an early habit of keeping journals, and the gradual discovery that I possessed a strong feeling for place. Only several years after leaving the academic arena did I begin shaping my accumulated bulk of notes and sketches into a form that is generally known as "the nature essay."

Such a hybridized history, like that of so many nature writers, is reflected in the awkward and unhelpful array of binomial name-tags that have been pinned on us. Nature writers are labeled variously as poet-naturalists, natural-history writers, literary naturalists, nature essayists, creative naturalists, and so on. The preponderance of double terms used to describe the genre's practitioners suggests, I believe, some inner dichotomy in the minds of those who use them, some not-quite-comfortable amalgam of the humanities and science. This confusion reaches even to *Walden*, that supreme icon of American nature writing, which has remained something of a wandering orphan on the shelves of most libraries. One might think it could always be found under American Letters, but over the years I have found it shelved with general nature writing, New England regional literature, personal essays, travel, philosophy, economics, science and technology, limnology, even pets (well, Thoreau *did* keep some ants inside for a while . . .).

What is nature writing anyway? Like fall warblers, works of nature writing are not always easy to recognize. From a distance their characteristic outlines may seem distinct, but individual birds tend to be difficult to identify. I suspect that, in addition to *Walden*, most readers would agree to include under the general rubric of nature writing such works as Gilbert White's *The Natural History of Selborne*, Charles Darwin's *Voyage of the Beagle*, John Muir's *My First Summer in the Sierra*,

Mary Austin's *The Land of Little Rain*, Aldo Leopold's *Sand County Almanac*, Loren Eiseley's *The Immense Journey*, Edward Abbey's *Desert Solitaire*, and Barry Lopez' *Arctic Dreams*. But what about Coleridge's *Anima Poetae*, or Mark Twain's *Life on the Mississippi*, or Gerard Manley Hopkins' journals and diaries, or Isak Dinesen's *Out of Africa*, or D.H. Lawrence's *Etruscan Places*, or Norman Maclean's *A River Runs Through It*? And should we mention *Moby-Dick*, *Leaves of Grass*, or the novels of Willa Cather and William Faulkner? Clearly nature writing is not simply a question of subject matter, but of the writer's intent and treatment of that matter.

Consider for a moment those two "facts" about wind I cited at the start of this essay. What they have in common is not just the same environmental vector but a more significant characteristic. In each case scientific information is coupled with a peculiarly human element: wind force defined on one hand by human spit and on the other by man-made machines that are themselves overwhelmed by the very power they are designed to measure. These, I would suggest, are the kinds of "natural facts" that attract nature writers—data or experiences with human meaning attached to them, or on which they can bring some human meaning to bear.

John Steinbeck illustrates this idea in his introduction to *The Log from the Sea of Cortez* (1951), an account of an expedition with his friend, the biologist Ed Ricketts, to study the marine life of the Gulf of California. He also points toward a definition of nature writing by focusing on the crucial distinction between scientific and literary natural history:

> We wanted to see everything our eyes would accommodate, to think what we could, and, out of our seeing and thinking, to build some kind of structure in modeled imitation of the observed reality. We knew that what we would see and record and construct would be warped, as all knowledge patterns are warped, first, by the collective pressure and stream of our time and race, second, by the thrust of our individual personalities. But knowing this, we might not fall into too many holes—we might maintain some balance between our warp and the separate thing, the external reality. The oneness of these two might take its contribution from both. For example: the Mexican sierra has "XVII-15-IX" spines in the dorsal fin. These can easily be counted. But if the sierra strikes hard on the line so that our hands are burned, if the fish sounds and nearly escapes and finally comes in over the rail, his colors pulsing and his tail beating the air, a whole new relational externality has come into being—an entity which is more than the sum of the fish plus the fisherman.

In other words, both scientists and nature writers impose patterns upon their subjects. But it is the nature writer's deliberate intent to include that "relational externality" between self and nature, to filter natural experience through an individual sensibility, that makes the undertaking a literary one.

Yet despite the high literary caliber of such contemporary practitioners as Wallace Stegner, Annie Dillard, Barry Lopez, Peter Matthiessen, John Hay, John Fowles, Edward Hoagland, and John McPhee, many critics still seem uneasy evaluating nature writing as literature. Rather, its authors tend to be judged on such things as their perception and sensitive recording of natural fact ("Her book contains a wealth of observation on the little-understood ecosystems of southern Minnesota"), their defense of endangered species ("An eloquent effort to understand a despised, feared and heavily mythologized beast"), their philosophical and moral stands on current environmental crises ("An important warning towards an uncertain future")—even for their ability to chop wood or survive alone in the desert or build a birch-bark canoe, things most of them are not especially good at. Though token acknowledgment is frequently given to an author's style ("Fleshy, quite often rapt"), nature writers are too seldom recognized for being—as much as any lyric poet or short-story writer—conscious literary craftsmen, shapers of experience.

What sets off nature writing from all other kinds of writing about nature, I think, is that it tries to suggest a relationship with the natural environment that is more than strictly intellectual, biological, cultural, or even ethical—though it pays due attention to these aspects. This is not to denigrate other forms of natural history, especially the basic field research that provides much of the grist for the contemporary nature writers' mills. But nature writers tend to see nature as more than a subject for scientific research or a life-support system for human society which must be managed wisely, more than a source of aesthetic and recreational pleasure or a topic for philosophical speculation, more even than something which has basic "rights" and "values" and which we have a moral obligation to protect and pass on to posterity. Rather, they sense that nature is, at its very heart, an enduring mystery—a mystery, as Henry Beston put it, for which "poetry is as necessary to comprehension as science." They sense a fundamental connection in the physical and biological world not just with human existence but with human identity. They suspect that, despite the urban lives most of us live today, we must look to the sounds and images of unedited natural experience for the true sources of our emotions, our impulses, our longings—even for the very language of imagination itself. In other words, what the nature writer seeks is as whole and immediate and integrated a response to nature as most other writers seek with other human beings, real or fictional.

This is why nature writers, as opposed to environmental writers, tend to have no agenda—no theory to test, no point to prove, no program or plan for salvation to push. Or if they do, as in a book like Farley Mowat's *Never Cry Wolf*, the agenda tends to be subordinated to or eventually overwhelmed by the larger human experience related. This is why, in my mind at least, Rachel Carson's *Silent*

Spring is important as a work of environmental writing, but *The Edge of the Sea* stands as one of the finest books of twentieth-century nature writing.

This is not to say that the propagandist or the moralist does not often exist within the same set of covers with the nature writer. Thoreau himself was no slouch at lecturing the reader, and part of the pleasure of reading a writer like Edward Abbey is being hit full in the face with his unbridled and outrageous Old Testament fury. But at its core, nature writing does not so much seek to express didactic certainty, or even unambiguous meaning, as to find imaginative connection with what D.H. Lawrence called the "circumambient universe"—the plants, animals, and natural forces with which we share existence.

This desire to restore nature to its central place in individual, personal experience can be seen as part of a broader attempt by writers from many fields to bridge the notorious "science/humanities gap," first popularized three decades ago in C.P. Snow's *The Two Cultures* (although the discussion actually goes back at least to the lectures of Thomas Huxley and Matthew Arnold over a century ago). Nature writing in a sense serves as a melting-pot genre where scientists and humanists can meet on congenial terms. Of course, during the golden age of natural-history writing—the later eighteenth and early nineteenth centuries— there was no such gap to be bridged. Pick up a volume from any of the leading naturalists of that era—John or William Bartram, Mark Catesby, Alexander Wilson, John James Audubon, Philip Gosse, Louis Agassiz, Charles Darwin, Thomas Nuttall—and you will find a human sensibility, a full and engaging personality, behind it. Here, for example, is the final paragraph from Darwin's *The Descent of Man* (1859):

> Man may be excused from feeling some pride at having risen, though not through his own exertions, to the very summit of the organic scale; and the fact of his having thus risen, instead of having been aboriginally placed there, may give him hopes for a still higher destiny in the distant future. But we are not here concerned with hopes or fears, only with the truth as far as our reason allows us to discover it. I have given the evidence to the best of my ability; and we must acknowledge, as it seems to me, that man with all his noble qualities, with sympathy which feels for the most debased, with benevolence which extends not only to other men but to the humblest living creatures, with his godlike intellect which has penetrated into the movements and constitution of the solar system—with all these exalted powers—Man still bears in his bodily frame the indelible stamp of his lowly origin.

What unabashed humanity there is in a passage like this!—so full of personal humility, racial hubris, deliberate rhetorical flourishes, compassion, and a sense of the enormity of his subject. One can easily forgive what now seem its faults—

such as its ingrained Victorian sense of progress—because of Darwin's fullness of response to the philosophical as well as the scientific implications of man's evolutionary nature. It is ironic that the man who was responsible for the transformation of the study of modern biological science employed language in his landmark works that today would be "unacceptable" in most scientific papers.

Earlier I suggested that the awkward hybrid terminology that has evolved to describe nature writing implied a more profound and disturbing dichotomy in our contemporary concept of nature. If the underlying intent of the genre is, as I have said, to reintegrate the human personality in its response to nature, then one reason why nature writing has been so difficult to categorize (and why there has been such resistance to its acceptance as genuine literature) may be precisely because it threatens to break down traditional Western categories that we have come to hold dear: the divisions between literature and science, between fiction and nonfiction, and above all, between human culture and nature.

There is now almost universal intellectual acceptance of the premise that humanity is a part of nature. Yet every day, as global ecological crises worsen, we wonder why we have paid little more than lip service to that idea in our individual and communal actions. It is easy enough to point the finger at the vast structure of vested economic and political interests, or at the apathy and sense of helplessness of the individual in the face of overwhelming environmental problems. But I think there is a more fundamental problem in our refusal to internalize what we know to be true. There seems to remain, on a deep emotional level, something in us that does not want the barriers broken down, that resists the notion that we are, in the most literal sense, not only a part but a *product* of physical creation. Nature writing poses problems beyond those of classification or evaluation by touching something extremely basic in the human psyche. The nature writer is not merely exploring the natural world and offering an individual response; he is asserting his, and our, undeniable connection to that world—which is nonhuman, which is otherness, which is *not us*.

We resist this connection in large part because we recognize in the natural a world where human moral structures and value systems do not apply, at least as we usually apply them. It is this sense of an unbridgeable gap—between ourselves and a natural order which seems to fly in the face of human sensibilities—that leads most of us to attempt to view nature with scientific detachment, to imbue it with human values, or simply to avoid it. Yet it is this same simultaneous gap/connection between the human and natural world that nature writers both delight in and recoil from. The best are honest enough to record and explore both responses. At one place in *Pilgrim at Tinker Creek* Annie Dillard can say, "The great hurrah about wild animals is that they exist at all." In another, after watching a praying mantis devour its mate during the act of copulation, she can protest that "The universe that suckled us is a monster that does not care if we live or die . . . we can only try to outwit it at every turn to save our skins."

The naturalist imagination always makes the basic assumption, first deliberately tested by Thoreau, that nature (or the nonhuman environment) has something fundamentally important to teach us about ourselves as human beings—not because of its scientific or poetic potential, not as anything that we can directly use, but precisely because we have fundamental connections to it. Nature is the source from which our consciousness and identity have sprung— and which still informs them, whether we recognize it or not.

John Hay, one of our finest contemporary nature writers, put the intent of much nature writing in a nutshell when he wrote, "One ought to be able to say, Here is a life not mine, I am enriched." This, I think, expresses the essential task of nature writers. Nature is a continual challenge to our very image of ourselves, to all we have created and set apart from it. Our instinct is to hide from nature by covering it up with our works or our words, to control it with our simplistic technology or our narrow ideas, to cut it down to our size—which, as Hay says elsewhere, may be making too little of too much. The nature writer's job is not to limit or encompass nature, not even necessarily to explain or interpret it, but to show it to us in all its scope: its beauty and repulsiveness, its sociability and its utter alienness, its nurturing and its destructive elements, its immeasurable providence and (more terrifying than any malice) its indifference to human aspirations—and in so doing to extend our own humanity.

But this, after all, has always been the job of artists everywhere: to make us see in new ways, to make us comfortable with the uncomfortable and uncomfortable with the comfortable, familiar with the unfamiliar and unfamiliar with the familiar, responsive to what we have ignored and skeptical—or at least questioning—of what we have loved without examination. This is at once the challenge, the risk, and at times the great reward of the nature writer. For he is always putting his human values on the line, always placing himself and his viewpoint at the center of the universe (though aware of the immense folly of doing so), and then waiting with glad suspense, open-eyed, with pencil or word processor in hand, to see which universal force—an earthquake or an ant—will be the next one to knock him right back on his assumptions.

GARY PAUL NABHAN

Hummingbirds and Human Aggressions

A View from the High Tanks

I

This is not exactly what I'd call a resort, nor have I come here for sport. Instead, I've pulled into a pit stop on the devil's highway, in February 1991, for a reckoning of sorts. I've come to see if anything grows in the tank tracks scarring the desert floor, to watch creatures battling for riches in patches along dry washes, and to reflect upon human aggression.

My camp in Arizona's Stinking Hot Desert is more than twenty-five miles away from the nearest permanent human habitation, but less than four from a stretch of international border. That stretch, among the hottest on earth, has pulled me into its camps six winters over the last sixteen. This year differs in a subtle manner; I feel a tension carried in the atmosphere which I have failed to observe before. I sense this weight in the air is somehow balanced by the war in Kuwait. I am not sure, however, whether I am the one bringing this tension along, or whether it is endemic to this land of little rain but remained hidden from me in the past.

The origins of this tension have become my consuming passion. Like a lab scientist peering through a microscope to identify some debilitating disease, I've fixed on a global issue through concentrating my attention on this desert microcosm. I hope to discover a morality that is not an abstraction, one that emerges out of the local ecology, and that I can adhere to in this place. This morality must address a fundamental issue, "Are human societies fatally stuck in a genetic script of aggression against one another, whether or not such behavior is now adaptive?"

With every step I take around camp, I seek clues. I find myself kicking up bones, grave markers, ammunition shells, historic warheads, and missile debris. At night, I glimpse vapor trails of various nomadic tribes, coming in for a little water; the cliffs echo with the calls of owls, these hooting souls reminding me of their presence.

Maybe I can echo-locate myself for you. I'm below an ancient watering spot along the Camino del Diablo, where over four hundred deaths have been recorded during the last century and a half. Some of these wayfarers died of thirst, some from broken dreams, some from ambush. Here, it is not hard to imagine hunters in pursuit, and the hunted in hiding or in flight. Over millennia, various tribes have converged here as their migration routes intersected. They bartered, haggled, or battled over scarce resources, and they shifted the boundary lines of their territories. My camp below High Tanks is loaded with the dispirited bodies of these past encounters, for the historic cemetery and much of the prehistoric archaeology once evident here have been bulldozed and tank-trampled by more recent military maneuvers.

I should explain, by the way, that I speak of two sorts of tanks. The latter are those of the U.S. Marines, armed and armored all-terrain vehicles. The former, the High Tanks, are usually called *Tinajas Altas*, as they were named in Spanish prior to the battle of the Alamo, when they were still part of Mexico. The High Tanks form a series of nine plunge pools, waterholes no bigger than bathtubs, naturally carved into the bedrock of a shady drainage that cascades five hundred feet down an abrupt granitic ridge.

Such cascades are seldom covered by waterfalls here in southwestern Arizona, where precipitation is so variable from year to year that all averages and ranges have lost their currency. Rain may fail twenty-six months at a time, but bombs fall out of the sky quite frequently, because the tanks lie in a bombing range jointly administered by the Marine Corps Air Station in Yuma and a Bureau of Land Management office in more distant Phoenix. The area is often closed to "public access" during periods of bombing exercises, tank maneuvers, and mock battles. Here, in the late 1970's, the U.S. military reputedly prepared for the ill-fated helicopter raid into Iran's arid turf to free American hostages, and more recently it prepped for Operation Desert Storm.

I ponder that operation and my own genetic history as an Arab-American. A week before missiles were exchanged across the Saudi Arabia-Kuwait border, a Middle Eastern geographer sent me a few pages from Sir Arnold Wilson's 1928 history, *The Persian Gulf*. I was simultaneously intrigued and appalled to read how, eleven centuries ago, a state of anarchy prevailed from Oman to Basra. Taking advantage of the general chaos, Muhammad bin Nur wrested control of the region: "He cut off the hands and ears, and scooped out the eyes of the nobles, inflicted unheard-of outrages upon the inhabitants, destroyed the watercourses, burnt the books, and utterly destroyed the country." Nur's tyranny was met with "the vengeance of an infuriated people," who disposed of his deputies but then went through seven Imams of their own in less than thirty years. The area continued to be fraught with "intestine quarrels," Wilson tells us; then, "about the middle of the twelfth century, the Nabhan tribe acquired the ascendancy and ruled over the greater part of the interior of the country until the reestablishment of the Imamate in A.D. 1429; this tribe, however, continued to exercise considerable influence for quite two centuries longer . . . until . . . finally suppressed."[1]

Stunned, I learned how my own Nabhan kinsmen fought off Persian invaders, skirmished with a petty sheik from Hormuz, and then dealt with the dread Mongols who, at one time, held nearly all of Asia Minor. During this epoch, a few lasting monuments were introduced: underground *qanat* waterwork technologies, stone dams, arid-adapted crops, and Persian-influenced temples. To be sure, the long chronicle of bloodletting, upheaval, and desert destruction dwarfs these material accomplishments. My paternal ancestors had no doubt been as absorbed in the warring, the warding of territory, and the hoarding of resources as any of them. Do genes for pugnaciousness lie latent within me? How much of the same bellicosity can be found in the history of Everyman?

I ask these questions to the desert, not rhetorically but literally: to the desert that is an open book waiting to be read, the desert that so casually pulls up its shirt, like Lyndon Johnson, to show us its scars. And I ask these questions to the Sonoran Desert in particular—but because the Sonoran is hitched to every other desert in some essential way, the answer I hear has bearing on the Persian Gulf.

II

The sound of divebombing jars me from my slumber. Some hummingbirds call this place home, others migrate through it, but they all fight tenaciously for its resources. I hear metallic shrieks and zings—the latter not unlike the sound of glancing bullets—as they dive or chase one another. I try to roll over and cover my ears, but the high-pitched chittering has penetrated the tent walls. I must get up, go out, and face the music.

The morning sun has not yet come over the Cabeza Prieta range across the valley from us, but the fighting began well before daylight. I am camped in a wash that is a haven for hummingbirds, but to arrive here they crossed a veritable hell, virtually devoid of the nectar and insect foods which their hyperactive metabolisms require. For miles in any direction, the surrounding desert flats and rocky slopes have little to offer the migrants of late winter. However, along a couple hundred yards of superficially dry watercourse leading down from the *tinajas* into the desert valley, the shrubbery is unusually dense. The native bushes form nearly impenetrable hedges of foliage along the banks of the wash, and some of these verdant walls look, at first glance, to be splattered with blood. But the color in fact is supplied by thousands of crimson, floral tubes of *chuparosa* for which the shining warriors battle.

Chuparosa simply means "rose-sucker" or "hummingbird" in Spanish. I am speaking of flowers so custom-fit for pollination by hummingbirds that they bear the bird's name wherever they grow. The chuparosa flower is elongate for hummingbird bills and tongues, a chalice filled to the brim with nectar each dawn. The bushes bloom through late winter in frost-free zones, tiding the birds over until the coming of spring stimulates other plants to blossom. Their bright color can attract hummingbirds from some distance away. In turn, the winged creatures transport the "sperm of floral sex" from one bush to the next, ensuring crosspollination. The birds' iridescent heads become discolored by the thousands of pollen grains plastered onto them as they probe the flowers, hovering at their entranceways.

As I marvel over the perfect fit between hummer and blossom, another hummer comes along—and a high-speed chase begins. The Rufous Hummingbird and Costa's Hummingbird dogfight over the flower that is seemingly suited to fit both their needs, while I wonder how their belligerence is viewed by the Bambi Bunch, those who see all animals as cute, cuddly, or constantly in balance and at peace. In the blazing sun of a Tinajas Altas morning, I take a hard look at the desert, its creatures and flowers, trying to keep my own rose-colored glasses from tainting the picture, from stereotyping as nature films and glossy magazine features so often do. I concede that Nature behaves unlike model members of either the Tooth-and-Claw Hunting Club or the Benevolent Sorority of Nurturing Networkers. Nature, to my knowledge, has not recognized that adherence to any anthropomorphic construct is a requisite for existence. I try to put such filters aside, wanting to read the desert's own patterning without superimposing others upon it.

So I walk up and down the wash looking for hummingbirds, soon catching a flurry of avian activity in a dense patch of chuparosa bushes. I go and sit upslope between two battlefields, and not far away from a third chuparosa. At one, a male Costa's is perching on a mesquite branch overlooking a mound of flowers. He darts out to hover in front of a blossom or two and sucks up their nectar. Then, he suddenly turns to chase away another small bird. I watch as he whips away after another Costa's male or possibly a Black-chinned. Minutes later, he chases an Anna's that ventures too close to his treasure. Although Costa's adults are somewhat smaller than these other species, they are roughriders, well adapted to such desert conditions. It is not surprising that they are the most abundant warriors in this wash.

I guess they must already be nesting and mating here. Down the wash a little way, I spot the purple throat (characteristic of Costa's) on a bizarre dancer; he is flying a huge U-shape, an arc perhaps sixty to eighty feet from tip to tip. He hovers at the end of the arc, high up, then swoops down to the ground with a high-pitched buzz; soon, he begins again, tracing the same arching pathway. From my vantage point, I can't see a female at the base of his courtship loop, but suspect that this aerial ballet is not being done to flatter *me*.

In the next patch over, I'm having trouble telling who has been holding the territory most of the time. Whenever I can identify the actors in a Painted Desert drama, a Rufous male has the upper hand over a Costa's.

Rufous Hummingbirds do not nest here; they migrate up through California when the ocotillo blooming begins, and some continue as far as Alaska. The wandlike ocotillos are spread widely over the rocky ridges and flats of the Sonoran and Mojave deserts. Their populations burst from bud sequentially—south to north—providing migrants with a bridge extending northward. Sometimes, when cold winter weather has postponed ocotillo flowering several weeks, the hummers try to migrate anyway—in advance of peak flowering. Ocotillo fruit in these years are left with low reproductive success when their pollinators miss their date.

The ocotillo-flowering fest is an event that will begin here in another week or so. In most years, I recall, migrants such as Rufous arrive in late February just prior to the opening. They pack into the chuparosa patches already occupied by Costa's and Anna's, adding to the territorial tension. Physiologist William Calder, who discovered a remarkable lifelong fidelity of hummingbirds to their nesting sites, has also observed Rufous individuals allegiant to particular stops along their normal migration route. Even though Rufous do not nest at Tinajas Altas as do Costa's and Anna's, their stake in this place is more than a one-shot deal. Unlike certain birds that become territorial only around courtship, breeding, and nesting, Rufous Hummingbirds even lay claim to sets of resources en route to their breeding ground. Accordingly, they fight tenaciously to keep other hummers out in the cold.[2]

This fact struck me as curious, for I had supposed that birds become territorial only when needing to exclude other males of their own species from access to potential mates, or to guard enough food to raise a brood. Melees between migrants didn't make sense at first. I wove my way down the wash, wondering about this seeming incongruity. I then recalled that a mentor of mine, avian biologist David Lyon—who had introduced me to the subversive science of ecology two decades before—probed this very problem three hundred miles to the east of Tinajas Altas, in the Chiricahuas[3]

When I contacted Lyon later on, he responded to my questions on hummingbird behavior with the fine particularism that characterizes the best of ecologists: "Where *were* you?" he asked. "There are great differences in territoriality in the winter depending upon the area. But all of these little rascals are opportunistic and will set up territories any time of the year if rewards are sufficient."

If rewards are sufficient. Lyon views the driving force of hummingbird territoriality as the defense of dense caches of food during times of the year when there are few alternative energy resources. Because hummers must consume close to half their weight in sugar each day to maintain normal activities, finding a concentrated source of food for their fifty to sixty meals per day is a palpable problem. Territories at the Tinajas, then, should be most pronounced when chuparosa nectar production is sufficiently high to make the exclusion of other birds worth the price of the energy expended in defense. Imagine a chuparosa patch oil field thick with wells, in a country with few other energy resources developed. That's where the troops will hover.

I had a chance to explore Lyon's notion a month later when I returned to my camp, not long after the peak of ocotillo flowering on the surrounding flats. The wash so aggressively and noisily guarded in early March was quiet as a reading room in April. There were still hummers around, but no frenzy of flowering attracted them as before. Most of the resident birds had dispersed after nesting to draw upon the widely scattered ocotillo blossoms that remained. The migrants had moved on, so the number of competitors for any single patch of flowers was low. Territorial shows, for the most part, were canceled.

Lyon himself had tied the story down another way. He verified that territoriality among different species of hummers was truly adaptive, and not simply a misdirected means of venting innate aggression on other species that a male has mistakenly identified as competing for his potential partners. For his test, Lyon enticed a Blue-throated Hummingbird to establish a territory in an area circumscribed by ten sugar-filled feeders, two placed in the center of the area and eight in a circle on the periphery. Over the following period, he held constant the amount of sucrose available to the bird, but once a day he moved the eight on the periphery farther out from the midpoint, enlarging the area over which the sugar sources were distributed.

Lyon was not surprised when the Blue-throated male took to chasing other hummers out of the artificial territory, regardless of the area it covered. In fact, this male at first spent twice as much time in dogfights around the hummingbird feeders as males typically spend defending natural patches of flowers. The trouble came as the feeders were spread over a larger area. The Blue-throated initially attempted to defend the expanded arena, but the number of competitors entering it increased to two-and-a-half times what they were in the original small territory. In the smaller arena, the territorial male chased after the majority of all hummers trespassing into his turf, irrespective of their species identity. When the sugar was set out over the largest area, he was forced to become more selective in his combat; he needed more time to pursue competitors across the longer distances between feeders, and more time flying to reach the various feeders to refuel himself.

The Blue-throated male shifted his strategy. Rather than wearing himself out with incessant jousting, he opted for adaptability. He had tolerated the presence of females of his kind all along, but now he also permitted Black-chinneds to forage on the periphery. Although they outnumbered the other hummers at this time, Black-chinneds were small and therefore the easiest competitor to expel when resources became scarce. Magnificent Hummingbirds, another species slightly larger than Blue-throateds, posed more of a threat. And yet, by afternoon, most of the Magnificents in the oversized territory were tolerated as well.

At last, defense against all comers became tenuous. A few competing Blue-throated males were allowed to feed without being ejected. Still, whenever other Blue-throated males were chased, they were pursued a greater distance than that flown to repel other species. If another bird was seen as a competitor for *both* food and sex, the aggressive tendency of territorial males toward him remained in place.

Place per se is not what the birds are defending. They are after a finite amount of nectar, pollen, and bugs required to stay alive and to pass on their genes. If they can glean those foods without much territorial pyrotechnics, they will do so, whether from a small area or a large one.

Their lives cost something, as do ours. On a late winter day, an Anna's Hummingbird must spend one minute out of every nine feeding in order to fuel its metabolism. Its hovering and flying demand ten times the calories per ounce of flesh that people need when running at full clip. If you give a hummer a feeder full of "junk food," it will reduce its foraging effort to a tenth of what it would be otherwise. Nonetheless, a male does not fill up all this newly found "leisure time" with warfare. Even when you give him a territory literally dripping with sticky-sweet sucrose water, his foraging efficiency increases tenfold while his time pestering intruders only doubles.

Put in terms of an ecological maxim, a male hummer will defend a patch of riches only to the extent that it is truly "adaptive" to do so. When battling becomes too costly relative to the food security it brings, he will relax what many observers have assumed to be unrelenting, genetically determined hostility. Here is where the genetic determinists (and fatalists) have led us astray: they claim it is our "animal nature" to be aggressive, yet even animals stereotyped as interminably warlike can suspend their territorial behavior. They opt for peace whenever their essential needs are met, or when the cost of territorial behavior becomes too high. And as ornithologist Amadeo Rea has pointed out to me, "hummingbird fighting, warfare, etc., are not really homologous to human activities of the same name. How many dead hummers do you find in the chuparosa patch? How many bloodied, maimed victims? Their fighting . . . is probably only to exclude, not destroy, a rival male."[4]

The Aztecs called the hummingbird *huitzitzil*, "shining one with (a weapon like) a cactus spine." Yet for all its feistiness, the hummingbird does not embody the incessant irascibility attributed to it by certain historic and modern observers. Do such ascriptions actually tell us more about the Aztecs—or the sociobiologists—than they do about the bird itself? If human warfare is not homologous to that found in other animal species, what is its derivation? Is it somehow peculiar to the genes of Homo sapiens, or is it false to claim fatalistically that human aggression is genetically determined? I go back into the desert to answer these questions, a colorblind botanist seeking clues that those with normal vision may not be able to detect. And I turn my vision from the hummingbirds—most of which have taken flight by this time—to the human being, whose tracks are still evident all around me.

III

Now it is April. I'm up above the desert floor on the ridge overlooking the High Tanks. Last night, I tucked my sleeping bag into a rock shelter, a cave-of-sorts shared with an old friend and a few packrats. We had hoped to see desert bighorn come in for water. This niche in the granite formerly kept O'odham hunters out of sight until they were ready to jump the wild rams and ewes trapped in the canyon. I dream of seeing sheep approach, and I imagine myself a primitive hunter from centuries past, hot in the pursuit of big game.

Suddenly, I am jogged from my reverie by the realization that we are being pursued. My friend Susan has noticed that an armored vehicle has lumbered up out of a wash, heading straight toward our parked pickup truck on the desert floor below us.

We watch, silent, hidden in the rocks, as the tanklike all-terrain vehicle stops fifty yards away from our truck. Its passengers do not immediately get out to breathe the fresh morning air. We wait for the doors to open. More than a minute passes.

Simultaneously, all the doors swing open and six soldiers land on the ground, automatic rifles in hand, spreading out. They slowly stalk the truck, fingers ready on the triggers. Forming a semicircle ten feet out from the back and sides of the truck, weapons aimed at all openings, the men look ready to move in for the kill.

"Campers!" I yell, immediately regretting it. In the folk taxonomy of the military, the word "campers" does not necessarily conjure up a contradistinction to "drugrunners," "wetbacks," or "Arab undercover agents." It does not bring the same sigh of relief that "garter snake" brings, when the other choice might be "sidewinder." Half the armed men now point their weapons toward the wash from which they sense my yell was emerging. I wince, remembering another time on the Camino del Diablo when a border guard held me at gunpoint, my hands behind my back, belly to the ground, for a half hour of questioning. He had been sure that I was a drug smuggler, unconvinced that anyone who arrived on his borderline beat at dawn was there merely to watch birds. From that distasteful experience, I knew that I had to assure the boys below that they were not stalking aliens from another planet or continent.

"Campers! It's okay! It's okay!" I yell again, waving my Panama hat back and forth, in case they needed a moving target. The echoes must have confused them, as they have confused me when I have tried to locate a calling owl while standing near its position below the cliffs. Then, one of the GI's spots my movement, raises field glasses to his eyes, and gives Susan and me a quick once-over. Another lowers his rifle, and raises his binoculars as well. There is some talking, largely below earshot, all beyond our comprehension. They all release their fingers from their triggers and sulk back to the armored vehicle. Another minute passes, and they are gone.

The season of heightened hummingbird aggression has passed, but my preoccupation with human aggression is bursting its buds. The military visitors to Tinajas Altas departed silently, without incident. Still, that did not leave me much solace. As Susan and I descend into camp and return to the truck, the air there is choked with a sense of aggrievance. It is perhaps like the feeling of violation that one feels for months after one's house has been robbed; physical violence may have been avoided, but any measure of psychological peace has been shattered.

At the same time, I feel foolish for expecting human presence in a place such as the High Tanks to have any smackings of tranquility. As my mind rolls over just a few of the incidents that have been staged here over the years, I realize that there are few desert routes in the world that have been soaked in as much blood as has the Camino del Diablo. I remember how Teddy Roosevelt's son Kermit described Tinajas Altas and its desperados during a hunting trip in the August heat of 1910:

> This is a grim land, and death dogs the footsteps of those who cross it. Most of the dead men [buried below the Tanks] were Mexicans who had struggled across the desert only to find the tanks dry. Each lay where he fell, until, sooner or later, some other traveller found him and scooped out for him a shallow grave, and on it laid a pile of rocks in the shape of a rude cross. Forty-six unfortunates perished here at one time of thirst. They were making their way across the deserts to the United States, and were in the last stages of exhaustion for lack of water when they reached these tanks. But a Mexican outlaw named Blanco reached the tanks ahead of them and bailed out the water, after carefully laying in a store for himself not far away. By this cache he waited until he felt sure that his victims were dead; he then returned to the tanks, gathered the possessions of the dead, and safely made his escape.[5]

Add to the human corpses at least twice as many livestock carcasses, and you've arrived at a paradise-and-lunch for vultures, were it not for the long wait between courses. When carrion feeders were not enticed to dine in such an out-of-the-way place, the flesh slowly sizzled to beef-jerky consistency on the skillet-like desert pavement. I've measured temperatures of 170 degrees at ground level near here, on a summer day that was not particularly hot. In 1861, when New York mining engineer Raphael Pumpelly rode the Camino during the period of peak heat, he wondered if he had stepped beyond the familiar into another world. The following is from his *Across America and Asia*, published in 1870:

> We were approaching the Tinajas Altas, the only spot where, for a distance of 120 miles, water might at times he found. It was a brilliant moonlit night. On our left rose a lofty sierra, its fantastic sculpturing weird even in the moonlight. Suddenly we saw strange forms indefinable in the distance. As we came nearer our horses became uneasy, and we saw before us animals standing on the side of, and facing the trail. It was a long avenue between rows of mummified cattle, horses and sheep.[6]

Pumpelly's handwritten journal, not published until 1918, gives the incident in more detail:

> The pack animals bolted and Poston and I rode through with difficulty. Ten or twelve years before, during the time when meat was worth in California almost its weight in gold dust, it paid to take the risk of losing on this desert nearly all of the herd, if a few survived. If no water was found at the Tinajas, most of all of the

animals and some of the men would die. In the intensely dry and pure air there was no decomposition. All the dead simply became mummies. The weird avenue had been made by some travelers with a sense of humor and fertile imagination which had not been deadened by thirst. . . .[7]

A thirst of another sort drove miners and buckaroos across the desert, and moved Blanco the Bandito to empty all the water out of the plunge pools: greed. Life did not matter as much as money or material possessions. Those who rode down the Camino del Diablo did not care about the places they were passing through or the life that they might encounter along the way. Some of the native O'odham, first recorded in residence at Tinajas Altas in 1699, had adopted the same attitude by the midnineteenth century. They had made a pastime out of robbing, and infrequently killing, Forty-Niners en route to California.

Such conduct disturbed their neighbor Tom Childs, the first white man to marry into the Sand People or Hia-Ced O'odham. Tom finally asked one of the Indian bandits, José Augustin, "Why did you kill the Camino travelers?"—and Augustin responded with matter-of-fact brevity: "For their sugar, tobacco, and coffee."[8]

This quip must have struck Childs as anomalous, for the O'odham—including the Sand People—have been known for a century and a half as "the Peaceful People." In anthropologist Ashley Montagu's global search for cultural models of nonaggressive behavior, the historic O'odham were included among the two dozen societies least prone to violence.

Despite recent rises in family violence where substance abuse has affected them, the O'odham people as a whole can still be characterized as one of pacific temperament. I have had the good fortune to have worked, eaten, and slept in the homes of several O'odham families over the last sixteen years, and I have been moved by their peaceable nature: a humility and a live-and-let-live commitment to conflict evasion underscore most of their cross-cultural interactions with neighbors and visitors. The historic literature on the "Pima, Desert Papago, and Sand Papago," as they were formerly called, reiterates an O'odham avoidance of violence.

During World War II, with the support of their elders, the young men of an entire village refused to be inducted into the military. Other O'odham, of course, have dutifully participated in the Armed Services rather than raise a ruckus, the best known being the Pima Indian hero at Iwo Jima, Ira Hayes. Like Hayes, however, many came back from the service profoundly disturbed by what they had participated in, and some died from the alcohol or drugs taken to deal with the cultural collisions. Anthropologist Ruth Underhill has argued that for the traditional O'odham, "War . . . was not an occasion for prestige as with the Plains tribes nor of booty as with the Apache. It was a disagreeable necessity. The enemy . . . or anything that had touched him, was taboo. Therefore all booty was burned and the man who had killed an enemy or who had been wounded by him had to go through a long ordeal of purification."[9]

These words are echoed by those of ethnohistorians Clifford B. Kroeber and Bernard L. Fontana, who worked together for three decades on the major work—*Massacre on the Gila*—concerning intertribal warfare among Southwest Indians: "While they were perfectly capable of taking the offensive, Pimas and Papagos [O'odham] seemed to have done so only when revenge was called for or as a counter-offensive to protect lives and property. There is little to suggest that northern Pimans ever made raids for the sole purpose of obtaining booty. . . . Neither does it appear that northern Pimans engaged in ritualized formal battles with their Apache and Yavapai enemies [after] 1698."[10]

Indeed, the first O'odham raids on Camino del Diablo travelers may have been in response to finding a year's supply of water consumed by cattle, horses, and journeymen during a single day's stopover. When Padre Kino came into the area around 1700, his livestock drank dry one tinaja after another. In response, the able-bodied O'odham men did not immediately fight, but fled instead, leaving only the smallest children and infirm elders to be baptized by the Jesuit father. It was not until Anglos and Mexicans began draining the plunge tanks of the Camino with frequency—during the California Gold Rush—that the O'odham sought to discourage travelers along the route.

Like the !Kung Bushmen of the Kalahari and Australian aborigines of the Red Centre, the O'odham of the Sonoran Desert developed traditions which put a damper on aggressive behavior, and a premium on cooperation. *In Anger: The Misunderstood Emotion*, psychologist Carol Tavris writes of desert nomads so dependent upon unpredictable environments that "Their only insurance against hard times is each other. No individual can lay-in a supply of frozen pizzas and beer in the event of famine and drought, and no individual could long survive on his or her own. . . . Under such conditions, any antisocial or angry outbursts threaten the whole group; so it is to the [desert dweller's] interest to avoid direct physical confrontation or violence, and to be suspicious of individuals who cannot control their behavior or their tempers."[11]

Further, Tavris sees nothing innately aggressive in human beings: "It is the world, not the genes, that determines which way it will go." Yet I've recently come to realize that such an issue has become a virtual battleground within academia. Sociobiologists such as E.O. Wilson (in his *On Human Nature*) still maintain that "human beings have a marked hereditary predisposition to aggressive behavior."[12] Wilson does concede, however, that aggression is not tied to a single gene, adaptive syndrome, or racial lineage, and he also expressed other ambivalences; he argues that our territorial expressions are often responding to the same resource-scarcity problems that direct other animals toward territoriality, but at the same time he is convinced that our aggressive expressions are peculiar. "Most significantly of all," he asserts, "the human forms of aggressive behavior are species-specific: although basically primate in form, they contain features that distinguish them from aggression in all other species" (p. 99).

To my mind, Wilson shifts between two parallel ruts, arguing that we have aggressive (animal) responses but that our scholars and political leaders can lead us into more diplomatic resolutions of conflict if they choose pacifism as a goal. He hardly takes into account the vast terrain between these ruts. His scientific parables are fixed on the notion that our behavior can be explained by understanding the evolutionary history we share with other species. While rightly emphasizing that we respond to many social or environmental stresses and conflicts much the way other organisms do—there are only so many options—he often glosses over critical differences in context and intent.

Nevertheless, one of Wilson's paradigms may shed light on the hummingbirds which become territorial around dense patches of chuparosa in the middle of nowhere, and on the O'odham who do the same with plunge pools. A territory, Wilson notes, invariably

> contains a scarce resource, usually a steady food supply, shelter, space for sexual display, or a site for laying eggs. ... [T]erritorial behavior evolves in animal species only when the vital resource is economically defensible: the energy saved and the increase in survival and reproduction due to territorial defense outweigh the energy expanded and the risk of injury and death.... [I]n the case of food territories the size of the defended area is at or just above the size required to yield enough food to keep the resident healthy and able to reproduce. Finally, territories contain an "invincible center." The resident animal defends the territory far more vigorously than intruders attempt to usurp it, and as a result the defender usually wins. In a special sense, it has the "moral advantage" over trespassers.

I tend to agree with Wilson that it is somehow "natural" for indigenous desert people to defend a waterhole from intruders, much the same way we accept the territorial pugnaciousness of hummingbirds. But because such aggressiveness is oftentimes relaxed when resources become more abundant or widely dispersed, neither the hummers nor the hunter-gatherers seem inexorably fixed on fighting. Be that as it may, cross-cultural comparisons suggest that most societies fight for reasons other than those obviously related to their immediate physical survival. Only ten percent of so-called primitive cultures maintain a constant peace with their neighbors. For sixty-four percent that skirmish with neighbors at least once every two years, many but not all of their conflicts are concerned with competition for basic resources. Cultural evolution has left us with tensions not easily explained by addressing only the driving forces of natural selection: the need for food, water, and shelter; the urge to reproduce and keep our genes "alive" in the form of offspring.

That is why there is something profoundly disturbing—perhaps unprecedented in mammalian evolution until 10,000 years ago—about Blanco the Bandit. By draining the plunge pools, he left all later travelers without access to an essential resource. If there is something peculiar about us latter-day human beings, it is our ability to opt for destroying a resource essential for everyone's survival, rather than simply controlling a competitor's access to it. In this new game—untried in an evolutionary sense—neither the resident nor the intruder ultimately wins. As the resource vanishes, all potential users are inevitably vanquished.

IV

For weeks, the tension had mounted. Young, hormone-charged men stood on the south side of a line, like so many hummingbirds waiting for the ice to break up north, for the season to burst with activity. First Lieutenant John Deedrick likened the mood on the front lines to the waiting in a blind while hunting deer: "Just like being in a tree stand. You're cold and miserable and you just have to wait."

Then, the Desert Storm let loose like an ejaculatory release from an eighteen-year-old: after an all-out war of some one hundred hours, the boys were done. The troops were coming home, having freed the oil fields of Kuwait from a despot's control. American soldiers were regaining the solid manly image that had been deflated during the sixties. "By God," George Bush exclaimed, "we've kicked the Vietnam syndrome once and for all!"

Lingerie sales in America reached a new all-time high, as women swooned for the victors. The boys were a bit embarrassed: "I think its kinda shallow that a girl might want to make it with me just because I was over there. . . . Fun, but shallow."[13]

As anthropologists Fontana and Kroeber see it, ever since farming overtook hunting as society's primary means of support, young men have been trying to figure out what they can excel at that women cannot. The hunter's prowess, tenacity, and dignity, which once won him access to the most attractive and fecund mates, evaporated when both men and women began to share in the chores of agrarian society. Women had already been tending plants for centuries, domesticating them and possibly bringing in far more calories than male "breadwinners." As landscapes became tamed and men spent less time on the mythic wild proving grounds, they abdicated a primordial connection that had given them their meaning. What many people came to feel, Kroeber and Fontana have recently said aloud: "Women could do all the work necessary for society's physical survival. Males were potentially persons of great leisure. Or . . . ," as they rather bluntly state, "males were potentially all but useless."

Men swerved off course, from the sacramental and nutritionally justified bloodletting of hunting to that of warfare, even when the gains did not justify the risks. Another hunger grew in men's loins that made them want to taste blood, to be on top. And this hunger, seldom satisfied, sticks with many men today. Never in history have men been so useless; a woman can now go to a sperm bank and be fertilized without ever having to touch her child's biological father. No wonder Robert Bly's "Gathering of Men" has captured center stage in a formerly floundering men's movement. It sees the male loss of meaning beginning with the Agricultural Revolution, which took men out of contact with the wild, disbanding the fraternity of the Big Woods.

No boot camp or campus fraternity hazing has ever made up for that lack. Far from the mythic rite of passage that it once was for males in many societies, military service too has become an objectified routine of monitoring computer printouts and calculating missile trajectories from remote locations. The bombing of targets has become so depersonalized by the jargon that one might as well be playing Pac-Man. The young technicians simply "took out targets" and euphemistically referred to any human presence in those debilitated places as "collateral damage."

American audiences responded to the Gulf War with much the same fervor they usually reserve for the made-for-TV Super Bowl. Arab-bashing has become a new spectator sport: "Operation Desert Storm" cards come with bubble gum in packages remarkably similar to those in which our boys find the faces of Larry Bird, Bo Jackson, and Michael Jordan.

Even if the government's pathological lies about the war disturbed some Americans, it was fortunate for Bush that Saddam Hussein still seemed downright evil, while we only seemed sick. Of course, that perception was largely influenced by the White House media machine. Who else could be better cast in the role of Blanco the Bandit than Saddam Hussein himself? Rather than emptying out the tinajas of all their water, he shrewdly set fire to the scarcest resource underpinning our global economy: fossil fuel. While more than five hundred wells burned like battle torches day after day, enough oil was going up in smoke to meet a tenth of the world's daily consumption.

"If Hell had a National Park, this would be it," mourned the Environmental Protection Agency's director William Reilly on the *Today* show just after his return from Kuwait on 7 May 1991, hardly two months after the Gulf War "cease fire." The fires, of course, had not ceased: it would take months to extinguish all of them, and as each month passed with the blazes unabated, they added to the atmosphere as much as a million tons of sulfur dioxide, a hundred thousand tons of nitrogen oxides, and 2.5 million tons of oil soot—the latter amount being more than four times the monthly emissions from the entire United States. All told, the war contributed four percent of the world's total carbon release by the end of 1991, thereby accelerating global warming over the long run.[14]

And yet, President Bush still claims that Desert Storm made the victory swift, and the long-term damages minimal. Unfortunately, his antiseptic war was never that at all; over a hundred thousand were dead within a month, with twice that many wounded, crippled, or contaminated with toxins. Many more people were deprived of potable water and food for months on end, and it is now estimated that only one tenth of the deaths occurred during the "official" war. Environmental destruction proceeded on an unprecedented scale and left unsanitary remains that will persist indefinitely.

To console us, William Reilly announced in doublespeak (during that same *Today* interview) that "President Bush cares as much about the environment as he did about winning the war."

However, the current condition of the fragile desert left behind by a million troops does not give credence to this platitude. Scars left by helter-skelter driving of military vehicles will be seen in the vegetation and soils for anywhere from 100 to 1,000 years. In some places, observers found the desert biologically sterile following the war; elsewhere, remaining plants were covered with a crust of soot, oil, and wind-drifted sand. Massive defense berms interrupted watercourses, and countless bomb craters were not exclusively the result of Iraqi actions. Further, the U.S. Air Force admits that it left behind nearly nine thousand tons of undetectable explosive materials in desert areas. In terms of exploded refineries and burning lakes of oil, the culpability is blurred. "Who knows who set what off?" asked Tony Burgess during a telephone interview. Burgess is a desert ecologist who spent three weeks with Friends of the Earth in the Gulf assessing environmental damage: "The country was so trashed. It literally was a vision from Hell."[15]

We have only an inkling of how far that hellish apparition will spread, but Burgess has assured me that the oil fires are bound to have profound, pervasive global ramifications. Using the greasy soot particles resulting from the burning oil fields as but one example, Burgess told me that "effects from the Kuwaiti smoke plume have already been picked up in Australia and Hawaii," more than eight thousand miles away from their source. From the snows of the Himalayas to the headwaters of the Blue Nile, acid rain and carbon soot have been accumulating at unprecedented levels.

Petroleum engineer John Cox regards the magnitude of carbon soot from Kuwait, Iraq, and Saudi Arabia to be more concentrated and therefore more devastating than what would be expected were a nuclear winter to occur. He explains why the Kuwaiti smoke plume has already been so widely dispersed: "If you are in a rainy area, a very high proportion of the smoke is going to be washed out. If, however, you are in an area that is already dry—and the microclimate around Kuwait is very dry—and you have an intense temperature, then the chances are that the smoke cloud will go to a much greater height than the nuclear war simulations suggest.... [There will be] a major effect upon the growth of vegetation and crops."[16]

This is not the maverick opinion of one self-styled expert, but that of the Greenpeace organization as well, which claims that the Gulf War already ranks as one of the most ecologically destructive conflicts ever. According to Andre Carothers, Kuwaiti officials have begun to concede that the environmental damages of the war have been more crippling than any material losses incurred during the hundred days of armed conflict.[17] And that, to my mind, is the fatal deviation, the divergence of our path from that of our sometimes pugnacious biological ancestors and neighbors on this planet. Although sociobiological scholars may still smugly argue that "we are far from being the most violent animal," the damage our kind has done is suffusive enough to be all-encompassing.

Hummingbirds skirmishing over chuparosa, O'odham and Quechan Indians vying for a waterhole, or Kuwaitis and Iraqis battling over an oil field may appear to be parallel parables of territorial disputes over scarce resources in the desert. But the latter battle has the capacity to damage a broad range of resources required for life now and in the future—indeed, to damage irreparably the capacity for life support within our planet's atmosphere. Gone are the days when ritualized warfare affected control over only one waterhole, one food-gathering ground, one territory.

The verbal antagonism between Saddam Hussein and George Bush on television was a pathetic throwback to esoteric jousting by medieval sportsmen, who lived in a time when the stakes were low and the damage local. We can no longer speak of competition for a single, concentrated resource; a life-support system dependent upon widely dispersed, vitally important resources is now under threat. Compared to other centuries, the number of wars within and between nations has increased during this century, despite pacifying efforts by the United Nations and other mediating bodies. If Bush or Hussein had the mentality of a hummingbird, it would be clear to them that the resources crucial to our survival are no longer economically or ecologically defensible through territorial behavior. These resources are too diffuse, too globally interdependent, to be worth the risks both leaders have placed before us. But what a hummingbird can surmise with its senses in a matter of hours or days, our species must muddle through, argue about, and even shed blood over for decades.

V

I am back, in the dead of the summer, on a desert wash near the international border where hummingbird bushes like chuparosa exhibit a few last, ill-fated flowers withering in the heat. A fire has burnt a patch along the border today. Dusty whirlwinds are everywhere, turning and churning in the drought-stricken air. A hummingbird whirrs by me. I turn to see if he is being chased, then back to see if he is in hot pursuit of another. He is not. We stop on opposite sides of the wash, which is wide enough to let us pause for a moment without feeling on top of one another.

As I pause, I think of the O'odham name for Tinajas Altas: *O'ovak,* "Arrowhead Sunk." The Sand People tell about two of their fellow O'odham who climbed to one of the ridges overlooking the steep-sided canyon where the precious pools of water are found today. One of these two warriors challenged the other to a contest: who could shoot an arrow all the way across the canyon to the far ridge?

As my O'odham friends tell it, the first man's arrow cleared the canyon, but the other's did not. Instead, it glanced against the bedrock in the drainage, skipped along, then sunk into the granite. Wherever it had struck the rock, however, a pool of water formed, and the O'odham and their neighbors have used these plunge pools ever since. Retelling this story, my friends express their gratitude for the unlikely appearance of water, wherever it emerges in the desert.

I turn to the hummingbird and think, "Who, then, won the contest? The warrior demonstrating the greatest facility with weaponry, or the one who helped make a lasting resource for all people?" Laughing at myself, at the long and winding trails my answers take, I leave the wash with one last gesture to the hummer. "You must be my teacher," I offer, palms open to his direction. "We're here together." I am beginning to learn what we share in common—this earth— and what differences in behavior I cannot bear to let come between us.

NOTES

1. London: George Allen and Unwin, pp. 82–83.
2. William A. Calder, III, et al., "Site-fidelity, longevity, and population dynamics of Broad-Tailed Hummingbirds: a ten year study," *Oecologia* 56 (1983), 359.
3. David L. Lyon, James Crandall, and Mark McCone, "A test of the adaptiveness of interspecific territoriality in the Blue-Throated Hummingbird," *The Auk* (July 1977), 448–49.
4. Rea, a retired curator of birds and mammals at the San Diego Museum of Natural History, made this remark to me during a telephone conversation in May 1991.

5. *Happy Hunting-Grounds* (New York: Charles Scribner's Sons, 1920), pp. 73–74.

6. New York: Leypoldt & Holt, p. 105.

7. My Reminiscences (New York: Henry Holt).

8. Wilton Hoy, *Organ Pipe Historical Research* (Lukeville, Ariz.: Organ Pipe National Monument, 1970), p. 71.

9. *Social Organization of the Papago Indians* (New York: Columbia University Press, 1939), pp. 128–29.

10. Tucson: University of Arizona Press, 1986, p. 56.

11. New York: Simon and Schuster, 1982.

12. Cambridge: Harvard University Press, 1978, p. 100.

13. Unidentified serviceman, speaking in the spring of 1991 on a radio call-in program, "The Jones and Boze Show," broadcast over station KXCI in Scottsdale, Arizona.

14. Tony Burgess, "Trip report to Saudi Arabia and Kuwait, for Friends of the Earth," unpublished manuscript.

15. Information and statistics in this paragraph were gathered during a telephone conversation with Tony Burgess in June 1991.

16. "Waging War against the Earth," *Environmental Action* (March/April 1991), p. 22.

17. "After the Storm: The Deluge," *Greenpeace. Magazine* (Oct./Nov./Dec, 1991), 17.

Skunk Dreams

When I was fourteen, I slept alone on a North Dakota football field under the cold stars on an early spring night. May is unpredictable in the Red River Valley, and I happened to hit a night when frost formed in the grass. A skunk trailed a plume of steam across the forty-yard line near moonrise. I tucked the top of my sleeping bag over my head and was just dozing off when the skunk walked onto me with simple authority.

Its ripe odor must have dissipated in the frozen earth of its winterlong hibernation, because it didn't smell all that bad, or perhaps it was just that I took shallow breaths in numb surprise. I felt him—her, whatever—pause on the side of my hip and turn around twice before evidently deciding I was a good place to sleep. At the back of my knees, on the quilting of my sleeping bag, it trod out a spot for itself and then, with a serene little groan, curled up and lay perfectly still. That made two of us. I was wildly awake, trying to forget the sharpness and number of skunk teeth, trying not to think of the high percentage of skunks with rabies, or the reason that on camping trips my father always kept a hatchet underneath his pillow.

Inside the bag, I felt as if I might smother. Carefully, making only the slightest of rustles, I drew the bag away from my face and took a deep breath of the night air, enriched with skunk, but clear and watery and cold. It wasn't so bad, and the skunk didn't stir at all, so I watched the moon—caught that night in an envelope of silk, a mist—pass over my sleeping field of teenage guts and glory. The grass in spring that has lain beneath the snow harbors a sere dust both old and fresh. I smelled that newness beneath the rank tone of my bag-mate—the stiff fragrance of damp earth and the thick pungency of newly manured fields a mile or two away—along with my sleeping bag's smell, slightly mildewed, forever smoky. The skunk settled even closer and began to breathe rapidly; its feet jerked a little like a dog's. I sank against the earth, and fell asleep too.

Of what easily tipped cans, what molten sludge, what dogs in yards on chains, what leftover macaroni casseroles, what cellar holes, crawl spaces, burrows taken from meek woodchucks, of what miracles of garbage did my skunk dream? Or did it, since we can't be sure, dream the plot of *Moby-Dick*, how to properly age parmesan, or how to restore the brick-walled, tumbledown creamery that was its home? We don't know about the dreams of any other biota, and even much about our own. If dreams are an actual dimension, as some assert, then the usual rules of life by which we abide do not apply. In that place, skunks may certainly dream themselves into the vests of stockbrokers. Perhaps that night the skunk and I dreamed each other's thoughts or are still dreaming them. To paraphrase the problem of the Chinese sage, I may be a woman who has dreamed herself a skunk, or a skunk still dreaming that she is a woman.

In a book called *Death and Consciousness*, David H. Lund—who wants very much to believe in life after death—describes human dream—life as a possible model for a disembodied existence:

> Many of one's dreams are such that they involve the activities of an apparently embodied person whom one takes to be oneself as long as one dreams.... Whatever is the source of the imagery ... apparently has the capacity to bring about images of a human body and to impart the feeling that the body is mine. It is, of course, just an image body, but it serves as a perfectly good body for the dream experience. I regard it as mine, I act on the dream environment by means of it, and it constitutes the center of the perceptual world of my dream.

Over the years I have acquired and reshuffled my beliefs and doubts about whether we live on after death—in any shape or form, that is, besides the molecular level at which I am to be absorbed by the taproots of cemetery pines and the tangled mats of fearfully poisoned, too-green lawn grass. I want something of the self on whom I have worked so hard to survive the loss of the body (which, incidentally, the self has done a fairly decent job of looking after, excepting spells of too much cabernet and a few idiotic years of rolling my own cigarettes out of Virginia Blond tobacco). I am put out with the marvelous discoveries of the intricate biochemical configuration of our brains, though I realize that the processes themselves are quite miraculous. I understand that I should be self-proud, content to gee-whiz at the fact that I am the world's only mechanism that can admire itself. I should be grateful that life is here today, though gone tomorrow, but I can't help it. I want more.

Skunks don't mind each other's vile perfume. Obviously, they find each other more than tolerable. And even I, who have been in the presence of a direct skunk hit, wouldn't classify their weapon as mere smell. It is more on the order of a reality-enhancing experience. It's not so pleasant as standing in a grove of old-growth red cedars, or on a lyrical moonshed plain, or watching trout rise to the shadow of your hand on the placid surface of an Alpine lake. When the skunk lets go, you're surrounded by skunk presence: inhabited, owned, involved with something you can only describe as powerfully *there*.

I woke at dawn, stunned into that sprayed state of being. The dog that had approached me was rolling in the grass, half-addled, sprayed too. The skunk was gone. I abandoned my sleeping bag and started home. Up Eighth Street, past the tiny blue and pink houses, past my grade school, past all the addresses where I had baby-sat, I walked in my own strange wind. The streets were wide and empty; I met no one—not a dog, not a squirrel, not even an early robin. Perhaps they had all scattered before me, blocks away. I had gone out to sleep on the football field because I was afflicted with a sadness I had to dramatize. Mood swings had begun, hormones, feverish and brutal. They were nothing to me now. My emotions had seemed vast, dark, and sickeningly private. But they were minor, mere wisps, compared to skunk.

I have found that my best dreams come to me in cheap motels. One such dream about an especially haunting place occurred in a rattling room in Saint Thomas, North Dakota. There, in the Potato Capital of the World, I was to spend a week-long residency as a poet-in-the-schools. I was supporting myself, at the time, by teaching poetry to children, convicts, rehabilitation patients, high-school hoods, and recovering alcoholics. What a marvelous job it was, and what opportunities I had to dream, since I paid my own lodging and lived low, sometimes taking rooms for less than ten dollars a night in motels that had already been closed by local health departments.

The images that assailed me in Saint Thomas came about because the bedspread was so thin and worn—a mere brown tissuey curtain—that I had to sleep beneath my faux fur Salvation Army coat, wearing all of my clothing, even a scarf. Cold often brings on the most spectacular of my dreams, as if my brain has been incited to fevered activity. On that particular frigid fall night, the cold somehow seemed to snap boundaries shift my time continuum, and perhaps even allow me to visit my own life in a future moment. After waking once, transferring the contents of my entire suitcase onto my person, and shivering to sleep again, I dreamed of a vast, dark, fenced place. The fencing was chain-link in places, chicken wire, sagging X wire, barbed wire on top, jerry-built with tipped-out poles and uncertain corners nailed to log posts and growing trees. And yet it was quite impermeable and solid, as time-tested, broken-looking things so often are.

Behind it, trees ran for miles—large trees, grown trees, big pines the likes of which do not exist in the Great Plains. In my dream I walked up to the fence, looked within, and saw tawny, humpbacked elk move among the great trunks and slashing green arms. Suave, imponderable, magnificently dumb, they lurched and floated through the dim-complexioned air One turned, however, before they all vanished, and from either side of that flimsy-looking barrier there passed between us a look, a communion, a long and measureless regard that left me, on waking, with a sensation of penetrating sorrow.

I didn't think about my dream for many years, until after I moved to New Hampshire. I had become urbanized and sedentary since the days when I slept with skunks, and I had turned inward. For several years l spent my days leaning above a strange desk, a green door on stilts, which was so high that to sit at it I bought a barstool upholstered in brown leatherette. Besides, the entire Northeast seemed like the inside of a house to me, the sky small and oddly lit, as if by an electric bulb. The sun did not pop over the great trees for hours—and then went down so soon. I was suspicious of Eastern land: the undramatic loveliness, the small scale, the lack of sky to watch, the way the weather sneaked up without enough warning.

The woods themselves seemed bogus at first—every inch of the ground turned over more than once, and even in the second growth of old pines so much human evidence. Rock walls ran everywhere, grown through and tumbled, as if the dead still had claims they imposed. The unkillable and fiercely contorted trees of old orchards, those revenants, spooked me when I walked in the woods. The blasted limbs spread a white lace cold as fire in the spring, and the odor of the blossoms was furiously spectral, sweet. When I stood beneath the canopies that hummed and shook with bees, I heard voices, other voices, and I did not understand what they were saying, where they had come from, what drove them into this earth.

Then, as often happens to sparring adversaries in 1940's movies, I fell in love.

After a few years of living in the country, the impulse to simply *get outside* hit me, strengthened, and became again a habit of thought, a reason for storytelling, an uneasy impatience with walls and roads. At first, when I had that urge, I had to get into a car and drive fifteen hundred miles before I was back in a place that I defined as *out*. The West, or the edge of it anyway, the great level patchwork of chemically treated fields and tortured grazing land, was the outside I had internalized. In the rich Red River Valley, where the valuable cropland is practically measured in inches, environmental areas are defined and proudly pointed out as stretches of roadway where the ditches are not mowed. Deer and pheasants survive in shelter belts—rows of Russian olive, plum, sometimes evergreen—

planted at the edges of fields. The former tall-grass prairie has now become a collection of mechanized gardens tended by an array of air-conditioned farm implements and bearing an increasing amount of pesticide and herbicide in each black teaspoon of dirt. Nevertheless, no amount of reality changed the fact that I still *thought* of eastern North Dakota as wild.

In time, though, *out* became outside my door in New England. By walking across the road and sitting in my little writing house—a place surrounded by trees, thick plumes of grass, jets of ferns, and banks of touch-me-not—or just by looking out a screen door or window, I started to notice what there was to see. In time, the smothering woods that had always seemed part of Northeastern civilization—more an inside than an outside, more like a friendly garden—revealed themselves as forceful and complex. The growth of plants, the lush celebratory springs made a grasslands person drunk. The world turned dazzling green, the hills rode like comfortable and flowing animals. Everywhere there was the sound of water moving.

And yet, even though I finally grew closer to these woods, on some days I still wanted to tear them from before my eyes.

I wanted to *see*. Where I grew up, our house looked out on the western horizon. I could see horizon when I played. I could see it when I walked to school. It was always there, a line beyond everything, a simple line of changing shades and colors that ringed the town, a vast place. That was it. Down at the end of every grid of streets: vastness. Out the windows of the high school: vastness. From the drive-in theater where I went parking in a purple Duster: vast distance. That is why, on lovely New England days when everything should have been all right—a spring day for instance, when the earth had risen through the air in patches and the sky lowered, dim and warm—I fell sick with longing for the horizon. I wanted the clean line, the simple line, the clouds marching over it in feathered masses. I suffered from horizon sickness. But it sounds crazy for a grown woman to throw herself at the sky, and the thing is, I wanted to get well. And so to compensate for horizon sickness, for the great longing that seemed both romantically German and pragmatically Chippewa in origin, I found solace in trees.

Trees are a changing landscape of sound—and the sound I grew attached to, possible only near large deciduous forests, was the great hushed roar of thousands and millions of leaves brushing and touching one another. Windy days were like sitting just out of sight of an ocean, the great magnetic ocean of wind. All around me, I watched the trees tossing, their heads bending. At times the movement seemed passionate, as though they were flung together in an eager embrace, caressing each other, branch to branch. If there is a vegetative soul, an animating power that all things share, there must be great rejoicing out there on windy days ecstasy, for trees move so slowly on calm days. At least it seems that way to us. On days of high wind they move so freely it must give them a cellular pleasure close to terror.

Unused to walking in the woods, I did not realize that trees dropped branches—often large ones—or that there was any possible danger in going out on windy days, drawn by the natural drama. There was a white pine I loved, a tree of the size foresters call *overgrown*, a waste, a thing made of long-since harvestable material. The tree was so big that three people couldn't reach around it. Standing at the bottom, craning back, fingers clenched in grooves of bark, I held on as the crown of the tree roared and beat the air a hundred feet above. The movement was frantic, the soft-needled branches long and supple. I thought of a woman tossing, anchored in passion: calm one instant, full-throated the next, hair vast and dark, shedding the piercing, fresh oil of broken needles. I went to visit her often, and walked onward, farther, though it was not so far at all, and then one day I reached the fence.

Chain-link in places, chicken wire, sagging X wire, barbed wire on top, jerry-built with tipped-out poles and uncertain corners nailed to log posts and growing trees, still it seemed impermeable and solid. Behind it, there were trees for miles: large trees, grown trees, big pines. I walked up to the fence, looked within, and could see elk moving. Suave, imponderable, magnificently dumb, they lurched and floated through the dim air.

I was on the edge of a game park, a rich man's huge wilderness, probably the largest parcel of protected land in western New Hampshire, certainly the largest privately owned piece I knew about. At forty square miles—25,000 acres—it was bigger than my mother's home reservation. And it had the oddest fence around it that I'd ever seen, the longest and the tackiest. Though partially electrified, the side closest to our house was so piddling that an elk could easily have tossed it apart. Certainly a half-ton wild boar, the condensed and living version of a tank, could have strolled right through. But then animals, much like most humans, don't charge through fences unless they have sound reasons. As I soon found out, because I naturally grew fascinated with the place, there were many more animals trying to get into the park than out, and they couldn't have cared less about ending up in a hunter's stew pot.

These were not wild animals, the elk—since they were grained at feeding stations, how could they be? They were not domesticated either, however, for beyond the no-hunt boundaries they fled and vanished. They were game. Since there is no sport in shooting feedlot steers, these animals—still harboring wild traits and therefore more challenging to kill—were maintained to provide blood pleasure for the members of the Blue Mountain Forest Association.

As I walked away from the fence that day, I was of two minds about the place—and I am still. Shooting animals inside fences, no matter how big the area they have to hide in, seems abominable and silly. And yet, I was glad for that wilderness. Though secretly managed and off limits to me, it was the source of flocks of evening grosbeaks and pine siskins, of wild turkey, ravens, and grouse, of Eastern coyote, oxygen-rich air, foxes, goldfinches, skunk, and bears that tunneled in and out.

I had dreamed of this place in St. Thomas, or it had dreamed me. There was affinity here, beyond any explanation I could offer, so I didn't try. I continued to visit the tracts of big trees, and on deep nights—windy nights, especially when it stormed—I liked to fall asleep imagining details. I saw the great crowns touching, heard the raving sound of wind and thriving, knocking cries as the blackest of ravens flung themselves across acres upon indifferent acres of tossing, old-growth pine. I could fall asleep picturing how, below that dark air, taproots thrust into a deeper blankness, drinking the powerful rain.

Or was it so only in my dreams? The park, known locally as Corbin's Park, after its founder Austin Corbin, is knit together of land and farmsteads he bought in the late nineteenth century from 275 individuals. Among the first animals released there, before the place became a hunting club, were thirty buffalo, remnants of the vast Western herds. Their presence piqued the interest of Ernest Harold Bayne, a conservation-minded local journalist, who attempted to break a pair of buffalo calves to the yoke. He exhibited them at county fairs and even knit mittens out of buffalo wool, hoping to convince the skeptical of their usefulness. His work inspired sympathy, if not a trend for buffalo yarn, and collective zeal for the salvation of the buffalo grew until by 1915 the American Bison Society, of which Bayne was secretary, helped form government reserves that eventually more than doubled the herds that remained.

The buffalo dream seems to have been the park's most noble hour. Since that time it has been the haunt of wealthy hunting enthusiasts. The owner of Ruger Arms currently inhabits the stunning, butter-yellow original Corbin mansion and would like to buy the whole park for his exclusive use, or so local gossip has it.

For some months I walked the boundary admiring the tangled landscape, at least all that I could see. After my first apprehension, I ignored the fence. I walked along it as if it simply did not exist, as if I really was part of that place which lay just beyond my reach. The British psychotherapist Adam Phillips has examined obstacles from several different angles, attempting to define their emotional use. "It is impossible to imagine desire without obstacles," he writes, "and wherever we find something to be an obstacle we are at the same time desiring something. It is part of the fascination of the Oedipus story in particular, and perhaps narrative in general, that we and the heroes and heroines of our fictions never know whether obstacles create desire or desire creates obstacles." He goes on to characterize the Unconscious, our dream world, as a place without obstacles: "A good question to ask of a dream is: What are the obstacles that have been removed to make this extraordinary scene possible?"

My dream, however, was about obstacles still in place. The fence was the main component, the defining characteristic of the forbidden territory that I watched but could not enter or experience. The obstacles that we overcome define us. We are composed of hurdles we set up to pace our headlong needs, to control our desires, or against which to measure our growth. "Without obstacles," Phillips writes, "the notion of development is inconceivable. There would be nothing to master."

Walking along the boundary of the park no longer satisfied me. The preciousness and deceptive stability of that fence began to rankle. Longing filled me. I wanted to brush against the old pine bark and pass beyond the ridge, to see specifically what was there: what Blue Mountain, what empty views, what lavender hillside, what old cellar holes, what unlikely animals. I was filled with poacher's lust, except I wanted only to smell the air. The linked web restraining me began to grate, and I started to look for weak spots, holes, places where the rough wire sagged. From the moment I began to see the fence as permeable, it became something to overcome. I returned time after time—partly to see if I could spot anyone on the other side, partly because I knew I must trespass.

Then, one clear, midwinter morning, in the middle of a halfhearted thaw, I walked along the fence until I came to a place that looked shaky—and was. I went through. There were no trails that I could see, and I knew I needed to stay away from any perimeter roads or snowmobile paths, as well as from the feeding stations where the animals congregated. I wanted to see the animals, but only from a distance. Of course, as I walked on, leaving a trail easily backtracked, I encountered no animals at all. Still, the terrain was beautiful, the columns of pine tall and satisfyingly heavy, the patches of oak and elderly maple from an occasional farmstead knotted and patient. I was satisfied and, sometime in the early afternoon, I decided to turn back and head toward the fence again. Skirting a low, boggy area that teemed with wild turkey tracks, I was just heading toward the edge of a deadfall of trashed dead branches and brush, when I stared too hard into the sun, and stumbled.

In a half crouch, I looked straight into the face of a boar, massive as a boulder. Cornfed, razor-tusked, alert, sensitive ears pricked, it edged slightly backward into the covering shadows. Two ice picks of light gleamed from its shrouded, tiny eyes, impossible to read. Beyond the rock of its shoulder, I saw more: a sow and three cinnamon-brown farrows crossing a small field of glare snow, lit by dazzling sun. The young skittered along, lumps of muscled fat on tiny hooves. They reminded me of snowsuited toddlers on new skates. When they were out of sight the boar melted through the brush after them, leaving not a snapped twig or crushed leaf in his wake.

I almost didn't breathe in the silence, letting the fact of that presence settle before I retraced my own tracks.

Since then, I've been to the game park via front gates, driven down the avenues of tough old trees, and seen herds of wild pigs and elk meandering past the residence of the gamekeeper. A no-hunting zone exists around the house, where the animals are almost tame. But I've been told by privileged hunters that just beyond that invisible boundary they vanish, becoming suddenly and preternaturally elusive.

There is something in me that resists the notion of fair use of this land if the only alternative is to have it cut up, sold off in lots, condominiumized. Yet the dumb fervor of the place depresses me—the wilderness locked up and managed but not for its sake; the animals imported and cultivated to give pleasure through their deaths. All animals, that is, except for skunks.

Not worth hunting, inedible except to old trappers like my uncle Ben Gourneau, who boiled his skunk with onions in three changes of water, skunks pass in and out of Corbin's Park without hindrance, without concern. They live off the corn in the feeding cribs (or the mice it draws), off the garbage of my rural neighbors, off bugs and frogs and grubs. They nudge their way onto our back porch for catfood, and even when disturbed they do not, ever, hurry. It's easy to get near a skunk, even to capture one. When skunks become a nuisance, people either shoot them or catch them in crates, cardboard boxes, Hav-A-Hart traps, plastic garbage barrels.

Natives of the upper Connecticut River valley have neatly solved the problem of what to do with such catches. They hoist their trapped mustelid into the back of a pickup truck and cart the animal across the river to the neighboring state—New Hampshire to Vermont, Vermont to New Hampshire—before releasing it. The skunk population is estimated as about even on both sides.

We should take comfort from the skunk, an arrogant creature so pleased with its own devices that it never runs from harm, just turns its back in total confidence. If I were an animal, I'd choose to be a skunk: live fearlessly, eat anything, gestate my young in just two months, and fall into a state of dreaming torpor when the cold bit hard. Wherever I went, I'd leave my sloppy tracks. I wouldn't walk so much as putter, destinationless, in a serene belligerence—past hunters, past death overhead, past death all around.

BARRY LOPEZ

Replacing Memory

I

Manhattan, 1976

The hours of coolness in the morning just before my mother died I remember for their relief. It was July and it had been warm and humid in New York City for several days, temperatures in the high eighties, the air motionless and heavy with the threat of rain.

I awoke early that morning. It was also my wife's thirtieth birthday, but our celebration would be wan. My mother was in her last days, and the lives of all of us in the family were contorted by grief and tension—and by a flaring of anger at her cancer. We were exhausted.

I felt the coolness of the air immediately when I awoke. I walked the length of the fourth-floor apartment, opened one side of a tall casement window in the living room, and looked at the sky. Cumulus clouds, moving to the southeast on a steady wind. Ten degrees cooler than yesterday's dawn, by the small tin thermometer. I leaned forward to rest my arms on the sill and began taking in details of movement in the street's pale light, the city's stirring.

In the six years I had lived in this apartment as a boy, from 1956 until 1962, I had spent cumulative months at this window. At the time, the Murray Hill section of Manhattan was mostly a neighborhood of decorous living and brownstone row houses, many of them not yet converted to apartments. East 35th Street for me, a child newly arrived from California, presented an enchanting pattern of human life. Foot-beat policemen began their regular patrol at eight. The delivery of residential mail occurred around nine and was followed about ten by the emergence of women on shopping errands. Young men came and went the whole day on three-wheel grocery cart bikes, either struggling with a full load up the moderate rise of Murray Hill from Gristede's down on Third Avenue, or hurtling back the other way, driving no-hands against light traffic, cartons of empty bottles clattering explosively as the bike's solid tires nicked potholes.

In the afternoon a dozen young girls in private-school uniform swirled in glee and posed with exaggerated emotion across the street waiting to be taken home. By dinner time the street was almost empty of people; then, around eleven, it was briefly animated again with couples returning from the theater or some other entertainment. Until dawn, the pattern of glinting chrome and color in the two rows of curbed automobiles remained unchanged. And from night to night that pattern hardly varied.

Overlaying the street's regular, diurnal rhythm was a more chaotic pattern of events, an unpredictability I would watch with unquenchable fascination for hours at a time. (A jog in the wall of The Advertising Club of New York next door made it impossible for me to see very far to the west on 35th Street. But if I leaned out as far as I dared, I could see all the way to the East River in the other direction.) I would study the flow of vehicles below: an aggressive insinuation of yellow taxis, the casual slalom of a motorcycle through lines of stalled traffic, the obstreperous lumbering of large trucks. The sidewalks, with an occasional imposing stoop jutting out, were rarely crowded, for there were neither shops nor businesses here, and few tourists. But with Yeshiva University down at the corner of Lexington, the 34th Street Armory a block away, a Swedenborgian church midblock, and 34th Precinct police headquarters just up from Third Avenue, I still saw a fair array of dress and captivating expressions of human bearing. The tortoise pace of elderly women in drab hats paralleled the peeved ambling of a middle-aged man anxious to locate a cab. A naïf, loose-jointed in trajectory down the sidewalk, with wide-flung strides. A buttonhooking young woman, intently scanning door lintels and surreptitiously watching a building superintendent leaning sullenly against a service entrance. Two men in vested suits in conversation on the corner where, rotund and oblivious, they were a disruption, like a boulder in a creek. A boy running through redlighted traffic with a large bouquet in his hand, held forth like a bowsprit.

All these gaits together with their kindred modulations seemed mysteriously revealing to me. Lingering couples embraced, separated with resolve, then embraced once more. People halted and turned toward each other in hilarious laughter. I watched as though I would never see such things again—screaming arguments, the other-worldly navigations of the deranged, and the haughty stride of single men dressed meticulously in evening clothes.

This pattern of traffic and people, an overlay of personality and idiosyncrasy on the day's fixed events, fed me in a wordless way. My eyes would drift up from these patterns to follow the sky over lower Manhattan, a flock of house sparrows, scudding clouds, a distant airplane approaching La Guardia or Idlewild with impossible slowness.

Another sort of animation drew me regularly to this window: weather. The sound of thunder. Or a rising hiss over the sound of automobiles that meant the streets were wet from a silent rain. The barely audible rattle of dozens of panes of glass in the window's leadwork—a freshening wind. A sudden dimming of sunshine in the living room. Whatever I was doing, these signals would pull me away. At night, in the isolating light cone of a streetlamp, I could see the slant, the density, and sometimes the exact size of raindrops. (None of this could I learn with my bare hands outstretched, in the penumbral dark under the building's cornices.) I watched rainwater course east in sheets down the calico-patched street in the wake of a storm; and cascades of snow, floating and wind-driven, as varied in their character as falls of rain, pile up in the streets. I watched the darkness between buildings burst with lightning, and I studied intently the rattle-drum of hail on car roofs.

The weather I watched from this window, no matter how wild, was always comforting. My back was to rooms secured by family life. East and west, the room shared its walls with people I imagined little different from myself. And from this window I could see a marvel as imbued with meaning for me then as a minaret—the Empire State Building. The high windows of its east wall gleamed imperially in the first rays of dawn, before the light flared down 35th Street, glinting in bits of mica in the façades of brownstones. Beneath the hammer of winter storms, the building seemed courageous and adamantine.

The morning that my mother would die I rested my forearms on the sill of the window, glad for the change of weather. I could see more of the wind, moving gray clouds, than I could feel; but I knew the walk to the subway later that morning, and the short walk up 77th Street to Lennox Hill Hospital, would be cooler.

I had been daydreaming at the window for perhaps an hour when my father came downstairs. The faint odors in the street's air—the dampness of basements, the acrid fragrance of ailanthus trees, the aromatics in roof tar—had drawn me off into a dozen memories. My father paused, speechless, at the foot of the stairs by the dining table. As determined as he was to lead a normal life around Mother's last days, he was at the beck and call of her disease almost as much as she was. With a high salute of his right hand, meant to demonstrate confidence, and an ironic grimace, he went out the door. Downstairs he would meet my brother, who worked with him, and together they would take a cab up to the hospital. My brother, three years younger, was worn out by these marathon days but uncomplaining, almost always calm. He and my father would eat breakfast together at the hospital and sit with Mother until Sandra and I arrived, then leave for work.

I wanted an undisturbed morning, the luxury of that kind of time, in which to give Sandra her birthday presents, to have a conversation not shrouded by death. I made breakfast and took it into the bedroom. While we sipped coffee I offered her what I had gotten. Among other things, a fossil trilobite, symbol of longevity. But we could not break the rind of oppression this terminal disease had created.

While Sandra showered, I dressed and returned to the window. I stood there with my hands in my pockets staring at the weathered surface of the window's wood flame, with its peeling black paint. I took in details in the pitted surface of the sandstone ledge and at its boundary, where the ledge met the color of buildings across the street. I saw the stillness of the ledge against the sluggish flow of early morning traffic and a stream of pedestrians in summer clothing below. The air above the street was a little warmer now. The wind continued to blow steadily, briskly moving cloud banks out over Brooklyn.

I felt a great affection for the city, for its tight Joseph's coat of buildings, the vitality of its people, the enduring grace of its plane trees, and the layers of its history, all of it washed by a great tide of weather under maritime skies. Standing at the window I felt the insistence and the assurance of the city, and how I was woven in here through memory and affection.

Sandra touched my shoulder. It was time we were gone, uptown. But something stayed me. I leaned out, bracing my left palm against the window's mullion. The color I saw in people's clothes was now muted. Traffic and pedestrians, the start-up of myriad businesses, had stirred the night's dust. The air was more rank with exhaust. A flock of pigeons came down the corridor of the street toward me, piebald, dove gray, white, brindled ginger, ash black—thirty or more of them. They were turning the bottom of a long parabolic arc, from which they shot up suddenly, out over Park Avenue. They reached a high, stalling apex, rolled over it, and fell off to the south, where they were cut from view by a building. A few moments later they emerged much smaller, wings pounding over brownstones below 34th Street, on a course parallel to the wind's.

I left, leaving the window open.

When Sandra and I emerged a half-hour later from the hospital elevator, my brother was waiting to meet us. I could see by the high, wistful cast of his face that she was gone.

II

Arizona, 1954

Our train arrived at Grand Canyon Village on the South Rim late on a summer afternoon. With my brother Denny and a friend of my mother, a young woman named Ann, I had come up on the Santa Fe spur line from Williams, a town about thirty miles west of Flagstaff. We had left Los Angeles the evening before, making a rail crossing of the Sonoran Desert so magical I had fallen silent before it.

The train itself was spellbinding. I do not remember falling asleep as we crossed the desert, but I know that I must have. I only remember sitting alone in a large seat in the darkened observation car, looking at the stars and feeling nearly out of breath with fortune—being able to wander up and down the aisles of the streaking train, sitting in this observation car hour by hour staring at the desert's sheer plain, the silhouettes of isolated mountain ranges, and, above, the huge swath of the Milky Way.

Near midnight we stopped for a few minutes in Needles, a railroad town on the lower Colorado across the river from the Fort Mojave Indian Reservation. The scene on the platform was dreamlike, increasing my sense of blessing. The temperature was over one hundred degrees, but it was a dry heat, pleasant. I had never been up this late at night. Twenty or thirty Indians—I didn't know then, but they would have been Chemuwevis as well as Mojaves, and also Navajos, who worked on many of the Santa Fe repair crews—craned their necks, looking for disembarking passengers or cars to board. Mexican families stood tightly together stolid, shy and alert. The way darkness crowded the platform's pale lamplight, the way the smoky light gleamed on silver bracelets and corn blossom necklaces, leaving its sheen on the heavy raven hair of so many women—all this so late in the heated night made Needles seem very foreign. I wanted to stay. I could have spent all the time I had been offered at Grand Canyon right here.

But we left. I returned to my seat in the now completely empty observation car. I am sure I fell asleep shortly after we crossed the river on the way to Kingman.

John, Ann's husband of only a few months and a seasonal ranger at the park, met the train at the canyon. My brother and I were to have two weeks with them before Mother came up to join us. (The three of them taught together in the secondary school system in Southern California's San Fernando Valley.)

On the way up from Williams, the train had climbed through piñon and juniper savannah. As I descended the train car's steps, I saw fully for the first time the largest trees I had ever looked at—ponderosa pines. In the same moment, their fragrance came to me on the warm air, a sweet odor, less sharp than that of other pines.

John embraced Ann fiercely and said, "I will never be separated from you, ever again, for this long." Their passion and his words seemed wondrous to me, profound and almost unfathomable. I stared at the huge ponderosas, which I wanted to touch.

During those two weeks, Denny and I traveled the South and East rims of the canyon with Ann while John lectured daily to visitors. The four of us lived in a small log cabin with a high-pitched roof. Sometimes I rose early, before the sun, and went outside. I would just stand in the trees or wander nearby in the first light. I could not believe the stillness.

A short distance from the cabin was a one-room museum with an office. I spent hours there, looking at pinned insects, stuffed birds, and small animals. Some of these creatures seemed incredibly exotic to me, like the Kaibab squirrel with its tufted ears—perhaps a made-up animal.

I read pamphlets about the geology of the canyon and its Indian history, and I went with my brother to some of John's lectures. The most entrancing was one in which he described the succession of limestones, sandstones, and shales that make up the visible canyon walls. The precision and orderliness of his perception, the names he gave so easily to these thousands of feet of wild, unclimbable, and completely outsized walls, seemed inspired, a way to *grasp* it all. I think this was the first such litany I committed to memory:

> Kaibab, Toroweap,
> Coconiño, Hermit;
> Supai, Redwall,
> Temple, Muav.
> Bright Angel.
> Tapeats.

On John's days off we drove out to picnic at Shoshone Point, a place on the East Rim set aside by the Park Service for its employees. Here, far from the pressing streams of visitor traffic, the silence within the canyon reverberated like silence in the nave of a large cathedral. The small clearing with its few picnic tables was a kind of mecca, a place where the otherwise terrifying fall-off of the canyon seemed to comfort or redeem. I saw a mountain lion there one afternoon. It leaped the narrow road in one long bound, its head strangely small, its long tail strangely thick, a creature the color of Coconiño sandstone.

I did not go back to the canyon after that summer for twenty-six years. In the spring of 1980, I joined several other writers and editors at a workshop there in the Park Service's Albright Training Center. I arrived at night by plane, so did not see much until the next morning. I got up early, just after sunrise, thinking I would walk over to the El Tovar Lodge on the rim of the canyon for breakfast. The walk, I thought, would be a way to reenter the landscape, alone and quietly, before the activities of the workshop caught me up in a flow of ideas and in protracted discussions.

I didn't remember the area well enough that morning to know where I was, relative to the cabin we'd stayed in, but I set off through the woods toward what felt like the canyon's rim. The gentle roll of the land, the sponginess of ponderosa needles beneath my feet, familiar but nameless odors in the air, the soft twitter of chickadees up ahead—all this rounded into a pattern my body remembered.

At a certain point I emerged from the trees onto a macadam road, which seemed the one to take to the lodge. I'd not gone more than a few yards, however, before I was transfixed by the sight of a small building. It was boarded up, but it had once been the museum. An image of its interior formed vividly in my mind—the smooth, glass-topped display stands with bird eggs and prehistoric tools, the cabinets and drawers full of vials of seeds and insect trays.

I walked on, elated and curiously composed. I would come back.

At the foot of the road was a wide opening in the trees. Once it might have been a parking lot. I was only part-way across when I realized that the young pines growing here were actually coming up between train rails. Again I stood transfixed. It was here, all those years ago, that I had gotten off the train. I held tightly to that moment and began stepping eastward along the tracks, looking up every few steps to pure stands of ponderosa growing a hundred feet away to the south. Then I recognized a pattern in the trees, the way a dozen of the untapered, cinnamon-colored trunks stood together on a shallow slope. It had been here exactly that I had stepped off. I stared at them for many minutes, wondering more than anything at the way memory, given so little, could surge so unerringly.

I walked up to the trees and put my fingers on the bark, the large flat plates of small, concave scales. Far above, the narrow crowns were still against the bluing sky.

On the other side of the tracks I walked past the entrance to the lodge and stood at the edge of the canyon before a low, broad wall of stone. The moment my knees touched the wall, my unbounded view was shot with another memory—the feel of this stone angle against my belly when I was nine, and had had to hoist myself up onto the wall in order to see deep into the canyon. Now, I stood there long after the desire to gaze at the canyon had passed. I recalled suddenly how young ponderosas, bruised, smell like oranges. I waited, anxious, for memories that came like bursts of light: the mountain lion in its leap; the odor and jingle of harness mules and saddle horses in the hot sun at the top of Bright Angel Trail; my brother, light footed as a doe, at the wall of an Anasazi ruin. These images brought with them, even in their randomness, a reassurance about time, about the unbroken duration and continuous meaning of a single human life. With that came a sense of joy, which I took with me to breakfast.

III

Bear River, Idaho, 1991

Cort bought a potted sulfur buckwheat in the Albertson's in Jackson and he and John and I left for Idaho by way of Afton, Wyoming, passing through Montpelier and then Paris, Idaho. We turned off the main road there, drove west through Mink Creek and then Preston and swung north on U.S. 91, crossing the bridge over Bear Creek, where we pulled off.

Cort had been here before. Neither John nor I had, but I had wanted to see the place for a long time. In this river bottom, rising away from me to the Bannock Range in the northwest and, more precipitously, to the Bear River Range behind me in the southeast, several hundred people had been violently killed on a bitter cold morning in January 1863. This obscure incident on the Bear River, once commonly called a "battle" by Western historians, has more often been referred to in recent years as a massacre, an unnecessary killing. Twenty-two men of the Second Cavalry and the Third Infantry, California Volunteers, under the command of a Col. Patrick Connor, were shot dead by Northern Shoshone. No one knows how many Shoshone were killed, but most estimate it was well over three hundred—more Indians than were killed in any other massacre in the West, including those at Sand Creek, Colorado (1864), Washita, Oklahoma (1868), or Wounded Knee, South Dakota (1890).

Connor's stated reason for bringing three hundred troops north from Salt Lake City that winter on a forced march was to protect the Overland Mail Route. The incident that triggered his decision was the death of a white miner in a skirmish involving several miners and Indians near Preston, a few days after Christmas, 1862. In his official report, Connor said he meant to "chastise" the Shoshone. He permitted a federal marshal to accompany him, carrying arrest warrants for three Shoshone men reputedly involved in the fatal incident with the miners, but Connor told the marshal it was not his intent to take any prisoners.

The Shoshone, 400 to 450 of them, were camped in willow thickets at the mouth of a ravine formed by Beaver Creek, several hundred yards short of its confluence with the Bear River. The spot was a traditional winter campsite, well protected from a prevailing north wind, with hot springs and with winter grazing for about two hundred horses. The night before the massacre, a man named Bear Hunter was in the nearby village of Franklin with his family, purchasing and loading sacks of wheat. He saw Connor's troops arriving, surmised their real purpose, and brought word back to the encampment.

Early the following morning, realizing he had lost the advantage of surprise, Connor massed his cavalry openly on the south side of the river, across from the Indian camp. The temperature was probably in the low teens. Connor then waited impatiently for his infantry, which had bogged in heavy snow on the road out of Franklin.

The Shoshone were by now all awake and digging in, for Connor's intentions had become plain. (Connor, of course, had no evidence that these particular Shoshone people had done anything wrong, only the suspicion that the men the U.S. marshal wanted were among them.) One of the Shoshone men shouted out in perfect English, "Come on you California sons-of-bitches. We're ready for you." Provoked by the remark, Connor surged across the icy river and ordered the cavalry to charge. Fourteen of his soldiers were cut down almost instantly. Connor retreated to regroup and to help his foot soldiers, now arriving, get across the river.

Once they were over, Connor divided his forces, sending one column up the west slope of the ravine and another up the east slope, achieving a double flanking of the Indian camp. From these elevated positions the soldiers raked the camp with a furious, enfilading fire. The Shoshone, lightly armed, fought back with sporadic shots and in hand-to-hand combat for three or four hours, until late in the morning, by which time most of them were dead. Connor ordered his troops to kill every wounded Indian and to set fire to all seventy tepees, scattering, burning, or fouling all the food they could find as they did so. (Historians believe as many as sixty Shoshone might have escaped, most of them by swimming the partly frozen river.) In the final stages of the fight, Shoshone women were raped. Bear Hunter was tortured to death with a white-hot bayonet.

Connor reported 224 Indians killed. Residents of Franklin, six miles away, riding through the smoldering camp and into the willow thickets the next morning, counted many more dead, including nearly one hundred women and children. They took a few survivors back, housing them and treating their injuries. Connor, who returned immediately to Salt Lake City, denounced the Mormon people of Franklin in his official report as unhelpful and ungrateful. For their part, the Mormons may only have been heedful of Brigham Young's official policy: it was better to feed Indians than to fight with them.

John and Cort and I read in silence the historical plaques on a stone obelisk at the roadside. I felt more grief than outrage, looking across at the mouth of what is no longer called Beaver Creek but Battle Creek. An interpretive sign, erected in October 1990 by the Idaho Historical Society, seeks to correct the assumption that the fight here was a battle. It calls the encounter "a military disaster unmatched in Western history." A 1990 National Park Service plaque, designating the undistinguished ravine across the river bottom as a National Historical Landmark, says with no apparent irony that the spot "possesses national significance in communicating the history of the United States of America."

We left the highway, drove up a dirt road, and parked at the site of the encampment, which is not signed or marked. Where the Shoshone tepees once stood, in fact, the creek is now clogged with debris and refuse—a school locker, a refrigerator, a mattress, scorched magazines and tin cans, lawn furniture riddled with bullet holes. Violet-green swallows swooped the muddy water, only eight or ten feet across, On what is today called Cedar Bluff—the west side of the ravine—an iron-wheel combine and a walking-beam plow stood inert in sage and buckbrush. Overhead we heard the mewing of Franklin's gulls. From bottom flats near the river came the lowing of beef cattle.

Cort took the sulfur buckwheat from the truck, and the three of us started up the east side of the creek. The ravine, crisscrossed with horse and cattle tracks, was badly eroded. A variety of exotic grasses barely held in place a fine, pale tan, friable soil. Suddenly we saw a red fox. Then a muskrat in the water. Then the first of nine beaver dams, each built with marginal materials—teasel stalks and shreds of buckbrush, along with willow sticks and a few locust limbs. As we moved farther up the creek we heard yellow-headed blackbirds and mourning doves. In the slack water behind each succeeding dam, the water appeared heavier—silt was settling out before the water flowed on to the next dam, a hundred feet or so downstream. The beaver were clarifying the watercourse.

We finally found a small, open point of land near the creek. Cort put the buckwheat down and began to dig. He meant the planting as a simple gesture of respect. When he finished, I filled a boot with water and came back up the steep embankment. I poured it through my fingers. slowly, watching the small yellow flowers teeter in the warm air. Cort had gone on up the creek, but I met John's eye. He raised his eyebrow in acknowledgment, but he was preoccupied with his own thoughts and stepped away.

I climbed to the top of the ravine on the east side and walked north until I came to a high bluff above the creek where hundreds of bank swallows were nesting. I sat watching them while I waited for my friends to emerge from the willow thickets below. A few months before, Cort had lent me his copy of Newall Hart's scarce history, *The Bear River Massacre*, which contains reproductions of military reports and other Primary materials. He recommended I read Brigham Madsen's *The Shoshoni Frontier and the Bear River Massacre*. Cort himself had written about the incident in his *Idaho for the Curious*. When he and John joined me, Cort said he wanted to cross the creek and look over a section of Cedar Bluff he'd not walked on an earlier visit. I wanted to watch the swallows a while longer. John essayed another plan, and we each went our way again.

I worked back south along the creek bottom, pausing for long moments to watch for beaver, which I did not see. Frogs croaked. I came on mule-deer tracks. The warm air, laced with creek-bottom odors, was making me drowsy. I climbed back to the top of the ravine at the place where we had planted the buckwheat. A road there paralleled the creek, and its two tracks were littered with spent 12-gauge shotgun shells, empty boxes of .308 Winchester ammunition, and broken lengths of PVC pipe. I followed a barb-wire fence past a bathtub stock tank to the place where we'd parked.

I opened Hart's book on the hood of the truck. Tipped against the back end-sheet is a large, folded plat map of the "Connor Battle Field," made in 1926 by W. K. Aiken, the surveyor of Franklin County, Idaho. I oriented it in front of me and began matching its detail to the landscape—Aiken's elevations, the sketchy suggestion of an early road to Montana, and a spot to the south where Aiken thought Connor had caught his first glimpse of the Shoshone encampment that morning. In the upper-right corner of his map Mr. Aiken had written, not so cryptically, "Not a Sparrow Falls."

The river's meander had since carried it nearly three-quarters of a mile to the south side of its flood plain. Otherwise the land—ranched and planted mostly to hay crops, dotted with farm houses and outbuildings, and divided by wire fences—did not, I thought, look so very different. You could see the cattle, and you could smell pigs faintly in the air.

John came back. He took a bird guide out of the truck and began slowly to page through it. Cort returned with the lower jaw of a young mule deer, which we took as a souvenir. We drove back out to the road and headed north for Pocatello.

IV

Southern California, 1988

Sandra and I were in Whittier, California, for a ceremony at the town's college. It was the sort of day one rarely sees in the Los Angeles basin anymore: the air gin-clear, with fresh, balmy winds swirling through the eucalyptus trees, trailing their aromatic odor. The transparency of the air, with a trace of the Pacific in it, was intoxicating.

As we left the campus, Sandra said she could understand now what I meant about the sunlight, the clear air of my childhood.

"Yes," I answered. "It was like this often in the spring, after the rains in February. Back then—well, it was a long time ago. Thirty years, thirty-five years ago."

It was obvious anyway, she said, how this kind of light had affected the way I saw things.

I told her something Wallace Stegner wrote: whatever landscape a child is exposed to early on, that will be the sort of gauze through which he or she will see all the world afterward. I said I thought it was emotional sight, not strictly a physical thing.

The spanking freshness of the afternoon encouraged a long drive. I asked Sandra if she wanted to go out to Reseda, where our family had lived in several houses, starting in 1948.

In November 1985 I had come down to Los Angeles from my home in Oregon. I was meeting a photographer who lived there, and with whom I was working on a story about the California desert for *National Geographic*. Flying into Los Angeles usually made me melancholy—and indignant. What I remembered from my childhood here, especially a rural countryside of farms and orchards out toward Canoga Park and Granada Hills, was not merely "gone." It had been obliterated, as if by a kind of warfare, and the remnant earth dimmed beneath a hideous pall of brown air.

A conversation with people in Los Angeles about these changes never soothes anyone. It only leaves a kind of sourness and creates impedence between people, like radio static. On the way to eat dinner with my friend, ruminating nevertheless in a silent funk about the place, I suddenly and vividly saw a photograph in my mind. It was of a young boy, riding the cantilevered support of a mailbox like a horse. On the side of the mailbox was "5837." I wrote the numerals down on the edge of a newspaper in my lap. I was not sure what they meant, but I recognized the boy as myself.

During dinner, I just as suddenly remembered the words "Wilbur Avenue," a street in Reseda. We had lived in three different houses in that town, the last one on Calvert Street. I had visited it several times in the intervening years, but hadn't been able to remember where the other two houses were.

The next day I rented a car and drove out to the Calvert Street home. Some thirty citrus and fruit trees my brother and I had planted in the midfifties had been dug out, and the lot had been divided to accommodate a second house, but parts of the lawn we had so diligently watered and weeded were still growing. I had raised tumbler pigeons here, and had had my first dog, a Kerry Blue terrier.

I inquired at a gas station on Victory Boulevard and found I was only a few blocks from crossing Wilbur Avenue. I made the turn there but saw the house numbers were in the six thousands and climbing; coming back the other way, I pulled up tentatively in front of 5837. I got out slowly, stared at the ranch-style house, and was suffused with a feeling, more emotion than knowledge, that this had been my home. Oleander bushes that had once shielded the house from the road were gone, along with a white rail fence and about fifteen feet of the front yard. In the late forties, before flood-control projects altered the drainage of this part of the San Fernando Valley, Wilbur Avenue had been a two-lane road with high, paved berms meant to channel flood water north to the Los Angeles River. In those days it also served as a corridor for sheep being moved to pasture. Now it was four lanes wide, with modest curbs.

One walnut tree remained in the yard, and a grapefruit tree closer to the house. I glimpsed part of the backyard through a breezeway but kept moving toward the front door, to knock and introduce myself.

There was no answer. I waited awhile and knocked again. When no one answered I walked around to the breezeway, where there was a kitchen door. I nearly collided with a small, elderly woman whose hands flew up involuntarily in defense. I quickly gave my name, explaining I had grown up here, that I only wished to look around a little, if I could. Fright still gripped her face.

"Do you know," I said to her, "how, from the family room, you have to take that odd step up to the hallway, where the bedrooms are?"

Her face relaxed. She waved off her anxiousness, seemingly chagrined. She explained that the owner of the house, a woman named Mrs. Little, was inside, dying of cancer. I remembered the name. She had lived out near Palmdale when we rented the house. I said that I was sorry, that there was no need for me to go inside.

"Well, please, have a look around," she said. She was relaxed now, serene, acting as though we were distant relatives. She walked into the backyard with me. At nearly each step, having difficulty stemming the pressure of memories, I blurted something—about a tree, about a cinderblock wall (still unfinished) around a patio. I pointed to some aging apricot and grapefruit trees, and to a massive walnut tree. We were standing on a concrete path, where I squatted down to peer at a column of ants going in and out of a crack. I had watched ants in this same crack forty years before. These were their progeny, still gathering food here. The mystery of their life, which had once transfixed me, seemed in no way to have diminished. I felt tears brim under my eyes and spill onto my cheeks. The woman touched my forearm deliberately but lightly, and walked away.

The horse stalls, a barn, and a row of chicken coops were gone, but I found scraps of green rolled roofing and splinters of framing lumber from them in the tall grass. I remembered mischief I had created here as a five-year-old. And then, like a series of sudden inflorescences, came memories first of the texture of tomatoes I had raised in a garden beside the chicken coops, and then of the sound of bees—how my friends and I had dared each other to walk past a hive of feral honeybees behind the barn where it ran close to the back fence.

Tempted to pick apricots and a grapefruit, I decided I had no right to do so. I said goodbye to the woman and asked her to convey my good wishes to Mrs. Little, whom I could not think would remember me.

Driving straight from the house to Anza-Borrego State Park in the western Sonoran Desert, a hundred and fifty miles away, I felt a transcendent calm. I promised myself I would return and try to find the first house, the location of which was lost to me.

Sandra and I came over from Whittier on the freeways, turning north off the Ventura onto Reseda Boulevard, then cutting over to Wilbur, which ran parallel. The house could not hold for her what it held for ne, and I felt selfish using our time like this. But I wanted to share the good feeling I had had. The neighborhood still has about it something of the atmosphere of a much older San Fernando Valley—a bit run-down, but with no large housing developments, no landscaped and overwatered awns. I drove past the house and had to turn and come back. The mailbox with its numbers was gone. The lot was empty: the house and all the trees had been razed; the bare, packed, red-brown earth had been swept clean. Only the tread marks of a single tractor were apparent, where it had turned on soft ground.

I got out of the car and walked back and forth across the lot, silently. On the ground near a neighbor's cinder-block fence I saw an apricot pit. I put it in my pocket.

"I've been thinking," I said to Sandra, once I was standing beside the car again. "The first house may have been way out on Wilbur, toward the Santa Susannas." She looked off that way.

"Would you mind driving? That way I could look. I might get the pattern of something, the way it looked."

"Yes," she said. "Certainly."

We turned around and headed north on Wilbur, windows open to the fresh breeze. We drove past the house where my friend Leon had lived, where I had first bitten into the flesh of a pomegranate, and then slowly past other places that I knew but which I could not recognize. The air all around was brilliant.

SYDNEY LEA

On the Bubble

Early June of 1992, below Stonehouse Mountain, Grafton County, New Hampshire—a place and time in which snowsqualls, routine enough just weeks ago, will at last deserve the name freakish. In freshet beds where waters flared and vanished, frail shoots of jewelweed declare themselves; grass bursts the voles' winter tunnels; geese trail the Connecticut northward; the buck deer's antlers are in velvet; the woodchuck's busy to double in weight; trout sip the ponds' ephemerids; everywhere, the lovesick insistence of birds.

Our family has lived ten years on this foothill's flank, but soon after dawn this morning—beckoned by the full day ahead—I hiked down from its mild summit for perhaps the last time. The ramble, especially under such circumstances, brought back the many I'd made there, in company or alone, one recollection summoning another, and that one still another, till outward prospects opened onto vaster, more labyrinthine inward views.

I suddenly found myself at the June of 1989, three years gone. Unseasonable as any late spring's for a hunt, that forenoon had still invited my scout's eye; for companions therefore I had my gun dogs, two of them dead since. And because I'm also forever scouting more than game—no easy name for it—I'd also brought along my third-born, Jordan. He'd turned five less than a month before; I would manage to haul him in his riding pack through one more year.

As soon as we struck height-of-land, my boy reached into his jacket and fetched out paraphernalia for blowing bubbles. What few he managed were pea sized and, hustled by a hard wind, quickly burst against the granite moraine where we stood. Jordan, however, is more stubborn a soul than I will ever quite understand—no matter that, despite its costs, I share the quality myself, in spades. For all my untypically rationalistic discouragement, he persisted until in a momentary lull he somehow produced one outsized sphere. Perhaps six inches around, it lifted off his dipper, fighting like a hot-air balloon for altitude—which it couldn't sustain. As my son watched in agony between rage and sorrow, the great thing sank slowly toward stone. On lighting, though, it remained miraculously intact—tenuous, quivering. I could actually hear the catch in Jordan's breath as he beheld in its film the reflections of a whole domain: high blue crossed by thunderheads, skinny black upland spruces, weathered crags and windfalls, glyphs of animal trails.

He and I would miss all this directly.

Then the bubble vanished. No obvious pop, only evanescence. And in the after-moment, by quenchless habit I began to conjure metaphors. The perdurability of the mountain, the transience of human constructs, the rest. But all sorts of things—inner and outer, gross and subtle—blocked my scheme, and I gave it up. If I've discovered nothing else, I know that one can't simply will his figures.

Besides, there seemed enough in the plain spectacle of the child, dazed by these quicksilver splendors and their disappearance, to cause a familiar commotion. I was moved by more than his mere smallness, the puff of his bewildered lips, the way his pale, forgotten hand spilled the bubble jar's contents. I felt, almost physically, the curse fallen on his parents' wish for him and his sisters and brothers: that we might leave these young spirits among the apparent unchangeables that had nourished our own. This wish in fact had moved us all to Stonehouse Mountain, whose very name seemed auspicious. Between eternities of stone and mountain, a house might nestle for good.

Not that I'd left my former town, some miles to the south, altogether cheerfully, having cherished it so for the preceding decade and a half. Yet after that time, I watched the village and its surroundings transform themselves, overnight it seemed, into a sprawl of bedrooms for the burgeoning college-and-commercial cluster downriver. The jobs—far scarcer in actuality than in developers' fabulations—had arrived and departed so quickly that, on looking up one day, I found native families gone, their farms become "grounds."

Eighty-year-old Harry Franklin, among the few who stayed, put matters succinctly: "We're just like anyplace else now."

This morning's reverie on my son's bright bubble must have established a motif of fragile glories, that motif in turn leading to further recollections, which otherwise seem willy-nilly, or at least nonchronological. I shortly found myself leaping to the autumn of 1991. That was a fall like many another in obvious respects: fragile, yes—flares of maple racing into the umbers and beiges of oak or beech; short summer shadows stretched suddenly long after noontime; big-fingered ferns gone arthritic as the swamps showed the first pale ice at their margins. But even more than usual, I'd been out and busy. From the final weekend of September till the middle one in November, I chased birds pretty much every day. Nasty work, of course, but necessary: my two youngest pointers were just at field-training age. If, as usual, I lamented the headlong rush of those weeks, it was as much because the pups deserved more exposure than I could cram into a season as because of my ineradicable elegiac streak.

Therefore, when it came to deer season (which, precisely for being dogless, shakes less passion from me anyhow than the grouse months), I hunted too rarely and casually. But this was of necessity, too. A part of me would choose to spend as much time year-round in the wild as it had done all fall with the pointers, yet I must now and then come indoors, there to ponder other things: my children growing up; my wife aging into a greater and greater handsomeness, in every sense of that word; reflections like these passing—so far as possible—into articulation.

In short, as the eleventh month of '91 advanced on the twelfth, I spared only an hour here and another there to follow the whitetail, preoccupied as I was with separate pursuits. Such an approach may reap results in places like Pennsylvania or Texas, but in my edge of New England—herd thinner, woods thicker—it's apt, barring dumb luck, to end in failure.

It did. It didn't.

My first morning out was all Indian-summer crackle underfoot, but by the second, several days later, conditions had turned ideal: a light snow fallen on unfrozen ground, sign would be clear, the going quiet. Moreover, though as always I'd cherished October's game more than the bigger game of the moment, there was and is something about November that exerts a stronger aesthetic appeal. I know that to say so puts me in a distinct minority, but the austerity of that period just before real snow—of sharply contoured branch and trunk, granite and cloud—oddly braces my soul.

I recall setting off in that second dawn at a brisk clip, which I meant to keep till I came on something interesting. This didn't take long: less than a mile from home, on a brushed-over twitch road at the north end of Stonehouse, I fairly struck a turnpike, deer tracks everywhere. Mostly skippers and does, of course, but one heel-heavy trail, too, fresh as paint, every third print ruddy with rut. I wondered for the hundredth time how a buck can manage to produce so much of that dribble—as if this were the chief internal mystery in such a creature.

There's a certain special outcropping on Stonehouse Mountain which, though short of the summit, provides as bold a view: the loftier Whites to northeastward in the distance, and—closer below—that bijou, Mason Pond. Flush with first settlement here, my wife and I happened onto this ledge in one of our early, desultory explorations. No sign of human presence around us or in the vista, we found it hard to suppose that a lone soul knew or remembered this corner of forest, which then belonged, technically, to an unknown out-of-stater.

We spoke of rigging a sledge some winter, dragging materials to the site for a shack, even installing our extra woodstove. Then we'd make occasional getaways. If our cabin were found and dismantled, what harm? We'd have had it for a spell anyway.

These musings preceded our small children. And someone else soon bought that flank of mountain anyhow, for which he now plans fifteen "luxury estates." Thus our musings turned to idle dreams before we owned a prayer of making them otherwise, but neither dream nor prayer will utterly die; we still name that spot "The Shack." It stays on, somehow, as a place in mind. Yet how can we pass such inner property down to those same children?

I'd been saying something else, however, before sorrow and anger broke in. Taking the buck's track last fall, I shortly found myself exactly at The Shack. Perhaps that very sorrow and anger distracted me; in any case, I relaxed concentration as one so easily does, and I missed my deer until too late. A good buck, right enough. Although I couldn't count horns, of course, there looked like a thicket of them as he bolted into softwood cover: I could see that much, and the bulk of him, and the almost black color which typifies our trophy ridge-runners. I could have shot—and would have, in my youth—yet I knew that it would be no more than luck if my slug hit, that it would go in from behind. It would ruin a share of venison, and might do far worse: I'll haltingly acknowledge some atavistic excitement in following a blood trail—but not a long one.

I performed an old charade of rage, complete with misdirected oaths at the vanished prey: "Why, you son of a bitch! I'll fix you!" But in truth I remained happy at my own calm and resignation; I'd rest the fellow a spell and then pick him up again. Brushing the scarf of snow from a blowdown, I sat and lit a pipe. When I checked my watch, though, it astonished me as ever: two full hours gone, all I'd allotted for this morning's chase. No, I wouldn't fix that buck, not today. Instead I'd follow an arc down to our house, semi-alert, just in case I jumped something else on the way. But that would be accident, too, and in any case my thoughts had already gone elsewhere.

The younger children must be getting up about now; it pleased me to imagine them at a front window, frowzy, curious, and then the sleep in their necks a warmth against my cold face. They'd grow up so soon. The thought of my first-born Creston, off at college just now, was bittersweet: how thoughtful and decent and *interesting* a man he'd become; yet how wouldn't I miss the vanished little boy in him? And the next child, Erika, was already fourteen, bright and beautiful.

I'd have stopped the whole lot in their tracks if I could, or maybe even moved them backwards in time-back to Jordan's age, or three-year-old Catherine's, or even to the age of the next tiny mystery, who'd arrive in his or her splendor a month from that deer-hunting day. I'd load each one by turns in the battered old pack, heft them, march them with me into the wonderful highlands. We'd see things together again.

By a cellar hole in a certain burntland, an abandoned Model A lay for decades: we named the place Henry's Clearing, after the car's inventor. I have a picture of my oldest son astride the wreck's springless seat. He's ten. Beside him, a popple sapling has grown through the floorboards; it rests a feathery branch on the rust-orange dashboard, as a slim, slightly apprehensive adolescent girl might rest her fingertips. The skins of child and tree seemed translucent that morning and—far more than in the photograph—they remain that way to my interior eye.

Six months ago my big boy turned twenty. His companion popple is dead, scalped by the local developer when his crew removed the jalopy as an eyesore. One of his intended access roads will pass through the old burn. As I approached Henry's Clearing, I imagined gleaming foreign sedans, run hub-deep into March goo and left to replace the Model A. Such a fantasy made me grin—but only momentarily. Pavement would follow, sure as death.

Just east of Henry's, I froze—my impulse strange but familiar to anyone who's hunted long enough. I felt sure a deer stood somewhere near. Don't ask how. It couldn't have been my hearing, which is not worth much (and which forty years of shooting haven't improved). In my time, if children contracted ear infections, they went to a doctor and got them lanced. That fact is worth remembering, perhaps, while I rhapsodize on bygone days: I seem to have had those infections every other week, so my aural channels are a maze of scar tissue. Even though my sons and daughters appear equally susceptible to their father's old malady, they will never, like him, confuse some inward clatter of the eardrum with duck flight, some high whine through it with a building wind, some uncertainly located pop with the far report of a firearm. None will wonder, as I soon did near that burn, whether an actual or illusory squelch sounded in dampening snow.

I chose, at least for the moment, to believe in the sound's reality, and I felt gratified once again that a belief could still make my heart rap. I smelled an odor like the ozone warning of electrical storm. My mouth went cotton. Slowly I settled my backside onto a boulder, watching until my eyes teared and I had no choice but to blink. Then I watched some more, shivering, willing the deer of my intuitions around the shoulder of the knoll and into Henry's Clearing—broadside, big. My younger son, seven by now, could eat four chops at a go.

A different man would have waited even longer. I, however, began in due course to doubt my own instincts, even if I'd had reason to curse such reckless doubt in the past. But as I say, I had home on the brain by now, and was unsure anyhow that I wanted a buck I'd done so little to deserve, supposing he *were* on hand. As the game thins out, its supporting habitat savaged by conspirators in greed, a hunter should place demands on himself; he should do things right or not at all.

In 1991, that ravenous seven-year-old fairly wriggled with enthusiasm for the woods and the quarry. Stuck unmoving to my perch, I remembered the same fever from my childhood. With him, flesh of my flesh, I could somehow chafe again for a first armed trip to the field. I too could hang on a porch door, awaiting a parent's return from his hunt. Then I could smell the cold dirt on his dogs, the humid stench of bird-feathers in the gamebag. My father would suffer my slow services: I could kneel and undo his bootlaces, the aroma of man falling all over me.

It had only been four short decades before, after all, that I'd done and felt these things. But when four more had passed, when the boy had reached my age, when it was 2031, what of this sort would thrill him, in fact or imagination or memory? What would keep him watching as I watched, even as a chilly dampness climbed through pantswool into my bones? *Where* would he sit, and what would he pass on to his own children? What could I myself pass on—from here, from there?

I needed to disrupt my own mood, and so—the wind northwest, straight in my face—I decided to sneak over for a look through the burn, a mere twenty yards from my stand. I took most of that distance easy, little at a time, eyeing the spot where I'd have to scooch to keep my profile under the slope's, injuries to each knee speaking more sternly now than in the sports-crazy boyhood that produced them.

Step, stop, wait. Step, stop, wait.

I flinched as a raven *whoof-whoof-whoofed* low overhead, across the fire-cleared ground and gone. The bird left a deeper quiet than the one it had broken, and I lingered within it till by God I did hear something! A small racket in brush around the corner. I sucked my teeth, trying to swallow but trying also to reason: if I'd heard a deer at all, odds favored a doe; or it might as easily turn out to be a plain old red squirrel, famous for disproportionate ruckus in a calm woods.

Five squatting steps further on, inch by inch I straightened. Over the knoll's rim, some forty yards down the former tote road, sure enough I detected fur and motion. A flag? No. Though I couldn't yet tell to what else, it belonged to no deer. Wrong color for a start: chocolate brown, highlit by cinnamon.

At length the animal slipped from brush and showed its shape entire. Still unable to identify it, I could see it was large. I stood fixed as a pillar while it made its unmistakable way toward me. The wind had picked up some, but kept moving toward me too. Better and better.

Then, something familiar but inexplicable: rather than growing bigger, my creature began to shrink as it came on. Noting the fussy lope of the weasel family, I thought: Well, I'll be damned, an otter! I'd happened on such apparent strays before, especially in the cold months, far from any watershed worth the name. Better and better.

Then I noticed the too-prominent ears, and I briefly imagined: *marten*! But this fellow, even as he got smaller, looked heavier than martens, which in any case, alas, had vanished from virtually all of New Hampshire some time ago. And yet since he is to the more common black as one to five, the pure-brown fisher— as he eventually became—proved no disappointment, especially as he kept up his nosy progress. The wind from behind him blew more insistently now: I could see back-hairs ruffle like a field of late hay, and vague cloud-shadows skidding past m the coarse wet turf.

A good hound couldn't have smelled me from that animal's quarter; but just as the human, without any sensory clue, may occasionally surmise the nearness of the nonhuman, so now my fisher felt something out of the ordinary, stopped in his tracks, raised his head, sniffed the useless air.

We were in full sight of each other, but my eyes were the better. How many minutes, then, did we stand like that? One? Four? Ten? We stayed equally motionless, but my mind continued to run anyhow. And the fisher's? Were there images in his brain too, and if so, how did they look? How had it happened that a man could see his boy blow soap bubbles in another season and another niche of this very mountain, and still somehow be here this morning? Was my wife happy enough with our life together? Did the fisher believe he'd find hare in Henry's Clearing? Had he found them before? Did he store that experience? How? Was he in fact a she? Who had owned the Model A? Would anyone store memories of me? Did God really count each bird that fell and, having counted, what did He conclude? Why does blue show up under scarred paper birchbark like that tree's five yards to the animal's right? What made this particular scar? Did you feel the cold in Idaho, say, as you did in New England? Could a person go on fathering children and still complain about his world's crowding?

Perhaps I didn't think these exact thoughts just then. I mean to present less my mind's content than the way it kept filling with things apparently random and unaccountable. What had any to do with an outsized weasel, to whom I was about to wave or speak, excited as always to witness a wild thing's most frantic flight? No time to say. Suddenly, the big wind blew a gap in the overcast, and a filament of sun struck the fisher. The guard hairs of his coat became a numinous, gilded aura, I gasped, the cloud cover sealed itself again, the creature bounded into near woods and took to the treetops, leaping from one to another out of sight.

I stayed on for a spell, some bloodheat distracting me from weather's authority. But the wind soon gathered a few horizontal rainsplots, and I came to: my knuckles ached on the rifle, my wet bottom burned with the cold, and a gloom descended, which was instantaneous as the clouds' return and sadly common in my middle life. In what direction would my fisher's children fly, and my own, once the 'dozers had coughed and quit, the backhoes dug and gone?

Oh, I'd seen something that morning. I'd see it till my own dark hole got dug. And after that?

The adored father who was my first guide died in the February of my twenty-third year. I married the following June, though my better soul found something wrong in taking such an important step while still gripped by a mourning so heavy and confusing. I'd never been a deliberate boy, never would be; but even I had enough sense to know I was acting unsensibly.

Why, then, did I let things proceed? Well, however much I'd played the hell-raiser from earliest schooldays, I'd often likewise shown counter-instincts toward politeness. To this day I retain both these sides of my character, neither a pure virtue nor a pure vice, and each still in periodic, painful contest with the other. In 1966, wedding day approaching, I felt compelling reasons to stop the whole business, even if that meant sabotaging everybody else's plans. But my mannerly disinclination to rock boats prevailed: I stayed the good boy. How, after all, could I break off an arrangement that appeared to gratify my mother so? Hadn't she suffered enough for a spell? Wouldn't I likewise insult the memory of her husband, who'd been similarly fond of my bride-to-be? ("I've known you all your life," he joked to me when I announced our engagement, "and this is the first really *bright* decision I've caught you at.")

Monkeysuits and gowns—all fitted. Preacher, organist, orchestra—all hired. On and on, and no decent way out, I imagined; no time even to decide whether I really wanted a way. And thus, in the confidence of my sublime ignorance, I concluded that I could always divorce if married life didn't work out.

Sixteen years and two children later, my wife and I did part company. Because of that son and that daughter, I will never seriously unwish those years; but they were undeniably hard for me in many respects, and surely more so for my spouse. At length I believed, and still do, that no solution other than divorce would leave us both sane; yet the pain of it overwhelmed me. What hurt, above all, might I bestow as inheritance? The agony of that time lives on in me, though I soon remarried (more happily than anyone deserves), and have remained in a contact with those first children as close and loving as with the three who have followed.

These are thoughts, however odd, that I *do* know I had as I lingered on Stonehouse Mountain this morning, recalling a bubble and a brown fisher. And I thought of how, from an astonishingly young age, I'd vowed to find a region—some beautiful and intriguing country, home to fleet, wild things—and marry it. I thought how I'd courted the wilder parts of Maine, New Hampshire, and Vermont all through my adolescence and then, in my twenties, tied the knot with upper New England.

And I thought, as the poet wrote, of "failings from us, vanishings."

For a long stretch, I'd remained so in love with this Grafton County that even on the worst day of mudtime my heart would stutter at the simple sight of a certain slope or tree or stream. The stubborn green of an October sidehill surrounded by darkening woods seemed a marvel that all by itself proved life worthwhile. I remember a July moon over Kenyon Hill so apparently near that my first little girl, not yet two at the time, made clutching gestures toward it, imagining candy. I remember my oldest son's wide-eyed, slack-jawed stare at the bank of Trout Brook, from which a January mink had just scampered into nearby jack-firs. I remember the scarlet tanager that came daily out of yellow May woods to a maple by the bedroom where my wife nursed another baby son. I remember that son's little sister, giggling as we cracked the skim-ice on a late March pool with pointy sticks. And now the newest baby goes cross-eyed and furrow-browed as a sulphur butterfly lights on her carriage. In mind it's as if in all seasons the wide, good universe were there for the sake of each child alone.

In recent years, though, my love affair has found itself in trouble. I can no longer take its passions straight, because for every moment of the old exaltation—for every field or moon or mink, every bird or puddle, every blue butterfly or sun-dazed fisher—there comes a grimly compensating recognition. All these glories are under attack as never before.

But have I another divorce in me? And if so, on what grounds? Does one abandon the love of one's life because she's been assaulted? Doesn't one defend her to the death? Here, while so accurate in other respects, the marriage analogy fails. Though I can cherish the lands and waters and animals of a place with a human affection, none will ever *become* human: indeed, that their inner lives remain so irretrievably otherwise is the greater part of their seductiveness to imagination.

But let my puny allegories stand or fall as they will. How little they matter anyhow. I have fought as hard as was in me against those luxury "estates" I mentioned earlier, to the extent that on several occasions I've scarcely restrained myself (or been restrained by others) from physical violence. In company with my wife and friends and neighbors, I have poured cash, time, and fervor into the battle, and as I write our side has happily prevailed. Yet I have also read my *mene, mene, tekel, upharsin*: the town planning board's rejection of a swinish proposal takes note of the dirt-road intersection below us, which the members consider too tricky for such sudden increase in traffic. Nothing noted of the greater, the more obscene peril: that in future deliberations an unencumbered mountainside will be considered not a wondrous treasure but a chunk of real estate.

When things have reached such a turn, "conservation"—however ardently I practice and support it—looks depressingly irrelevant to a stubborn fool like me, because by then something is already past conserving, irretrievably lost. Something spiritual: once banished, no *genius loci* accepts reinvitation; we're mucking around with eternals here.

For all of that, there will doubtless soon be talk of compromise. (One vociferous—and almost marvelously featherheaded—townsman who spoke all along in the project's favor has lately been elected as a "planner.") Perhaps the developer will settle for seven luxury homes on the wild side of Stonehouse, not fifteen; perhaps he'll put aside a larger segment of his property for conservancy, the one that from the start he has called a park (the very word suggesting the awful diminishment I speak of). Not that my mind will disapprove these enforced concessions, which will be better than nothing. It's only that my heart is an absolutist: mere terms having changed, this stretch of woods and hillside will never again suffice for me and my family.

It's time to go.

For a long while, I pledged I'd never inhabit ground I couldn't pee on in broad daylight without worry over observation. Whatever burdens it imposes on her for obvious reasons my wife has joined in the oath. The day the developer filed his plan with the town, we vowed we'd resist it to the end; but we also put our Stonehouse home on the market and went looking for a bigger spread somewhere else, outside the gentrifying web, affordable. The spot we found sits a good way upriver, and in one respect I should be satisfied for a long time: with nearly three hundred acres of scrub and ledge to choose from, I'll relieve myself where I damned well please.

Yet my old stipulation, which I once considered a telling metaphor, seems the palest of whimsies now. Even after we discovered the new site—full of game and cedar swamp, bordered by granite palisade, barely dotted by a bungalow and workshop—I recognized for my own part that our move could at best be a holding action. One can piss his bladder out on the earth and still be shriven of all that really matters. The breadth and situation of the place will ensure privacy, but this isn't what we're after. It is not only that both my wife and I relish the human connectedness of a true community, the kind of community that so-called development does much to sunder; it's also that if we reach the point of valuing privacy over other qualities, we will have admitted defeat, will have bought a mere illusion. If ours becomes the last domain of apparent wildness in the county or state, then we'll live in a park ourselves, as artificial as some millionaire's fenced-in preserve or that biospheric bubble one lately reads of. We may not see another soul from where we live, but as I say, the very air will have changed.

What on earth can I want, then? I ask the same of myself, to the point of hysteria; and in answering I sometimes recall the title of a poem by an unlikely hero, insurance executive Wallace Stevens: "The Pleasures of Merely Circulating." Or I summon the closing passage of yet another of his poems, "Esthetique du Mal":

> And out of what one sees and hears and out
> Of what one feels, who could have thought to make
> So many selves, so many sensuous worlds,
> As if the air, the mid-day air, was swarming
> With the metaphysical changes that occur,
> Merely in living as and where we live.

I want to live where a meeting with a brown-phase fisher is never a commonplace, but always a *possibility*. I would a hundred times prefer to encounter that creature on home ground than travel to Kenya or wherever to behold a basking leopard. Tourism won't do: to thrill at that leopard, I'd have to inhabit his landscape. I'd rather wander a path across the very landscape I dwell in, certain that by such mere circulation, however stealthily undertaken, I might slip among its secretive, metaphysical wonders, as I've done for so much of my life.

Where on the planet can such country lie anymore? That, of course, is the rub. The leopard's every move has been charted by the organizers of the photographic safari; the guests will not fail to snap him from their Land Rovers. Amazing, then, that I recall dim markings on maps of Africa, representing—we were told—places untrod by human feet. Though our teachers betrayed, needless to say, their Eurocentric notions of humanity, notions whose political implications still prove enormous, I—as a child of European extraction myself—must admit my childhood enchantment with these obtuse descriptions. As a grownup I wince to know that someone may have fitted the big cat with a radio transmitter, kin to the cassette players in the native villages where young men pass in knock-off Michael Jordan basketball shoes. So much for what we called darkest Africa, whose very undarkening, whose whitening, fits my mood of disaster.

More locally, how staggering to read New Englander Ralph Waldo Emerson's claim of a bare hundred and sixty years ago—less than twice the span of his own rich lifetime—that "*Nature*, in the common sense, refers to essences unchanged by man; space, the air, the river, the leaf."

Fifteen luxury estates on Stonehouse Mountain.

From the White Mountains to the Black Forest, foliage shriveling in its acid bath.

The "blue Danube," so thick you can almost walk across it.

The crew of the spaceship Atlantis—one member no doubt on watch for orbiting junk—beams congratulations to *Star Wars* director George Lucas at the goddamned Academy Award ceremonies.

For me such bad news underlies even a fair amount of good news: for example, that the frightening hole our ingenuity has rent in the ozone layer can perhaps be patched up by the same ingenuity. Logic requires me to rejoice at such a prospect, but I claim no logic for my feelings: should *human* nature repair what it has wrought in nonhuman, there will no longer *be* such a thing as the nonhuman. The heavens themselves are park enough as it is. That moon's no magical candy for a daughter, even in my fancy. And though she and her sisters and brothers have all been keen for evening hikes to high prominences, they've never looked on stars that kindled in a truly unknown realm. I feel almost cursed to have been so blessed myself as a child.

And yes, how stubborn old blessing has made me! On the day that a rocket flew up to probe Venus, two grouse flew up ahead of my great bitch Bessie. Don't ask me to name that rocket nor say what of use its crew brought home; but until I die I'll remember each inch of the joyously arduous trek up the maple-crazy slope above Pony Hill, and Bessie's point on that double.

"Does No One at All Ever Feel This Way in the Least?" asked Robert Frost in a poem so entitled, one already quaint by 1952. And quainter still, I answer him *yes*:

> And now, O sea, you're lost by aeroplane.
> Our sailors ride a bullet for a boat.
> Our coverage of distance is so facile
> It makes us to have had a sea in vain.
> Our moat around us is no more a moat,
> Our continent no more a moated castle.

I know the argument—to which, again, I can offer no logical counter—that it's as much a "natural" thing for human speculation and endeavor to keep broadening themselves as it is for my fisher to root a hare from under some fallen hemlock, or for me to fire on a pair of game birds; and that the 747 has its roots in the warrior's chariot—not to mention that my precision-made Winchester looks back on his pike. Perhaps some son or daughter will delight, as many people obviously must, in a naturalism so conceived. I recognize here that I speak, as one tends to do, of things that have charged my *own* imaginative life, things whose alteration feels like painful, personal attack, and whose disappearance bodes a death.

So mortally wounded, I come back and back to the same painful stand: What father am I? What vision do I leave behind?

It may sound as though my restlessness were new, and my younger love for this north country the emotion of a naïve boy. But my only genuine naïveté lay in a radical underestimation of the *speed* with which today's remote New England corner—let alone those dark African map-splotches—would become tomorrow's suburb or resort. Although I began to dream of Idaho when the very first fern bar opened in the nearest town of size, it was a bit as I'd dreamed of divorce even as I married for the first time: my innocence, as I say, was to feel no immediate urgency in either speculation.

I had spent a good deal of time in the West, and had loved every minute; yet there existed something deep within me that clove to the density, the greenery, the variety of the woods and even of the much maligned weather in the upper Northeast. What could be more beautiful than the Yellowstone reaches of Montana, the Green River valley in Utah, the Wind River Mountains in Wyoming, the Sangre de Cristos in New Mexico, the Maroon Bells of Colorado? But I remained no more than a rapt visitor among these intoxications, and while I got a kick out of cowboys, I identified, however presumptuously, with backland Yankees.

I did recognize, for all of this, one powerful advantage the Western mountain states held over my beloved trio of Maine, New Hampshire, and Vermont. They were, so to say, a little closer to dark old Africa. That is, even if they were equally prey to the international conspiracy against beauty and wonder (indeed, perhaps more so: once, seeing a Wyoming strip mine, I imagined my damnation in advance), those states beyond the Mississippi had *size*. If a pustule like Aspen popped up and festered, that still left a hell of a lot of Colorado; so did Rocky Flats. For every Jackson Hole and every wretched mineral operation, there existed a hundred barely populated hamlets to east or south or north. Once the cake got frosted near Santa Fe, you could trek back into mountains that made our own look like loaves on a shelf.

And since I'd for some reason never been to Idaho, nor ever heard it much spoken of by exactly the wrong people, it became a new place in mind. Vague, latent.

That Idaho.

I finally visited the state late last summer, and at least where I roamed, it looked all the Idaho it ever could. I found things that have long bound me to the East—forests, chiefly, and none restricted like many Western stands to single species—combined with a superb, non-Eastern vastness. I even came on a stretch of river that would serve: not blue-ribbon stuff, but its trout being wild it was good enough, in part precisely for being yet undiscovered by the blue-ribbon crowd in their spanking Orvis duds. Though all my reserves had been poured into the new property back home, I did discover a modest riverside farm, for sale at a beggar's price. Someday, maybe, I thought—before it's too late.

It was too late already. Not long after getting home, my brain crowded with fantasies which I believed I'd sobered out of, I read the inevitable, crushing article in one of my conservation magazines. There was furor in good quarters over a proposed development (what a word! as if God had left the job undone) on the fabulous Snake River. The golf course; the jetboat marina; the complex of condominiums with twenty-four-hour security. This horror will quite likely fail to go through, but there will be another compromise, and, for all its hard effects on my soul, something in my blood—the very blood I've passed on to five children—will not be compromised.

And yet it must.

I look out the window of a house laid bare: high on Stonehouse Mountain, where the foliage comes late, the scrawny hardwoods have just started to show their meek pastels, which they seem to pull back into themselves whenever a cloud sails over. In our driveway my truck cringes under its burden of furniture, books, dog crates, crockery, firearms. Orts and fragments.

Suddenly I recall one more walk, with my fourth child Catherine in the venerable riding pack. It was the sort of languid August midday when the woods go silent as a cave, so that the little girl's voice seemed to fill the countryside. *Yesterday*, she sang, *all my troubles seemed so far away. / Now it looks as though they're here to stay. / Oh, I believe in yesterday.* She was three years old, and the song but a song; yet I needed to labor some against my own tears, her tune ringing truer than she could yet know.

Within my lifetime no jetboat will roil the waters beside the farm I found in Idaho. But once my children live there, they'll hear such a snarl in their own— the *tock* of the clubbed ball, the growl of the patrolling Rottweiler. I whistle for the blonde son and daughter who want to ride north with me in the truck; I sigh and try to feel practical, since I know what I know: as well to move our paltry twenty-five New England miles as to wrench up stakes more radically.

There seems wrench enough, after all, in leaving one more local town where once we dreamed of permanence, where a handful of friends and a handful of wilds will remain. The prospect of hunting up their replacements elsewhere seems sufficiently daunting too. Inner lives, both human and natural, will reveal themselves at a slow pace; that's the rural New England manner. Yet the greater ache is that those lives, like the ones we abandon today, may prove as fragile as our boy's one bold and bright expression, a few short hours past, up there at height-of-land.

EMILY HIESTAND

Watershed

An Excursion in Four Parts

> The idea of nature as a well-balanced machine
> has been replaced by complicated talk of
> dynamic and multiple equilibriums, chaotic
> systems, and other unsettling notions that
> undermine all the conditioning we received
> at the hands of Disney nature films and Mark
> Trail comic strips. Nature, we are learning,
> is enormously untidy and rarely predictable.
> Change is the rule, stability the exception.
>
> —PAUL SCHULLERY, *Searching for Yellowstone*

Part One | Street

Like travelers who want to keep some favorite place from being discovered, the residents of our neighborhood sometimes confide to one another in a near-whisper, "There's no other place like this in the city." It's not a grand neighborhood, only a modest enclave on the fringe of the Boston metropolis, but visitors who chance upon our streets are routinely surprised. They remark on the quiet of the area; on the colonnade of maples whose canopies have grown together into a leafy arch over the street; on the many front porches (which older residents call their *piazzas*), and on the overall sense of being in a little village.

This small urban village is situated in the territory long represented by the late Thomas P. "Tip" O'Neill, who served in the U.S. Congress for thirty-four years, nine of them as Speaker of the House. Our streets are part of his "lunch-bucket liberal" district, a working-class neighborhood located on land that formerly held such things as the city's poorhouse, blacksmith shops, and tanneries. The earliest inhabitants of our streets were predominantly French-Canadians, families and young men fleeing British persecution, streaming south from Nova Scotia, Quebec, and the Iles de la Madeleine. That early history explains why our inland houses and streets feel curiously like a small fishing village; the architecture, exterior stairs and porches, even the way the houses are sited—close to the sidewalks with miniature front yards—are all transplants from the maritime villages of Acadia.

Immigrants from several other countries were also lightly represented in the early history of this neighborhood. The streets immediately surrounding the French-Canadian enclave were home to Irish, Italian, and West Indian immigrants, and to African Americans migrated and escaped from the South. From the beginning the neighborhood had a diverse population. Universally, older residents who grew up here recall that these streets were not contested territory, something of a rarity, then and now.

Together, the varied people of this end of town created a way of life based on dogged work and devotion, donuts from Verna's coffee shop, tolerance, fraternal clubs, church, and church bingo. The early neighborhood tone can be gleaned from one widely observed tradition, which was a principal entertainment on summer evenings. The activity consisted of residents sitting on their front porches after supper and talking to one another and to passersby. "Sitting out," they called it. The close-set houses with facing porches, rows of shade trees, and the intimate scale of the streets all contributed to making this neighborly activity possible. These physical conditions are among those championed by today's New Urbanists, the movement of architects and urban planners whose recipe for reviving community life calls for porches, trees, density, and services within walking distance.

At the end of a road, on the edge of town, our neighborhood was long a modest backwater, sociologically and geographically remote from other parts of Cambridge. As our neighbor Alice, who has been living here for seventy-eight years, puts it: "No one came down this way unless they lived here." But Speaker O'Neill, a pure product of these streets, took the local, big-hearted ethos national, where it made a difference across the length and breadth of the land.

The bones of the early demographics of this street are still visible where the names on scattered mailboxes still read Beauchemin, Arsenault, and Ouellette. In keeping with its original character as a portal into the city, our neighborhood has more recently become home to new citizens from India, Haiti, China, and Cape Verde, as well as to writers and artists seeking affordable housing. It is also a peaceful place to work, the quiet engineered by a rabbit warren of one-way streets that deters incidental traffic from attempting the neighborhood, creating a precinct that is, by city standards, serene.

By day you can hear the tinkle of a small brass bell tied to the door of the mom & pop store across the street; by night, the lightly syncopated jazz of crickets and katydids rises from our small yards. Not too quiet, though. The bells of St. John the Evangelist peel on the quarter hour, and Notre Dame de Pitié rings its three great Belgian-made *cloches*—bells named Marie, Joseph and Jesus. At Christmastime Notre Dame plays the carols *"Venez Divin Messie"* and *"Dans Cette Étable."* Several times a day, a train hurtles through the crossing, blowing a classic lonesome whistle; and at night teenagers sometimes roil along our sidewalks, releasing barbaric yawps.

Oh, way beyond yawps, my husband Peter reminds me. Completely over the top in the case of the five teenage girls with boom boxes who brought many sleepy citizens onto our balconies one morning at 3 am. In the late afternoons, younger children come by our house: the girls wearing plaid skirts and singing; the boys bouncing basketballs en route to the hoop in the corner park, where on any given summer day the wading pool is full of toddlers whose sleep-deprived parents sit conferring on nearby benches. Recently, we have also experienced a brand-new sound.

The new sound arrives about nine o'clock on summer evenings. It is audible first as a low rumble several blocks away, more a feeling than a sound. You might think it is the beginning of a minor earthquake. Slowly, the sound grows louder, coming closer, until, as it passes our house, it has grown into a glass-rattling, rhythmic, ultra-low-frequency pulse. It's not an earthquake, it's a car. Peter, who is a musician, explains the phenomenon to me. "It's kind of a guy thing," he says, which much I had guessed. To achieve the effect, young men retrofit automobiles with high-powered amplifiers—one for treble, one for bass, and several additional ones for each channel. They also install a couple of very large Bazooka brand loudspeakers, and then hook the assembly up to a CD player. The resulting system is intended for a kind of music called "house music," a subset of rap.

"House music," Peter continues, "is made up of long dance jams of sampled loops and effects. It's heavily percussive, with huge bass sounds created by combined synthesized and electric bass, and drum machines. A common technique is to have two or three drum sounds all hitting at the same time, which gives a fatter, chord-like sound. What these guys have learned is that if you take a plain eighty- or one-hundred-cycle tone, and hook it up so that it triggers simultaneously with a kick drum, it gives a massive low end."

"Are they doing this to attract girls?" I ask. "Well, sure," Peter replies. "But on some level they're doing it to try to impress everybody. They want people to notice, to say 'There goes Ron, he's got the loudest car in the neighborhood.' It's like hot-rodding a car, only instead of speed you're looking for more noise, more bass. They like to stop at lights, meet at certain places, sort of joust to see who can make the most booming sound."

Does such loud rumbling sound actually appeal to girls? Hmmm, hard to say. But something like it does appeal to female katydids. The journal *Nature* has reported that the rhythmic night chirruping of male katydids—the resonant sound which the males accomplish by rubbing their front wings together—is not a cooperative effort. Though it sounds like one of nature's most harmonious sing-alongs, the katydid nocturne in our summer grasses is the by-product of intense competition. Researchers have found that male katydids who can chirp only a few thousandths of a second ahead of others attract "most of the females."

Some of the sounds that most appeal to me are my husband's voice reading Wodehouse's pitch-perfect comedy, Alberta Hunter singing on Amtrak Blues, and Schubert's E-flat Trio. Although I am not the most likely fan of the rumbling vehicles, it sends me to realize what is happening: as the gear and recordings cause the metallic car body to vibrate, the whole vehicle becomes a resonating shell for sound. These young men are not merely installing a musical device in a car; they are transforming the car itself into an instrument.

Not far from our street there is a lumberyard, a Big & Tall men's shop, two grand churches, the best Greek restaurant in town, and two fortune-telling parlors. There is a genetics lab in our neighborhood, close to a Tex-Mex bar and grill where any escaping DNA on the lam could probably hide for days. There are fishmongers, lobster tanks, and think tanks here, and a storefront dental office with a neon molar in the window. There is a candy jobber and the Free Romania Foundation. There used to be a fast-food shack, named Babo's, that had a sweeping modernist roof designed by the young Saarinen. There are sushi bars with sandalwood counters, pizza parlors, and, recently, several nail salons. It is a dense, urban neighborhood, baroque with energies, more than anyone could ever say. Just last year we were all stunned to hear that a call-girl ring was operating on a block not too far from ours. According to the immensely surprised neighbors, the people who ran it were "very polite." Even more surprising, to me, was the discovery that most of our neighborhood exists on land that was—not so very long ago—a vast and ancient swamp.

Part Two / Swamp

The vast wetland began just north of the clam-flats along the Charles River, and lay about nine miles inland from the coast. The Great Swamp it was called by the earliest English settlers who inked its features on their maps. It was not a very imaginative name, but an accurate one for the acres of glacially sculpted swampland, a place laced with meandering slow streams and ponds, humpbacked islands that rose from shallow pools fringed by reeds, and brackish marshes home to heron rookeries, wild rice, fish, and pied-billed grebes. For some ten thousand years, the swamp had been evolving, preening, and humming.

The conditions for a swamp of such magnitude emerged as the last North American glacier melted and retreated, and the bowl-like shape of our region (the Boston Basin) became a shallow inland lake, an embayment contained by surrounding drumlin hills. Most locally, the waters were corralled by a recessional moraine, whose gentle bulk still slants across our city, and by beds of impervious blue clays under layers of gravel and the watery surface. The first human beings to arrive in this watershed would have found the vegetated marshes and swampland sprawling around two largish bodies of water, one of which is the amoebal-shaped pond known today as Fresh Pond.

I have lived close to Fresh Pond for most my adult life, and had frequented its shores for years before I came to know about the former swamp. If pressed, I suppose I would have realized that *something* must have formerly existed in the place where there is now a megaplex cinema and an organic market where the cheese department carries small, ripe reblachons that delight my husband. I don't think that I would ever have guessed that the shopping plaza was formerly a red maple swamp, a distinctive area within the larger swamp, with smatterings of rum cherries and tupelo trees, with water lilies, pickerel weed, and high-bush blueberries "overrun," said one habitué, in vines of flowering clematis.

I first learned about this former reality from the journals of William Brewster, a late 19th century Cambridge native and ornithologist, and curator of birds at the Museum of Comparative Zoology at Harvard. Not long after learning about the swamp, which Brewster explored throughout his life, I had occasion to drive to the Staples store in the Fresh Pond Shopping Mall. There, walking across the parking lot, I noticed my mind half trying to believe that if we could jackhammer up the acres of asphalt, underneath we would find—oh, not entire squashed red maples and blueberry bushes, but some incipient elements of a swamp, some slough or quagmire or marshy sponge—something of the liquid world lost to the single, dry word *mall*.

In truth, I like the mall, or at least I don't stay away. Its designers thought too little about the pleasures of shadow, light, and coincidence, and visually, this standard shopping center seems unworthy of replacing a notable red maple swamp. But the mall faithfully serves up shelves of many excellent goods: pens and paper, goat's milk soap, native corn, good running shoes, French wine, and radio batteries. There are birds-of-paradise flowers at this mall, and a newspaper-vending box whose door opens on papers resting inside in a trusting stack. I also am glad for the adjacent utility station whose gray transformer towers carry the cables that step down voltage from the Northeast grid to a pulse our local wires can handle. There is a word to be said for the cement-block home of Intermetrix, and the eight gold ballroom-dancing trophies on the sill of one of the company's windows, and another word for the restaurant that squats over a one-time rookery serving desserts named Starstruck Sundae and Chaos Pie.

Certainly, by middle age one knows that ours is a paradoxical paradise, that all times, all lands, all selves are an alloy of scar and grace, that blight may turn to beauty and beauty to blight, like mischievous changelings teasing the stolid. Certainly, we all know that our land is one supple carnival of misrule, a mesh of redemptive improbability and change. Still, this particular news—a whole gorgeous swamp gone missing—hit me hard. I am very fond of swamps. My mother was conceived in one, and I inherited the gene for liking to spend time in marshes and estuaries, floodplain forests and cypress swamps. The Great Swamp of this region had the usual wetland virtues (functioning as a nursery for life, an aeration, and a sponge that prevented flooding), and it presents my mind with a nice conundrum to realize that the construction of our neighborhood contributed to the demise of this wonder.

Perhaps I brooded over the great lost swamp because I had attained an age when sympathy for vanished things comes easily, when we are aware of mortality as real and not some absurd concept that has, in any event, nothing to do with ourselves, our only parents, and our irreplaceable friend. Certainly, I was beginning to like the past more as people, places, and ambitions receded into it and became its populace. And perhaps that is why I began to go on long walks around the former contours of the swamp, seeking its traces and remnants.

As it turns out, a glacial work is impossible to eradicate entirely. It is true that we are not going to find any quick phosphorescence of life under the asphalt that covers so much of the former swampland. But vestiges of the swamp survive in a brook trickling through a maintenance yard, in slippery gully of jewelweed, a patch of marsh, in the many wet basements of our neighborhood, and small stands of yellow-limbed willows. Great blue herons spend weeks on the river that runs alongside a local think tank, and there is still a lek ground where woodcocks perform their spiraling courtship flights. Wild Saint-John's-wort, healer of melancholy, grows here, also tansy and yarrow (*Achillea millefolium*), the spicy-smelling plant that sooths wounds—recently introduced species mingling with older ones. Killdeer, muskrat, and ring-necked pheasant (the last a twentieth-century arrival) have been seen in a small floodplain forest not far from the commuter trains, and against all odds, alewife fish run in the spring as they have for millennia, coming upriver from the ocean to spawn in the dwindling freshwater streams. Here and there, in a secluded patch of these old wilds, it is possible to get lost.

One afternoon as I was driving home along a road that passes a mucky pond behind the Pepperidge Farm outlet, something huge began to lumber across the road. I stopped my car and watched a low, round, dark creature—it was a snapping turtle—walking slowly across the road, going directly toward a roadside barbershop. The turtle was so large, with a shell easily four feet around, that it seemed to belong in a more exotic habitat, in a place like the Galapagos. Concerned about what a highway and a trip to the barbershop could hold for an old turtle, I was even more astounded to discover that our present-day city contained such a being. It walked deliberately, unaware of the dangers on every side, huge and unassimilated, a tragic-comic amalgam: Mr. Magoo and Oedipus at Colonus. As one by one the cars on that road came to a halt, and all the drivers got out, we stared together as the creature crawled across the macadam, lumbering like memory out of an unseen quarter.

cccccc-

"We will never know," says Professor Karl Teeter, a linguistic anthropologist who lives across the avenue, and next door to our friend, the historian Judith Nies. It's an early fall afternoon and I am talking with Professor Teeter about our pre-European predecessors on this watershed, the Pawtuckeog tribe. For many thousands of years, the Pawtuckeogs migrated annually between the inland forests and the coasts of an area they called Menotomet. Their sensible, appealing seasonal rhythm was to spend winters sheltered in the forest, then move to set up summer camps close to the clam-flats and the swamp that provided fish and fowl, waterways, and silt-rich land for corn and beans. Karl Teeter has spent his adult life studying the Algonquian family of languages, to which the Pawtuckeog language, Massachusett, belonged. Sadly, no living speakers of Massachusett survive, but Karl explains that the language is similar to the one spoken by the Maliseet-Passamaquoddy of Nova Scotia. He shows me how close the Massachusett word for "my friend," *neetomp*, is to the Maliseet word *nitap*. When I ask my learned neighbor if he knows any native Massachusett names for the Great Swamp or its features, he says, "Place-names are the hardest to recover, and the swamp landscape has changed so much now that I cannot even speculate." We sit for a while turning the pages of a large green book that holds the Pawtuckeog vocabulary. Karl says some words, and I pronounce them after him: *kushka* (it is wide), *(nu)keteahoum* (we cured him), *kohchukkoonnog* (great snows).

As the native Pawtuckeog culture reeled and collapsed in response to European diseases and violence, the swampland lay shimmery and resistant to the colonizing touch for another century. Europeans settlers were revolted by the miasmic terrain, and their disdain made the swamp a natural ally in the cause of American independence. It was on the swampy outskirts of the Newtowne settlement, safe from the Royalists who lived on high ground, that the patriots could meet to plan their revolution. The gift of protection was not returned however; as soon as technology permitted, the victorious Americans began to eradicate the wetlands. Handsome orchards were the first incursions, then a single road built through the marshes—the "lonely road," one writer called it, "with a double row of pollard willows causewayed above the bog." Shortly before it began to disappear in earnest, the swamp found its poet in William Brewster, a shy boy who grew into one of America's finest field ornithologists, and taught himself to write a liquid prose:

> When there was a moon, we often struck directly across the open fields, skirting the marshy spots . . . Invisible and for the most part nameless creatures, moving among the half-submerged reeds close by the boat, or in the grass or leaves on shore, were making all manner of mysterious and often uncanny rustling, whispering, murmuring, grating, gurgling and plashing sounds.

In that passage, Brewster was remembering his boyhood days. Later, just after the turn of the century, when the wide river that had drained the swamp was narrowed and straightened, and began to receive the discharge of a city sewer, Brewster had to write: "Thus has [the Menotomy] become changed from the broad, fair stream . . . to the insignificant and hideous ditch with nameless filth which now befouls the greater part of the swampy region through which it flows."

Only naturalists like Brewster and the rare person not enamored of the industrial adventure sorrowed when a stand of pines and beeches was cut to make way for an abattoir, and again when Fresh Pond was surrounded by icehouses and machinery, when ice was cut in blocks and sailed in sawdust to Calcutta, Martinique, and Southern plantations. Rail lines appeared just before midcentury, and the story goes quickly then: more swamp drained for cattle yards and carriage factories, and, after vast beds of clay were discovered, acres covered in the pugging-mills, chimneys, and kilns of a brickworks that turned out most of the bricks that built red-brick Boston. Close by the brickyards, workers constructed modest wooden cottages on the edge of the dry, sandy plain adjacent to the swamp. The malarial epidemic of 1904, and its many small caskets, aroused the Commonwealth to civil engineering projects designed to eliminate what remained of a wetland then commonly referred to as "the menacing lowlands" and the area of "nakedness and desolation." Streams were channeled and sunk into culverts; one large area was dredged and filled to make the site for a tuberculosis sanitarium. Over the next decades, the ever-dwindling wetlands were filled for pumping stations, suburban subdivisions and veteran's housing, for chemical plants, office parks and playing fields, a golf course, a gas storage depot and a major subway terminal. In a nod to an earlier incarnation, the terminal is named "Alewife," for the small, blear-eyed herring that was the fertilizer for the cornfields that sustained both native and early European settlements.

Laying a modern map of our part of the city on Brewster's ink map, I can cobble together an overlay. Where the older map reads "large oaks & willows" is the site of Porter Chevrolet. Where it says "muskrat pond" is the Fresh Pond Fish store. Where it says "heronry of night herons" is the Bertucci's Pizza parlor in the Alewife T-Station complex. "Pine swamp" is a grid of two-family houses. Each change was welcomed, was cheered, by the bulk of the population in a country where land seemed unlimited, where swamps were vile and filling them an act of civic heroism.

ꞔꞔꞔꞔꞔꞔ-

Once people hear that you are out walking around the neighborhood, nosing into the past, they send you pieces of folded, yellowed paper, copies of photographs and letters, and bits of stories. "I'm not a historian," I had to say, "I'm not writing a proper history." But people are generous; they want to help make your picture clearer, and they want a repository for memory. I also received a very old, red brick stamped with the letters NEBCO, which stands for New England Brick Company, and one of the horseshoes that my neighbors Toni and John found while digging in their garden. The day they gave it to me we stood in their backyard passing around the piece of rough iron, turning it over in our hands as Toni told me they had learned there was once a blacksmith shop on the site of their house. From another neighbor, I learned about a great-uncle from Barbados who had worked at the rubber factory. At the pizza parlor an elderly diner told me, "This was Lynch's Drugstore. You could get a lime rickey." At the electrician's office, where a neon fist holds a bolt of blue lightning, the polite young electrician who is not one bit afraid of electricity but terrified of flying, says, "This was the Sunshine Movie Theatre."

One day the mail brought a photocopy of a newspaper clipping from 1908. The headline read: "Famous Horses Raced Here." And that is how I came to know the names Flora Temple, Black Hawk, and Trustee—some of the great trotting race horses of their day—and the greatest of them, Lady Suffolk, a horse descended from the legendary Messenger. Trotting horses are the kind whose jockeys ride in the small, light vehicles called sulkies. Lady Suffolk, was also apparently a saddle racer because the article mentions that her time for a mile "under the saddle" was 2:26, a time then considered so fast that the reporter gushed that it made her name "imperishable." I mention her story to do my part to make that so.

My neighbor Joan, a woman who would be a leading member of the Society of Those Still Living in the House in Which They Were Born (if it existed), remembers other now-vanished features of our landscape, including swimming ponds. "We used to swim in one of the clay pits after it flooded," Joan tells me. "The one along Rindge Avenue, we called Jerry's Pit. I remember my father sitting on the beach of Jerry's Pit, bare-chested and showing off his tattoos. He had an Indian maiden on his shoulder, a goddess jumping rope on his arm, and a navigational star just above his thumb. By the time I was girl, all of the brickyards but one had closed, and there was trash and white powdery stuff lying around the yards. One summer, in the place where the apartment towers are now, the owners put up a sign that read 'Clean Fill Wanted.'" Later that week, at night, someone dumped a dead horse in the pit. I can remember my mother and her friends laughing at that joke until they cried. There was not much sympathy for the owners of the pits because of the trash and the chemicals they had left on the place. Then there came the year the city closed our swimming pond because chemicals had leaked into it. The last clay pit closed in 1952, after it collapsed on a man. The collapse took the whole steam shovel that the man was operating, and the man himself. They could not rescue him. And that was the end of the clay pits. Later that pit became the town dump."

￼

By the 1970s, when I arrived in Cambridge, the dump has been operating for several decades, and had grown rolling foothills of unwanted material, dunes of newspapers and old appliances. Many of the trash hummocks smoldered with fires and all them were circled by scavenging gulls. There were sometimes human gleaners at the dump, a man or woman salvaging a child's highchair or a table. In the 1980s, after years of behind-the-scenes planning, the landscape began to change again, this time into a city park with playing fields, hills covered in wildflowers, a restored wetland swale, and paths made of a sparkling, recycled material called glassphalt. On a recent Sunday, a croquet match was underway—older couples in traditional whites, younger players in flowered shorts and retro Hush Puppy shoes. Not far under the decorous new lawn and the wickets lies the refuse of four decades, capped and monitored, and threaded with pipes that allow gases to vent.

On contemporary planning documents the former great swamp is now called the Alewife Area. It is a place where a modern land-use opera continues to rage, a public policy drama complete with mercantile princes, dueling experts, public officials, citizens for whom the natural world is itself a form of wealth, and at least one man who sits with binoculars, at a high window of the apartment towers, scanning the landscape for barred owls.

The other day I went to the site of the former muskrat pond to rent Bertrand Tavernier's brooding 1986 film "Round Midnight," in which jazz great Dexter Gordon plays the role of saxophonist Dale Turner, a fictional character based on Bud Powell and Lester Young, and their years at the Blue Note jazz club. The center of gravity may be the scene in which Gordon stands by his Paris hotel window talking to a young fan and aspiring musician. In a voice gravelly with age and hard living, Gordon tells the young man about the essence of creativity: "You don't just go out and pick a style off a tree one day," he says, "The tree is already inside you. It is growing, naturally, inside you." Isn't that always the hope: that the things we make and build will be as right as rain, as a tree, or a glacier coming, gouging, then melting into something great.

Part Three / Alluvial Fan

By far the largest remaining feature of the Great Swamp is Fresh Pond itself, a 55-acre kettle hole lake surrounded by 160 acres of land. For more than twenty years I have circumnavigated Fresh Pond in all seasons, weathers, and moods, running or walking the serpentine path that winds around the water. I have run with various companions: an energetic Dalmatian named Gus; Anne, who was shedding weight and the wrong husband; and Jim, who joined me on night runs during which we admired how Porter Chevrolet's sign laid streamers of color over the black sheen of the pond. Recently, I walked around the pond with my husband, Peter, and smiled to hear him use the word "rip-rap," a word that public works *cognoscenti* use to describe the rocks placed along a shore. Hearing Peter use that word, casually, reminds me that he is still something of a public works hound, having started his career as a reporter covering a suburban public works department. During those years he often returned home from embattled, all-volunteer board meetings exhausted but enthralled by some exotica of the municipal infrastructure. The word also transports me again to the places Peter arranged to take me during our courtship: tours of waste-water filter systems for the whey runoff from ice cream factories; state-of-the-art silicon chip factories; the power station at Niagara Falls. At the Niagara facility, we were given hardhats to wear, and I was allowed to touch one of the three-story-high steel cylinder turbines that generate the power for the northeast corridor. (Talk about romance.)

Most often my companion on walks at Fresh Pond has been the surrounding land—filled with deciduous woodlands, a stand of white pines, and a small bog with yellow-limbed willows—and, of course, the pond itself, on which ice sheets rumble against the shore in winter and canvasbacks bob for their favorite food, wild celery, in fall. From time to time I exchange rambles at Fresh Pond for lap swimming, weight training, and a sauna. The health club in which these activities are accomplished has a skylight over the pool through which a backstroker can admire moons, clouds, pigeons, and falling snow. Handsome palms surround the aqua water. A nice person at the desk gives you a piece of fresh fruit. Driving away from these rituals, I have but a single thought (if you can call it a thought), namely, "Everything is fine." The effect is testimony to the health club's powers, and bringing any calm into this society is good, but the influence of Fresh Pond is even more salutary.

Circling Fresh Pond in all seasons has immersed me in a nuanced portrait of the year, and the pond's fable of constant change within continuity has voided several slings and arrows of outrageous fortune. You can never predict what you will find: a sprawl of tree limbs after a storm; white cattail seeds streaming on a breeze; a sodden creature darting from the pond into the woods; crows cawing over glare ice. A place like Fresh Pond schools the eye, teaches one to expect surprise, and to rely on minute things—a dark red leaf encased in ice—to unlock meaning for the metaphor-loving mind. The patterns of light and shadow, thickets and tangles into which we can see but partially, the unspoken-for patches, the water surface that skates toward the horizon—all these are forms and shapes that offer possibilities for mind, for ways of being.

Technically however, Fresh Pond is a terminal reservoir and purification plant for the city water supply, and that is why it survives. A greensward at the entrance is named Kingsley Park for a famous Victorian president of the Cambridge Water Board. The Honorable Chester W. Kingsley tells his story of the Fresh Pond water works somewhat wistfully, as a man who loves his work and finds few souls able to appreciate the grandeur of an infrastructure: "I have never before had a chance to inform so many on this subject," he writes, "and never expect another such opportunity." Kingsley was president of the Water Board for fourteen years; during his tenure, in 1888, Fresh Pond was ceded to Cambridge by the Commonwealth, the surrounding land included in order to preserve the purity of the water. "The City," writes Kingsley, "has taken about 170 acres, and removed all buildings therefrom. The pond contains 160 acres, and a fine driveway has been constructed all around its borders, nearly three miles long. With the water area and the land taken, this makes a fine water park of 330 acres. The surroundings of the park are being graded and laid out in an artistic way, beautify-

ing the whole region and making it one of the most attractive places in the suburbs of Boston." He continues, "It will thus be seen that in an abundant supply of
excellent water . . . Cambridge presents one of the strongest inducements . . . for
any who may be looking for a home where good water and good morals prevail."

A water park. The phrase conveys the Victorian confidence and expansive
gesture of a people for whom civic works embodied the democratic ideals: proper
comportments of land and water would invite city dwellers into vital and uplift-
ing pleasures, even moral life. It is not hard to imagine Chester Kingsley, bewhis-
kered, appearing at civic parades in a Water Board Officer's jacket. Kingsley's
comrades in civic proclamations sound the same pleased, confident note: of one
scheme for a riverside esplanade, the Cambridge park commissioner envisions
that "launches may run from city to city" that "men [may benefit from] this little breathing-space . . . among beautiful surroundings." It was not only a sweet
boosterism that led to these claims. The Victorian planners, guided by Frederick Law Olmsted, had noticed the link between qualities of landscape and human
well-being.

Reading the Victorian's plans, their bursting pride and energetic efforts, one
cannot but feel a tender spot for these city-builders who were helping to finish
off the exquisite meadows and wetlands. It is hard to fault them when even today many seem not to have understood that only an astonishing one percent of
the earth's water is fresh. As the original wetland filtering system was destroyed,
modern water planners turned to extraordinary engineering to deliver safe and
plentiful water to the city.

One day in the winter of 1995, I visited Mr. Chip Norton, the Watershed Manager of Cambridge, in his offices on the east side of Fresh Pond. The Water Department building is a fine old thing from the 1920s. It has Palladian windows
and a lobby that is a near-museum. The space is untended and empty save for
a large yellow map of the reservoir mounted on the wall above a fading, dusty
model of same, and a very dead rainforest plant near a peeling radiator. The floor
is swaddled in brown linoleum, the walls painted pale pink with aqua trim, the
effect one of bleak assurance that not one dime of tax money has been wasted
here. From the back of the lobby comes a luxurious sound—the rush of fast water spilling from three holding basins over aerating tiles.

To be greeted by the roar and rush of water is the most brilliant possible
entrance to a water department. In the upstairs rooms, city servants are outfitted with carpets, recessed lighting, and the hum of computers, which is well and
good, but one prays that the city will have the sense to keep the aura of faded sanitarium that it has going downstairs in the lobby. (At least if this treasure has to
yield to renovation, move it to the Smithsonian as Calvin Trillin's entire writing

office was moved when *The New Yorker* moved from one side of 43rd Street to the other.)

As I pore over the dizzying engineering and planning reports that Mr. Norton has placed on a table in a small reading nook near the reception area, a woman behind the partition is talking on the telephone about where to get some chicken salad sandwiches for lunch. She recommends Armando's Pizza. Long silence. Next she offers to go to Sage's Market, where, she says, they make a delicious chicken salad. Another long silence. Armando's comes up again; the deliberations continue. From behind the other side of the nook a youngish woman sasses a walrus of a man who has apparently asked her to do some extra task. She replies that she has much more work to do than he does, and besides she has housework on top of that. "Peg always does your housework, I'm sure," she says tartly. The man agrees, takes the comments in stride, sighs, says that it's going to be that kind of day, and then, after a long awkward silence, that it's time for a cigarette.

Other than these essential bureaucratic activities, the municipal water system seems to work by such devices as: having bought water rights a hundred years ago to sources in outlying suburbs; an underground eight-mile-long pipe; gravity; the chemicals alum and chlorine; testing; sedimentation beds and flocculation chambers; sand and charcoal filtration; monster pumps; holding tanks in Belmont; shut-off valves; and more gravity. Mr. Norton lucidly explained all the workings in front of an enormous, wall-size hand painted map of the twenty-three-square-mile watershed for which he is responsible. Merely to gaze on the territory gives one a feeling of expansiveness and excitement—like that associated with mounting a campaign or planning an adventure meant to prove something. The watershed is twice the size of the city it serves, and the wall map reaches well beyond the city, north to the Middlesex Fells, where Mr. Norton used to work and upon which he looks wistfully, recalling how peaceful life was in that rural outpost. In its scale and precision, the map gives the Water Department antechamber the air of a war room, the territories of conquest displayed in crystalline detail. But what makes this map wonderful is that its mission is the peaceful delivery of water for washing babies and boiling potatoes—well, for MIT's little nuclear reactor, too, but mainly for aiding the daily lives of citizens.

Perhaps a woman who considers her bathtub the single most important device in the home, whose favorite work is watering plants, and whose day begins with cups of Assam tea can be forgiven for looking on Mr. Norton a bit dreamily as he pours forth the story of our city's water. Like Mr. Kingsley before him, Mr. Norton's chief responsibility is to protect the water quality within his watershed; at Fresh Pond, every use of the land must, he emphasized, be compatible with this goal. Once, while explaining that Fresh Pond is the only place in the state ("maybe in the world, save for the Ganges," his look implied) where dogs are allowed to range freely near a public water supply (thus, swim in and befoul it), the watershed manager let a wry look stroll across his face as he added, "But this is Cambridge." He said this with a complex tone that bodes well for his tenure. As we spoke about the reservoir, I was also impressed by Mr. Norton's crisp analysis of what we can and cannot control. "We cannot," he said, "control the past, or birds, for instance. But we can control dogs."

This seemed as he said it like a gnomic reduction of wisdom, and I felt immediately relieved by the idea that the past can be let go of (as far as us controlling it), and also by the clear, calm way he said it. That's right, I thought, admiringly, the past is over. What's done is done. Later I recalled fiction, Proust and Nabokov, and the fact that modulating our idea of the past alters the present. But I know perfectly well what Mr. Norton means. He means, rightly, that he's got a dealt hand. And he is especially not going to be able to control what happened to his watershed and Fresh Pond during the Pleistocene. It was while sitting quietly at the metal table in the Water Department office, studying a heap of maps and surprisingly passionate master plans, with talk of chicken salad sandwiches in the air, that I suddenly, unexpectedly found myself descending again on the plumb line of time, plummeting far past the Great Swamp and its lost heronries to arrive in an entirely other incarnation of our neighborhood.

One Newton Chute provided the geology for the 1944 surficial geologic map of our area. Glancing back and forth between Chute's map and his report, I slowly grasp that Fresh Pond exists, and that Peter and I make our home on what was the eastern slope of a river valley. That is: where now exists the ground on which have variously stood drugstores, dray horses pulling blades, and apples in blossom was once merely a volume of air above an enormous river valley that ran southward from present-day Wilmington to the Charles River (which had not yet come into being). A rock terrace at about eighty feet below present sea level was the bottom of this deep, broad valley; the valley also held an inner gorge that cut down another ninety feet. The presence of the inner gorge indicates to Chute and his colleagues that "at least one important uplift of the land or lowering of sea level occurred during the formation of the valley."

In part, it may be a recent appointment with my dentist, Dr. Guerrara, in which he filled an unusually deep cavity—first boring it out, then filling it in discrete stages with various substances—that makes me riveted by the geological process by which glaciers filled the deep valley. As you may know, the modern human tooth cavity is filled first by a layer of calcium hydroxide, a liquidy paste like Elmer's glue that hardens quickly on the floor of the prepared cavity; then with a thin, cool varnish, painted on to seal the tuvuals; finally, with the silver amalgam (copper, silver, tin, mercury) that is tamped in, carved, and burnished. The gorge in one's mouth—as these minute spaces feel to the tongue—is topped up. This is very like what happened all over New England about twenty thousand years ago, in the Pleistocene.

Chute identifies ten principal events in the centuries-long process by which an old valley was filled with successive layers of till, clay, peat, and gravel—materials pushed, trailed, and extruded by a glacier advancing and retreating over the land, moving south and east, a chthonic grading of the surface. Chute accompanies his glacial geology with a map that shows which of these glacial fill events figure on the current surface, and where. With mounting excitement, I locate the area of our street on the map: our home ground is Outwash 4, the eighth event, an outwash of sand and pebble-sized gravel that occurred as a large alluvial fan spread southward over the "rock-flour" clays deposited in the exciting seventh event, the clays that would have such consequences for our neighborhood. A small ridge two blocks away, which we now know as Massachusetts Avenue, is thought to be "too high to be part of the fan" and probably was overlayered by its powerful flowing outwash.

I sit back in the Water Department's chair, nearly faint from the morning's events, and my idea of home rearranges itself once more, assimilating the knowledge that we live not only atop a lost swamp but also over a buried river valley and on an alluvial fan. It changes things—everything somehow—to know that during all the years I have yearned for life in a bucolic valley my wish has, if prehistorically, been true. And what shall we make of the news that we dwell on an alluvial fan? While the fine sandy fan was spreading out, Fresh Pond must have still been entirely occupied by a stagnant ice block, for, as Chute reasons, "if the fan had been deposited after the ice block had melted, the depression occupied by the pond would have been filled."

Even the alluvial fan does not prepare me, though, for the fact that our neighborhood, our city, indeed the Eastern Seaboard from Virginia to Nova Scotia, takes place on a crust of earth that was once the west coast of Africa. The crust is named Avalon, and it arrived when a piece of Gondwana, ancient continent, broke away, swept across the ocean (not the Atlantic yet, but Iapetus), and collided with the old North American continent. Our most local crust came from the part of the earth that is today Morocco (and which shares with the Boston Basin the lumpy-looking rock we call puddingstone). It has been quite a long while since these mighty things took place, and it is hard to say what, if anything, they have to do with the realpolitic taking place on the underlying Avalon. But, as always, the familiar when closely observed reveals itself as an exotic.

Beyond its transforming information, a U.S. Geological Survey report enthralls because of the language scientists use to convey glacial events: here there are "geophysical raverses," "faults in overridden sand," "uplift of the land," and "marine embayments." The souls who spin off these phrases in longish sentences that describe—calmly—seismic events that rumbled over millennia, sound as if they know what they are talking about, as if they know what is going on under there down deep, at the level of *accurate subsurface information* where knowledge is grounded.

Although I was born decades after early twentieth-century physicists had their near-nervous breakdowns at the implications of relativity, the fluid epistemology implied has come only slowly and imperfectly into my psyche, which seems to cling to a pre-modern, limbic hope for solidity. As my life's education has proceeded, each new knowledge gradually reveals that it too rests on gossamer metaphor. Reading the geologists, I feel the tantalizing hope that with this vocabulary I might grasp the real nature of things. Perhaps here are the minds and ways of talking that take one through loose gravel, till and sand, through bands of clay, to bedrock. And if it all be gossamer, what better gossamer than bedrock?

Part Four / Navigable

One afternoon, circumnavigating Fresh Pond with a photocopy of an 18th century map in hand, I see that our local pond was once linked by a series of rivers to the Atlantic Ocean, that for all but the last hundred years of its existence our inland region had a direct channel to the sea. On the old map, the river Menotomy rises out of Fresh Pond, winds through the Swamp, joins the Little River and flows into the Mystic, which empties into the Atlantic. I also see that some vestige of that former water route would still be navigable by canoe. The Little River is extant, and flows into a stream called Alewife Brook, formerly the last stretch of the Menotomy. A present-day river guidebook tersely describes Alewife Brook as "not recommended," but Peter and I cannot resist taking our canoe down the pungent, olive-brown stream. As we float past half-submerged shopping carts and debris, we will be moving along the oldest artery of our watershed.

The route will take us through a lock at the Amelia Earhart Dam on the Mystic River. Studying the route, Peter says, "We should get an air horn to signal the lock keeper." I say, "Great," because I have learned that Peter is always right about gear. There was the time in the Everglades with the maglight, the extra bike tire that saved the day, the boxes of Happy Lamp fireworks. Many times I have owed my happiness—and once my life—to Peter's gear and his skill with it. He selected an air horn at the sporting goods store and together we read the instructions, which were very explicit, saying in essence: Do Not Ever Use Your New Air Horn. It Will Destroy Your Ear Drums, So Do Not Use Under Any Conditions. "Oh, they have to say that," Peter said, hefting the little horn. "Some rude people take them to sporting events."

The only other special thing we will need for this journey is an idea about where to land a canoe in a big-city working harbor. The canoe is seventeen feet of a dull green material called Royalex, a stable boat with a low-slung profile, named in honor of the Victorian traveler Mary Kingsley, who liked to paddle in African swamps. We want to land the *Mary Kingsley* somewhere along the banks of the inner harbor, near the Tobin Bridge. On the early summer evening that Peter and I scout the harbor, we discover not a single take-out site for a canoe, but many other interesting things, including a marine shipping terminal, the titanic legs of the Tobin Bridge, a burned-out pier, the U.S. Gypsum Company, and a mountain of road salt recently offloaded from an Asian freighter. Near sundown, an oblique red light slants over pools of steamy gypsum tailings. This extravagant light and the sheer muscle of the place make for a romantic landscape. As is often the case, Mr. Emerson has been this way before, admiring the potentially fine face of industry:

> It is vain that we look for genius to reiterate its miracles in the old arts; it is its instinct to find beauty and holiness in new and necessary facts, in the field and road-side, in the shop and mill. Proceeding from a religious heart it will raise to a divine use the railroad, the insurance office, the joint-stock company; our law, our primary assemblies, our commerce, the galvanic battery, the electric jar, the prism, and the chemist's retort. . . . The boat at St. Petersburg, which plies along the Lena by magnetism, needs little to make it sublime.

On the other side of the river lies the city of Chelsea, nearly all galvanic battery, a welter of scrap metal yards, weigh stations, warehouses, sugar refineries, gas yards—the last a sinuous complex of pastel pipes. As night comes, and a hazy fog begins to materialize, we happen on the Evergood Meat Packing Company, where beams of light from mercury vapor arc lamps rain down on a parking lot, carving the lot out of the night and lighting up this scene: three meat packers in long white butchers' coats, the men running through the lot passing a soccer ball back and forth expertly. The ball bounces from a corrugated wall, skims under the axles of a fleet of trucks. The long white coats are brilliant in the vapor arc light, the fabric flowing, flapping like wings. It is the quickest glimpse, and now the road climbs a dark hill. From the summit, the city's financial district is visible across the river, its lights flickering, cleaning crews at work. Down the hill, on the river itself, and moored to the bank, we see the object of our search: a small pavilion and public dock.

ﾟﾟﾟﾟﾟﾟﾟﾟ

The most succinct account of our river journey is that we launched a canoe amongst somnolent lily pads and took it out near a Brazilian cargo tanker. Our paddle begins on the Little River, where, passing the mouth of a narrow, brown ditch full of appliances and engine parts, a sodden teddy bear, we are passing the paltry remains of the wide Menotomy. Along one stretch, the Little River is so shallow that it is more a skim-coat of water than a channel; the dorsal spines of carp crest the waterline, giving the river the eerie appearance of being alive with silver grey eels.

As it deepens again, the Little River becomes Alewife Brook, and when we pass the gas station near Meineke Muffler, we are at the old site of a basketry weir, a spot that both native Americans and settlers used for harvesting shad and alewives—the latter plentiful still enough in the nineteenth century to move one observer to write, "I have seen two or three hundred taken at a single cast of a small seine." Up to the present day, new citizens come to this watershed in spring to catch alewives. On another day at the Mystic Dam, we meet three slender Cambodian men whose fishing gear consists of a box of large pink garbage bags. The men are barefoot, wearing dated bell-bottoms and white dress shirts (vintage Goodwill), and they fish from slippery rocks, dipping the pink plastic bags into the causeway spill. Although the numbers of the fish are greatly diminished, at this dam in spring they look abundant, flowing over the spill into the thin plastic bags like grains of rice from a bulk bin.

An alewife is an *anadromous* fish ("running upward"), and its presence in our watershed is known as *ephemeral*. The fishes are seasonal transients, coming from the ocean to freshwater to spawn. Continuing south now on the Mystic River, we are following the young alewives' fall route back to sea. They would pass, as we do now, backyard barbeques and hammocks, and then the backside of a downtown, where retaining walls read "Dragons Rule," where a crumbling infrastructure crawls with organic patterns, subtle grays and browns, white encrustations—a spectacular topography of decay and struggle.

Here and there, trees overhang the river, dappling its surface of lily pads and oily gloves. As the river widens the tree break disappears. We pass by an Edison power plant, and under a bridge that bears eight lanes of interstate traffic. The

Amelia Earhart Dam comes into view. Peter readies the air horn, and when the dam is close, he presses the small button. It delivers one of the loudest bursts of sound I have ever heard—next to the time a lightning bolt hit the house and made me wonder, for a second, if I had been shot. The lock keeper likes the air horn, likes being hailed in the proper nautical way, and gives Peter a crisp salute. As *Mary Kingsley* glides into the narrow chamber, two powerboats hurry in behind us. The doors of the lock slide closed, the water rises, and when the lock opens again, the still, olive river water has vanished and we are in an ocean-blue chop with whitecaps.

The powerboats take off like rodeo cowboys on broncos, and I am wishing that we had something with a throttle too. As the wind picks up, first tugboats, then small freighters appear. Conveyor belts, rigs, and tall booms are cantilevered over the water; an inverted silver dome built to cover twenty tons of unrefined sugar glints on the bank. By the time the big bridge looms into view, our canoe has shrunk to a bobbin—a bit of flotsam below the gantry cranes. We are gawking at the cranes like rubes on Broadway when a rogue ocean swell rises out of nowhere, tosses the canoe four feet into the air, spins us a little, breaks across the side, slaps us full-face with salty water. The pavilion and dock are just visible now on the other side of the river, and as we struggle toward the landing in the chop, we marvel at the people who took their thinner, lighter canoes out much farther, into open ocean, and up and down the Atlantic coast.

At the dock we are met by two small boys, brothers, who shyly stare and smile at the canoe, and within seconds of our invitation are in it, are touching its sides, gripping the paddles, putting on lifejackets, and not sitting too still but gently rocking the boat to get a feel for it. Their names, the boys tell us, are Ulysses and Erik.

I wouldn't dream of making that up, and where else but a big-city waterfront would you expect, these days, to be met by the two chief heroes of epic seafaring? True to their names, the boys cannot take their eyes off our boat. They are intrigued by paddles. Fascinated by the weight and color of life jackets. Overjoyed by ropes, by tying knots. Desirous to know what the canoe is made of. Running their hands over the cane seats and wooden thwarts. In love with all things nautical. Beside themselves with happiness when their father says, yes, they can take a short ride with us, just around the perimeter of the dock, not far. And when at last we must head home, the legends (as bold, as clever as ever) cajole us, insist on hauling some of the gear up the slight incline to our waiting car, where they are further enthralled by the every detail of mounting a canoe on a Subaru: how the canoe is lifted up by two people, how it is strapped onto the roof of the car, how foam clips are slipped over the gunnels, how ropes are laced and tightened.

Ulysses and Erik tell us that, yes, they were born here, in this city, but home is an island far from here, somewhere over the water. They each point out to sea, not exactly in the same direction. When the canoe has been secured in place, and all the gear stowed, the hero-boys shimmer away, are last seen lying flat on their stomachs, their arms submerged in water up to the shoulder blades—as close to being in the ocean as boys on dry land can be.

Refugium

At first I think I'm seeing a small cat doing a weak imitation of an inchworm. It undulates in a strange combination of hunch-and-slink along the edge of Cranesville Swamp. Covered with dark fur, its chin dabbed with white, it reminds me of what theologians say about the life of the personality being horizontal, craving community, and that of the soul being vertical, needing solitude. Crouching behind some shrubs, I finally see that it's a mink, moving from one alder to another. It manages both landscapes, traces with its lustrous back a pattern of swell and subside, evokes an image of Muslims prostrating and standing, Catholics kneeling and rising, pale green inchworms arching and stretching along my forearm. We are gardeners, all of us, our hands broadcasting seeds in the spring, our arms in autumn clutching the harvested wheat. We mingle and retreat, seek company and refuge.

I have been thinking a lot about refuge, how what makes the swamp a safe hideaway also makes it dangerous, a paradox for all the scoundrels and saints, artists and hermits, victims and perpetrators who have fled there. And how, for all of them, the most difficult question in the end might not be about safety but about duration—how long to stay, how to know when a temporary refuge is about to become a permanent retreat without exit. The mink, a solitary creature who tolerates other minks only enough to breed and give birth, lives on the edge of this soggy Nature Conservancy land on the western border of Maryland. Cranesville Swamp is a valley between two Appalachian ridges, a high bowl with poor drainage. Its ground is spongy, its vegetation matted and damp. I am with a hermit friend who has sold his house and is dismantling his identity as an artist by living at the edge of the swamp. When he sold his studio a nearby gallery took his work, including a drawing in which the hair of a goddess's attendants is replaced by a waterfall. You can study it and try to puzzle out where their heads end and the waterfall begins.

Michael is after an intimacy in his life that has nothing to do with sex. It's a bit disconcerting to sit with a man—his hazel eyes clear, his beard and hair neatly trimmed—who has no concerns about mortgage payments and insurance premiums or how he'd introduce himself at a campground social. Everything I feel about comfort starts to rattle. He tells me, quietly, *I want to live like an animal, close to the earth, self-sufficient, doing as little harm as possible.* Then, ten minutes later: *And I want to live like Christ, close to God, detached, finding refuge in the unknown.*

We talk for hours on the deserted boardwalk at Cranesville. Michael isn't going into hiding; he's retreating from a path that wasn't headed toward what, for him, is being fully human. He's not sure what that means except a quiet letting go, a deliberate choice to go toward some kind of refuge that nourishes his spirit. All the great spiritual leaders have done it, from Buddha to Christ to Mohammed. They've withdrawn to sit in caves and under trees, to wander in deserts, packing as little as possible into their knapsacks. They were after, I think, some moments of trackless quiet; a chance to blur their footprints, the sense of having been someplace, of having some place to get to; a chance to see what happens when the past and the future stop tugging on the leash and the present opens like a well.

Those who are fond of various retreats—writers, ecstatics, parents with young children—often comment on the silence such time away allows. Silence becomes something present, almost palpable. The central task shifts from keeping the world at a safe decibel distance to letting more of the world in. Thomas Aquinas said that beauty arrests motion. He meant, I think, that in the presence of something gorgeous or sublime we stop our natterings, our foot twitchings and restless tongues. Whatever our fretful hunger is, it seems momentarily filled in the presence of beauty. To Aquinas' wisdom I'd add that silence arrests flight, that in its refuge our need to flee the chaos of noise diminishes. We let the world creep closer; we drop to our knees as if to let the heart, like a small animal, get its legs on the ground.

The mink disappears into the underbrush. If I had been blindfolded and plunked down in this pocket of cool air and quaking ground spiked by tamaracks and spruce, home to hermits and minks, and tried to figure out just where I was, I would have guessed a bog in Canada somewhere, far north of the bustle of Quebec and Montreal. And Canada was probably the original home of this bog. We don't think of landscapes being on the run, though we know birds fly south in the fall, mountain goats trek up and down the Rocky Mountain passes from season to season, and eel journey from the Sargasso Sea in the middle of the Atlantic to North America or Europe in search of fresh water. But stand back far enough in geologic time and you can watch ecosystems migrating north and south across the globe as giant glaciers drag and push up and down the northern hemisphere. Almost 20,000 years ago the last intrusion shoved a wide band of boreal forest south to the mid-Atlantic region. When the glacier withdrew, some 10,000 years later, most of those dark forests withdrew also, reestablishing themselves in Canada while southern deciduous forests reclaimed their usual position here in Maryland. But in a few isolated pockets protected in high-altitude bowls surrounded by higher ridges, boreal forests hunkered down, sank their damp feet into poorly draining clay and rock, and stayed.

Now they couldn't migrate north if they wanted to, for around them is a hostile world—too warm, too dry, the water flushing too fast through the underground aquifers. Dug up and replanted just a mile to the south, the tamaracks would wither, cranberry and sphagnum would curl and crisp, cotton grass would scorch and wilt in what would feel like brutally tropical air. This is an area known as a refugium—a particular localized ecosystem that cannot survive in surrounding areas.

Historically, refuges are retreats in human terms—shelters for protection from danger or distress—and a refugee is one who flees to such shelter for safety. Something in the "outside" world threatens, presses too close, cannot accept the refugee's color or ethnicity or religion or eccentricity, his or her need for so much water and cool air. Something in the refuge spells protection. If you can hack, float, stagger, or climb your way into the jungle, swamp, desert, or mountain, the color of your skin and how you worship won't matter. But something else will. Mohammed in his cave knew this, and Jesus in the desert, and the Buddha under the Wisdom Tree. Michael in the swamp does, too.

Refuge means an escape from what frazzles and buzzes, from what sometimes reminds me of the continuous replay of the final minutes if a tied Super Bowl game—bleachers sagging with hoarse spectators whooping and jeering, the players' one-point attention on flattening whatever comes between them and the triumph of a square yard of pigskin flying over the goal line. On an ordinary day, the human ear is bombarded with sound—anything and everything: the neighbor's lawnmower, a ratchety clock movement, sirens, car engines, and the popping roll of tires on hot pavement. Our minds, of course, automatically filter much of this hubbub. But at what cost? What happens to that filtered material?

Cleaning the lint trap in my dryer yields a fuzzy bedding of dog hair, threads, shredded Kleenex, and, once, a striking black and white feather, small and striped, cleaned and surely destined for more than the trash. I run my fingers across the trap, gathering the clean down. Scraped and softened linen like this was once used as dressings for wounds—a buffer between raw flesh and the barrage of bacteria. Too much lint, though, and the wound can't breathe, the dryer will catch fire, your house will burn down. Does the human mind work the same way? Are there long screens we occasionally need to pull from our heads and run our fingers up, gathering into a pleated, linty accordion the excesses of noise and activity we haven't processed? Do we occasionally need the silence of refuge for the way it lets our minds breathe a bit more easily?

The summer I was twelve, I broke both bones in my right leg. Instead of practicing bull's-eyes at archery camp and swimming laps at the local pool, I read for months. I got out of setting the table, folding laundry, and raking grass to sit on the screened-in porch and plow through biographies and mysteries from May until September. When I lifted my head long enough to regain my bearings, it wasn't to wonder what all the other kids were doing but to imagine what kind of summer my splintered leg would be having if it had its own ears. I reckoned that noises from the outside—clinking dinner forks, whoops from neighborhood kids playing kick the can, the spit of gravel under tires on the shoulder of the road—would have been muffled by all that cast, the thick white walls. I sat in a chaise longue trying to visualize my bones, tender and traumatized, swathed in gauze and then locked into a white plaster tunnel nothing could enter. I thought of how those slim bone stilts had for years propelled me down school hallways, across hockey fields, along wooded paths—and now must lie languid and lazy for three months, lounging inside padded walls with nothing to do but knit back together.

Maybe it was this experience that later led me to find refuge behind the attic insulation. When I shared a bedroom with my twin sister in a house in the suburbs outside of Philadelphia, I found a way to unstaple the insulation in the attic, slip between the two-by-fours, and crawl into the space under the eaves behind the attic's knee wall. The process was like crawling into a long, cottony, pink tent—quiet and dark, an unlikely hiding place. I felt the way I imagined my healing bones had—hidden in a padded world with nothing pressing to do but heal. So long as I could tolerate the itching that the pink fiberglass fired in my arms, I reveled in the silence, the guaranteed lack of interruption. Sometimes I took a book to read or a notebook to scribble in, but often nothing, sitting for hours in the darkness.

My childhood wasn't full of trauma I needed to escape. My father worked hard and my mother tended to us children; there was always a beloved dog around, sometimes a rabbit, and, for a while, a couple of roosters. We ate dinner together every night—roast beef and mashed potatoes or hamburgers done on the grill. My twin and I fell asleep holding hands across the space between our beds, and my father made sure to close the windows when a storm came up in the night. But something in me craved a getaway. From a very young age, I was hungry for the privilege of not being interrupted, for a sanctuary nobody else could enter, for a place to which I could retreat, yank those lint screens from my mind, toss them, and then wander or sit with fewer and fewer filters.

Part of the appeal of a refuge is surely its isolation. There nobody can see you still weeping over a lover who hunched off with another some thirty years ago. Nobody is there to notice whether you stand straight or slouch, or how you suck your stomach in. Or don't. A refuge is like a locked bathroom door where you can practice the fine art of extending your tongue until you can finally touch the tip of your nose, which you also feel free to pick as thoroughly as you want. Nobody's watching; you can do whatever you want.

Consider, for instance, the hermit found in 1975 in Florida's Green Swamp by a sheriff and his deputies. This solitary Asian man had been so overwhelmed by metropolitan chaos, he'd fled to the cypress and black water a few miles from the roller coasters and virtual reality of Disney World and lived on alligators and armadillos. Hiding with white ibis and leopard frogs among wild orange trees, he was dubbed "Skunk Ape" by the few who had spotted him. I like to think he earned this nickname, that in the relative safety of the Green Swamp he indulged in some childhood fantasies of branch swinging and chest beating, that it was his dark silky hair against a pale back that people saw as he scurried away. Nicknames don't always trivialize and they aren't always meant to humiliate. Consciously or no, perhaps the puzzled observers named his most salient characteristics, the ones that needed the tangled and private understory and the mournful cry of night herons in order to surface.

That need for privacy and a less encumbered life might be what Michael's after, too. In addition to his car and his bike, he's sold his kayak, the one he used to launch by the church at the edge of the swamp and paddle around in, gliding eye to eye with skunk cabbage. He wants to be unburdened. For the Buddhists, taking refuge in the dharma means cutting the ties, letting go of whatever hand you've been clinging to, whatever boat you've been floating in. It means shedding your armor, letting what's underneath soften, grow squishy, and open. It means, as Pema Chadron, a Buddhist nun, says, relaxing with the ambiguity and uncertainty of the present moment without reaching for anything to protect ourselves . . . total appreciation of impermanence and change. Monks must have loved a swamp. Sometimes I think that their ancient texts must have risen like vapors straight out of the middle of places as wobbly as Cranesville. That the monks, lifting their robes up around their knees, might have simply looked at where they were wading, said, Yes, I see, and written it all down. Surely there is no better place than a swamp or bog to learn about uncertainty, to notice how we feel when the ground under our feet literally moves, what small boats or dogma we cling to, what we must let go of when we look down and learn to trust that which is holding us now. Something in us gives over to the place, the lines relax, the definitions go mushy, the body goes limp with this landscape—itself so limp and ill-defined. Such paradox that, in a groundless refuge, what has been tight and willed relaxes until fear begins to dissipate.

Whether we head to a swamp's isolation with spiritual intentions or a predator close behind, most of us fear the first step onto that other ground. And why not? Longfellow, in his famous poem "The Slave in the Dismal Swamp," describes a place "where hardly a human foot could pass / or a human heart would dare," a morass of gloomy fens, strange lights, and gigantic mosses. Many a human foot has stepped into forbidden territory, but harder than that is to make the heart go too. You stand with one foot on firm land, the other in a canoe. Behind you is light, the expected horizon of your life; in front of you the green overhead hunkers down, crouches over its waters, and you're startled that you could even think of putting your body into this lightweight snippet of rolled aluminum and then paddling, heart in mouth, towards what the Irish poet John O'Reilly branded a "tragedy of nature."

All the ingredients that make the swamp a place of refuge are the same ingredients that make it dangerous: cottonmouths, saw grass so razor sharp it can slit a horse's legs, alligators that can devour a human whole, a sense of the plant-sky bearing down, the need to stay crouched and wary. If you add to the poison the sedge swords, and to the carnivores the prospect of being lost for days or decades, it's easy to see why, no matter how determined your pursuer was, he often paced at the edge of the swamp, plucking off leeches and wondering whether plunging into such unmapped, trackless territory was worth it. Of course, the same concerns ought to arise for you. In a canoe, you watch the water close silently behind you. On the ground, you watch your footprint in the mud fill and vanish.

It doesn't matter who's the hero or who's the villain. The swamp will protect and threaten both. In Cold Spring Swamp in New Jersey during the Revolutionary War, a bunch of men who called themselves the Refugees, who thought of themselves as British loyalists but were, in reality, a band of thugs, terrorized housewives and stagecoach travelers and then hightailed it back to the swamp to gloat over their booty. Scoundrels all, they counted on the inaccessibility of their hideout on a small island in the middle of the swamp.

Also during the Revolutionary War, soldier Francis Marion eluded the British in Four Holes Swamp of South Carolina. Known as the Swamp Fox, Marion could disappear into the cypress with his band of men and stay hidden for weeks. Further north, the Narragansett Indians holed up in the Great Swamp of Rhode Island beyond the reach of white men bent on retaliating for raids—until December of 1675, when the swamp froze over in an early New England cold snap and what had been almost impenetrable to the white men was transformed, overnight, into a smooth array of patios and sidewalks. The whites simply walked in, and what followed was the greatest massacre in Rhode Island history.

Runaway slaves, hidden for years in the Great Dismal Swamp making shingles, knew about their own swamp fears and those of their pursuers. And so did the Seminoles who fled into the Everglades after the white man booted them from their homes in the Okefenokee of south Georgia. Unwilling to negotiate, surrender, or flee, the Seminoles took advantage of the white man's horror of the infested waters of the Glades. They established villages on hammocky islands in the midst of quagmires, built small canoes that could glide over shallow water, and used the dense vegetation for cover. In pursuit, the U.S. Navy in the 1830's sent a Lt. Powell, whose men tried pushing and poling their boats, their boots and sticks slurping and sucking in the mud, the vast prairie sea of saw grass closing in on them. When a Lt. McLaughlin tried to succeed where Powell had failed, he led his men into Big Cypress Swamp on the western side of the state, where dense overhead vegetation blocks sunlight and the still water is thick with spinachy trailings. When the men in their big boots stirred the dark water, they kicked up noxious vapors that made them retch. Even more disconcerting, the circuitous streams destroyed their sense of direction. They wandered, retracing and detouring, unable to use the stars as navigational help because the canopy was so thick. Where water was low, they portaged again and again, stumbling over cypress knees and dead stumps, always on the lookout for snakes. Mist rose, steamy and blinding, from the muck; when it cleared, the men had only the labyrinthine mirrors of black water, the almost impenetrable green walls of Spanish moss and cypress, with no way to distinguish "here" from "there." From the top of a pine one of the men might climb, he'd gaze down on a maze of channels—a nightmare of fractals and mirrors, a kaleidoscope of water and thicket that disorients not because it shifts at the far end of your telescope but because it doesn't—and still you don't know where you are.

Under *disorientation*, my thesaurus lists *insanity* first, followed by *lunacy*, *bedlam*, and that charming phrase *not all there*. In psychiatric terms, we think of fugue, dissociation, amnesia, confusion, a dream state. But my favorite option is from the dictionary, which defines *disorient* as *to turn from the east, as in the altar of a church. Hence to cause one to lose one's bearings*. To turn from the east. How curious. If I had to label a swamp's aesthetics and philosophy as primarily eastern or western, I'd say eastern without question. A swamp is receptive, ambiguous, paradoxical, unassuming. There's no logic, no duality, no hierarchy. But does immersion in a swamp have anything to do with turning a person from the altar of a church—especially an eastern church? Try this: Buddhists say that if you meet

the Buddha on the road, you mustn't prostrate yourself in front of him, light in-
cense, ring temple bells, count your breaths, or begin chanting. You should kill
him—because any naming, any clinging, can too quickly become dogma. The
point is to let go of everything. In a spiritual swamp, there's nothing to hold on
to. Everything is fluid, mercurial. You're on a small tussock one minute, chanting *Hail Mary* or *Om Mani Padme Hum*, fingering your rosary or mala, offering dollars or marigolds and rupees. As in the first moments of most flights to safe ha-
vens, you're basking in some feeling of grace until you notice that everywhere
you turn, the altars keep slipping under the surface, and the next minute there's
a copperhead at your ankle and you're fleeing through the sedges, leaving a trail
of stirred murk and sludge.

Like most refuges, the swamp makes a poor permanent retreat. You can't stay
too long without the risk of its becoming a trap with no way out. The dilemma
is recognizing the right moment for return. At the exact midpoint of the *I Ching*,
the ancient Taoists provide counsel on the wisdom of temporary retreat, which
they imagine as the creative heavens balanced on a mountain—an image of stillness. Such provisional retreat demonstrates strength, they say, while perpetual
flight signals weakness. Retreat is never meant as escape, a permanent disappearance. In fact, its purpose is restorative: that which retreats is strengthened
by a conscious decision to rest. Retreat can be a wise pulling back, a temporary
withdrawal until it's time for what the *I Ching* calls the "turning point," the eventual countermovement and return. At some moment, the energy that has been
building underground or under the attic eaves, unseen and in private, turns to
resurface in the world. This is supposed to be a reversal of the retreat, a bringing
back into the larger community the wisdom gained in the quiet of contemplation. The danger, of course, is that the turning point may come and go unrecog-
nized. Those in retreat may miss the signal and go on fortifying the walls, flooding the moat, growing their own food inside the compound.

When scientists in the early 1800s first studied the bronzy-red and lippy
leaves of the pitcher plant, they noted the way it collects water in its base and
speculated that this wetland plant served as a refuge for insects eluding predators. Because the insect can actually crawl up the flared flap and hide inside, under the shadow of the hood, it could remain out of sight of any marauding bird
or bat. This theory, from early scientists who marveled at such cooperative effort,
was soon replaced by the realization that although the pitcher plant is designed
to look like safe harbor to fleeing insects, it is, instead, a carefully engineered lure
and deathtrap. The welcome mat on the flared flap is spiked with hundreds of
tiny hairs, all of them aimed downward, like trail markers, and designed to encourage the insect to descend into the pitcher. Once the visitor crawls or slides

past these tiny hairs, it slips into the slick, vertical throat of the plant and down into the main body of the pitcher, which is often full of rainwater. The hapless bug then spends the rest of its life, which isn't long, trying to crawl up the sides of the throat, to take off without a solid runway, to keep its exhausted head above water. Eventually, the insect drowns and the plant has its dinner. If the bug was anticipating an eventual return to leafy branches, a summer of night skies and porch lights, it missed the point of return, misjudged the way a trap can disguise itself as retreat. I think of the 450 or so Seminoles still living in the Everglades, generations of hunters and trappers still gliding their canoes through the saw grass as their ancestors did after fleeing from white men in the 1800's. What countermovement? What return?

Years ago I volunteered at a state hospital. My role was to hang around with a kid named Patty, who was maybe thirteen, her face blank and her tongue silent. We did nothing more than walk around the hospital for months. I don't recall that she ever said a word. I used to imagine that inside her mind was a busy port, a large ship unloading its wares with cranes clanking, foghorns out in the harbor moaning, and men on the docks with small carts, hollering and wheeling the cargo to somewhere else—and Patty's job was to not let anyone else know about the existence of this secret port. She was like the screening fog in a special-effects movie, the blank page that harbors invisible ink. I used to imagine that whatever this secret trading was, it needed a sanctuary, needed the fog screen of Patty so it could carry on its business. I didn't care what kind of business this was or whether it was legal. I remember feeling, more than anything, protective of Patty's silence, as if her retreat were more important than whatever handicap it caused for her in her dealings with the rest of the world. I was stupidly romantic: a part of me even envied Patty her ability to use silence to murder every Buddha in the shape of a psychiatrist who rounded the corners of her ward, clipboard in hand. I used to imagine she had befriended the dockworkers and sailors, that everyone in that fog-shrouded port trusted one another to keep the secret until the ship had offloaded whatever its mysterious cargo was, hauled its anchor up, and set out to sea again, lighter, with a lot more air in its holds and engine rooms.

Later, when I studied dissociative reactions in an abnormal-psych class, I thought of Patty and of Eve—the famous case of the multiple personalities who remained, for a while, hidden inside her because they did not feel safe in the noise and crush of the outside world. Therapy eventually helped them emerge and helped Eve live a more normal life, but nothing seemed to help Patty, who, as far as I know, still wanders the hallways behind locked doors. What counterpoint? What return?

The boardwalk at Cranesville wanders for about a half mile out toward clump of tamaracks where it slips underwater. No gate, no warning sign, no *This is the end! Turn around!* The crossboards simply disappear beneath the mud and water and, as far as I know, keep heading east. It reminds me of the bridge-tunnel spanning the mouth of Chesapeake Bay between Cape Charles and Norfolk. From the air, the bridge looks more like a causeway that abruptly halts partway out in the gray waters of the bay, then reappears a mile or two away. It's as if some engineer's calculations were horrifyingly off, but they went ahead and built the thing anyway. On the road, of course, you simply rise and drop as you climb bridges and descend into tunnels, and so this is what I think when I stand at the point where the boardwalk dips below water: I'll just keep walking and soon I'll enter a tunnel, a tube perhaps, dug out by some kind of shrew and then widened and braced with pressure-treated two-by-fours, and then I'll reemerge into the sunlight and sphagnum a mile or two further into the bog.

I think of the *I Ching*'s cheerful coaching: *It furthers one to cross the great water.* The ancient Chinese meant, I suppose, that it's important to persevere through danger and uncertainty, that such perseverance allows the eventual possibility of countermovement and return. But who knows if they had this tangled morass in mind? I inch my way along the disappearing boardwalk.

Michael has wandered off. I feel like an old woman alone on an icy ramp; I want handrails and a walker with ice grippers on its legs. I concentrate on keeping the soles of my sneakers in firm contact with the mud-slicked walkway, but when the water curls around my knees, the wood has softened into slime. My foot rummages around, backs up to the last known point of secure contact, inches forward again to find only velvety ooze. I can't tell if the boards simply stop or if they have sunk down under the mud. I can't see anything below my calves. Now what? The *I Ching* urges me on. Joseph Campbell whispers something about the hero's journey and the need to visit the underworld. My mind ratchets from philosophy and metaphor to the not-very-concrete world oozing around my legs.

Sometimes, Rilke says, a man has to get up from his table and walk. Walk where? And for how long? Moses and Jesus wandered into the desert. Mohammed hiked up the mountain. Michael is considering wandering from one swamp to another. *Solvitur ambulando*—the difficulty will be solved by walking. Rousseau knew this, as did Thoreau, Wordsworth, Nietzsche, and Austen. They walked out into the hills, country paths, and shorelines, philosophical tramps all, seeking some sort of refuge; some of them found it in the walk itself, some in the desert landscapes stripped of the extraneous where they wrestled with the holy, and others in the muck and ooze of swamplands from Florida to Rhode Island where they holed up in the thick entanglements, the mucky waters, the trackless shallows that twist and bend for miles among overhanging cypress.

What countermovement? What return?

I wonder whether Michael worries about his retreat being a one-way street. What if, twenty years from now, he wanders out of the swamp and finds so much of the world has changed that he cannot even buy a book without access to the Internet, which requires a computer, which he sold when he sold his house, his car, his bike, and his kayak. What if he emerges with a passion for hand-knotted Persian carpets and caviar and no way to make a living? Or what if he emerges and nothing, absolutely nothing, has changed?

Out of the desert Jesus emerged, the devil's temptations strewn and parched on the sands behind him. Out of the wilderness, Moses' people wandered into the Promised Land. Under the Wisdom Tree, the Buddha finally stood and stretched his legs. Out of its cocoon in the pitcher plant, the *Exyria rolandiana* moth unfurls its wings. It had found refuge there weeks ago and reinforced the safety of its retreat by spinning a tight girdle around the neck of the plant's hood. The girdling causes the hood to choke and eventually to flop over the throat, sealing off the pitcher from outside intruders, much like closing the hatch on a boat against threatening seas. Inside, the caterpillar spun its cocoon in a dry haven and waited for the right moment, emerging today with wings the color of claret, epaulets of saffron.

Standing at the vanishing end of this boardwalk, I think of the water shrew whose fringed hind toes can actually trap air bubbles that allow him to scamper across the surface of the water. A sort of built-in pontoon system that eliminates for him any need to stand here debating whether this is the turning point, the right moment to head back. The mink is hiding. Around the edges of the bog, the solitary white flower of *Coptis groenlandica* rises from its thready golden stem which runs underground in a vast, lacy interlocking, its juice a balm for canker sores and irritated eyes. And Michael has reappeared, knee-deep in the earth, to show me sundew plants, those glistening carnivorous circles the size of thumbtacks that look like the childhood drawings of hundreds of suns, cut out and glittered and strewn across the swamp.

PART TWO
2000–2017

DOUGLAS
CARLSON

"I am what is
around me"
—WALLACE STEVENS

In February 2016, then-editor Stephen Corey and I were considering Sean P. Smith's submission of "The Slow and Tender Death of Cockroaches." Part of our deliberation concerned whether we were repeating ourselves, if we had circulated the same themes that Smith was advancing in earlier essays, earlier issues. The answer, of course, was yes. And our conclusion was finally that we'd continue to do so until we had some sense that someone was listening. We published the essay, it won the 2017 John Burroughs Award for Nature Writing, and the world remained unchanged. Such is the condition of the essays in the second part of this collection; they dwell in despair and frustration brought on by the combination of clear vision and no return. Ann Pancake's essay title serves accurately as a title for the whole: "Creative Responses to Worlds Unraveling." To recall the turn-of-the-century milieu is to gain insight into how environmental writing was becoming an exercise in theme and variations, a statement of loss expressed in myriad ways, each essay finding the proper voice and imagery to express that loss. Much like the musical theme and variation form, which part 2 mirrors, individual works vary in style, tonality, modality, and—stretching the image—melody.

For the International Panel on Climate Change's climate assessment in 2007, thousands of scientists gathered what they termed *unequivocal* evidence that global warming is in progress and concluded that such warming was *very likely*—as in 90 percent likely—to have been caused by an increase in anthropogenic greenhouse gas concentrations. The panel developed complex scenarios of multiple futures, but more revealing than the careful diction of science was a private conversation between environmental activist Tim DeChristopher and Terry Root, one of the lead authors of the 2007 IPCC report. De-Christopher recreated the conversation when Terry Tempest Williams interviewed him in 2011 (see *Orion*, January/February 2012).

After attending an address by Root in 2008, DeChristopher asked Root about a contradiction he noticed: she had told her audience that, at best, carbon emissions could peak around 2030. The actual report, however, suggested that if they didn't peak by 2015 we "wouldn't even recognize the planet." DeChristopher wondered what he had missed. He found Root's reply "shattering": "You're not missing anything," she said. "There are things we could have done in the '80s, there are some things we could have done in the '90s—but it's probably too late to avoid any of the worst-case scenarios that we're talking about." When DeChristopher asked why Root didn't mention this in her presentation, her explanation was even more chilling: "Oh, I don't want to scare people into paralysis. I feel like if I told people the truth, people would just give up." Her apology was plaintive: "I'm sorry my generation failed yours."

A decade later climate activist Greta Thunberg, who was sixteen at the time, would tell the United Nations Climate Action Summit, "You are failing us. But the young people are starting to understand your betrayal. The eyes of all future generations are upon you. And if you choose to fail us I say we will never forgive you. We will not let you get away with this." For Terry Root, the disastrous global atmospheric CO_2 concentration was 385 parts per million (ppm). Scientists at that time believed that to preserve "a planet similar to that on which civilization developed," the amount had to be reduced to 350 ppm. As Greta Thunberg's protests were beginning to gain attention, the level had risen to 415 ppm.

The American literary response to a threatened and already diminished environment as seen in the *Review* presents a striking parallel to the Kübler-

Ross model of the five stages of grief as it pertains to a Western culture. *Denial* (missing here, the stage held by the ignorant and the terrified) is followed by reactions much in evidence: the *anger* of Ed Abbey's *Monkey Wrench Gang*, the *bargaining* seen in the hopeful exchange of recycling and other "green" activities for an unpolluted world, and the obvious *depression*. Each of the essays in part 2, on some level, is about facing loss. And to a varying degree, each reveals the fifth stage of grief: the *acceptance* that eases the paralysis of denial, anger, and fear.

Buddhist teachings, for example, encourage acceptance by asking if it's reasonable or natural to think we won't die. In his 2008 book, *The World We Have*, Buddhist monk and activist Thich Nhat Hanh asks that same question about our civilization. His essential position is this: things change; to live in denial of the impermanence of things is to live in dread, resentment, and despair. Living organisms obey their natural instincts to survive as a species. Some species succeed better than others by removing competition and maximizing their resources. Human beings, with their ability to adapt, are pretty successful, right up there with cockroaches. We will do whatever is necessary, even if we have to pull down the rest of the planet, roaches and all, until we reach the limits of our reources. It's only natural. Only *unnatural* behaviors of self-limitation could have stopped our kind before we drastically altered conditions on Earth.

After Tim DeChristopher internalized the notion of industrial civilization's collapse, he turned to action. "Once I realized that there was no hope in any sort of a normal future . . . of a career and a retirement and all that stuff—I realized that I have absolutely nothing to lose by fighting back." Thich Nhat Hanh suggests that before fighting back, environmentalists must first heal themselves. He offers this meditation: "Breathing in, I know that this civilization is going to die. Breathing out, this civilization cannot escape dying." But although this natural dying process can't be halted, it can be slowed and the quality of the planet's lives can be improved under conditions of acceptance and peace.

Within part 2 is the group of four essays written in response to Scott Russell Sanders's essay prompt that called for simpler and less intrusive lifestyles in response to global environmental threats. Within the four essays is the point at which the environmental writing in *The Georgia Review* experienced a sea change: Lauret Edith Savoy's "Pieces toward a Just Whole." In her essay, Savoy redefined the boundaries that had artificially limited the humans-on-Earth discussion and, thereby, redefined "environment."

Other responders' reactions to Sanders's call play like an accompaniment to Savoy's riff. They insist on the rejection of dualistic thought and emphasize responsibility. David Gessner writes, "What we need are artists wrestling with the human world, which is forever entwined with the so-called natural world because the two are one and the same." And Alison Hawthorne Deming: "What are the boundaries between my animality and the microbes that collaborate with my existence, between my voluntary and involuntary actions? There *are* no boundaries— only conflicts and resolutions, an endless process of mutual capitulation that keeps a person coasting along as if she were one discrete organism." This interconnectedness of all things demands the extension of universal rights. As Reg Saner declares, "Expecting environmental sanity to coexist with social injustice is the illogical equivalent of what physicists studying light call an interference pattern."

Savoy challenges the popular equation of Nature = Environment and its familiar trope of environmentalists saving forests and streams. More important, she repositions *environment* to include habitation, built spaces where people often live when they lack the opportunity or means to live elsewhere. Much has changed since Mary Austin and John Muir saw the environment that they wanted to preserve as an Arcadian escape, a balm. In her 1903 classic *The Land of Little Rain*, Austin wrote, "Come away, you who are obsessed with your own importance in the scheme of things, and have got nothing you did not sweat for, come away by the brown valleys and full-bosomed hills to the even-breathing days, to the kindliness, earthiness." By contrast, Savoy insists, "If we can imagine 'environment' broadly as sets of circumstances and contexts within which all of us intimately live and die, then the whole we must understand includes those lives whose experiences of place are displaced or alien, migrant or urban, indentured or enslaved, degraded or toxic." Or as Camille Dungy was to put it in a later *Review* essay, "Environment is a set of circumstances as mundane as the choice of paths we take to get home." In some cases, nature/environmental writers turned from science to sociology, from observation to theorizing. But more important, the genre, which began as an exemplar of privilege, has gradually begun the process of inclusion and compassion.

The second special feature represented in part 2, *I Am What Is around Me: Opening Up the Environmental Dialogue*, contains a broad compass of topics and approaches that share a deep background of imminent tragedy and its corresponding literary manifestation. More apparent than in earlier essays, however, is the element of social justice—a natural result of a genre moving from an exclusive author-versus-other understanding to a more inclusive *we*. In 1970, Earth Day founder Gaylord Nelson intended the day to be about "all of America and its problems." Nelson's vision serves equally well today. "Our goal is not just an environment of clean air and water and scenic beauty. The objective is an environment of decency, quality and mutual respect for all other human beings and all other living creatures." Other ideas conducive of a wider range of environmental work were in the air as well; thanks to quantum physics, the concept of a nonbinary universe had been in place since the early twentieth century. But it took the rising threat of the sixth extinction to make the connections necessary for environmental writers to fold notions of equality and community into the concept of the environment. Thus authors expanded the definition to one articulated by Camille Dungy: "What we decide matters in literature is connected to what we decide will matter for our history, for our pedagogy, for our culture. What we do and do not value in our art reveals what we do and do not value in our times. What we leave *off* the page often speaks as loudly as what we include." This, plus Wallace Stevens's "I am what is around me" equals Dungy's assertion: "All writing is environmental writing."

In general, mid-twentieth-century literary writing about nature and the environment often interacted in despair with the passing of something beautiful or wonderful. But anger and grief depend on an isolated self; there's no beauty or wonder without an observer. One can sense, however, a gradual lessening of the distance between nature/environmental writers and the more-than-human world. As threats to environmental wellness have increased in number and intensity, the culture has gradually awakened to their existence. Activist and environmentalist leader Bill McKibben has suggested that artists and writers are "the antibodies of the cultural bloodstream." And like antibodies rushing to an infected wound, artists and writers have clustered around various environmental damage points to a degree that the culture in general is finally beginning to grasp the issues at stake. Even politicians, whom McKibben categorizes as "lagging indicators," will occasionally gesture toward green considerations. Likewise, marketing has embraced the cause of clean and safe surroundings as advertising forage. Still to be generally understood, however, is that the issues are symptoms, not the problem. Turning away the offered plastic straw at lunch or buying products labeled "green" won't forestall environmental disaster. As Amitav Ghosh writes in *The Great Derangement*, "The scale of climate change is such that individual choices will make little difference unless certain collective decisions are taken and acted upon." At the nexus of Earth's predicament is a dominant culture that sees itself separate from its environment, both human and more-than-human. To surmount their despair, humans will have to achieve unity with what David Abram calls "the commonwealth of breath." The idea of such sharing took hold as the twentieth century waned; environmental writers opened their view of the environment to a more nondualistic understanding, extending the boundaries of their thinking to merge interior and exterior entities. For example, in "The Carcass Chronicle," which won the 2019 John Burroughs Nature Essay Award, Robin Patten writes of a "thin place"—an elk carcass site attended by ravens she has studied and with which she has achieved a bond. "A thin place," Patten explains, "occurs where the veil between our known, visible world and another realm—the invisible world, the eternal, the 'other'—diminishes, allowing a sense of what lies beyond our everyday existence." The self joins the intimate details of one's surroundings, enabling an environment that is complete and entire. By whatever means or intention, the best environmental authors write from a place in that world.

SCOTT RUSSELL SANDERS

Simplicity and Sanity

The first time I assigned *Walden* in an undergraduate class, I opened our discussion of the book by asking the students for their initial reactions. A man wearing a tie-dyed T-shirt quickly raised his hand to say he was surprised that a writer as famous as Thoreau would use so many clichés. When I asked for an example, the student answered, "Like, if you don't march along with everybody else, it's because you're stepping to the beat of a different drummer. My mom's got that one on a magnet on her refrigerator."

I agreed that the different drummer must be weary by now, having been called on so many times, but I pointed out that when Thoreau used the metaphor it was fresh and vigorous, for he had made it up. Indeed, I explained, Thoreau originated dozens of expressions that have become part of our common awareness, if not always of our common speech, and I rattled off examples. Then another student asked me a shrewd question: in composing his memorable phrases, was Thoreau voicing ideas nobody had ever thought of before, or was he just finding new ways to convey old truths? Having recently fallen under the spell of Thoreau, I answered that his thinking was as original as his writing. At the time, I understood *original* to mean unprecedented, something utterly new under the sun, roughly what my students and my hip colleagues meant by "cutting edge."

Over the years since then, having read more widely, I've realized that one could find precedents for virtually all of Thoreau's central ideas: from sources close to him in space and time, such as Emerson; from sources long influential in the West, such as the Greek philosophers or the Bible; and from more remote sources that were only just beginning to reach America, such as ancient Buddhist and Hindu thought. I also came to understand that originality does not mean novelty, but returning to origins. Thus, when Emerson demands in the opening paragraph of *Nature*, "Why should not we also enjoy an original relation to the universe?" he is exhorting us to encounter things *directly*, and not merely through scriptures or hand-me-down notions or intermediaries such as ministers or pundits. He is urging us to probe the depths of existence for ourselves, accepting nothing on hearsay or faith. The Latin root of *origin* means to rise, to give birth, to set in motion. To be original, therefore, is to seek the source from which all things rise. Thoreau was just that kind of seeker—not only for the two years and two months he spent living beside Walden Pond, but for his entire adult life. He was original in the deepest sense: a radical, one who delved down to the roots.

I suspect that Thoreau would have felt amusement mixed with scorn for those who brag of being "cutting edge" because they wear the latest fashions, own the latest electronic gadget, or spout the latest lingo. Novelty was never his goal; his goal was integrity. He strove for wholeness, the union of life and thought. The motive for his tireless observation, reflection, reading, and writing was not merely to gain a deeper understanding of our mysterious existence but to *practice* that understanding, to act it out, day by day. Of course, he did not act out his ideas or values perfectly; no one does. But he dramatized the effort with unrivaled power. We learn of his effort from the testimony of people who knew him and from biographies, but mainly from his own account, written in one of the most compelling prose styles ever created by an American writer.

The combination of radical thinking, deliberate living, and literary brilliance has drawn countless readers to Thoreau, especially those who sense there is something profoundly wrong with the vision of the good life offered by our industrial, technological, and materialistic society. In America one can trace a lineage of dissident souls—John Muir, Aldo Leopold, Helen and Scott Nearing, Anna and Harlan Hubbard, Thomas Merton, Edward Abbey, Wendell Berry, Annie Dillard, and a great many others—who found in Thoreau the confirmation, if not the inspiration, for their own efforts at rethinking the meaning and conduct of life.

I belong to this lineage of writers inspired by Thoreau, however humble my place may be. After forty years of reading him, I am more impressed than ever by the power of his example and the vigor of his prose, and I am at times astounded by the prescience of his social critique. To illustrate his uncanny relevance to our present dilemmas, I want to examine one key element in his philosophy—the call for simplicity.

His most emphatic use of the term appears in another passage that has been excerpted on posters and refrigerator magnets, this one from the second chapter of *Walden*, "Where I Lived, and What I Lived For":

> Our life is frittered away by detail. . . . Simplicity, simplicity, simplicity! I say, let your affairs be as two or three, and not a hundred or a thousand; instead of a mil-

lion count half a dozen, and keep your accounts on your thumbnail. . . . Simplify, simplify. Instead of three meals a day, if it be necessary eat but one; instead of a hundred dishes, five; and reduce other things in proportion. . . . The nation itself, with all its so-called internal improvements, which, by the way, are all external and superficial, is just such an unwieldy and overgrown establishment, cluttered with furniture and tripped up by its own traps, ruined by luxury and heedless expense, by want of calculation and a worthy aim, as the million households in the land; and the only cure for it, as for them, is in a rigid economy, a stern and more than Spartan simplicity of life and elevation of purpose. It lives too fast.

Since Thoreau wrote those lines, every threat he identified has become more acute—the multiplication of activities, the proliferation of technology, the accumulation of stuff, the accelerating pace, and the lack of any "worthy aim" for the whole frantic pursuit.

How might the embrace of simplicity counter these threats? Consider technology. Among the "internal improvements" Thoreau called into question were the telegraph and the railroad. It is an "illusion," he wrote in *Walden*, to assume that new technology, merely because it is new, represents "a positive advance":

Our inventions are wont to be pretty toys, which distract our attention from serious things. They are but improved means to an unimproved end, an end which it was already but too easy to arrive at; as railroads lead to Boston or New York. We are in great haste to construct a magnetic telegraph from Maine to Texas; but Maine and Texas, it may be, have nothing important to communicate. . . . As if the main object were to talk fast and not to talk sensibly.

Our current "pretty toys" make the telegraph and railroad seem quaint and slow, but they raise all the more forcefully the same questions. For example, to what extent do e-mail and cellphones enable us to say things worth saying, and to what extent do they "distract our attention from serious things"? If the Internet is used chiefly for peddling merchandise and pornography and propaganda, does it, on balance, represent a "positive advance"? If jet travel is depleting the ozone layer, burning up the last reserves of petroleum, and disturbing the climate, does it represent a net gain or loss? If television serves mainly to sell us stuff we don't need, exploit our taste for violence and sex, and steal our time, are we better off watching it on two hundred channels, in high-definition, on flat screens the size of a wall? There is no advantage in doing something faster, or doing it on a larger scale, if it is not worth doing to begin with.

The hucksters brag that electronic media have enabled us to create an "always on" society, with stimulation on tap twenty-four hours a day. This is a comical boast, given that we dwell in a universe that has been "always on" for more than thirteen billion years, casting up an unbroken stream of miracles, from quasars to fireflies, that make sitcoms and celebrity profiles and video games seem trifling by comparison. We have traded the nonstop spectacle of nature for a shabby electronic substitute, one that requires from us less effort, less skill, less reflection and responsibility. To hold us captive inside the media bubble, the vendors of virtual "reality" must keep increasing the level of stimulation, pumping up the volume, the speed, the violence, and the sex, lest we begin to wonder if life might have a purpose other than amusement.

In sentences immediately following the passage about simplicity quoted above, Thoreau remarks: "If we do not get out sleepers, and forge rails, and devote days and nights to the work, but go to tinkering upon our *lives* to improve *them*, who will build railroads? And if railroads are not built, how shall we get to heaven in season? But if we stay at home and mind our business, who will want railroads? We do not ride on the railroad; it rides upon us." For "railroad" one could substitute the name of virtually any coercive technology, such as television, computer, or automobile. In each case, our lives have been organized to accommodate the technology, rather than the other way around.

Anyone who has encountered an advertisement for skinny cellphones or brawny pickup trucks—which in the United States means anyone not living in a cave—realizes that our inventions are brazenly *sold* to us as pretty toys, all shiny and colorful and stylish, as if we were savages craving baubles. The principle of simplicity would urge us to resist the sales pitch and to ask of any technology: What is it for? What does it enable us to do that we can't already do, and should we be doing it? Who benefits from the new technology, and who suffers? What does it displace? What skills and workers does it render obsolete? How does it affect the people who use it, the community, and the Earth?

If we gave honest answers to these questions, we would build no more nuclear reactors or atomic bombs, and we would dismantle the ones we have. We would not allow snowmobiles in national parks, leaf blowers in neighborhoods, or junk food in schools. We would quit spreading poisons on our farm fields, quit raising chickens and hogs in cages, quit injecting cows with bovine growth hormone. We would not release genetically modified organisms into the environment without thorough, long-term studies showing they are safe, and without convincing proof that they serve human well-being.

The standard of simplicity would also prompt us to calculate the true cost of our luxuries, whether fresh strawberries on our plates in winter or golf courses in the desert or Hummers on the highways or McMansions in the fields. In another maxim that has become part of our common lore, Thoreau declared, "The cost of a thing is the amount of what I will call life which is required to be exchanged for it, immediately or in the long run." The life Thoreau had in mind, as the context makes clear, is that of the individual, and certainly one could apply his metric to assess the cost, to body and soul, of buying a larger house or a fancier car, say, or of taking a Caribbean cruise. But on a planet supporting more than five times as many people as there were in Thoreau's day, and with a vastly more powerful technology at our disposal, we must interpret "life" in a larger sense. We must ask, for example, how many people have been killed or maimed in Iraq to support our addiction to oil. How many people work in sweatshops to fill our stores with cheap goods? How many animals and plants die, how many species go extinct, to satisfy our appetite for lumber or coffee or beef? And as a result of our destabilizing the climate, how much suffering will our lavish way of life impose on future generations?

Americans are not alone in squandering Earth's bounty, but right now we are the ones doing so most recklessly. With not quite 5 percent of the world's population, our nation now uses some 25 percent of the nonrenewable resources consumed globally each year and produces more than 20 percent of the world's greenhouse gases. We also account for half of the world's annual military expenditures, chiefly to perpetuate our extravagance. And yet, judging by the rising incidence in America of depression and other emotional disorders, by the widening gulf between the rich and the poor, by the high levels of divorce, alcoholism, drug abuse, crime, and incarceration, and by the general malaise registered in poll after poll, this feverish consumption has not brought us happiness or health. Indeed, our headlong pursuits of material wealth, technological novelty, and militarism have caused grievous damage to persons and planet, as Thoreau could have predicted.

A century and a half after publication of *Walden*, what might it mean to practice simplicity? The answer will depend not only on one's values but also on one's circumstances. A middle-class American would have far different options—and obligations—than would a subsistence farmer in Peru, say, or a street peddler in India. Likewise, retirees living alone, parents rearing children, young professionals just launching their careers, and students enrolled in college might make quite different choices. So let me speak briefly of the choices my wife and I have made, not because our efforts are in any way a model, but because they may suggest a few modest moves in the direction of living more simply.

Ruth and I, married forty years, are in our early sixties; we have reared two children and now have three grandchildren. We both grew up in frugal households, with parents whose habits and values had been shaped by the Great Depression. Ruth is a scientist, I am a teacher and writer, and we have been employed at Indiana University throughout our careers, earning together more money than we've ever needed to spend. We have several times declined opportunities to relocate for higher salaries or trendier addresses. For the first six years of our marriage we lived in apartments, and then, soon after our first child was born, we bought a 1920s vintage house, where we have lived ever since. The house is 1,250 square feet, which was the average size of an American house in the 1950s; half a century later, the average size of a new house in America has nearly doubled, to 2,400 square feet. As many of our friends and colleagues moved to roomier digs in the suburbs, we chose to stay in our house in town—because of our affection for neighbors and neighborhood, because from here we can walk to work, and because more space for us would be more costly for Earth.

Although our house is small by middle-class American standards, we're well aware that it is a palace by comparison with the dwellings in which countless human beings must live. Over the years, we've made the house as energy efficient as we could by insulating from basement to attic and sealing every crack, planting trees for summer shade, installing double-glazed windows and a high-efficiency furnace, replacing incandescent lightbulbs with compact fluorescent ones, and replacing worn-out appliances with efficient and compact new models. To further reduce energy use, we've also adjusted our habits: in winter, we set the thermostat at 58 degrees during the night and 68 degrees during the day, and wear more layers of clothes; in summer, we open the windows and rely on fans for cooling, resorting to the air conditioner only on the most sultry days; we wash our clothes in cold water and dry them outdoors on a line; we take showers rather than baths, and we use flow-reducing shower heads and faucets; we turn off lights and appliances when they're not in use.

In our tiny yard, we have replaced all but a patch of grass with native plants, and that grass we cut with a push mower. We mix our kitchen scraps with leaves in a compost bin and use the resulting compost on our garden, where we grow salad greens, onions, garlic, herbs, and other small-scale crops. Most of our remaining foodstuffs we buy from local and organic growers, at the farmers' market and natural foods co-op, and we eat so far as possible the produce that is in season. Most of our meals are vegetarian, and the poultry and meat that we do eat are free-range and locally raised. We do not buy bottled water, although we do filter our tap water for drinking and cooking. By recycling everything that is currently recyclable in our city, we need to put out a can of trash for the landfill only about once every six or eight weeks.

Between us, Ruth and I drive just under 10,000 miles per year—the national average for two drivers is 24,000—and our car is a hybrid-electric vehicle that cruises forty-five miles on a gallon of gas—double the national average. We don't belong to a gym or a diet club, but instead climb the stairs of our two-story house, work in our yard, do our own cleaning, and walk. Ruth gave up bicycling a few years ago, but I still ride my bike on errands around town.

The net result of these and many other actions, all as common-sensical and routine to us as tooth-brushing, is that our ecological footprint—our use of non-renewable resources and our contribution to the release of greenhouse gases and other forms of pollution—is about half that of an average American couple and on a par with citizens of Japan, Germany, Sweden, and other affluent but less prodigal societies. Still, our way of life is extravagant by comparison with that of most of the world's people, and it is more extravagant than the Earth could support were all of the world's people to live as we do. We try to offset the impact of our carbon emissions by purchasing shares in wind farms and other renewable energy sources, but we realize that this is a palliative, not a solution.

To achieve a degree of material simplicity that could be shared with the nearly seven billion humans now alive as well as with our descendants, Ruth and I would have to make more difficult choices. We might have to pay fewer visits to family and friends who live at a distance. I might have to decline all invitations for readings or lectures or meetings that require air travel. We might have to entirely forgo out-of-season produce, as well as bananas, coffee, and other foods that must be shipped from great distances. We might have to unplug from the Internet, cancel magazine subscriptions, quit buying books and only borrow from the library. By moving into an apartment, we could free up our house for use by a family with children, but could we bear to leave our neighbors and garden? Could we move in with our children, or invite them to move in with us? Anyone who recognizes how thoroughly the human economy is degrading nature's economy must ponder such questions.

Our ethical dilemma is quite different from the one Thoreau faced. He did not practice simplicity because he worried about damaging the planet or depriving future generations, but because he wished to leave a broad margin to his life—a margin for exploring the countryside, for studying nature, for playing the flute and sauntering with friends, for reading and writing and thinking. After describing in *Walden* his custom of scouting the Concord landscape and imagining which farms he might buy—and where he might build a house, fence a pasture, or plant an orchard—he ends by forswearing all these acquisitions and chores because, he explains, "a man is rich in proportion to the number of things which he can afford to let alone." Here, as in many instances where Thoreau exaggerated his point so as to challenge conventional views, I want to qualify his claim. I want to protest that if no one planted orchards there would be no apples, and if no one cleared pastures there would be no milk or wool. I agree, however, with his central claim, which is that we are more likely to achieve happiness by decreasing our possessions and activities than by increasing them—not reducing them to zero but to a modest, manageable sufficiency.

One modern translation of the *Tao Te Ching* captures this insight exactly: "If you realize that you have enough, / you are truly rich." "Enough" is the key word. We live on a globe where perhaps a billion people, including most Americans, have far more than they need while some three billion people are destitute. In a just world, in a sane world, everyone would have a sufficiency: neither too much nor too little, but rather enough to lead a decent, healthy, secure life. Visionaries from the Buddha and Jesus to Gandhi and the Dalai Lama have called on us to work toward such a sane and just world. Like Thoreau, they have urged us to live in a materially simple way, not merely so that we might achieve happiness but so that Earth's bounty might be conserved and equitably shared.

Along with Amos and Jeremiah and other Hebrew prophets who preceded him, Jesus repeatedly warned against devoting one's life to piling up money and property. In a well-known example, a rich ruler came to Jesus and asked how he might attain eternal life. When the ruler assured Jesus that he had faithfully observed all the commandments, Jesus told him, "'One thing you still lack. Sell all that you have and distribute to the poor, and you will have treasure in heaven; and come, follow me.' But when [the ruler] heard this he became sad, for he was very rich. Jesus looking at him said, 'How hard it is for those who have riches to enter the kingdom of God! For it is easier for a camel to go through the eye of a needle than for a rich man to enter the kingdom of God'" (Luke 18:18–25, Revised Standard Version). In another familiar instance, Jesus told his followers, "Do not lay up for yourselves treasures on earth, where moth and rust consume and where thieves break in and steal, but lay up for yourselves treasures in heaven. . . . For where your treasure is, there will your heart be also" (Matthew 6:19–21, RSV).

Whatever else Jesus may have meant by heaven or the kingdom of God, I hear in these terms the promise of utter fulfillment. I imagine heaven to be not a place but an experience, the bliss of realizing our true nature, as in the Buddhist and Hindu vision of nirvana. Of all the distractions that might prevent us from realizing our true nature, none is more seductive, according to Jesus, than the pursuit of worldly wealth. One need not accept this pronouncement as divine to recognize it as psychologically sound. If, above all other things, we treasure money and what money can buy, our lives will be given over to securing, monitoring, and protecting our dragon's hoard of gold. Craving will consume us; multiplied a billionfold by a global population whose numbers Jesus could not have imagined, this craving, if unchecked by ethical or cultural restraint, will consume the planet.

When Jesus reminded his followers, "Take heed, and beware of all covetousness; for a man's life does not consist in the abundance of his possessions," he was recalling the last of the Ten Commandments. Stated twice, once in the book of Exodus and once in Deuteronomy, this commandment warns us not to covet anything belonging to our neighbor. Again, whether or not one considers this instruction to be divine, one can see that it is wise. Most human strife, from divorce to war, arises from the impulse to grab what belongs to someone else. To covet is to be enslaved by greed—for possessions, sensations, status, or power.

Now consider the logic of a capitalist economy. For profits and businesses to grow perpetually, our appetite for whatever the businesses sell must grow perpetually as well. The purpose of advertising is to provoke in us an incessant craving for more—more style, more speed, more dialing minutes, more hamburger for a buck, more horsepower, more sex appeal, more glamour, more laughs, more thrills. Twenty-four hours a day, through every medium of communication, our advertising proclaims: *Thou shalt covet!*

I would be hard-pressed to exaggerate the pervasiveness of advertising. Nearly every earthly surface is plastered with ads—bus shelters, gas pumps, the interiors of elevators, the shells of eggs in grocery stores, trays at airport security gates, room keys in motels, the paper sheets on doctors' examining tables—so that the built environment begins to resemble the costumes of race car drivers, with each square inch peddling some product. The Internet is tattooed with ads. Our e-mail in-boxes overflow with spam as our mailboxes bulge with catalogs. Radios broadcasting on some school buses now carry ads. Cellphone companies lower monthly subscription rates to customers in exchange for flooding their pocket-sized screens with ads. Public arenas carry the names of corporations. T-shirts have become moving billboards for brand names, and billboards themselves—always a blight—are becoming digital so that commercial messages can be changed every few minutes. And all of this is in addition to the tens of thousands of television ads the typical viewer watches each year. Market researchers estimate that an American city dweller now encounters some five thousand ads, in one medium or another, each *day*. The central purpose of all these blandishments is to make us hunger for something we do not already have, make us dissatisfied with our lives so that we will lay out money to compensate for the lack or the flaw. Since no purchase will ever quell that dissatisfaction, we will have to keep buying, urged on by ubiquitous ads.

Along with praising greed, this marketing blitz overturns several others of the Ten Commandments, such as keeping the Sabbath holy and shunning idols and telling the truth, and it encourages nearly all seven of the deadly sins, notably pride, sloth, envy, gluttony, and lust. Advertising does not create these impulses, of course; it merely exploits them, and it does so using the best talent and techniques that money can buy. How much money? In 2007, expenditures on all forms of advertising in the United States amounted to roughly $300 billion.

There is no comparably well-funded, relentless, and pervasive influence appealing to our benevolent impulses such as compassion, humility, generosity, prudence, fidelity, or thrift. The home might provide a counter to consumerism, but when American children spend, on average, fifteen minutes a day talking with their parents and six hours watching screens, it's clear that the family has been overshadowed by the market. By the time these children finish twelfth grade, they will have spent, on average, more hours watching television and surfing the Web than attending school. And most schools, when they are not dealing with the consequences of poverty, addiction, broken homes, child abuse, and other social pathologies, concentrate on preparing students to enter the workforce and become lifelong consumers.

Churches might be expected to counter consumerism, especially in this nation where more than three-quarters of the populace claim to be followers of Jesus. And yet, far from calling for material simplicity, many of the most vociferous Christians preach a gospel of prosperity. Televangelists assure their listeners that God wants them to be rich. Ministers in the fastest-growing churches have become entertainment impresarios whose main business is to fill their vast sanctuaries with high-paying crowds. Such ministers may swell the crowds by denouncing homosexuals or decrying abortion or vilifying welfare queens, but they are unlikely to whisper a word against recreational shopping or stock market gambling or the insatiable pursuit of wealth. I do not see how such a religion, or such an economy, can be reconciled with the teachings of Jesus.

Like Jesus, the Buddha would have seen the madness of an economy devoted to the endless expansion of desire. In his moment of enlightenment, the Buddha realized that human suffering arises from craving and clinging, for whatever we crave or cling to is bound to pass away, including the ravenous self. And so he dedicated the rest of his long life to teaching a philosophy aimed at curbing desire. He understood that our *wants* are potentially infinite, while our *needs* are few. We need nutritious food, adequate shelter, durable clothing, useful tools, medical care, companionship, intellectual stimulation, and art, all of which could be secured in a modest fashion without jeopardizing the prospects for future generations. Once our real needs are met, we could live in peace and contentment if we did not always yearn for something more.

Thoreau recognized this constant hankering for more as a driving force in the industrial economy of his day and as a perennial source of human misery. His title for the first and by far the longest chapter of *Walden*, "Economy," announced his intent to challenge the prevailing ways of getting and spending. In that opening chapter he examines one by one our basic needs, and he suggests how they might be met without exhausting ourselves or the world. Again and again he counters the yearning for excess with a call for frugality, as when he observes: "It is possible to invent a house still more convenient and luxurious than we have, which yet all would admit that man could not afford to pay for. Shall we always study to obtain more of these things, and not sometimes to be content with less?"

This man who was content with a diet of potatoes, rice, beans, and pond water knew that many people would regard his estimate of our basic needs as too austere: "There is a certain class of unbelievers who sometimes ask me such questions as, if I think that I can live on vegetable food alone; and to strike at the root of the matter at once,—for the root is faith,—I am accustomed to answer such, that I can live on board nails. If they cannot understand that, they cannot understand much that I have to say." Here again, if Thoreau exaggerates his austerity, it is by way of countering what he saw as the profligacy of his contemporaries. The profligacy of American society today would, I expect, dumbfound him, as it should dismay and dumbfound us.

To put a prettier face on our prodigal ways, apologists for consumerism have recently borrowed a key term from ecology and begun to speak of "sustainable growth" and "sustainable consumption." In ecology, a process may be legitimately described as sustainable if it can continue indefinitely without degrading or exhausting its biophysical sources. Thus a prairie is sustainable because it requires only rain, snow, sunlight, and a substrate of minerals to flourish over thousands of years. But there is no such thing as sustainable *growth*—not even in a prairie, where plants die back every winter and eventually decay, increasing the fertility of the soil. In nature, no organism or community of organisms expands forever; all growth is constrained by predation, climate, geology, the availability of moisture and nutrients, and other critical factors. Thus, even the grandest trees, such as redwoods, grow only as high as sap can rise against the pull of gravity; the size of insects is limited by the weight of their exoskeletons; and the bulk of birds is limited by the physics of flight.

The model that nature provides is not one of perpetual growth, as in a capitalist economy, but of perpetual *regrowth*. Up to a point, trees may be harvested from a forest, crops from the fields, and fish from the sea—and the regenerative power of nature will replace what has been taken away. If pushed far beyond that point, however, forests give way to deserts, as in North Africa; soils become sterile, as in much of the Middle East; and fish stocks collapse, as has happened recently to dozens of species, such as cod, that were once a mainstay of the human diet. No form of consumption is sustainable, therefore, if it exceeds the capacity of a natural system to replenish itself.

Thus it is nonsense to speak of sustainable consumption of materials that do not regenerate, such as fossil fuels. Once oil, coal, or natural gas is burned, it is gone. There is no regeneration of lead, iron, zinc, gold, copper, or any other metal crucial to industry. Once a wilderness is cut up by roads, oil-drilling platforms, landing strips, and toxic dumps, it will never again be wilderness, or at least not within many human generations. Once the top of a mountain is stripped away to extract coal and the rubble is shoved into valleys below, the landscape will be forever deformed. Rivers may eventually flow clear if they are protected from new sources of pollution, but the pollution already dumped into the ocean has nowhere else to go. Agricultural runoff flushed down the Mississippi River has extinguished nearly all life in an area of the Gulf of Mexico whose estimated extent ranges up to 8,000 square miles, according to a 31 July 2008 article in the *Washington Post*. More than a quarter of the world's coral reefs have already been destroyed by pollution, sedimentation, rising ocean temperatures, and the use of explosives and cyanide for collecting tropical fish.

The so-called "sinks"—the air, soils, and waters—into which we have been dumping our wastes since the beginning of the industrial revolution are finite. Their capacity to absorb and detoxify our waste is also finite, and for certain materials that capacity is effectively zero: there is no safe level for the dumping of radioactive debris, nor for the dumping of mercury, dioxins, PCBs, CFCs, and a slew of other industrial byproducts. Even relatively benign byproducts, such as the carbon dioxide released by the burning of fossil fuels, become dangerous when they exceed certain limits. The dynamic equilibrium of the biosphere has been created and maintained in part by biological activity, and it is the single most important factor in the continued flourishing of life on Earth. Any human activity that disturbs this balance, as by thinning the ozone layer or heating the atmosphere, is a threat not only to humankind but to every other species.

Near the end of his life, Thoreau observed that "most men ... do not care for Nature and would sell their share in all her beauty, as long as they may live, for a stated sum—many for a glass of rum. Thank God, men cannot as yet fly, and lay waste the sky as well as the earth! We are safe on that side for the present. It is for the very reason that some do not care for those things that we need to continue to protect all from the vandalism of a few." The vandalism of a few is still a threat to natural beauty, as witnessed in the push by a handful of corporations, lobbyists, and public officials to open the Arctic National Wildlife Refuge to oil drilling or to carve up the last remnants of old growth forests with logging roads. But today the vandalism of the many is the greater threat. Billions of ordinary people, obeying their appetites and the enticements of the marketplace, are laying waste to the sky as well as the land and sea.

Nature is already imposing limits on the human economy, through resource depletion and ecological breakdown. If we human beings were as wise as we claim to be in calling ourselves Homo sapiens, we would do voluntarily what nature will otherwise force on us. We would restrain our appetites and, over generations, reduce our population. We would fashion an economy based on needs rather than wants. We would measure every product, every technology, every private or public decision, against the standard of ecological and communal health.

As a first step in that direction, let us quit using the word "consumer" for a season and use instead the close synonym, "devourer." Thus, the Office of Consumer Affairs would become the Office of Devourer Affairs. In schools, the study of consumer science, which used to be called home economics, would become devourer science. Savvy shoppers would subscribe to *Devourer Reports*. Pollsters would conduct devourer surveys. Newspapers would track the ups and downs of the devourer price index.

The point of these substitutions is not mere wordplay. The point is to regain a sense of what our language implies. To consume means to use up or lay waste, as fire reduces a house to rubble and ash. We should resent being called consumers, and all the more so when those who apply the label suggest that they care only about our happiness and well-being.

Let us think of ourselves, instead, as "conservers". For conservers, the Earth is not a warehouse of disposable stuff, but the source and sustainer of life, surpassingly beautiful, worthy of love. True, we must draw upon the Earth in order to live, but we should do so gratefully, respectfully, and modestly, aiming to preserve rather than devour our planetary home. This is the ethical imperative at the heart of the call to simplicity.

Following his boast in *Walden* about a willingness to live on "board nails" if need be, Thoreau goes on to say this:

> For my part, I am glad to hear of experiments of this kind being tried; as that a young man tried for a fortnight to live on hard, raw corn on the ear, using his teeth for all mortar. The squirrel tribe tried the same and succeeded. The human race is interested in these experiments, though a few old women who are incapacitated for them, or who own their thirds in mills, may be alarmed.

We needn't share Thoreau's prejudice against old women owning shares in mills or his enthusiasm for emulating squirrels to recognize the value of experiments in simple living. In America, his sojourn beside Walden Pond is the most famous example of such an experiment, but there have been many others, including ones that lasted much longer.

We cannot expect to learn of experiments in simple living from the same media that promote extravagant living. But we may find stirring accounts in books, such as John Muir's *My First Summer in the Sierra* (1911), Henry Beston's *The Outermost House* (1928), Aldo Leopold's *A Sand County Almanac* (1949), Helen and Scott Nearing's *Living the Good Life* (1954), Mohandas Gandhi's *Autobiography*

(1954), Wendell Berry's *The Long-Legged House* (1969), Harlan Hubbard's *Payne Hollow* (1974), Annie Dillard's *Pilgrim at Tinker Creek* (1974), Gary Snyder's *Practice of the Wild* (1990), and William Coperthwaite's *A Handmade Life* (2002)—to name only a few books that have nourished me. We may also learn of experiments in simple living from magazines, such as *Orion* and *Resurgence*, and increasingly—and paradoxically—from the Internet. There are now hundreds of websites that advocate simplicity, some of them merely exploiting the term for selling products, but many of them, such as the sites for New American Dream and The Simple Living Network, offering sound advice.

All of these testimonies to simplicity deserve to be far better known, for they point the way to a more humane and hopeful future. The way is not easy: in comparison with consumerism, the simple life requires greater effort, courage, fidelity, and imagination. In the long run the industrial economy will undermine our ability to feed and clothe and shelter ourselves, but in the short run we are likely to find it easier and more convenient to buy groceries at the supermarket than to raise them in the backyard . . . to hop in a car and drive to work than to bicycle there or ride the bus . . . to turn up the thermostat than to feed a woodstove or put on an extra layer of clothes . . . to buy a new gadget or garment than to mend the old one . . . to sink into the couch and watch a music video than to learn to play the fiddle and gather neighbors for a dance. The practice of simplicity is more strenuous than the pursuit of luxury; it demands more of our attention, intelligence, perseverance, labor, and skill.

The reward for this effort is a more gathered and meaningful and joyful life. In a letter written the year after publication of *Walden*, Thoreau asked: "To what end do I lead a simple life at all, pray? That I may teach others to simplify their lives?—and so all our lives be *simplified* merely, like an algebraic formula? Or not, rather, that I may make use of the ground I have cleared, to live more worthily and profitably?" He sought to live in a materially simple way so as to create the conditions for spiritual and intellectual richness. The root of the word *simplicity* means all of a piece, single, whole; thus it is closely aligned with *sanity*, whose root means health or soundness. What generations of readers have found in Thoreau is a robust sanity, a harmony of action and values, an antidote to scatter, clutter, distraction, delusion, and sham:

> To be a philosopher is not merely to have subtle thoughts, nor even to found a school, but so to love wisdom as to live according to its dictates, a life of simplicity, independence, magnanimity, and trust. It is to solve some of the problems of life, not only theoretically, but practically.

Unlike Thoreau and his contemporaries, we now face problems that are global in scale, and so we need wise policies at the national and international level. But solutions even of global problems must begin with changes in the vision and practice of individuals. We arrived at our current predicament as a result of billions of individual choices. We can turn our civilization around and head in a new direction by making new choices, person by person, household by household, neighborhood by neighborhood, business by church by school. Beginning right now, we can choose to lead materially simpler lives, to conserve rather than consume, to own fewer things and give away what we don't need; we can undertake fewer activities, and those we do undertake we can pursue with more care and delight. We can move around less and pay closer attention to our home ground. We can draw more of our food and other necessities from local sources. Instead of chasing after manufactured sensations, we can revel in nature and community. Instead of distracting ourselves with novelties, we can seek what is enduring. We can strive to be, like Thoreau, truly original, and delve down to the wellsprings of life.

We need to launch our own experiments in simplicity. Living in such a way, we can promote both ecological health and equity in the sharing of the world's goods. We can preserve natural resources and resilient ecosystems for future generations, and we can thereby achieve greater security by reducing our dependence on a fragile, corrosive global economy. We can help alleviate the poverty, hopelessness, and suffering that lead to war.

No life is perfect, but every life can become nobler, finer, saner. Just because we can't live without doing harm doesn't mean we can't do *less* harm. The world's crisis is an opportunity—to reorient our lives away from material consumption and toward inner richness, to heal ourselves as well as the planet.

Culture, Biology, and Emergence

1.

Before Henry David Thoreau began his twenty-eight-mile walk along the Cape Cod seashore in October 1849, he stopped to witness a shipwreck at Cohasset. "Death!" read the headlines in Boston, "One Hundred and Forty-Five Lives Lost." Thoreau traveled among the many Irish, hundreds of them going to identify bodies, comfort the survivors, and attend funerals. "Many horses in carriages were fastened to the fences near the shore," he wrote, "and, for a mile or more, up and down, the beach was covered with people looking out for bodies and examining fragments of the wreck." The brig *St. John*, loaded with emigrants from Galway, Ireland, had broken on the rocks that Sunday morning, and the atmosphere was not of grief but of "a sober despatch of business" as coffins were filled, nailed shut, and carted away. Among the crowd picking through the wreckage were men collecting seaweed the storm had cast up, carrying it above the reach of the tide, after separating out fragments of clothing. The horror of turning up a human body in the wrack did not keep them from gathering the "valuable manure" of seaweed. "This shipwreck," Thoreau observed, "had not produced a visible vibration in the fabric of society."

He was not numb to the loss and misery of the wreck, but he admired the social whole and its ongoing pragmatism. He felt that the seashore acquired "a rarer and sublimer beauty" when framed by this event. He admired the industry of the fishermen, farther along on his journey, counting two hundred mackerel boats working offshore near Truro, another hundred on the horizon floating on this "highway of nations," and overall an astonishing 1,500 fishing rigs working out of Provincetown in the mid-1800s. Today one might see a handful, and those nearly always lashed bow and stern and spring lines to the wharf. Thoreau depicts the place with an eye to history, an ear to local story, and an implicit confidence in human enterprise.

Reading this account of his travels, I don't see him as recluse, Luddite, and misanthrope—the pacifist Unabomber of the nineteenth century—as those who grow cynical about human prospects might come to imagine. He is a man who seeks solitude in order to live deliberately and to pass the lesson on to others, a man who commits civil disobedience to goad injustice and advance moral philosophy, and a man who appreciates human thrift and industry.

Thoreau's *Cape Cod* makes a good complement to *Walden*, which grates on me for some of its stridencies, particularly Thoreau's ridicule of technology as "pretty toys" that "distract our attention from serious things." This strikes me as snobbish intellectualism, as opposed to the work's more dominant note of mindful curiosity. What has been more serious to human beings than technology since the first flint struck sparks? Maybe art. Maybe religion. This is the kind of animal we are: tool-making, art-making, symbol-making, and intensely social, engaged in a mutually reinforcing set of activities that make us speed-learners and obsessive connectors with one another. Technology may be sinking us now, but this need not be the case. The question is not whether we can live without technology, but whether we can live with technology in such a way that we do not destroy ourselves and the planet.

The communication and information technologies, in particular, strike me as markers of an emerging shift in consciousness. What kind of good thing might they be? What might be the adaptive aspects to this cultural movement? A form of collective intelligence that no one controls, it evolves in its own organismic way to egg us on toward greater connection, exposure, accountability, and collaboration. Sure, the Internet is full of trash and hype, but the freedom with which information can move makes censorship, deception, and totalitarianism much harder to inflict.

Scott Russell Sanders' "Simplicity and Sanity" makes an eloquent case for simplicity and the role of individual responsibility in facing the crisis of global climate change. I try to follow the principles he offers, taking pragmatic steps to reduce my weight on the planet. But the problems we face are of such profound scope that they cannot be effectively addressed by individual responses alone. The ultimate responsibility for reducing the effects of global climate change is a collective social responsibility that requires policy, regulation, alliance, and law—instruments our culture has failed to provide. I say "culture," not "government," because democratic government is, in theory, an instrument for realizing the will of the people. We do no good by acting as if we-the-people are virtuous while they-the-government are corrupt. The fabric of human culture is being frayed, stretched, and torn by our predicament. Values rule that none of us really believe in: profit trumps all, every man for himself, wealth is health, and—this is author William DeBuys' coinage at a recent symposium—"yoyo": you're on your own.

Not surprisingly, I am at odds with my culture. So many of us are these days, as we free-fall into ecological doom. Recycling, installing halogen bulbs, and writing letters to Congress seem pallid levels of activism when compared to the severity of our collective malaise. We live in a pathological culture that is sick with violence, greed, waste, contentiousness, and a sense of futility. We live in cities we despise for their ugliness, menace, and lack of community (though it's puritanical, I know, at such moments as this to deny the pleasures of the city). We have poor people whom we ignore, leaving them stranded on their roofs in a flood or cast out on the street. We ask their children to die in senseless wars. We have elected leaders who have no business leading, so lacking are they in wisdom and the capacity for reflective thought and empathy; their disdain for learning and scientific research, and their absurdly simplistic posturing about the state of religion in a pluralistic democracy, would make such leaders laughable if their actions were not causing so much anguish around the world and so much erosion of our sense of purpose at home.

No greater proof of our dissident relationship to our own culture is needed than the terrible moment we parents meet when we send our children to school, camp, movies, or a sleepover at a neighbor's house. We feel them slip from the embrace of family and plunge into the turbulence of society. We realize we cannot control the influences that will enter their minds and hearts. We feel sick with fear.

Raising me in the 1950s, my artistic parents wanted to protect me from the conformity of Connecticut's suburban somnolence. Raising my daughter in the culturally contentious sixties, I wanted to protect her from rednecks and the evangelical neighbors who said that her dreams of a beloved dead grandmother were visits from Satan. My grown daughter and her husband—a visual artist and a progressive pastor—struggle to raise their boys without taint of the violence, excess, and greed that surround them. We all come to the horrible awareness that we cannot protect our children from the culture in which they live. We do not trust it; we do not want to feel that we are part of it. Yet our children, too, will become creatures of their culture and their historical moment. They will have to learn for themselves what their values are, but we want desperately to *give* them their values, as surely as we gave them their names.

This alienation from and resistance to culture only serves to reinforce the value of bullish individualism, but no matter how much we do as individuals, the larger organism of culture remains impoverished. The old place-based cultures no longer work. John Donne wrote that no man is an island; now we know that no culture is an island, that to be alive cultures must be permeable. This lesson is one that First Nation peoples of the Americas have had to learn through the hardest of lessons. Today, war based upon conflicting fundamentalisms breaks out when people are unable to acknowledge and live with the permeability of culture. Yet the velocity of change is such that we do not know what verities to rely upon. What ideas about culture can we take up in good faith as part of our tool kit for rebuilding the "commons"—those aspects of nature and culture that cannot be owned—as a countervailing force to the market? What ideas about culture might help us to celebrate rather than bemoan the social whole of which we are a part?

2.

I return again and again to Edward Sapir's essay, "Culture, Genuine and Spurious," parts of which appeared in the English *Dial* in 1919, barely beyond the shadow of World War I. Sapir explores his "idea of what kind of a good thing culture is," defining *culture* as "any socially inherited element in the life of man, material or spiritual." It includes art, religion, science, inventions, domestic skills, and consumer goods, as well as such society-shaping ideas as democracy, imperialism, civil liberty, and social justice.

I often ask my graduate students on the first day of a creative writing course to write down their cultural influences. I do this because I find that the biggest problem in the student writing I see, other than poor mechanics, is their self-absorption. Too many of them write about personal wounds: drug and alcohol abuse, car wrecks, anorexia, dysfunctional and failed families, failed love affairs, depression, anxiety, and rage against feelings of powerlessness. I don't mean to suggest that these are not suitable catalysts for making literature, but my students tend not to see these stories within a social matrix or cultural lineage. They feel locked within themselves and think of artistic expression as a key that will let them into the kingdom of emotional freedom, rather than seeing art as a mindful reframing of experience and emotion through a forming intelligence. They write with too much "I" and no sense of "we." They can tell me what has happened to them—but they cannot tell me the significance, the moral and psychological consequences. They cannot step outside of their anguish to see the cultural context that shapes them. They just know that they, who are among the most privileged people who have ever lived on Earth, feel they don't belong anywhere.

So, I start out by asking them to write down what they see as their cultural influences within three frames of reference.

First, culture as a shared set of traditions and meanings. They can choose any context they wish: ethnicity, gender, race, nationality, sexual orientation, or faith community. They write about being Mormon, gay, goth, punk, jock, transgendered, Chicano, Navajo, or mixed blood. They display an impressive array of political and activist affiliations, holding passionate convictions about social, economic, and environmental justice. The interesting thing is that while some speak of nationality—those whose families have come in recent generations from Italy or Korea or Somalia—not one student has spoken about being American as a significant cultural influence. This just doesn't seem to occur to them—as if, once you get here, you can be anything you want to be, but you can't see yourself as part of the whole.

Second, I ask them to consider culture as artistic expression, and they offer up movies, video games, jazz, performance art, and photography. They seem surprised at how their stories open up when told within such a texture. I, too, can be surprised. A Navajo student who had been silent all semester while listening respectfully each week as other students made presentations on dance therapy, installation sculpture, and finger painting became eloquent when her time to present arrived.

"I don't really know what you mean when you say 'art,' because in my culture it's not separate from life," she said. She held up in her hands her ceremonial dress and silver squash blossom necklace, and she passed "kneel-down bread" to everyone in the room. She was very much a contemporary woman, a jeans and T-shirt fashionista, with a foot in each of two worlds. She described the history and use of the traditional items: Yes, she said, the workmanship of the dress and necklace was artful, and the technique she described in her grandmother's kneeling down to press flour into tortilla-like rounds was artful. But these were simply the way things were done on certain occasions in her culture. No one on the rez thought of them as art.

A woman from New Jersey had worked as a teenage prostitute. She left home in the morning wearing the pleated plaid skirt and tailored white shirt that were the uniform of her Catholic high school. She carried in her backpack a different outfit for her after-school job. This was not a glitz-and-power class of prostitution, but a lowlife massage parlor where she did hand jobs on lonely and powerless men. Do you prefer oil or lotion, she would ask. She'd been sexually abused by her father. This work was the first time she'd felt in control of men. Reading her essays was difficult and painful, in part because she felt so affirmed by having been a sex worker; her fellow students could not get past the feeling that she had been degraded. Then she wrote an essay that ventured beyond her personal experience, and the writing, for the first time, lifted off the page. She had framed her experience in the context of prostitutes in cinema. *Pretty Woman*, starring an effervescent Julia Roberts, was the whore-with-a-heart-of-gold du jour, an innocent and redemptive depiction that everyone loved. The student's essay brought reel after reel of such fictions to light, and suddenly I felt complicit in the cultural hypocrisy surrounding sex workers. I did not feel accused, I felt called to understand how a woman might choose such a path.

Third, I ask students to consider culture as a relationship between people and nature or people and a place. This yields stories about places that are lost— the family store run by Chinese-American grandparents on a street corner in Phoenix now devoured by a mall. Or the places people go to get away—the hike in the backcountry, the family cottage at the lake, the study-abroad trip to Malta. I have read no student essay that draws on the depth of experience on the land and in specific places that writers such as Scott Sanders, William DeBuys, Simon Ortiz, and Wendell Berry so richly portray. Perhaps it is unreasonable to expect such work from the new generation; culture as it has traditionally been shaped by the terms of nature and place is itself a permeable idea and is giving way to velocity, hybridity, and Google-ality.

Sapir describes culture as "the spiritual possessions of the group rather than of the individual." It is "a spiritual heirloom that must, at all cost, be preserved intact." Which heirlooms, the skeptic may ask. Few people would wish to preserve all aspects of their culture—assuming they could even define who they are as cultural creatures. Cultural identity is becoming a matter of individual choice, but cultural relativism does not have to mean that all cultural traditions are equal. It can mean that a person becomes more deliberate about which aspects of her tradition she wishes to take up and pass on. Vernita Herdman, an Inupiaq community advocate in Alaska, offers the apt metaphor of cabins circling a lake. We each bring our individual histories and cultural legacies to our sojourn in such a place, but at the center is the still and open water. We can look across the lake and see how others do things differently than we do. And we can choose. Herdman describes the tribal woman who walked several feet behind her husband, in deference to his authority and according to cultural tradition, until she saw that in other cultures a man and woman could walk side by side.

A genuine culture, says Sapir, is one in which nothing is spiritually meaningless. By this standard the Aztecs' culture was genuine, even though they were imperialists who continually waged war to capture victims for sacrifice. This practice was meaningful to them. They believed blood offerings completed a circle of reciprocal exchange—that life must be given in order to earn life. By Sapir's standard, the baiting and barking that passes for deliberation and decision making in Washington, D.C., is spurious because it is empty of meaning. It reflects only jockeying for position and power, not any of the ethical principles upon which our government was historically based. The Bill of Rights, the Civil Rights Act, and the Wilderness Act were genuine; the 2002 Authorization for Use of Military Force Against Iraq Resolution was spurious, based upon poor intelligence and false claims. "It is imperative," Sapir asserts, "if the individual is to preserve his value as a cultured being, that he compensate himself out of the non-economic, the non-utilitarian spheres—social, religious, scientific, aesthetic." The spurious culture is one in which people expect to be compensated financially for all wounds and losses.

Though my father was never a litigious man, he comes to mind here. He was charming and sociable, a man who loved people and entertained them as a radio and television personality. He took the measure of himself in the pleasure of human company and in his handiwork on gardens, stone walls, and brush piles. Yet at the end of his life, after his heart began to fail in his eighties, his days narrowed down to a card table where he sat filling out Publishers Clearinghouse Sweepstakes entries in hopes of an easy million. He still felt the world owed him something, and he did not know where else to look for compensation. By contrast my mother, who lies at the far edge of her life as I write this, suffers enough skeletal disintegration to make her days a torment, yet she has found nonutilitarian compensations that make the prospect of death something she meets with equanimity. She has spent her late nineties completing a sharply written memoir; at ninety-nine she is intrigued by the images that come in dreams, often columns of people dressed in ceremonial robes of shiny pastel colors, which we discuss during our visits as one of many marvels of the inner world, the imaginative process that seems to be guiding her on this most difficult of passages.

"Nature is God," she told me one day. "I don't need religion. I tried it when I was younger. There was nothing there for me. Just think about a seed—all that's packed into that little miracle and the beauty that will unfold."

I picture her examining the stamens and pollen hoards of wildflowers with a magnifying glass, as has been her habit, her eyes growing glassy in love.

"That's all the religion I need," she tells me with the conviction of one shaping final thoughts. She is making a private peace with the terms of her existence, though she too is at odds with her culture.

"The self," Edward Sapir writes, "must learn to reconcile its own strivings, its own imperious necessities, with the general spiritual life of the community."

I know this is necessary for us to do.

Culture is an emergent property of our biology. We are social creatures—the worst punishment we can inflict, short of the death penalty, is solitary confinement—and we are successful creatures, compared to many less fortunate species, because culture has made us speed-learners. The problem lies in the speed at which these two mechanisms—culture and biology—work. Culture is fast, biology slow.

Plastics offer a good example here. They are hydrocarbons, and we've made a lot of them. Plastic particles float in the ocean as vast islands of waste. No organism can metabolize this form of hydrocarbon; yet scientists suggest that, given enough time, microbes will evolve that can break the plastics back down into their chemical building blocks, and they will enter again into the molecular flow. This will be a long time coming, too long for the human species to sit back and wait. But in Earth's time, a biological solution will come for at least some of our cultural excess.

With our increasing awareness of the crisis of global climate change, the science thrust to the forefront of attention is, as J. Baird Callicott pegs it, "biogeochemistry, which reveals a Gaian Earth that is certainly systemic, holistic, internally related, and indeed self-organizing and self-regulating." This shift in awareness is forcing us to pose old questions about our own nature with increasing urgency: What kind of creature are we? What kind of creature might we become? What is given and what is learned? Must we operate on the principle of survival of the fittest or can we shift to survival of the most cooperative? What stories can biology give us that help us revise the story of who we can be?

3.

Nothing on this trip to San Diego last year was as I had expected. Why is it that my fantasies are so often stuck in the past? When I made the hotel reservations on the California coast, I pictured the place as it might have been a century ago. That small black dot on the edge of the map showed ocean blue on one side and forest green on the other, not the grid of freeways so entangled that places overlap and nothing has definition or limit. I pictured the classic stucco-and-mission-tile retreat, a place where the only shows in town are the sun-struck surf and forever blond sand, plus the bird-of-paradise flowers blooming with orange and blue plumage in December.

What I found was no small black dot, but a panic attack of intersecting velocities. Each town sold shirts wearing its name, and the shirts wore pictures of the classic stucco-and-mission-tile hotel. I found a flier advertising the Blessing of the Pets scheduled at St. Anne's Congregational Church, "all species welcome," with cut-and-paste computer art showing turtle, parrot, cat, iguana, and dog lining up for sanctification. I found sidewalks busy with pedigreed dogs boasting perfect hairdos as they walked with their owners in the glamour of California sunlight—canine celebrities such as the beauty queen Irish setter with her gleaming mahogany coat feathering off belly and legs like the chiffons of a veil dancer, and the attentive little corgi sitting upright in the driver's seat of a parked Range Rover as if he were ready to pull out into the flow.

I had come to California to observe the bonobos (*Pan paniscus*) at the San Diego Zoo. These seductive little apes, along with their cousins the chimpanzees (*Pan troglodytes*), are our closest primate relatives. We three species are descended from an alleged common ancestor, a woodland ape whose fossil remains have yet to be found, an animal dubbed *Pan prior* that lived about six million years ago. Traits carried by *Pan prior* come into the modern world—shape-shifted by time—in the bodies and minds of human beings, chimps, and bonobos. To see (more likely than not on tv) a chimp displaying and slapping his way into the social group, or a bonobo gossiping, hugging, and humping her way in, is like finding an old family photo album, the faces and behavior of strangers closely resembling living relatives.

Physical violence is common among chimpanzees. Primatologist Frans de Waal writes in *Our Inner Ape* that the chimpanzee "resolves sexual issues with power." The bonobo, however, almost never shows violence, but instead "resolves power issues with sex." Want a taste of your neighbor's food? If you're a bonobo, you don't steal it—you offer your rump, or hump your neighbor's thigh, or simply throw a reassuring arm around his shoulder. When groups meet in the forest they exchange constant chatter as if catching up on gossip. In captivity bonobos spend so much time grooming one another they may become temporarily bald. They laugh when tickled, they squeal in sexual pleasure, they have sex face-to-face—and in every other position imaginable—and they enjoy the solo delight of masturbation. Few bonobos are kept in captivity because they are rare and endangered: as far as I know, they are only in the zoos of San Diego; Milwaukee; Columbus, Ohio; and the Planckendael in Belgium. One can imagine the challenging staff meetings as zookeepers and handlers discuss the appropriate language for interpretive materials. What will we tell the children? That sex is fun and helps these creatures maintain a peaceful and egalitarian society? Perhaps this approach would play in Belgium, but with the abstinence-only regime ruling sex education in the United States, one imagines a somewhat stiffer word choice.

Although the fate of bonobos in the wild is grim, what might the story of their traits lend to our thinking about ourselves? True, we seem to have followed the pathway of the chimp with chest thumping, ground drumming, bullying, assault, and mutilation as very old habits in the primate line. That doesn't mean this is the only path we can follow through the genetic undergrowth. Our species is apparently the only one in evolutionary history to develop refined skills for language, self-awareness, and awe. Symbolic systems that embody these capacities may have developed on other worlds—worlds on which creatures have made it through the bottleneck of learning technological prowess without destroying themselves—but we are unlikely ever to know them. We're stuck with the wonder and challenge of us.

De Waal, studying social intelligence, has spent thousands of hours watching bonobos and other primates. He has been dissolving the distinctions between instinct and intelligence in our distant relations, finding that they, like us, are adept at taking cues from the social prompts surrounding them. Primatologists increasingly speak of "cultural" variability among primates, and this does not apply just to learned tool use and eating habits "such as chimpanzees cracking nuts with stones or Japanese monkeys washing potatoes in the ocean."

De Waal's most intriguing account is the experiment in which he put juveniles of two different macaque species together for five months: "The typically quarrelsome rhesus monkeys were housed with the far more tolerant and easygoing stumptail monkeys." The monkeys he expected to be aggressive clung fearfully to the ceiling of their cage, making a few threatening grunts. The stumptails weren't impressed, ignoring the challenge. De Waal writes, "For the rhesus monkeys, this must have been their first experience with dominant companions who felt no need to assert their position."

The rhesus monkeys learned the lesson "a thousand times over and also engaged in frequent reconciliations with their gentle oppressors." After five months the two species played, groomed, and slept together "in large mixed huddles." Most impressive was the fact that when the species were separated, the rhesus showed "three times more friendly reunions and grooming after fights than was typical of their kind." Peacemaking was shown to be a social skill rather than an instinct in these primates. Is there something in us then, older than our conflicts, that can bring us peace?

How it stands today:

Bonobos 10,000 (No reliable estimates are available, but according to the World Wildlife Fund, there may be as few as 5,000 and as many as 60,000; in any case, their numbers are declining rapidly.)

Chimpanzees 200,000 (The WWF estimates a midrange of 172,000 to 299,700; although they once inhabited twenty-five African countries they are now extinct in three or four of those and nearing extinction in many others.)

Human beings 6,700,000,000 (And ticking, according to the U.S. Census Bureau's World Population Clock.)

Pan prior 0

4.

The female beewolf, a European species of wasp, hunts honeybees. After paralyzing them with her stinger, she carries them to a chamber she has built in sandy soil. She paints the walls with white goo she has cultured in her antennae glands, a substance produced by *Streptomyces* bacteria that live in these glands, finding there a warm and moist habitat wherein they thrive. The beewolf lays her eggs in the nursery, where the goo prevents fungus from growing. When the young hatch, they eat the honeybees. They apply the antifungal goo to the threads of their larval cocoons, protecting themselves from the parasitic fungus that might find the warm and humid nest a welcome home. Solitary and commensal, attacking and harboring, learned and brainless, the beewolf is a study in contrasts. The beewolf *is* its relationships. It does not require thought, but it does require millions of attempts and failures at community among insects, fungi, and bacteria.

Is there sentience involved in this process? We cannot possibly know what the labor of the beewolf feels like. I can imagine the physical intensity of the hunt, the weighty work of flying the prey back to the nest, the fevered robotic housekeeping before the eggs are deposited. But I cannot imagine my way inside the beewolf's experience. Every creature, even a plant, has some degree of sentience, the capacity to read its surroundings and identify signs—"honeybee," "sandy soil," "strep goo"—that trigger what it has to do to survive. Even an amoeba can switch genes on and off in response to changes in its environment: slime your way over here for food; slime away from toxins. This is an elaborate enzyme activity based in chemistry and biomechanics. No consciousness. No decision making. No reflection. But I can't stop thinking how weird and marvelous it is that mere matter can conjure up such processes.

The simplest life form seems symphonic when I contemplate the unlikelihood of the complexity each creature embodies. If the amoeba is a symphony, then the human being ought to be a cacophony with its 10 trillion cells, 100 trillion synapses, and each neuron averaging 1,000 inputs. To really hear the noise of a single person, add to these human cells the 100 trillion live-in bacterial cells (10 trillion individual bacteria of 1,000 different species in the gut alone!), mostly friendly, collaborating in our bellies, hair follicles, tear ducts, and skin, each of them probably ecstatic in the fecundity of our bodies, each of them welcomed by our bodies (though our minds may find them disgusting) for the contribution they make to our well-being. Hookworms in the human gut, for example, appear to reduce the incidence of allergies. When I think about the complexity of my body, the biological community of my body, my idea of myself begins to wobble. I am essentially two creatures in one: the thinking, feeling, sensing creature I know as me, and the bundle of involuntary processes—electrical, chemical, cellular, rhythmic, and inter-organismic—that go smoothly along beneath my recognition.

This mess of collaboration feels to me like a musical masterwork, though I do not believe any master is involved in its creation. I believe that life is a self-generating, self-complicating, self-correcting, and often self-deceiving process. What are the boundaries between my animality and the microbes that collaborate with my existence, between my voluntary and involuntary actions? There *are* no boundaries—only conflicts and resolutions, an endless process of mutual capitulation that keeps a person coasting along as if she were one discrete organism. Why call it musical? I think of the jazz chords I've been learning for the past couple of years, the sevenths and ninths and thirteenths that add a crunchy dissonance to melody by rendering it more bittersweet and beautiful because they complicate the song, creating the tension that longs for resolution, the complexity that longs to know the simplicity of a major chord with nothing funky to challenge the ear. I find oddly comforting the fact that all my desires and sorrows and aspirations are nothing more than 10 trillion cells interacting with each other and with what they—in the guise of an "I"—encounter. My animal heart keeps the beat without anyone counting.

Biologist Ursula Goodenough writes:

> Life can be explained by its underlying chemistry, just as chemistry can be explained by its underlying physics. But the life that emerges from the underlying chemistry of biomolecules is something more than the collection of molecules. . . . Once these molecules came to reside inside cells, they began to interact with one another to generate new processes, like motility and metabolism and perception, processes that are unique to living creatures, processes that have no counterpart at simpler levels. These new, life-specific functions are referred to as emergent functions.

Emergent functions, Goodenough says, are "something more from nothing but." Emergence is nature's mode of creativity. Atoms made in stars possess emergent properties; planets and seas are emergent in star ash. Emergent properties abound in nonlife and life. When water turns to ice, it expresses the emergent property of buoyancy. Emergent outcomes in biology, such as motility or awareness, are called "traits." They mean that the organism has a purpose. Fly in tandem with the handful of starlings closest to your side, and the emergent property of flocking is expressed. Paralyze a honeybee and plant it with your young, and the emergent property of nurture is expressed. Write a book, symphony, sermon, or equation, and the emergent property of culture is expressed. Life insists upon purpose through a continual process of emergence.

The self does not feel like matter, but that is all it is. Brain-based awareness in human beings emerges to become language, language-based brains lead to an "I": "Something more from nothing but." Maybe it's just an accident that we have self-consciousness. Maybe the feeling we have that some people call "soul" or "spirit" is simply an intuition for the emergent, "the search for the adjacent possible," in Goodenough's words.

Where are we heading in this big symphony of emergent chords? With any luck, and given enough time to develop enough collaborative relationships, we are trying to get from "I" to "we" on a global scale: from self to culture, nation to planet, history to biology.

Stuart Kauffman's most recent book, *Reinventing the Sacred: A New View of Science, Reason, and Religion* (2008), explores the significance of the idea of emergence. Kauffman offers a comprehensive theory of emergence and self-organization that he says "breaks no laws of physics" and yet cannot be explained by them. "God," he writes, "is our chosen name for the ceaseless creativity of the natural universe, biosphere, and human cultures."

5.

On a 2008 visit to the Cape Cod National Seashore I heard a young naturalist speak about the condition of the piping plover, a species that nests on the beaches in May and June. I'd become interested after walking there and finding areas roped off for "bird use," where plovers had scratched out tiny basins in which to lay eggs perfectly camouflaged by the sand grains. The parent plovers worked the tidal wash for prey; a pair of turkey vultures scanned the shore for a shot at cleaning up. On Cape Cod this nesting behavior stirs up controversy akin to the trouble roused in the Pacific Northwest by the northern spotted owl. Select bumper stickers boast "Piping Plover: You Can't Eat Just One" and "Piping Plover Tastes Like Chicken."

Cape Cod fishermen pay dearly for off-road permits to drive their Jeep Cherokees and Dodge Rams along the beach and surf-cast for bluefish and stripped bass. Their beach roads coincide with the nesting ground, so the fight is on—birds versus men—though in truth the fight is between one group of citizens and another. I don't see why moderation cannot be a guide here. That appears to have been the course taken by the U.S. National Park Service with its gracefully worded sign, "Bird Use Area," that prods the visitor to consider the motto "Land of Many Uses" as incorporating the interests of species other than our own in our policies.

The lecturer, a young AmeriCorps volunteer doing noble service on behalf of ecological integrity, had been trained to foster audience participation. What I wanted were the facts, the latest research, details about what was at stake for the plovers and how they were doing against the human competition for beach space. But I bowed to the process, with one random half of the audience assigned to the "pro" plover position and the other half to the "con." I was among the pros. No contest in my mind, though I could not get anyone in my group to acknowledge that "all life forms are sacred" was an argument worth holding up to the policy fray. The cons argued "why interfere with the natural process of evolution?" and held forth that since we are the dominant predators and since we have paid good money for our off-road-vehicle permits, it is our right to unseat the nesters.

Our lecturer floated between the two groups. One of our pro colleagues, wanting to find something tangible to counter a fishing license, asked her, "Do they have a purpose? I mean, it would be so much easier, if the plovers had a purpose."

Like what, I wondered? Pharmaceutical production, or mosquito control, or the higher purpose that the religious see in life? I know some people see in the science story a life without direction or ethical dimension. Why are the plovers' actions what they are? What should their actions be? The facts of life do not answer, and the silence looms. I am not among such people. For me, as for my mother, the facts of life are enough of a miracle to induce religious feeling and a sense of purpose.

"No," our guide confided apologetically to the plover pros. "That's the hard part. They really don't."

I wanted to take her by the shoulders and shake her loose from this capitulation to the forces of doom, but I understood that my role here was not to be the hard-hat but to understand how very far my sympathies lay from the general drift of public sentiment.

"Of course they have a purpose," I shouted into my inner megaphone. "Their purpose is to be piping plovers and to make more piping plovers! That's a sacred calling. Life is its own purpose." I remained silent, considering how terribly well my own species had followed the dictates of this imperative to make more of itself. And I sat in the sadness that the argument was not at all a simple one for this random gathering of tourists assembled at the National Seashore on a May afternoon in the first decade of the twenty-first century. If everything is sacred, then how do we know which interests to protect? Our moral philosophy is not yet sufficient to give us clear guidelines.

6.

I cannot get out of my head the little Lucy-like hominids whose bones turned up early in the new millennium on the Indonesian island of Flores. Standing a meter tall and possessing a chimp-sized brain, *Homo flores* left remains that were similar to *Australopithecus afarensis*, the erect walking hominid that lived in Africa 3.5 million years ago. The team that discovered the skeleton in Ethiopia celebrated its find while sitting around a campfire listening to "Lucy in the Sky with Diamonds" on a portable tape player. That's how this relic of our deep ancestry got her nickname. But the new find suggested that a similar creature lived on an Indonesian island as recently as 18,000 years ago. An artist's rendering of *Homo flores* depicted him walking home for dinner with a golden retriever–sized rat slung over his shoulder. How many millennia had passed since his ancestors migrated away from Africa and Asia?

Three or four or five species of old world hominids were living at the same time. *Homo erectus* was the first colonizer, making it to Java around 1.8 million years ago, according to evolutionary biologist Francisco Ayala. Modern humans are not descendants of those early migrants. The diaspora of Homo sapiens from Africa to Asia came much later, starting about 100,000 years ago. The earlier migrants appear to have had a long and relatively peaceful tenure on Flores, and they represent a different branch on the tree of life than do our ancestors. They make us contemplate the possibility that, rather than a tree of hominid life, there was a thicket—many starts, many entanglements, many failures—and only we survived. (Unless, of course, you believe in Bigfoot.) Somehow this time-deep story grows more fascinating as our fear increases that our story may be growing short and that our species' resume may show us to have been terrible animals, heedless devourers of the beautiful Mother that gave all Earth's beings their lives.

But thinking backward in such a time frame also calls up the question of a symmetrically long future. What if we make it? What if learning how broadly destructive the human presence has been on the planet provides us with catalyzing self-awareness? What if this sensitivity to brokenness is tweaking our intelligence to make the next leap in our evolutionary history, a leap that turns the runaway force of human culture toward restraint and mutual aid, toward the acquisition of knowledge rather than junk, toward a ten-thousand-year project to restore Earth to a state as close to Eden as we could come, and to grow an outlying garden on Mars? Is that not an artful technological dream that we could love? I want this to be as possible as our doom. Ten thousand years from now, I want someone to say of us, "What amazing courage they had, and what spirit. How smart they were, how inventive—and how profoundly they must have loved Earth."

REFERENCES

Callicott, J. Baird. "What Can the Humanities Contribute to a New Consciousness in Harmony with Nature?" Paper presented at the "Toward a New Consciousness" conference at the Aspen Institute in Colorado, sponsored by the Yale School of Forestry and Environmental Studies, 2007.
Goodenough, Ursula. *The Sacred Depths of Nature*. New York: Oxford University Press, 1998.
Sapir, Edward. *Culture, Language, and Personality: Selected Essays*. Berkeley: University of California Press, 1985.
Thoreau, Henry David. *Cape Cod*. 1865. New York: Penguin, 1987.
Waal, Frans de. *Our Inner Ape*. New York: Riverhead, 2005.

REG SANER

Sweet Reason, Global Swarming

A half century ago Richard Wilbur's presciently ironic yet beautiful poem "Advice to a Prophet" addressed suggestions to a seer whose prophecies warn city after city of dire losses if environmental sanity is ignored. Already in the poem's opening stanza, however, he has grown "Mad-eyed from stating the obvious" and is begging his hearers "In God's name to have self-pity."

Alas, like Cassandra's foretelling Trojan doom, the prophet's wise counsel has apparently fallen on deaf ears, and the poem's tone implies that its own "advice" will fare no better. Feeling briefly clairvoyant myself, I now prophesy that except among a small percent of altruists environmental appeals to reason and enlightened self-interest will have little effect.

All the same, the persuasive good sense and exemplarily well-chosen detail of Scott Russell Sanders' argument in his essay "Simplicity and Sanity" carries me along like Plato's discoursing on the Good. After all, what should be more compelling than the health of our planet?

Sadly, however, the history of Homo sapiens reveals that voices as reasonable as that of "Simplicity and Sanity" evoke lasting admiration but little action. In all history, no great movement has ever been driven by intellect. Only emotion can do that, and at one juncture Sanders expresses just such a misgiving: "If we human beings were as wise as we claim to be . . . we would do voluntarily what nature will otherwise force on us." The sentence's first tiny word recalls Touchstone's shrewdly noting in *As You Like It*, "Much virtue in if."

On an April evening in 2007 I loitered in the foyer of my university's planetarium while awaiting the start of a show on what arguably has been the most brilliantly successful mission in NASA's history since humans landed on the lunar surface. Already the Cassini-Huygens vehicle had been orbiting Saturn for some weeks, and I was eager to see the results. Lest the post-show discussion go into overtime, my vatic powers suggested a quick visit to the men's room. There, an astronomer at the urinal next to mine excitedly told me of possible life on the

Saturnian moon Titan. "Wait'll you see the photos," he said. "They'll knock your socks off."

"Hm-m-m," I replied.

Despite my lifelong fascination with astronomy and cosmology, I deplore spending millions on quests for life elsewhere when—given our finite resources—Earth's plight should be our number one priority. Venus, Mars, Saturn, Jupiter, and Pluto won't wander off, but countless terrestrial species have done so, disappearing forever, and Homo sapiens may join them. How rational is it, therefore, to blow incredible wampum looking for life on other planets while blighting life on this one? We know our Earth so ill that we're totally ignorant as to what the daily loss of species after species may cost us.

Rather than enthuse over some hypothetical critter under the surface of Titan, I therefore thought, "Piss on it!" and did. Figuratively speaking.

Although I can't imagine any reader of Scott Russell Sanders' essay failing to admire both him and it, and thereby to some degree profiting from his example— or at least meaning to—I do wonder at his addressing us as reasonable creatures. Certainly I'm not such an oddity. Capable of reason, yes, but only spasmodically, with barely enough reason to suspect I'm not alone in that failing.

Recently I stood beside our local newspaper's *fashionista* as she stared into a shop window at a pair of sandals all aglitter with silver-and-turquoise insets. "Okay," I said, "if they're really 'to die for' why don't you just buy them?"

"Hah!" she huffed. "Are you balmy? They don't pay me that kind of money."

Some ten minutes later she walked out of the store with the sandals in a nifty Anthropologie shopping bag, and her Visa card in further weakened condition.

In 2008, for the second year in a row, *Forbes* magazine declared Boulder, Colorado, "the smartest city in the USA." Of its adults twenty-five or older, some ninety-three percent graduated from high school, fifty-three percent have a college degree, and one in twenty-five has a PhD. Big deal. We Boulderites were already immensely pleased with ourselves, so the announcement made little stir. The article also noted that our "overwhelmingly young adult population" takes advantage of Boulder's "many outdoor recreational activities." That explains our high percentage of joggers, fitness snobs, rock climbers, Himalayan adventurers, elite runners, elite cyclists, bike-to-work lawyers, and cars with kayaks atop—all giving rise to an amusing article in the *New York Times Magazine*, "The Town That Can't Sit Still." Right on. And then there's our "greener-than-thou" hauteur.

Too, we know how infallibly the forested mountainsides of our town's setting, with their soaring upthrust of great sandstone forms, excite the envy of visitors. Our pride extends as well to miles of beautiful trails winding among the ponderosa pines and Douglas firs of our Mountain Park, the nation's only such park within city limits. In fact, we're so proud of it all you'd think the rocks, trees, and summits had been our idea. There's even talk of putting a city official in charge of Smug Control.

One day, while waiting for a bus on our erstwhile mining town's busiest street, I tried counting SUVs. Traffic was flowing too fast along its four-lane thoroughfare for an accurate count, so I did it per cluster of ten or so vehicles at a go; even ignoring the scads of pickups, I finally guesstimated passenger traffic to be 60 percent gas guzzlers.

My interest was less statistical than botanical. The beauty of those steep, pine-forested slopes just west of where I was standing is threatened with potential blight by pine beetles. Until recent years, the beetles have been kept in check by winterkill. As our winters have warmed, however, more beetles have successfully survived them and thus have bred in greater numbers. Compounding the problem, hotter and drier summers have increased the count of stressed trees, lowering their resistance to infestation. So far, the beetles have specialized in lodgepole pines growing well west of Boulder and out of our sight. There, they've devastated lodgepole by the thousands of acres. Biologists now warn us that the combination of hotter summers, warmer winters, and the insects' own population pressure could impel them to feast on other species as well. That would uglify our mountain backdrop like an Old Testament plague. On great conifer swaths the green needles will turn rusty, then drop away, leaving a skeletal forest of the standing dead.

To compound the irony of teeming SUVs on the streets of "the smartest city," there's the fact that Boulder is home to the National Center for Atmospheric Research. Like Richard Wilbur's mad-eyed prophet, the center's world-class scientists began telling us *decades* ago about the possibility of global warming.

A long bowshot away from that busy street, astronomers and astrophysicists at my university eagerly search for their Grail: an extra-solar planet with liquid water. We've even a new degree program in astrobiology, so we're ready in case one is found. Thus far, however, aside from a couple of rocky possibles too torridly close to their natal star, no Earth-like, extra-solar planets have been detected, only gas giants similar to our Jupiter and Saturn. Meanwhile, one astronomer on the faculty awaits exciting data that should result when the space vehicle he and his collaborators designed at last begins orbiting Pluto. Even as I write this in the summer of 2008, yet another vehicle with ties to Boulder has successfully landed on Mars and begun digging for water ice. If found, it would imply that—once upon a time—life might have existed there. Meanwhile, right here on Earth species are going extinct at an alarming rate.

Despite knowing that each and every human is a bipedal paradox, can you imagine anything more paradoxical?

As Scott Sanders is the first to admit, his plea for sweet reason in our way of living has more precursors than Thoreau. We talk of "firsts," but of course no one is ever the first, so the fact that Thoreau's imperative "simplify!" is as old as philosophy doesn't make it less wise. Thoreau's cabin at Walden Pond and Diogenes' choice of a large tub for his shelter mark them as fellow contrarians, a kinship further proven by Diogenes' radical simplicity regarding true necessities, as well as by what a modern scholar calls "his fanatical espousal of the natural life." In *Walden's* first chapter, "Economy," Thoreau's debt to classical antiquity's philosophizing on the *summum bonum* is clear, and Sanders continues that tradition, though with a hugely crucial difference: neither the ancients nor Thoreau ever dreamed human activity could make Earth unlivable. Nonetheless, both "Economy" and "Simplicity and Sanity" are examples of moral philosophy's long speculation on how to live, what to do.

Natural or not, Diogenes' fanaticism wasn't nearly so cordial as the healthy sanity of Democritus. Born in 460 BC, almost two generations earlier than Diogenes, Democritus lived to be more than a hundred years old, and might therefore be said to have validated his view of happiness as the fruit and flower of a moral life. If we moderns know him at all, it's only as the ancient Greek who thought about atoms—but nearly every moral philosopher after Democritus followed his lead in considering happiness, the *summum bonum*, to be a consequence of virtue, and virtue a consequence of knowledge.

Democritus' view of evil is simplistic only in being so reasonable: "The cause of sin is ignorance of what is better." That's as hard to refute logically as is Socrates' equally rational argument that evil represents a failure of knowledge. You could even say the two epitomize a rationalist idea of moral wisdom.

On the other hand, a Pontius Pilate sort of cynic might counter, "And what is wisdom?"

Socrates would have a ready answer, which can be paraphrased thus: wisdom is knowing how best to use what we possess, whether material things or immaterial qualities. This too would be irrefutable if not for the fact that we so often know the better, yet choose the worse. In fact, isn't that half our history?

By Socrates' lights, blowing megabucks on frozen sterilities of the solar system while Earth's species dwindle by the minute amounts to, paradoxically, a failure of knowledge in the quest for knowledge. Agreed, science is only a collateral benefit of NASA's enterprises, whose true raison d'être lies in their military potential, but that doesn't alter the wisdom of putting our resources to their best use. As astronomers know well, and as the bumper sticker warns, "A Good Planet Is Hard to Find."

By way of urging their readers to make knowledgeable choices instead of short-sighted ones, Thoreau and Sanders both emphasize "the cost of a thing," which I've always called "learning to read price tags." Regardless of wording, the concept is ancient, perhaps most famously associated with Epicurus' idea of how to live, what to do. Thoreau's "Economy" and Sanders' "Simplicity and Sanity" are Epicurean in the philosophic sense, though certainly not the pejorative, popular one that takes lowercase "epicurean" to mean limitless swilling, coke snorting, screwing, and gourmandizing.

It's true Epicurus taught that happiness comes of minimizing pain and maximizing pleasure. Yet he also taught that doing so requires forethought amounting to wisdom, since short-term pleasures often prove painful in the long run—with addiction, venereal disease, obesity, and poverty being instances. For Epicurus "pleasure" meant pleasures of the mind. Thoreau, by favoring mindfulness over brain-numbing labor and routine drudgery, thereby gave his life "more margin," and implicitly agreed. So does Sanders in suggesting that hours spent needlessly acquiring more stuff, and on the lowbrow vacuity of tv (whose ads I call obedience training), would be better invested in learning a new language or skill.

Even the tale of the ant and the grasshopper is Epicurean. The fact that it's both old as the hills and relevant as sunrise tells us a good deal about reason's role in human nature. After all, the cumulative effect of sagacity from Democritus, Socrates, Plato, Aristotle, and Epicurus, on through Emerson, Thoreau, Scott Sanders, and other Western moralists—not to mention those of Asia and the Middle East—has been to leave Homo sapiens none the wiser. When Bernard Shaw first read Plato and discovered that—despite all the centuries between—the European mind hadn't progressed one whit, his faith in progress was staggered to the verge of a breakdown. The inescapable question is, "Why so slow to learn?"

First and foremost, we're talking about animals with claws on forefeet and hind feet, a spine ending in a tailbone, plus tufts of fur on top and in private places. Our evolutionary past encoded us to act on self-interest mainly in terms of immediate threats to bodily survival. The rational appeal of farsightedness remains by comparison decidedly tenuous, as is evident in a "smartest city" teeming with SUVs.

Every now and then, however, collective sanity can override our encoded myopia, as is evident in Boulder's sensitivity to environmental hot topics. Civic wisdom has created and funded a superb open space program that continues to be the envy of other cities degraded by sprawl, and our recycling facilities are among the best in the country.

So, yes, sanity can prevail, but it needs more than a little help. Compared with towns in the nation's Rust Belt, Boulder is awash with money. The town has banks enough to be a little Zürich. It can afford long views, whereas the dirt-poor peasants of Brazil still actively clear-cutting our planet's greatest rain forest cannot.

Expecting environmental sanity to coexist with social injustice is the illogical equivalent of what physicists studying light call an interference pattern. Similarly, a nation trying to work toward a low carbon footprint while doing nothing to check the growth of its population amounts to an interference pattern even more farcically myopic.

In the Midwest I came from, every other small town's city limits were marked with a sign saying something like, "Atwood / pop. 2500 / Watch Us Grow." Since thirteen colonies became the United States, two unexamined assumptions have been axiomatic among us. The first is that growth is not just good but our glorious destiny; the second is that North America's resources are limitless. Thus, when politicians inflate their lungs for the indispensable obbligato on "what made this country great" they never name the true cause: dumb luck, which gave "the greatest nation on Earth" a pristine continent to exploit, no matter how wastefully.

At our house I'm the recycle guy, from newsprint to cartons to plastic milk jugs, shopping bags, aluminum cans, and so forth. I'm also a little mad-eyed from invoking "waste not, want not," turning off unneeded lights and idling motors, buying secondhand where feasible, refusing to use chemical weedkillers, sticking to a push mower powered by granola, and rummaging in Dumpsters for reusable lumber. The latest addition to my basement is a combination worktable/tool cabinet built, except for its melamine top, from salvage. Last year our household's two vehicles logged a combined total of around 6,500 miles, which is far below the national average.

All that is as nothing compared to Sanders' example, but infinitely less than nothing compared to Earth's single most important issue: population, population, population.

When my wife Anne and I moved to Colorado in 1962, our new town held some 56,000 souls, a number now doubled. The entire state came to well under two million, but since our arrival has added another three million, and it shows. As if determined to validate the Malthusian prophecy that our species will inevitably breed beyond the ability to feed itself, world population has grown more in the past half century than in our species' entire history. Already, Paul Roberts'

The End of Food (2008) describes a global food system nearing collapse. In his and all such projections, accuracy depends on the underlying assumptions, which in turn depend on the impossible: reading the future. Nonetheless, the Population Division of the United Nations posts figures that suggest a doubling of world population every fifty years. Their analysis estimates that in 1950 our global numbers were considerably more than 2.5 billion and by 2000 were roughly 6.1 billion, with a projected 9.2 billion by 2050.

I'll continue to recycle, despite knowing we Earthlings can do so until "waste" is an archaic concept yet will still be overwhelmed by what I call global swarming. Some universities now have, literally, professors of population, so it almost passes belief that there is disagreement on what "exponential" means in relation to birthrates, much less on how many births is too many, even though—except in China—there is next to no agreement on what to do about it. Arithmetically, any continuous growth, however slight and variable the percent, must sooner or later double population.

Not to pussyfoot, I therefore declare that any religion whose creed is to breed qualifies, in the etymological sense of the word, as perfectly insane. So does "For the Lord will provide." And if He doesn't, who are we to question His mysterious ways? Besides, in the world after this one, He'll make it up to every innocent sufferer. After all, the United States is, nominally at least, made up of more than 90 percent believers, with family Bibles full of Old Testament begats inciting any amount of begetting. Dare any of our politicians speak against the Lord's fiat?

In the spring of 1990, while enjoying the fragrant May evening amid the formal gardens and tall cypresses of a villa on Italy's Lake Como, I fell to musing about the ancient Roman known as Pliny the Younger, who had built a summer home on that very promontory. What would he think, I wondered, if he could stand at my elbow and see the wide, white wake of the lake's hydrofoil whizzing past diesel-powered boats? Or watch a tourist-bearing pontoon plane land on the water, to say nothing of lakeside automobiles? Because I'd been chatting with a distinguished demographer, I asked her to prophesy what Lake Como with its surrounding mountain slopes and shoreline of luxury villas would look like in the year 2500. After all, her discipline dwelt on the temporal—the past, the present, and the future.

She gazed round that idyllic setting as if trying to see her way to an answer. Across the lake many lights began to wink on, their reflections rippling over the water. "In five hundred years?" she asked, then shook her head. "There's just no telling, even for the next hundred."

I first heard of Robert Malthus in the 1950s during a grad school seminar on English literature of the nineteenth century. In 1798 Malthus had published *An Es-*

say on the Principle of Population as It Affects the Future Improvement of Society, with Remarks on the Speculations of Mr. Godwin, M. Condorcet, and Other Writers. To Malthus, the "speculations" alluded to in his title carried an Enlightenment bias forecasting a rosy future, which he thought utopian. Thus Malthus' book said in effect, "No way!" He had been particularly struck by "unfettered growth" in the colonies that became the United States of America. There, the population was doubling every twenty-five years! He predicted if that continued, either there or anywhere else, such a people must inevitably outgrow their food supply.

I clearly remember our teacher's condescending tone as he encapsulated Malthus' argument for us students sitting around the seminar table. Influenced by Euro-American prosperity of the mid-fifties, he presented the man as a British eccentric relevant solely to ills of the Industrial Revolution and the London poor. Yet no sooner had I grasped Malthus' arithmetical logic on what's loosely termed exponential growth than I thought, "But he's right."

Contemporary gainsayers of the Malthusian view take what has been called the cornucopian stance: the more the better. I've even heard a lecturer on the subject of Earth's carrying capacity contend that doubling global population won't diminish prosperity but increase it. "Through what means?" I wondered. His answer was technology. Techie solutions would keep pace with growing birthrates and, despite lowering mortality, bail us out. I thought, "How very American."

Me, I'm Malthusian enough to predict the bleak opposite. I'm also Coloradan enough not to confuse material goods with quality of life. Full disclosure, however, obliges me to admit I've four day packs, five backpacks, and three fanny packs—but I must save an inventory of skis and snowshoes for a more convenient occasion. Already I've said too much.

My English expatriate friend Professor David Wrobel, a London native, seriously contends that the unimprovable panoramas of our American West can and should hold oodles more people. "But David," I tell him, "that's so beyond sick! Do promise me you'll get help." What's more, I remind him that Aldous Huxley, a fellow Brit, hadn't meant it only facetiously when he wrote, "The most wonderful thing about America is that, even in these middle years of the twentieth century, there are so few Americans."

Nearing the end of that century and foreseeing sprawl, I wrote a book of nature essays on the Colorado I had come to be gaga about, calling its in-progress version *Colorado Adios.* However, lest such a title mislead people to suppose the collection merely regional in scope, I renamed it *The Four-Cornered Falcon,* thereby alluding to its essay on survival of the peregrine; *Falco peregrinus* is found on every continent but Antarctica, and in 1990 it was still globally endangered. Apropos of our erstwhile wide-open West, the book also carried an epigraph from

Gertrude Stein: "In the United States there are more places where nobody is than where somebody is. That is what makes America what it is."

Were I into tattoos, I might wear those words on my chest.

Though believers may claim they've a sacred mandate to spawn, I propose a two-child limit on all marriages. After that, the male partner must have his tubes tied, or whatever it is the surgeons do down there where all the trouble starts. When it comes to being wise for others, reason is my middle name.

If we were wise we'd already have acted energetically on E. O. Wilson's dismay at the accelerating rate of extinctions. His little book *Biophilia*, written a quarter century ago, called for urgent measures in protecting the planet's diminishing species. Yet he ruefully conceded that "values are time-dependent." Wanting good things for ourselves and families, we also want them "for distant generations . . . but not at any great personal cost." And he predicted our present complacency: "The forests may all be cut, radiation slowly rise . . . but if the effects are unlikely to become decisive for a few generations, very few people will be stirred to revolt." Our evolutionary past simply didn't prepare us "to respond emotionally to far-off events and hence place a high premium on posterity."

Earth is now in a far more parlous state, yet for all the talk about it, our national response continues in slo-mo. Sanders quotes Thoreau on one of the causes: "most men . . . do not care for Nature and would sell their share in all her beauty . . . for a stated sum—many for a glass of rum." I honor Thoreau but doubt that any except alcoholics would trade all nature for rum. Even so, I *don't* doubt that tens of millions in the United States and countless other millions elsewhere will pay any amount of lip service to environmental sanity while privately thinking, "It'll probably last out my time. After that, who cares."

On my university's campus I often witness a different sort of swerving from rational action. During warm weather young women and men don swimsuits to lounge on the grass, inviting tissue damage from UV rays as they work on their tans. There, too, or for that matter anywhere else in "the smartest city," I also see cigarette smokers. Logically, we might suppose people who abuse their own bodies won't worry much about the world's body, but logic doesn't get us very far in understanding human behavior. Among the sun worshipers and smokers surely there are recyclers and contributors to environmental causes.

A likelier inference is that those risking skin cancer and lung cancer, to name but a pair of health hazards, let irrational optimism trump reason. This may at least partly explain the almost languid national reaction when it comes to the health of our planet: Americans are optimistic to a fault. Worse yet, our favorite food isn't apple pie—it's baloney, a preference exemplified by our incessantly referring to ourselves as "the greatest nation on Earth" and our cock-a-doodle-dooing about how "in this country there's no limit." (Even if not the greatest nation, we are far and away the most boastful.) Feel-good journalism and TV interviews have for decades so stuffed the public with vainglorious boosterism that we shouldn't be surprised if large segments of our population assume good old Yankee know-how will find a technological fix for any problem, global swarming included.

Some fundamentalist Christians declare that great natural disasters such as Hurricane Katrina, the lethal 2008 earthquake in Myanmar, and the recent horrendous cyclone in China (also 2008) are judgments of God. The evangelist Jerry Falwell has preached dismissively on environmentalism, claiming, "There's no need for the Church of Jesus Christ to be wasting its time gullibly falling for all of this global warming hocus-pocus." In Falwell's eyes and the eyes of his co-religionists, Earth is a mere steppingstone to heaven. Another evangelical leader, citing scripture, assures us the Almighty has promised to preserve Earth till Jesus comes again.

I agree that faith in a benign deity and a better world than this one does indeed afford solace to believers. Whether such faith, and organized religion generally, have done more harm than good remains an open question. Certainly the Old Testament fiat giving Adam dominion over the Earth has led to episodes of environmental arrogance, just as the biblical injunction to multiply has created shantytowns of appalling squalor and untold misery for millions of children. Only in the past decade or so have some United States churches at last begun adding a faint tinge of green to their moral spectrum.

Just where deities other than Yahweh stand on these issues I don't know, but according to me, Earth already holds a billion or more too many of us. I therefore offer this modest proposal: concern for our planet should carry the imperative force of a moral absolute. Making a case for such concern isn't necessary. To all reasonable Earthlings the cogency is self-evident—which leaves me only 6.5 billion votes short.

I shall respond to that landslide plebiscite with further foreseeing. We won't need an asteroid to do the job. Out-of-control global swarming by everyone's favorite weed species, Homo sapiens, will work its own ruin. Or will unless—as Malthus predicted—famine, war, and pestilence provide the bailout. Private virtue won't suffice.

Oh, yes, celebs and public pressure can make environmental sanity de rigueur. Give us celebs by all means, Hollywood hunks and bikini-clad hotties, though even they won't be enough. The sanity I'm proposing must become law, complete with jail sentences. Government simply must get real.

Otherwise, our disappearance will have been the grotesquely comic result of sheer timidity—our tippy-toe, temporizing reluctance to meet what ancient Greeks called *anankê*, "hard necessity," with a commensurately hardball decree: "Thou shalt not, under pain of law, have more babies than two."

How very un-American. And, oh, how hopelessly reasonable.

Against Simplicity

A Few Words for Complexity, Sloppiness, and Joy

"Let us settle ourselves, and work and wedge our feet downward through the mud and slush of opinion, and prejudice, and tradition, and delusion and appearance, that alluvion which covers the globe," writes Henry David Thoreau, building up steam as he begins one of the best, and certainly one of the longest, sentences in all of *Walden*. The same sentence ends, a good half page later, with Henry wishing for a very un-Thoreauvian-sounding gizmo—a device with a name straight out of a Hasbro commercial—called a "Realometer." As it turns out, the Realometer operates on the same basic principle as Hemingway's "bullshit detector," although unlike Hemingway's, Thoreau's device vibrates not at taurine excrement or at "shams and appearances," but when it encounters the hard rock of reality. Each of us comes equipped with a Realometer, of course, which helps us get to a place "which we can call *reality*, and say, This is, and no mistake," but to reach this reality we must wedge downward through the mush of "church and state, through poetry and philosophy and religion."

That's a pretty good list of the things that get in the way as we try to determine, Realometer in hand, what is true. But the list isn't complete, and one additional element that makes up the mud and slush I find myself working through is just the sort of romantic pastoralism that Thoreau unwittingly helped shovel into the world.

What was original in Thoreau has become less so in his literary descendants, and the nature-writing genre, which was young and flush when he created it, now suffers from hardened arteries. But even *Walden*, that beautiful, thorny book, holds its share of hokum. For instance, my own custom-made Realometer won't respond when I place it near Thoreau's notion of simplicity, an austere life pared down to the theoretical basics. The device's inactivity confirms something I have long believed: that there is no simple life, and that to wish for a simple life is to wish for unicorns or faeries.

This is not to say I wouldn't like to live, and benefit from, a *simpler* life. It's just that most of us dream of a simple life in the way that a busy person day-dreams of a cabin by a lake while staring out the office window during a crowded workday in the city. For the most part there is nothing pernicious about these daydreams, unless we take them too seriously. Then they might have the same effect as overactive fantasizing about another lover while in a marriage: making us sell short what we really have.

What most of us really have is complexity, not simplicity. What most of us have is the sloppy life, our minds hungry for more, never quite able to reduce the swirling mess of existence into solid Thoreauvian principles. In contrast to Thoreau's rock of reality, consider this A. R. Ammons line: "Firm ground is not available ground." At first this might seem a fairly pessimistic statement, but I believe that the path to mental health, and possibly even to some joy, lies in accepting a messy life rather than pining for something most of us will never actually have.

Thoreau argued, in what he called his "extra-vagant" manner, that it is better to be happy with less than to want more. This is a fine assertion, one that many spiritual thinkers have echoed, but how realistic is it for me and my fellow mass of men? To me the notion that we can weed out the desire for *more* is not a complex or accurate take on what it means to be a human being. I believe the best bet for us, and for our planet, is not a running away *from* but a deeper acceptance *of* the fact that we are driven creatures, always hungry and striving for more. I believe our personal and planetary health hinges on nudging that encoded desire for more in relatively healthy and creative directions, not in proceeding under the false notion that such desire can simply be extracted. Finally, I believe that our best role model for the trying times ahead may be someone other than an adolescent-minded, steel-willed loner named Henry.

Let me begin by defending my last point, before my fellow nature writers descend on me and beat me to death with their branches and rocks. Don't get me wrong: I know Henry Thoreau pretty well. Like so many others of my ilk, I have been deeply influenced by him: everything from my decision to become a writer to my love of nature to my choice to go jobless for long stretches of my life (so I could bring all my energy and concentration to bear on my writing) has sprung at least in part from an early reading of *Walden*. (A couple of summers back my wife and I visited Walden Pond with our then two-year-old daughter, and my wife, pointing at the cabin's foundation, said, "There's the house of the man who ruined Daddy's life.") But although the man has had a more profound effect on my life than almost any other writer, I have begun to note some temperamental differences between us, and I have begun to see that this prickly fellow might not always be the best of models. To put it simply, most biographers of Thoreau agree he was a born stoic, and having one meal of acorns each day was not so much a sacrifice as an expression of that natural stoicism. *Simplify, simplify* in Henry's hands might have some of the prescriptive qualities that Scott Russell Sanders attributes to it, but it also has the wild, braying quality of "This is who I am!"

As I grew older, I began to understand: this is who I'm not. "Excess is preferable to deficiency," said Samuel Johnson. *Amen.* Some of us like to eat and drink a lot, and to work on a dozen or so projects on various back and front burners. And I should add that some of us find that the most vital part of our lives, despite our love of the natural world and the private universe of our writing lives, is our sloppy and complex interaction with other human beings. Even when I first read Thoreau as an adolescent I understood that he and I parted ways here. "I have never wasted a walk on another," he crowed. I liked that line—it was funny in its extremity—but at the time I read it I was already wasting a lot of walks on girlfriends. As an advocate of nature and wildness, Thoreau was terrific. As an exemplar of human interaction, slightly less so.

Yes, his ideals about simplicity have helped give me focus and direction in my work. But what complicates and musses up those pristine ideals is the fact that I, like most of us, live in relation to a web of friends, family, and colleagues, people who are often, quite inconveniently, getting married or getting sick or in some other way needing help or companionship. One of the reasons that Thoreau was able to play by his own stringent rules, besides being temperamentally suited to do so, was that he was an antisocial crank and, furthermore, a *single* antisocial crank. Pardon me if I don't take as my role model a teetotaling, spartan, socially awkward virgin.

To borrow one of Thoreau's own metaphors, I tried his clothes on for a while and found they didn't fit. As I grew into myself I understood I had a taste for complexity and messiness and humor, not for simplicity and cleanliness and righteousness. I'll take a life of complexity any day of the week, a life of burgeoning multiple interests and comedy and tragedy and contradiction. Give me a few days in the woods alone and my head will implode. But give me a month there with a few engrossing projects, and with my wife (who will have a project or two of her own, of course) and my daughter (many projects, most of them involving Play-Doh), and I'll give you the closest I get to sylvan paradise. I have read all the biographies of Thoreau and have learned plenty, but when it comes to lives, I prefer the crowded hours of tough-minded realists like Samuel Johnson or Wallace Stegner or—to veer away from the literary—artistic politicians like Teddy Roosevelt or Winston Churchill.

"A change is as good as a rest," said Churchill, and the biographical pages prove it as we read about him leading his un-simple life, shifting from building a wall to writing a book to painting a watercolor to leading England through the war. Why did he leap from thing to thing? In large part because his mind could not keep still, a condition that I don't think was unique to that great man. Although it's true I may never be elected prime minister, I take some inspiration from this vital variety, born of an innate restlessness, as I try to balance things in my smaller worlds of writing, teaching, tree-hugging, and caring for my family.

I have also learned this: doing a lot turns out to be *fun*, particularly if you do it with gusto. For some of us, jumping from one thing to another is not such a bad way to be, as long as you give the thing jumped to your full attention. *Variety! Variety! Variety!* I crow along with my friend Winston.

Let me now address my conception of the human desire for more, which obviously clashes with the Thoreauvian philosophy of doing with less. My life's plot has not had the admirable steadiness and sense of Scott Sanders' description of his own history. Like many Homo sapiens, I have been plagued by anxiety, debt, poverty, depression, and illness, and buffeted about not just by circumstances but by my own appetites. Not the least of these appetites has been ambition, which for the purposes of this essay I will define as "wanting to be somewhere other than where you are." Few human beings, even the enlightened ones, are in the position to plot rationally the course of their lives in the manner that Thoreau claimed to have done, and most of us can at best wrestle with our circumstances, both external and internal. What would Sanders or Thoreau make of this line by another American artist, Bruce Springsteen: "Poor man wanna be rich, rich man wanna be king, and king won't stop 'til he got everything." I imagine they might argue that the desire for more is the root of the whole problem, and that, tempered by wisdom and daily readings of *Walden*, human beings could begin to make do with less, weeding out that nasty desire to be king. But I would argue back that for most of us this is a constitutional impossibility, that the urge for more is encoded in human DNA and can never be simply rooted out. The desire for more is a hunger that drives us onward and outward, a hunger that few of us can stifle.

More, however, can be redefined. It can also be inspired, turned toward art and toward ideals that transform *more* into *better*. Sanders has some fun with the word "consumer," but I would argue that "consumer" is not a bad or inaccurate description of most human minds in action. As a college student, still in the thrall of Thoreau, I had the good fortune to take a class with Walter Jackson Bate, who had just completed his monumental biography of Samuel Johnson. Bate, channeling Johnson, was a champion of common sense, which for me served as a corrective to Thoreau. Johnson's conception of the human mind was as a kind of living being—always hungry, always swallowing, always being colored by what it eats. This may seem a pessimistic view of human nature until we ask ourselves this: if we are what we eat, then who is to say we aren't in charge, to some extent, of what we feed ourselves? I believe that through our reading, our thinking, and most of all through the discipline and effort of repeated action we can begin to nudge ourselves in new and moral directions. But "effort" and "nudge" are the operative words here. Held up to the standard of purity that the model of Scott Sanders and Thoreau present, most of us would throw up our hands and quit. Change is often incremental, gradual, and grudging, and we are fighting a war in which altering one small habit constitutes a great victory.

Again, my language has turned martial, and there's a reason for that. I dropped Teddy Roosevelt's name above, and not just because he was Churchill's temperamental twin in the hyperactive pursuit of numerous activities in a strenuous, or *un-simple* life. I dropped it because this combative, complicated, simple but un-simple man was perhaps the single most effective conservationist in our country's history.

This is important, I think. Individualism and conservationism are always treated as if they are at odds, and to a certain extent they are, but we can turn our individualism toward the fight to conserve. Maybe it's too much to ask for some of us to change our basically excessive, competitive characters and turn toward the simple, ascetic life, but maybe we can turn our flawed, aggressive nature toward fighting good fights. After all, the man who preserved more land in this country than did any other was also an excess-loving, bloodthirsty, big-game-hunting, verbose, multi-tasking eccentric. And of course he was, like most of us, a hypocrite.

"We need more hypocrites!"

I recently heard those words come out of the mouth of Dan Driscoll, the man most responsible for the greening of the Charles River in Boston through the reclaiming of industrial land and the reintroduction of native plantings. Dan and I had just paddled the length of the Charles together, and what he meant when he spit out that sentence, he went on to explain, was that too many people judge their own lives and, deeming themselves environmentally unworthy and therefore hypocritical, decide that it would be wrong for them to take strong environmental stands. "But we need more hypocrites who fight for the environment," he continued. "We are *all* hypocrites anyway."

The point is that if we hold everyone up to a kind of environmental purity test, then the green movement will be made up not of millions, but of tens. I don't mind if Al Gore and Bill McKibben accrue thousands of frequent flier miles as they jet about to warn people of the dangers of overconsumption. They don't need to prove anything to me through some elaborate calculus with carbon footprints; they more than make up for all that air time by inspiring, by arguing, by cajoling—by describing for us, redefining for us, and pitching to us the idea of a new and better kind of human *more* that involves a whole lot of *less*. While they are busy doing this, I would not dare ask them to live up to Thoreauvian standards of purity because like most of us they have lives that are messy and complicated.

As I speak for complexity, for sloppiness, for necessary hypocrisy, I am perhaps overstating in my desire to make an emphatic claim, but I do so to counterbalance the words of the usual advocates of the simple life: the nature writer, the minister, the pot-smoking teenager, the daydreaming city dweller. "I'd like to dine with the poor, and speak with the simple," said David Garrick, the famous actor and friend of Samuel Johnson. Johnson replied briskly: "I'd rather eat with the rich and converse with the wise." Exactly! And I'd rather live the complicated life and do too much, as long as I do so guided by moral purpose. With apologies to Thoreau, I think the lot of adults, at least adults in the thick of their lives, is to do too much rather than too little. Recently my wife and I spent a week on vacation with a couple who have three children under the age of eight, and I imagine they dream often of the simple life, a life they won't be living for a long, long time. Dream on, I wanted to say, as long as it helps ease some of the burdens of your current frantic but often joyful reality. *What joy?* you ask from your cabin in the woods. The joy of clutter, the joy of creation, the joy of work, the joy of children. It's okay to dream of the simple life, I wanted to tell my friends—just don't live it.

I said that I have perhaps been overly emphatic, and I mean this. The fact is that I agree with Scott Sanders in more ways than I have let on, and although our means are different, our ends are similar. Not long ago I spent six years on Cape Cod, a kind of early retirement beginning when I was thirty-five, and during that time I reduced and simplified my life to writing and walking the beach—the closest I will ever come to living a Thoreauvian life, I suspect. After that period, I left Cape Cod and threw myself into a more complicated life, and perhaps my current defense of complexity reflects on my present circumstances. I should add that one of the main reasons I left my simpler life was to become a teacher, and in doing so I had a great model: Scott Russell Sanders.

Some years earlier I had had the good fortune of being his teaching apprentice at a writing conference, and watching him work fired my imagination. He was extremely generous—which of course meant he was also extremely busy. The Scott Sanders I was lucky enough to meet, the Scott Sanders I got to know when I was a young writer, might have spent hours insulating the attic and quoting Thoreau, but he spent more hours writing books, helping students, raising his kids, fighting local and national fights, involving himself with his university (and, I suspect, his church), going to dull meetings for the common good, and throwing himself into his life in a hundred other complicated ways. He was more

Stegner than Thoreau, and though he will not like to hear this, when we met I found him, despite his calm demeanor, a little *harried*. But it was a good sort of harried, a kind of harried that I now wear with pride as I proceed with my life of doing too much. *Complexity! Complexity! Complexity!*

I am thankful that even though Scott Sanders likes talking about a simple life, he didn't choose to live one. For my part, I will continue to argue that some of the value of his life has been in precisely the way he is *unlike* Thoreau. I bet that there were plenty of times when Sanders, trying to balance his writing with his devotion to his family, teaching others to write, and fighting for the environment, dreamed of a simpler life—but, luckily for the world, that was a dream he didn't follow. I will even go a step further and say that Scott Russell Sanders is a good man for the ideals he espouses, but what makes him a great man is the complex, messy, and deeply generous way he has lived.

Though people often read *Walden* that way, it is not a self-help book; and though Thoreau is often treated that way, he is not an ascetic Tony Robbins. What makes the moralist Thoreau interesting, and what makes *Walden* literature, is that the moralist is in conflict with—or at the very least coexisting next to—several other Thoreaus, including his primal opposite, a wild man with a glimmer in his eyes who occasionally feels the urge to mug a woodchuck and devour it, not for sustenance but for "the wildness it represented."

Of course, *Walden is* a kind of self-help book, but on a level that's complex, wild, and subtle because Thoreau wasn't a life coach or minister or even a philosopher, but an artist. Joseph Wood Krutch, in his beautiful biography, stresses that Thoreau's portrait of his own contradictory self, rather than a coherent argument of philosophy, is what lifts *Walden*—and that, for all of Thoreau's bursts of emphatic confidence, he often lived (like all artists) in restless uncertainty. Krutch writes:

> No doubt he was, as he himself insisted, a happy man; but he was not settled or certain. A hunger and a thirst are elements in his happiness and make it something other than mere content. And it is the hunger and thirst which are responsible for the excitement of his writing.

We read Thoreau for that excitement and restlessness, not for the finger wagging. Too often elements in his work that are sparked by his inner tensions have been reduced by other authors, in the century and a half since *Walden* was published, to clichés of the nature writing genre. When I read the books of some contemporary nature writers, the mystery is gone for the simple reason that I know the plot: they will worship their homeplace and abhor development; they will love the small and hate the big; and they will set down, either through exhortation or example, a way of being that, in contrast to most modern lives, is quiet, modest, calm. And I completely agree with them, finding their ideas morally correct and unassailable; but, at the same time, I too often find the writing overly predictable and overly simple, and I too often find it relying on conventions as calcified as those of Victorian poetry. The sentiments of Thoreau are there, but the tension, art, and conflict have gone missing. The genre feels settled in a way the artist never was. And when I take out my Realometer and wave it over many of the conventions, it doesn't vibrate or ping or tingle, but instead is rendered a dead and lifeless stick.

Why should this concern me? Because I agree with Scott Russell Sanders that we are in the midst of not just an environmental crisis but a moral one. This crisis will require a potent language to match it, and I worry that the musty language of nature writing is not up for the fight. We need prose that is as alive and complex as we are, that recognizes human beings respond best to something other than dry moral instruction sheets or mystical mumbo jumbo. This will also be a language, if I have my way, that acknowledges the "true natural state" of man is not a utopian wild kingdom of lion lying with lamb, but a conflicted place where we are as often buffeted by competitiveness, fear, and self-interest as by conscious efforts toward a moral life. In fact, there is something pernicious and dishonest about a language that doesn't start with an acknowledgment of our darker, more troubled selves. There are no more cabins in the woods, and we don't need modern Thoreaus piping on flutes and boasting about being in the present moment, whatever that is. What we need are artists wrestling with the human world, which is forever intertwined with the so-called natural world because the two are one and the same. We need artists fighting to find and make something called home, cabin or no cabin, and wrestling with the deepest of questions: how to be in the world. And it is out of that wrestling, often anguished, that a new language can be forged, a language contradictory and wild enough to speak to us and, miracle of miracles, transform our lives.

That this last phrase is not mere romantic fluff is backed up by some personal evidence I have already noted: my own life was forever changed when I first read *Walden*.

I am a daily beach-walker, and I have often thought that the most comical beach people, funnier even than the nearly naked who purposefully burn their skin or the bird geeks like me with our binoculars, are those solitary nutjobs who wave their metal detectors over the sand. These are the guys who wear Bermuda shorts and work shoes and black socks, trudging down the beach as they search for buried treasure or, at least, a lost dime or two. They might not seem like appealing models, but theirs is the role I will now embrace, substituting my Realometer for a metal detector, and searching the sands of nature writing rather than those of the beach. And just what will I be searching for? Certainly not a plank or a platform, or obvious moral instruction, or a reiteration of Thoreau, or the rallying cries of politicians or environmentalists or journalists. Rather, I will be seeking an un-simple and unsettled language that reflects my own un-simple and unsettled life. I won't mind if that language is moral, but it will have to have a complex morality created out of confusion, a rhetoric that matches the life. If it is not complex, then my Realometer will not ring or vibrate or hum or do whatever such a device does—which is fine with me, at least for now, because that negative data will help prevent me from digging for anything that is false.

False to me, I mean—false to what I feel is my experience on this earth. I don't know what answers I'll find, if any, but I know they won't be simple ones. That's not a very conclusive conclusion, but it's all I've got, and if you'd like to discuss it further you know where you can find me. I'm the guy in the funny shorts and black socks, out there on the sand, restlessly waving a long-necked gizmo back and forth, hoping for words and sentences that make my Realometer hum.

LAURET EDITH SAVOY

Pieces toward a Just Whole

Memory: the summer we stayed home. Not that we traveled more than a week or two any summer, if at all, but in 1968 we *stayed* home, in Washington, D.C. To the child I was, the weeks from April through June weighed ugly, and for the adult I am, memory stays sharp: the morning news sputters black-and-white from the television I watch over a bowl of cereal. I ask my parents in the other room, "Why is Bobby Kennedy lying on the floor?" Daddy's words run in with him: "Not again."

Other memories of that time don't let go. A little boy, a classmate, calls across the schoolyard to me, "*Ugly nigger, colored nigger.*" This will not be the only time. In my child–mind's eye "colored" had meant that sun lay in my skin and sky flowed in my veins. Even though I run home to hide, the sounds of *that* word made ugly, and of the uglier word, cling like spittle. I am eight years old when I learn what I cannot understand.

On 5 April 1968, the day after Martin Luther King Jr. was killed and two months before Robert F. Kennedy's own death, the senator addressed the City Club of Cleveland on one of his presidential campaign stops. Instead of discussing politics he spoke on the "mindless menace of violence" that had stained "our land and every one of us" the previous day in Memphis. This menace degrades the nation, Kennedy said, as "we seemingly tolerate a rising level of violence that ignores our common humanity and our claims to civilization alike. We calmly accept newspaper reports of civilian slaughter in far-off lands. We glorify killing on movie and television screens and call it entertainment." Kennedy also identified "the violence of institutions," which is characterized by "indifference and inaction and slow decay. This is the violence that afflicts the poor, that poisons relations between men because their skin has different colors. This is a slow destruction of a child by hunger, and schools without books and homes without heat in the winter."

Not again. Colored. Nigger. In 1968 my innocent sense of fairness and of good in the world began to erode.

Scott Russell Sanders' essay "Simplicity and Sanity" urges all of us, all Americans, to rethink our conduct in life, our "vision and practice," as an initial step to ending "the vandalism of the many" in our wasteful, wealth-and-technology-driven, environment-damaging society. Inspired by Henry David Thoreau's thinking and words, Sanders asks each of us to choose to lead materially simpler lives, "to conserve rather than consume," and "to launch our own experiments in simplicity" while minding the word's root: "all of a piece, single, whole."

Yes. I offer a wholehearted "Yes, thank you," but . . . still . . . I feel a troubling unease. What of those Americans who don't have the freedom, agency, or economic privilege to choose? What of Americans whose lives and experiences have been poverty-bound or degraded?

For Gunnar Myrdal, writing more than six decades ago in his massive study *An American Dilemma: The Negro Problem and Modern Democracy*, the paradox was that this nation "believes in and aspires to something much higher than its plane of actual life." Writing now, forty years after 1968's spring of assassinations, I grieve for a nation that remains accustomed to what should be unacceptable. Huge disparities in opportunity and income remain, with protected, vested wealth for a few. Violence continues against people who are often out of mainstream-media sight—whether in ghettos, barrios, reservations, labor camps, prisons, or elsewhere—and thus not heard. America's invasions of other lands for resources and power are cloaked as wars for peace and democracy, and thereby prioritized over the basic human needs of our own citizens. The dilemma that Myrdal observed remains: How does one reconcile ideals and principles of freedom and justice with actual life in this nation—that is, how does one move beyond hope and lip service to principled engagement?

Wendell Berry wrote *The Hidden Wound* half a year after Robert Kennedy was assassinated, while secluded in Stanford University's library over the 1968–69 winter holiday. Influenced by what he called "the civil rights agitation" on campus and elsewhere, this descendant of a Kentucky family that had enslaved African Americans tried to face his and his ancestors' unspoken complicity in history and thereby heal in himself the diseased hidden wound of racism. Berry recognized that our public language "conveys what we *wish* had been true" and that the too-common "lack of critical self-knowledge . . . is the historical and psychological vacuum in which the Walt Disney version of American history was not only possible but inevitable." I think self-protective denial and silence have kept too much of America from knowing who "we the people" really are, thereby keeping our vision and language of possibility impoverished. Such denial, such not-remembering, *dis*-members us. There is no single coherent American society, no homogeneous melting pot. We are not whole.

The fulfillment of Euro-America's exploration and empire-building—land acquisition and use, with the expansion of a new nation on what was believed to be a clean slate of wilderness—owed much to colonization, enslavement of Africans, and the dispossession and forced removal of indigenous people from homeland to reservation. There was a time when only white, property-owning men could vote; women and people of color were thought incapable or undeserving, and an enslaved African American was declared only three-fifths a man, not a citizen. (Words such as *white*, *race*, and *slave* are deceptive in that they are far more ambiguous, complicated, and fraught than their generally casual, unquestioned acceptance and use would indicate. The reader should assume quotation marks around my use of these words.)

We face many crucial challenges, including global climate change, as well as the loss of biological diversity and ecosystem integrity. The question we all need to answer is this: how, if at all, can the deeply rooted values and economic norms that institutionalized the exploiting and manipulating of the natural world be separated from what marginalizes human lives? Elemental to *our* American past and present are the omissions that have allowed separatisms by race, class, and gender, inequities in privilege and power, to remain.

The complexities and ambiguities of this nation's intercultural past and present, and the ways in which white America has perceived, used, or impacted the Earth, cannot be separated from what drives racism and other inequities in political and economic power. If seen in terms of process and response, the dynamics of the past several hundred years on this continent have yielded very different kinds of estrangement for those in power and those at the margins. Although it may be desirable to think of the past as long over, we all carry history within us, our pasts becoming present in what we think and do, in who we are.

Consider that America has been a land of enslavers and enslaved for much more of its existence than not—that in 1790, at the birth of this new republic, about one-third of America's population was enslaved. Chattel slavery produced the large-scale agricultural crops (tobacco, rice, sugar, cotton) that plantation owners sold on international markets. By both providing a labor force and bringing capital into all of the colonies and new states, slavery and its profits largely funded the nation's infrastructure—not just the South's—until the Civil War.

Slavery's profits and privilege are limited neither to the South nor to the past. Major American financial institutions such as predecessor banks of J. P. Morgan Chase and Bank of America, institutions of higher education such as Brown and Yale universities and Williams College, as well as newspaper, tobacco, textile, and railroad companies, either amassed their wealth from or were otherwise supported by slavery and/or the trade in enslaved human beings. To condemn chattel slavery while ignoring what originally made the system possible and has continuously fed a caste system up into the present seems an all too common practice, even among liberal Americans. A refusal to acknowledge how privilege connects with historical injustices is difficult to dismantle. Even the ways most Americans talk about skin color and race is residue of centuries-old ideas grounded in, and ground down by, stereotypes.

A supposed absence of obvious de jure discrimination today, and the presidential election of Barack Obama, might suggest that racism is a thing of the past—or that we have achieved, at least, racial neutrality if not equality. But the removal of barriers via legislated equality is a fiction we live by while our judicial system in fact weakens—by not enforcing and by narrowly interpreting— key laws enacted during the civil rights movement of the 1950s and 1960s. The federal government's failure to enforce such laws is at least as old as its abandonment of Reconstruction with the 1876–77 presidential election.

Perhaps it is easy for some to think that the inequality experienced by African Americans ended with the Jim Crow era. However, even as civil rights activists in the early 1960s struggled daily and risked their lives, much of so-called white America perceived no need for change. Tim Wise, educator-activist and author of *White Like Me: Reflections on Race from a Privileged Son*, reports that of white Americans polled by Gallup in 1962 about whether they thought black children had equal educational opportunities in their communities, almost 90 percent said yes. Polled in 1963 about whether they thought racial minorities were treated equally in their communities, four-fifths said yes. Wise also notes that two-thirds of white Americans polled by *Newsweek* around the time of the March on Washington in 1963 said Dr. King and the movement were pushing too far and asking for too much, too soon, too fast.

Robert F. Kennedy continued his speech to the Cleveland City Club by saying that when we are taught "to hate and fear" we "learn to confront others not as fellow citizens but as enemies—to be met not with cooperation but with conquest, to be subjugated and mastered. We learn, at the last, to look at our brothers as aliens, men with whom we share a city, but not a community, men bound to us in common dwelling, but not in common effort."

Can we work toward simplicity without community or common effort? Can we be whole if structural elements of America's daily motion—including education, employment, health care, immigration policies, public housing and transportation, and the criminal justice system—are not neutral? As human-rights and social-justice advocates repeatedly point out, blind interactions of existing policies, practices, and institutions tend to perpetuate injustice and barriers.

Education, for example, is not a fundamental right under the Constitution, and public schools are now more segregated by class and race than in 1970, before the Supreme Court approved busing. Public school enrollments in most major cities—New York, Chicago, Detroit, and Los Angeles among them—are three-quarters or more African American and Latino. Jonathan Kozol calls this "educational apartheid," as public schools once integrated (by law or voluntarily) resegregated, and schools already deeply segregated remained so. He also cites a legacy betrayed as schools named for civil rights leaders often are the most segregated, underfunded, underserviced, and poorly maintained. For example, Manhattan's Martin Luther King Jr. High School, located in an upper-middle-class white neighborhood, was once a hope for true community integration in the best sense. Today it is separate and unequal, with few white children.

Inequity continues in many other areas as well. More than forty-five million Americans have no health insurance, according to the Census Bureau in 2007, with the percentage of uninsured people of color twice that of whites. The highest number of housing discrimination complaints on record to date came not years ago but in 2006 and 2007, and most of them were related to disability and race. The recent environmental-justice study *Toxic Waste and Race at Twenty, 1987–2007*, published by the United Church of Christ, reports that more than half of the nine million people living within two miles of hazardous waste sites across the country are people of color. The Southern Poverty Law Center counted 888 active hate groups in the United States in 2007, an increase of nearly 50 percent since 2000 driven largely by anti-immigrant movements. Federal laws do not protect migrant workers from unfair labor practices, nor do they provide for overtime pay or even a guaranteed minimum wage.

We can also consider a single place, such as New Orleans, to see the breadth and embedded depth of injustice through time. The aftermath of Hurricane Katrina in 2005, particularly the levee failure, points to a long history of de jure and de facto segregation along the Gulf Coast. Although some affluent white communities, like Lakefront in New Orleans, were devastated, the disproportionate burden fell on poor people of color more vulnerable to flooding by living in lowland areas and having limited access to evacuation, rescue, recovery, and rebuilding efforts. This pattern is not new along the Gulf Coast, as those without forewarning, mobility, access to shelter or higher ground, or adequate relief assistance—from enslaved Africans to migrant workers—have suffered disproportionately over centuries. Before the mid-1960s, lawful segregation of public housing and transportation further entrenched the region's geography of poverty and race.

All told, the hurricane and its aftereffects displaced more than a million people, dispersing not just families but a deeply rooted culture. Of the impacted people of color, many were home renters, most were uninsured, and most did not own or have access to a car. *Reconstruction* in this place and context is a burdened word—and current efforts by both the public and private sectors still fail to address the existing risks, vulnerabilities, and inequalities of an infrastructure already weakened by racism. In New Orleans, building permits are less common in the lowest-income areas. Rents are climbing beyond reach while state programs tend to help property owners return to their homes, but not renters who couldn't afford to own. Thousands of public housing units have been demolished.

When polled on whether Hurricane Katrina and its impact pointed to persistent racial inequality, fewer than half of white Americans thought it did, while over three-quarters of African Americans in the country said yes.

In his chapter "Economy" in *Walden*, Thoreau wrote, "The cost of a thing is the amount of what I will call life which is required to be exchanged for it, immediately or in the long run." Rightly, as Scott Russell Sanders points out, the measure of cost (life required) should extend beyond the context of an individual and his or her property if we are to understand our larger impacts in the world. But shouldn't this critical metric also be applied across different scales of time, geography, and human institutions to recognize and include distinct interactions of race, class, gender, power, and privilege? How, for example, might thinking in terms of migrant labor define at least some of the costs (life required in exchange) of producing and consuming?

The *ecological footprint*, commonly described as a "sustainability indicator" or a "resource management tool," is a measure of the resources people consume and the wastes—including carbon emissions—that they produce, expressed in terms of the amount of productive land and water needed to provide those resources. Such measurements are typically done for an individual, for the "average" American couple or family or other group, for a country, and for the global impact of the human race. According to the public-policy institute Redefining Progress, that global impact has now exceeded Earth's ecological limits by more than a third. The World Wildlife Fund agrees that "humanity is no longer living off nature's interest, but drawing down its capital," noting that the United States has the largest per-person footprint of any nation.

Key to this measure is the word *resource*, the root of which comes from the Old French (from Latin) meaning "to rise again, recover." Dictionary definitions in common use refer to a stock or supply of materials or assets that can be drawn on, or a country's collective means of supporting itself or becoming wealthier, as represented by its minerals, land, and other assets.

A wiser measure of our ecological footprint would also include human beings and their cultural histories, or at least their labor, and would factor in the losses of lifetime relationships with land, losses of self-determination, and losses of health or life. What if this footprint measured, over time, upon whom and what the nation's foot has trod—that is, at the cost of whose lives has America's relative prosperity evolved? We need to know the cumulative ecological footprint of our long-term consumption of others' labor, land, and rights. Consider the energy derived by the undervalued toil of others: enslaved plantation labor, migrants, sharecroppers, and today's guest-worker labor. Consider the resources acquired through a sanctioned dispossessing of others, which would include "natural resources" gained from the many removals of the continent's indigenous nations, as well as the ongoing estrangements from homelands owing to environmental and health impacts, such as those of uranium mining and unreclaimed tailings on native peoples in the American Southwest.

In early spring 1968, Dr. Martin Luther King went to Memphis to support 1,300 sanitation workers on a sixty-four-day strike for better working conditions, improved wages, and some tangible recognition of their worth as human beings. I still recall those images of *I AM A MAN* on countless signs floating above crowds walking shoulder-to-shoulder. Recognizing how violence—including the undeclared war in Vietnam—linked with poverty in America, King had planned a "Poor People's Encampment" in Washington, D.C., for later that year. Among his last public words, in that last speech given in Memphis: "All we say to America is, 'Be true to what you said on paper.'"

If we can imagine "environment" broadly as sets of circumstances and contexts within which all of us intimately live and die, then the whole we must understand includes those lives whose experiences of place are displaced or alien, migrant or urban, indentured or enslaved, degraded or toxic. How and where we all live, the means and costs of living, must become part of the measure. Each of us must resist a monochromatic sense of culture and knowledge, must recognize human diversity across history and the nation. We and our experiences have direction and magnitude, as vectors in motion across generations.

Land conservation, for example, is antithetical to many communities because for them it has often meant land grab, dispossession, and graft as tools of oppression. It has meant status quo or further exclusion for the poor and for many people of color. Beyond open space, green space, and rural land, we must also consider urban, built environments and include spheres of justice, sustainability, inclusion, and democracy. But how can we reimagine through the dangers of socially constructed definitions, perceptions, and lenses to more accessible and larger frames—toward a true whole? What is possible?

In his 1967 book *Where Do We Go from Here: Chaos or Community?*, Dr. King observes, "So much of modern life can be summarized in that suggestive phrase of Thoreau: 'Improved means to an unimproved end.'" A superficial way of living affirms the "external"—"that complex of devices, techniques, mechanisms and instrumentalities by means of which we live"—while it devalues the "internal"—"that realm of spiritual ends expressed in art, literature, morals and religion." King goes on to say that "our hope for creative living in this world house that we have inherited lies in our ability to re-establish the moral ends of our lives in personal characters and social justice. Without this spiritual and moral reawakening we shall destroy ourselves in the misuse of our own instruments."

The lineage of dissident Americans who have tried to rethink the meaning and conduct of life is long, with many branches. Thoreau sought an original relationship with Earth and life, an *ab*-original connection. Something can also be discovered from Frederick Douglass, a man born within a year of Thoreau but under very different circumstances, who asked and answered, "What to the American slave is your Fourth of July?" Or we can learn from Margaret Fuller, a Massachusetts neighbor to Thoreau who was a proponent of women's rights and social reform, as well as coeditor (with Ralph Waldo Emerson) of *The Dial: A Magazine for Literature, Philosophy, and Religion*. So, too, can we learn from countless others who didn't write books but sought answers to the timeless questions of our souls in oral histories and narratives.

After hearing my father's "not again" on that early June morning in 1968, my child–mind's eye began to see the world as empty of goodness. As a young teenager I began to wonder if those who call themselves "white" really had the luxury of not needing to know, or to care about, the truths and realities of those with darker skin—or if the wealthy didn't need to consider those in poverty. I thought that if those without economic power were ignorant of the privileges and power of whiteness, they would find it impossible to survive in this country. Now, years later, I know the edge between despair and hope can be very thin.

I recently visited Canterbury Village, New Hampshire, one of the earliest and longest-standing Shaker communities in the country, active since 1792. Those followers of Ann Lee challenged almost every mainstream ideal of American society with their communitarian ethic. They said, "Do all your work as though you had a thousand years to live and as you would if you knew you must die tomorrow." Something in the peace on that hillside, in addition to Shakerism's call to simplicity, stirred in me a heart memory that beliefs in justice and equality, reverence and trust, *could* be lived largely.

Simplicity: *all of a piece, single, whole.* Having fewer possessions, consuming less energy, having a smaller ecological footprint—all of these are necessary to living simply, but still more is required of us. Appeals to conscience or responsibility will fall short—as will prescribed solutions of what we could, should, or must do—unless "we the people" face honestly all of what we are. Muriel Rukeyser, writing shortly after the end of World War II, declared in *The Life of Poetry*, "We are a people tending toward democracy at the level of hope; on another level, the economy of the nation, the empire of business within the republic, both include in their basic premise the concept of perpetual warfare.... Simply, the line of culture was begun in America at a point of open conflict."

The difficult things for us to cultivate are the expansiveness of spirit and heart necessary to respond to life fully and imaginatively—assumptions and stereotypes put aside—and a capacity to ask significant questions about our lives and about lives not our own. We benefit when we acknowledge and honor difference as enriching and at the same time find, across divisions, common interest and common humanity. I believe that we exist in relation—to each other, to the Earth and its inhabitants. We might do well to regard such relation and responsibility as life itself.

By considering geography, race, class, gender, issue, and time, we might come close to being "conservers" as Scott Russell Sanders suggests, but conservers of dignity, people, and communities as well as of land, water, and other so-called resources—especially where a community does not own or control the land and resources. In this sense, being a "conserver" also means resisting the unacceptable degrading of life, as well as holding to account those who profit from violence and poverty and disintegration.

This, perhaps, is life's task without end: to bear witness, to give testimony, to act with respect. The health of the land may reside in its capacity for self-renewal; the health of the human family may, in part, reside in our capacity for locating ourselves within many inheritances, across generations, as citizens of the land, of nations, and of the Earth.

REFERENCES

Berry, Wendell. *The Hidden Wound*. New York: North Point Press, 1989.
Bullard, Robert, and others. *Toxic Waste and Race at Twenty, 1987–2007: Grassroots Struggles to Dismantle Environmental Racism in the United States*. Cleveland, Ohio: United Church of Christ, 2007.
Kennedy, Sen. Robert F. "On the Mindless Menace of Violence." Speech to the City Club of Cleveland, Ohio, 5 April 1968. www.rfkmemorial.org/lifevision/onthemindlessmenaceofviolence/.
King, Martin Luther, Jr. *Where Do We Go from Here: Chaos or Community?* New York: Harper and Row, 1967; Boston: Beacon Press, 1968.
Kozol, Jonathan. "Still Separate, Still Unequal: America's Educational Apartheid." *Harper's Magazine*, September 2005. www.harpers.org/archive/2005/09/0080727.
Morse, Reilly. *Environmental Justice through the Eye of Hurricane Katrina*. Washington, D.C.: Joint Center for Political and Economic Studies, Health Policy Institute, 2008.
Myrdal, Gunnar. *An American Dilemma: The Negro Problem and Modern Democracy*. New York: Harper and Row, 1944.
Pastor, Manuel, Robert Bullard, and others. *In the Wake of the Storm: Environment, Disaster, and Race after Katrina*. New York: Russell Sage Foundation, 2006.
Rukeyser, Muriel. *The Life of Poetry*. New York: William Morrow and Co., 1949; repr., Ashfield, Mass.: Paris Press, 1996.

CATHERINE REID

And after a Sweet Singing Fall Down

1.

Blowing out eggs is a delicate affair, which I know from handling those of chickens, during the summer we cured a flock of eating each others'. We blew out the contents—a pinprick in each end, a tight seal with the mouth—then squirted in hot sauce, waxed over the holes, and returned the transformed eggs to their nests to watch the hens fall for the trick.

The stakes are, of course, higher with the shells of wild songbirds. The collector, in this case my great-grandfather, first had to know which week a certain migrant returned in the spring, and where it took up residence, and how quickly it built nests and laid eggs. He had to know the fields and woods the way some people knew about migration through a close reading of scripture: phoebe in the alders, snow geese overhead; "Yea, the stork in the heaven knoweth her appointed times"—Jeremiah 8:7. And he had to do it all during the busiest time in a farmer's year.

He must have collected hundreds, for surely some were too old and already contained embryos; or they broke in his coat pocket as he scaled a fence or crawled through scrub; or he pressed his lips to the egg and his pinch was too hard, his breath too strong, and the fragile shell gave way beneath his working man's grip.

But dozens survived, from warblers and thrushes and sparrows and finches, and these he carefully labeled and nested in excelsior, the boxes packed as though readied for shipment to a museum. He didn't record the narratives—the swale where a rare bird's nest was found, the tree he had to climb, the angry parent he had to duck; those stories died with him, and then the eggs were just eggs, and years later my grandmother, the logical inheritor, quietly and efficiently destroyed them.

She never said whether or not it was a hard thing to do; she may simply have become aware that it was illegal to hunt or own migratory birds or to keep any part of them in personal collections. Or she may have found it a burden—having married by then and had two children of her own—in a world where nostalgia or sorrow had no role. Still, I wonder what passed through her mind as she obliterated the hollow eggs. Was it like the letting go I have had to do in the months since she died, of old notes and letters and slips of papers she kept, listing birds she had seen on certain summer days? Was it a last goodbye to the private conversations she and her father had shared—and that soon she and I would share— talks coded in bird names and habits and habitats?

Or had they simply become dusty, fifty-year-old eggs that ceased to suggest journeys or the potential for wild, vibrant lives?

2.

Spring birds sweep through the skies, hundreds of thousands in all colors and sizes. The nights are as busy and loud as the days while South and Central America empty of their transients. Sleep is difficult, and I want to spend all the lit hours on the deck of my small house, made smaller by the sheer volume of bodies passing overhead—warblers and thrushes and orioles and tanagers. Then I hear the chittering of freewheeling chimney swifts, a call easy to distinguish above other neighborhood cries, and I let them embody the flurry and pace of the season.

The swifts' shape limits and makes possible everything they do, from their darting-fast flights to their dependence on vertical walls. This last fact I learned as a child at my grandparents' cottage, on a day too cold to be outside for long. We had built a fire in the fireplace and gathered in front of it with games, unprepared for the fall of several baby birds and their thin nest onto the ashes, the twigs shiny with the saliva the parents had used to glue them to the flue. We hadn't known the birds were there nor that they relied on chimneys and thus on us—an ignorance that for a while made us feel clumsy and brutal. But then, of course, we were kids and, until the fog lifted, there was Monopoly to play, and Crazy Eights, and soon enough we were back in the tidal pools or digging enough sea worms so that Grampa would take us out to the number two buoy, where flounder might bend our poles into flailing half circles.

The pirouetting birds I watch now make flight look as easy as blinking— which, for them, it is. It's what they do. Nearly tailless, with feet designed for clutching walls instead of walking, they spend their entire waking lives on the wing. They eat and drink, court and mate, in flight; they break off twigs for their nests while flying past bushes, and they keep track of each other across great stretches of sky. When it comes time to die, they even do that in the air. Rachel

Carson, who wrote about them while working for the U.S. Fish and Wildlife Service, asserts in "Ace of Nature's Aviators" that the chimney swift may be "less aware of the earth and its creatures than any other bird in the world."[1]

At night, the swifts come to earth and settle into chimneys or hollow trees, leading a communally lived life except during the four to six weeks shared primarily with a mate. At sunset, anywhere from a few dozen to several thousand can pack, shoulder to shoulder, into a single flue—pulsing, restless bodies that breathe together until dawn. Then, one by one, they lift through the opening and scatter, their voices and flight patterns forming a wide net above us.

Such lives spent in uncluttered space may account for their seeming absence of fear, which, for the earthbound, is a tough trait to fathom. Yet by all accounts I've read, when a swift is caught and handled, it tries to cuddle rather than fly. Arthur Cleveland Bent found that particularly odd and unsettling, a standout in his life devoted to the study of birds. When he writes about the swifts some children once found on the ground, the birds snuggling into the kids' hands or dangling like pendants when the kids let them clutch clothing, he sounds both disbelieving and sad. The terror seen in most caught birds wasn't present—the racing-wild heart, the flailing attempts to escape. The swifts simply waited until they could be airborne again.[2]

But even the sensitive and brilliant Bent didn't know the answer to another mystery about swifts, one that fostered lively speculation about how and where they spent their winters. Perhaps their chittering couldn't be heard above the din of a rain forest, or the canopy was too thick for observers to make out a stubby five-inch-long shape above it. But their annual absence from the United States kept alive the question, and "even eminent naturalists of the past generation," as Carson reminds us, "fell back on weird Medieval theories, such as the one that the birds buried themselves in the mud of swamps and hibernated until spring."[3]

3.

By the time I was six and old enough for dawn walks with my grandmother, she had discarded my great-grandfather's eggs and spent years studying with a handful of serious birders. The eight of them were competitive enough to be excellent, but so cohesive as a group that they made sure everyone saw everything—even me, the lone kid, the few times I accompanied them on bird walks, and I learned more from their remarks than I did from poring over field guides.

Each of those people would surely have scoffed at the idea of birds overwintering in mud or otherwise hibernating in frigid states, just as did the naturalists who preceded them—Izaak Walton, Gilbert White, William Bartram, Robert

MacLeod. Yet each of that latter group also hesitated to deny that such a possibility might exist. Too many sane and sober people had borne witness, they said; or, as MacLeod once wrote, "If reputable persons have not lied to me, then swallows do pass the winter like frogs." Maybe, just maybe, there really was a *hybernaculum* nearby, for no sooner would someone insist that the belief was as idiotic as the one about birds wintering on the moon than a handful of chilled swifts would be found in a chimney pipe, lifeless until warmed by the fire; or a tree would be felled in February, packed with stone-cold swifts that came alive as soon as they were warmed in a hand; or swallows appeared near a brook in the spring, and no one could explain why they looked so slimy and disheveled.[4]

A mental scrambling had to occur for those who looked on. It is, after all, cold-blooded things that freeze—like the spring peepers that wait, still as ice in the leaf litter, until the nights become mild enough to release them into action. Birds, for the most part, evolved to depart when cold arrives and food supplies dwindle, migrating thousands of miles to find warmth and good living. The ones that stay have to maintain active, heat-producing states, like the chickadees that pick around for seeds and insects all winter.

Or at least that was the long-held belief.

4.

When swifts mate, the event is so brief that it's hard to believe anything happens. I have to watch for several hours to confirm that moment of contact, when the V of one bird fits into the V of the other—a quick, cupped affair, before each darts away as though nothing had transpired. The speed is typical of all they do, single swifts having been clocked at 100 mph, which made their daytime habits hard to study, their winter whereabouts even harder to determine. "For five months [the swift] vanishes as utterly as though he were wintering on Mars," wrote a *New York Times* reporter in 1915. "Did they drop in the water or hibernate in the mud . . . their obliteration could not be more complete."[5]

Their night-roosting habits, however, make them easy to capture, which is what researchers finally did, for ten years during the 1930s and early '40s, in what was, at the time, the largest study of birds ever undertaken. Balanced on rooftops in cities across the eastern United States, dozens of volunteers captured and banded swifts as they departed their chimneys for the day. All told, close to 375,000 birds were tagged, though it took nine years from the project's start before the results finally came in—thirteen bands delivered to the American Embassy in Peru, all from birds shot in the Amazon delta. According to Rachel Carson, death brought "ornithological fame" to those thirteen, for in their dying they "filled in the missing paragraphs in the biography of their race." A sigh of relief must have passed through the scientific community, for this, Carson was convinced, would put to rest once and for all the myth of bird hibernation.[6]

5.

I think it's fair to say that my grandmother had no apparent wish to practice or know feelings, having grown up in rural New England in a family where hard work and education were the primary ethos. The loss of two younger brothers, each dying shortly after birth; the stillness of the quarantines she twice had to endure; and the solitary days spent as a new wife, forced to give up her teaching career as soon as she married, must have confirmed the pointlessness in cultivating emotions. I saw her cry but once, when her husband of seventy years died; and my siblings and I, along with our mother before us, knew to be wary when describing the dramas of our lives, because a bird flying by could end a conversation, everything stopped until she could name it and make its connection.

How much better, then, to join with her in her interest rather than compete with birds for her attention. I grew to like the ways they pulled her outside and into new places, and I ceased to mind the fact that birds proved more fascinating than the feats or deeds of our family, because there they were: Geese that can reach altitudes of thirty thousand feet! Terns that can travel fifty thousand miles in a year! Shorebirds that can fly for nine days without food or drink or rest!

"The more astonishing, the more true," as Andrea Barrett's characters say in "Rare Birds," a short story I wished I had discovered in time to share with my grandmother, especially those last months of her life when I often read aloud to her.[7] Still, I like to link my grandmother to the main characters, two women whose friendship blossoms through their shared love of natural history, and who bristle together at the notion that birds are able to spend their winters on lake bottoms.

Applying Barrett's twentieth-century logic to their eighteenth-century dilemma, the women set out to prove that birds cannot survive prolonged submersion. Their scheme is relatively simple: hire the gardener's son to capture swallows at night, then empty his sack into a barrel of water, enclosing the birds with a net over a floating board. ("Everything happens so fast, a flurry of hands and cloth and netting and wings, loops of string and snagged skirt.") The next morning they slip back to the stables and find just what they expected: twisted bodies sprawled at the bottom of the cask. The women's work is not yet done, however, for then they roll up their sleeves, scalpels in hand, and prove the bodies contain no means to maintain life underwater.

Though triumphant in disproving the men of their time, including the much-esteemed Linnaeus, who believed in subaqueous hibernation, they cannot prevail over a more insidious belief, which was that the findings of two women could not be taken seriously, and so they pack their bags and leave town, with no forwarding address, and we're left to wonder why so little changed in the subsequent centuries.

6.

When my mother was first in college, in the heady postwar years, she fell deeply in love. Exuberance was in the air, as were triumph and possibility, and she and her lover caught that joyous wave, headed for a sure future of sustained domestic bliss—except that one night, when she and he were walking hand-in-hand down a snowy road, a car hit them, throwing her to her knees and killing him on impact. Just like that, the dream was snuffed out, and she was left alone to figure out a new one.

She left college for a while and stayed at home, seeking solace in the passage of time and in what had once been familiar. She found some of that in her father, who one night laid his hands on her shoulders, as she sat at the table, and let her know through his touch that such sorrow made sense. Her mother, however, before leaving the room, simply remarked that it was late and they should all go to bed.

In my understanding of the story, this was not my grandmother's only departure at a crucial moment in my mother's life, for when she first learned about her daughter's new lover, and their happiness and all they hoped for, she waited until my mother had finished sharing the news and then pointed out a bird flying by the window.

7.

I have held wild birds in my hand and felt their fierce will to flee, and watched them try to find an exit from a house they had erred in entering, and heard them call in the predawn dark, so loud and alone that it seemed they would be owl meat soon, only to hear the same bird call again the next day. I know them as much by their vitality as by their coloring and size, which means I share the surprise of the man who recounted, in a recent post on a birder's listserv, putting a gravely injured nighthawk in his freezer to speed up its dying, and the next day he took it out and it moved in his hands.

This seemed implausible and yet I believed him; I had no reason not to, especially with his story ending well, the bird flying away once he brought it outside. Had I been alive in earlier times, I might even have believed the stories then circulating, such as the account of two men digging in a salt marsh near Cambridge, Massachusetts, (in February 1760) when "they dug up a swallow, wholly surrounded and covered with mud. The swallow was in a torpid state, but being held in their hands, it revived in about half an hour. The place where this swallow was dug up, was every day covered with the salt water, which at every high tide was four or five feet deep." A historian—Samuel Williams, a Harvard professor and a man of facts—recorded the event, which had a definite impact on his subsequent readers.[8]

But I might have been more leery of the descriptions by Olaus Magnus, author of *History of the Northern Peoples*, a fabulous mix of Scandinavian lore, customs, and history. So much of what he chronicled proved true, and he had a remarkable ability to create accurate maps, but who knows what he saw or heard in the early 1500s that shaped his understanding of the way certain birds prepare for winter. Swallows, in particular, he writes, were known to "clap mouth to mouth, wing to wing, and legge to legge, and so after a sweet singing fall down into certain great lakes or pooles among the Canes from whence next Spring they receive a new resurrection."[9]

8.

The January nights were bitter and brilliant when my grandmother lay dying. The full moon lit up the snow and created a soft glow in her room, especially around the one window she kept open when she slept. The family maintained a vigil by her bed for the long days of her letting-go, and I took the night shift for its stillness and the chance to spend such silent time with her alone. The dining room clock chimed the quarter hours, and occasionally she uttered something—"David," when her son told her he was leaving for the evening; "Catherine," when he told her I was staying; and, at one point, when snow blew around the house and the light outside was glittery and sharp, "It was a beautiful day; I spent it on Plum Island," and I could see her in the much loved place, wandering the fine sand beaches in search of terns and gulls and sandpipers; or taking a trail through the woods in search of warblers or an owl; or setting aside her binoculars on the slower summer days to fill a basket with the beach plums that she would later make into jelly.

Her breathing ebbed as the days drew on, and my youngest brother joined me at midnight, a welcome added presence in the long stillness. We took turns putting lotion on her skin, wetting a sponge to soothe her mouth, or reciting a favorite Psalm in the tick of slow minutes.

Little seemed to matter in the last hours of her life but that we be there, especially after that moment when, my hand on her shoulder, she turned and said, "Don't leave me." For the most part I didn't, until that last day when I had to head out before dawn to teach the new semester's classes. But others arrived and were there when her body finally surrendered, which I sensed on my drive home, catching sight of a bit of rainbow through the flurries—the only color in the sky, illuminating a feather-shaped cloud.

She, of course, would have registered no reaction had I mentioned such a sighting, just as in those times when I brought up dreams or talked hunches or bent down for a four-leaf clover, knowing a dose of luck could only help. She would have let the moment pass and then resumed an earlier conversation, one about the health of turkey poults or the complications of global warming or the effect of a cold front on the next wave of migrating warblers.

9.

The poorwill, a night-flying, insect-eating bird, pirouettes nearly as fast as a chimney swift but has a much larger mouth, which functions as a scoop. In the 1940s, in the Chuckwalla Mountains of California, naturalist Edmund Jaeger found a torpid poorwill tucked into a crack in the desert's rock walls. He sought it again when he returned a few weeks later with several students; they found and handled one, shouted at it, and opened and closed its wings. The bird, however, couldn't be roused. Jaeger soon learned that the Hopi name for poorwill is "the sleeping one," and a Navajo boy, when asked for the birds' whereabouts, indicated that they could sometimes be found fast asleep between the rocks.[10]

This was a radical finding, proof at last, he believed, that birds can hibernate. Others remain skeptical, even with the advent of tiny transmitters, which, tucked into almost as tiny backpacks, have confirmed what the Hopi already knew. In a study of poorwills, in the hills of southern British Columbia, a researcher caught and outfitted the birds with transmitters, finding that at night their body temperatures dropped a staggering 63°f (from 104°f to 41°f), a cascading that would kill a human being. A related study, of poorwills near Tucson, found that they can remain in such a chilled state for weeks, in a kind of Rip-Van-Winkle stasis, with no apparent delays when shifting from stalled state to full functioning.[11]

In the years since, experiments have taken place around the world: birds chilled in labs and deprived of food (they settle into a sleep state); torpid birds targeted with loud noise or sudden bright lights (they might briefly open an eye);

sleeping birds knocked over on their perches (they don't let go). The list of species believed to hibernate keeps growing, and ornithologists now suspect that hummingbirds may enter torpor every night of their lives.[12]

None of this can explain Magnus' operatic farewell—the in-sweep of wings like the closing of a cloak—but many puzzle pieces have fit together at last. When temperatures drop, some birds may appear dead, only to resume active life when there is warmth and food again.

Yet much of the puzzle still confounds: What do we make of the stories of birds seen underwater, clutching grasses in their bills as the waters raced by; or of birds dug out of river mud in the coldest days of winter? What can't we believe about the thing that animates them, our disbelief perhaps blinding us to all they're able to do?

10.

One doesn't really cry when a one-hundred-year-old person dies; the reaction is more of a tender farewell that was long in the forming. Yet hardly a day goes by that I don't miss her—when I sit at the drop-front desk I inherited, near her pens and careful cursive; or hear the swifts overhead, queuing up for their autumn trek to Peru; or follow a link to a website she would have enjoyed, as when I found the slowed-down version of a veery's song, one of our favorite birds, with its startlingly complex interior melody, harmonies the human ear is unable to hear without the aid of computers.[13] She and I may not have been able to tell one another much about the matters of our hearts, but in the language of birds we shared plenty.

I think of her now as I do of the swifts, with their spit-and-twig nests and their preference for sky over land, and I know my ache when missing her is akin to that of Arthur Cleveland Bent as he struggled to make sense of the swift's lack of interest in people: "How do we regard this bird that does not know we are on earth? . . . It is a guest that does not know we are its host. We may almost think of it as a machine for catching insects, a mechanical toy, clicking out its sharp notes."

His tone of lament is as much for their indifference as for the ways they remain beyond our knowing.

NOTES

1. Rachel Carson, "Ace of Nature's Aviators," in *Lost Woods: Rediscovered Writing of Rachel Carson*, ed. Linda Lear (Boston: Beacon Press, 1999).

2. Arthur Cleveland Bent, Smithsonian Institution United States National Museum Bulletin 176:271–93. United States Government Printing Office, 1940.

3. Rachel Carson, Department of the Interior, Fish and Wildlife Service press release, 12 November 1944, www.fws.gov/news/historic/1944/19441112.pdf.

4. Robert MacLeod, quoted, along with accounts of Walton and Bartram, in W. L. McAtee, "Torpidity in Birds," *American Midland Naturalist* 38, no. 1 (July 1947). Gilbert White suggests the presence of a nearby hybernaculum in *The Natural History and Antiquities of Selborne* (London, 1789).

5. "U.S. Studies Bird Migration. 500,000 Facts, Many Hitherto Unknown, Are Collected by Federal Officials on Flights of Feathered Myriads," *New York Times*, 20 June 1915.

6. Rachel Carson, Fish and Wildlife Service press release, 12 November 1944.

7. Andrea Barrett, "Rare Bird," *Ship Fever: Stories* (New York: Norton, 1996).

8. Samuel Williams, *The Natural and Civil History of Vermont* (1794); quoted in Elsa Guerdrum Allen, "The History of American Ornithology before Audubon," *Transactions of the American Philosophical Society*, New Series, 41, no. 3, 1951.

9. Olaus Magnus, quoted in Elsa Guerdrum Allen.

10. For Edmund Jaeger's work on poorwills: www.jaeger.ws/poorwill/index.html.

11. For Mark Brigham's research on poorwills in British Columbia: www.livingland scapes.bc.ca/thomp-ok/goatsucker/index.html.

12. Claims about hibernating birds are still handled cautiously, and the definition of "hibernation" is still in flux. Cf. Elke Schleucher, "Torpor in Birds: Taxonomy, Energetics, and Ecology," *Physiological and Biochemical Zoology* 77, no. 6 (Nov.–Dec. 2004). "Recent reports on patterns and occurrence of torpor and other natural hypothermic states in birds have prompted a revision of many longstanding opinions."

13. For a slowed-down version of the veery's song, see David Rothenberg's website www.whybirdssing.com, a supplement to his book *Why Birds Sing: A Journey into the Mystery of Bird Song* (New York: Basic Books, 2005).

ELIZABETH DODD

Isogloss

Language and Legacy
on Mount St. Helens

Nothing standing aboveground today was here thirty years ago. The ground it-self wasn't here. Oh, there was ground, but much of it lay below the surface where my boot soles slip a little in the loose pebbles of pumice. Rolling on loose rock and big ideas, for a moment I lose my sense of balance, glancing first at the sky above, then at the nearby peak of Mount St. Helens as if to stabilize myself. When we stop on the trail and gaze toward Spirit Lake, I try to make sense of things. There—blue water reflecting a bright sky. The bottom of that lake, the one I'm working to bring into focus in binoculars, now lies well above what was the ear-lier surface. The very idea sounds like an elementary problem in philosophy: if each constituent bit of an individual has changed, can it be said to be itself? I try to remember what I've heard about cell replacement in the human body, but that's no help. Yesterday's scraped skin is already healing; the cartilage in my knees will never regrow.

I've always thought of myself as a person of sedimentary landscapes. Sand-stone, limestone. Slow, slow, the accretions of dross, the bodies in sea-water, sand under waves. Erosional water clocks; time locked in rocks. From my child-hood in Appalachia: coal, the precipitate of rot, the metamorphosis of swamp to fire. There are magmatic intrusions into all this deep-time meditation—the granitic uplift of the Rockies and their alluvial spill back downstream into the wind-plied mat of prairie grass—but for most of my years, I've lived along varia-tions of horizontal accretion. And rock, we all know, is ancient stuff, the mineral evidence that our own soft selves are impermanent fluff like clouds in the atmo-sphere. When even carbon dating won't do—the ashes we leave at our campfires and kitchen hearths, the paint laid on cave walls or cliffs—we must turn to the longer-lived radiometric tick of the rocks.

"No vestige of a beginning," wrote James Hutton in *Theory of the Earth* (1788), considering stone and its witness of the great age of this earth; "no prospect of an end."

But this morning, on the mountain's northern flanks, I'm walking through fields first of lupine and then penstemon, broad swaths of purple atop a landscape gray with pumice and tephra, ash and dust. "Purple is the color of early seral stage succession," someone said yesterday, and now I see why it's so. (*Sere* in this context doesn't mean "dry," though I think the silvery leaves of the lupine can look like sage against the pebbly ground, and the wide vista, enlivened with ankle-high bloom, reminds me of the desert southwest. Here, *seral* means one-in-a-series, the way one plant community cedes the ground to the next.) I've been talking with biologists, botanists, geologists; the scientists outnumber the writers at the 2010 Mount St. Helens Field Pulse by more than ten-to-one, so I'm recalibrating my vocabulary, constantly at something of an intellectual jog, trying to keep up. While some of these scientists come to the mountain every summer for their field studies, this organized gathering takes place every five years. This year twelve writers were selected nationally to participate, through a program cosponsored by Oregon State University's Spring Creek Project for Ideas, Nature, and the Written Word; the Andrews Forest Long-Term Ecological Research Program, and the Pacific Northwest Research Station with funding from the U.S. Forest Service. We're here to reflect, but so far I've hardly been able to pause long enough to catch my breath and scrawl some notes. And I love every minute of it.

Photographs of the mountain before the 1980 eruption show old-growth forests, a land of thick duff and humus with a refractive brilliance of snow on the peak above. The alpine lake is like so many that I've slept and cooked by, or jumped into for the brief, shrieking shock of snowmelt-cold water. *Is* in the photographs, *was* on the ground. Some of the others camping here this month remember that earlier world: John, who cut logs for Weyerhaeuser decades ago; Christine, whose family cabin was shaded by the big trees; scientists who knew the pre-blast landscape and have returned throughout their careers.

From my Kansas home, I know some rhythms of ash and sprout. Some days in spring I touch flame to the standing senescence of tallgrass and watch fire encircle the flint-and-limestone hills—slow landswells of sediment—until the watershed sends up small cyclones of hot air and ash in a headfire with wind at its back. In the wake of the flame, bunch grass and bison dung smoke like tiny geysers. Finger-lengths of charred grass hang in the air. The first time I saw acres of burned-over prairie, I thought of destruction: the black of ashes and the pale rock outcrops like bones, an occasional charred snake still and crisp at my feet. But then, in less than a week, it all began to come back with verdant slivers of new grass just as Walt Whitman said, though he'd never seen it like this, the "uncut hair of graves."

Like photographs by Ansel Adams where the chemistry of black-and-white heightens his "patina of light on rock," the images taken immediately following the eruption are elemental: air and ash, sunlight and pumice. They also remind me of photographs of the Dust Bowl: the spill of ash like dust, half-burying behemoth logging trucks. The great flotation of blast-felled trees drift and shift across Spirit Lake's new surface, a forest transformed to lighter-than-water bones.

But the lake, for all its symbolic and suggestive beauty—sapphire in an asymmetrical setting, ill-shaped eye glaucomaed by those pale drifts of trees— is not what I'm working hardest to consider. What has me always on the verge of exclamation is the *youth* of the stone. Jeanne, our guide, points to a rounded lobe on the mountain's east rim—"The Sugar Bowl," she tells us. It's no more than eleven hundred years old. We can't see the lava domes within the volcano's crater yet, but the entire visible cone—the mountain along whose north flank we're crossing right now, tiny figures in the summer sun—was formed in the last twenty-five hundred years. When I look up, wondering if that's snow blowing from the crater's rim, or dust, or ash, or steam—dust, it turns out, from continuous rockfalls on the inner west rim that send up these signals of gravity's pull— I'm gazing at rock just a few hundred years old.

In the 1970s geologists mapped out the life of Mount St. Helens, a timeline that is utterly historic—contained within the urn of human events. After some four millennia of quiescence, the mountain entered five distinct periods of eruptive activity punctuated by no more than a few centuries of calm. Charcoal caught in the pyroclastic flows yielded specific carbon dating, pinning down each event of char and sear with real precision. I study the graph the geologists produced, a series of dots and dashes representing eruption or calm: it looks like Morse code on the page, spelling out messages.

All week the scientists have spoken of legacies—biological legacies from the as-if-miraculously protected refugia where life survived the scrape and scour of the volcano's blast: pocket gophers in the Pumice Plain whose subterranean burrows saved them from the searing 1,300-degree heat; isolated stands of trees near Meta Lake where the unexpected shelter of late-lying snow patches held vegetation in frozen stasis; fireweed and its resilient seed. Farther east, at Ghost Lake, we studied the topography's contours, imagining how—somehow—a particular curve in the hill, right there, across the water, sheltered a stand of conifers, though to see them we would have to stand shoulder-high in young willows and clamber over fallen trees four or five feet in girth. We could see the past mapped onto the landscape, the shapes of its stories draped over the earth.

One morning at breakfast there was much discussion of where the research will go in future years. Many of these men (they're mostly men) began their work here in 1980 as graduate students or junior faculty members, and they were now looking for younger scientists to whom they can bequeath their data to continue long-term studies in the next generation. Two in particular, Joe and Don, had been squiring around a younger scholar, Lisa. They study the effect of tephra falls on the surrounding old-growth forest's understory: the damage to moss and herbs, the flexibility with which the plants responded to their changed environment. First came the pummeling and heat of the eruption itself. Then, for years, they studied the varying depositional depth: a finger-width of ash here, a cement-like crust of snowmelt and tephra there. Talking about their research over burned camp coffee in the chilly morning, Joe appeared wren-like in his animation, while Don spoke with such understated calm that I could sometimes hardly hear him.

Language is a legacy, too, a data set that stretches back through generations, linking each breathing, speaking moment in the sunlit camp with—yes—millennia of shared thoughts, the communal embers culture kindles in the surrounding dark. And that legacy is what I have brought to the table, quite literally: with a notebook in hand bearing a few lines of a poem, a list of vocabulary I'm still trying to learn.

As the 2010 summer opened, volcanic eruptions in Iceland stilled European and some American air travel, reminding those of us who live at a distance from such places that ice and fire do meet and clash. I did a little reading about the rift valley where tectonic plates are moving apart at an infinitesimal rate of three millimeters per year—on one side Eurasia, on the other the Americas. In the basin of this slow divergence, the Icelandic transplants from Scandinavia gathered together to knit their social world. At what is now called the Þingvellir, Germanic-speaking people came for the Alþingi, the parliament for making laws and meting out justice. Twelve hundred years ago, people would step up on the Lögberg, the orator's rock. I wonder about vellir—in Old Norse völlir meant an untilled field or a plain, so I think of vale and valley, wold and wald. Along these lines of linguistic thought, the forest is a thing untilled. I think of Thing—it meant court or legal principle as well as object, a collection of concepts housed in both Old Frisian and Anglo-Saxon nouns.

This etymology seems to reach far back, through that intelligent window of Latin's tempus, to some Indo-European root where time and place converge.

It's an etymology I feel, somehow, tenderly close to. Haploid plus haploid, I am a partial sum of my parents' genetic bequest. Pale skin, the legacy of mostly Northern European forebears, obscures our family's Native American legacy—a bloodline that has lost contact with the cultures it once propelled. Mine is an uncertain inheritance—but isn't almost everyone's? I like to think about language and landscape, laid out across the planet's infinitesimally slow movement.

Mountains are the strongholds of wilderness, spikes of untamable terrain. To the east of Mount St. Helens, Mount Adams lifts its snow-covered dome, and between them these mountains suspend the green drape of the conifer canopy, the Gifford Pinchot National Forest and the Mount Adams Wilderness. I imagine a cornucopia of Germanic wild-words spilling across the rumpled topography, phonemes sliding and pooling around the rocks and in the draws: *weald, wald, wold, wilde.* All these words speak from somewhere in the past when the forests of Europe were not all felled. Amid thickets of etymology and the aging morphemes' mold and duff, Celtic *gwher* reaches even farther back to make connection with Latin's *ferus. Wild* and *fierce,* beyond the safety and civility of the city-state.

But *this* mountain is younger even than the presence of cities on the planet by as much as a thousand years.

Those cities, of course, were in another world—ancient Mesopotamia, a land of rivers and desert, birthplace of both agriculture and writing. Despite modernity's links to that ancient cradle, one of the first tongues of those cities, Sumerian, seems to have been an isolate, unrelated to Indo-European and Semitic languages. Unlike both of these families, Sumerian made no root distinction between nouns and verbs. *Dug,* the people would have said, meaning both speak and speech, with syntax or additional syllables indicating the sound's contextual role. If today we were in the company of Sumerians, hiking over the Pumice Plain or, to the east, the Plains of Abraham, they'd say *kur,* pointing toward the mountain. Two mountains? *Kur-kur,* repetition signaling the plural. Another tongue, called Harappan by archaeologists, remains only on inscribed fragments of pottery—illegible now along the banks of the Indus River. "Several respected experts have denied every possibility of deciphering the Indus script," writes Asko Parpola, the leading expert on ancient writing from the Indus Valley. "None of the crucial keys that have opened other unknown scripts is available.... Even the affinity of the Harappan language and the type of writing system represented by the Indus script are much debated." The Harappan script is extinct, a linguistic dead end.

Etymology's pathway takes one back beyond horizons into landscapes familiar or unknown. The Indo-European roots of English trace through the family tree something like five thousand years to pastoral people who spoke of axes and wheels and horses and crops—and, of course, mothers and fathers—with words that linguists have plotted out in illustrative tables. I think the work of comparative grammar, the painstaking comparisons of lexicon and phoneme, word-hoard and sound-scape, is a little like the lesson in plant surveying I saw this week beside Meta Lake.

Mark, the botanist, laid down a meter-square frame of white PVC pipe. "Let's bust out a micro," he said. (This means, it seems, to survey a microplot—one of several such the researchers examine, Mark explained.)

Pearly everlasting, *Anaphalis margaritacea*: 2 percent coverage. Woodland strawberry, *Fragaria vesca*: 2.5 percent coverage. Fireweed: .5 percent coverage. Quickly, the scientists estimated these proportions—plotting the plants against the totality of soil. Why, I wanted to ask, did they never switch into Latin for fireweed—*Epilobium angustifolium*? Maybe there's a special, filial fondness for fireweed—the first plant to be found punching its resilient, primrosey stems up through the scorched waste of tephra and ash. Maybe Mark just likes the sound of the name in isolation. I wondered whether the next step, back at the lab, might be population genetics, assessing the invisible-to-me diversity within each species counted in the researchers' string of beads. How many parent plants, or their seeds, made it through the blast? How many have been brought in this year, or last, by migrating birds?

But Mark broke off his explanation as he stepped closer to consult with his students about their rough estimates, and I didn't interrupt.

When we reach the end of the trail on the Pumice Plain, we're still hundreds of feet below Loowit Falls. I can't feel its spray; from here, I can no longer see the stretch marks and rock dust of the glacier itself. We're caught, now, in the continuous present.

It's lunchtime. From our backpacks we pull out sandwiches and fruit. Jeanne tells us about a climber who fell to his death in the crater last February. Simmons takes photographs of the falls, of Spirit Lake, of the group of us posed on the rocks. Jolie and Derek are talking about something that must be interesting, but for the moment I am not listening. I look over the erosional edge where Loowit Creek carves its way down—down through the blast debris, down to the horizontal sweep of the Pumice Plain.

When I look down, everything in sight is young enough to be my own child.

This is such a bizarre notion, I keep trying to catch hold of it for better examination. I pick up pebbles of pumice, cup my hands around them. I toss a rock the size of a volleyball into the air. Around us, stretching from what the map calls, remarkably, "The Breach" (where the mountain burst open with what must have been a terrifying roar) to as far as the southeast shore of Spirit Lake and the upper North Fork of the Toutle River, lies a generation of stone, six square miles of it. Coursing against bare rock and debris, the water plunges from the glacier above, where ice has circled the young lava domes in a collar of white, blue, and gray—a rough herringbone pattern I scan with binoculars, watching for movement. But there isn't any—only dust rising from those intermittent rockfalls. And since in fact I have no children, this moment of maternal metaphor-morphosis is doubly hypothetical: as if, if, if . . .

When rock takes on such an intimate, human scale, slipping free from the stern cloak of eons and ages, you have to pay attention, take note. Maybe this is no big deal for people who live in actively volcanic regions. Maybe it only seems especially significant to me because of my own meditative attention to time and to place, the way I've been trying to inscribe some understanding of my own brief existence onto the mental map of everywhere I've traveled recently. Maybe it's because so often I find the very idea of the near future almost mind-numbing with promised disappearance: landscapes likely will morph and torque in ways that even the assiduous work of climate change researchers can't fully envision— landscapes I love and others that I'll never glimpse. In the relative climatic calm, the bright temporal meadow that has been the Holocene—our geologic era, in which most of the cultural precursors that most deeply feed us were tilled—the familiar biomes became home to the world's peoples and languages.

My thoughts are clumping together. Landscape change, climate change. Biotic community, linguistic community. They are distinctly different things, I know, but I feel they're all converging on the open space beneath this mountain, here between the ash and spray of the waterfall and the rumpled hummocks— clumps of hills—where the breached volcano's load fetched up: Loowit.

The name on the map appears differently in a story told by an elderly Cowlitz tribal leader and collected in *Salish Myths and Legends: One People's Stories* (2008). *Lawelatla*, the storyteller calls the peak, instead of Loowit, and he says she is a wife of *Takhoma*, Mount Rainier. In his tale it's not a human person but that mythic figure, Coyote, who observes the mountain's eruption, and yet the power of the volcanic peak is utterly familiar. "Once in the long ago time Coyote was going up the Seqiku, the Toutle River, and he heard a great rumbling. He perked up his ear and realized that it was Lawelatla. She was very angry. Soon he heard another great rumbling coming from another direction, and he realized that it was Takhoma, who was also very angry. They were having a husband and wife argument, and he was in between them. Soon he saw Lawelatla blow her top and knock off the head of Takhoma."

A few years ago, on a trail above the tree line, I stood beside my brother as he pointed to the visible high peaks and told me their names in Salish. I remember them vaguely: *Pahtu* was Mount Adams. *Takhoma*, Mount Rainier. *Wyeast* was Mount Hood. If he mentioned Lawelatla or Loowit—Mount St. Helens, the exploding mountain—the syllables didn't catch hold in my memory. Then, I gazed breathless from beneath my backpack's weight at the landscape of enormous trees and sudden white peaks. Now, I wonder about the way language must have spread out across that enlivened topography, pooling into distinct dialects separated, like watersheds, by slopes or ridges. Around Mount St. Helens, two languages embraced the terrain: Cowlitz, a Salish tongue, and Yakama, a Sahaptin language related to Nez Perce. A person living along the Cowlitz River in previous centuries might have spoken both, and the stories of the landscape would reflect both land and language, teller and tale.

What about this place name, Loowit? While preparing for the Pulse, I found the tale that calls the mountain Lawelatla, not Loowit. I thought maybe Loowit was an Anglo-American corruption of the Salish, and launched into months of lexical obsession, interlibrary loan, and attempts to speak a smidgen of Salish and Yakama. I looked first at a dictionary including several dialects of the Salish language, Lushootseed. But the words for different sorts of mountain—hill, ridge, snow-covered peak—are nothing remotely like the fluid sounds of that exploding mountain, Loowit, and I could find no words for *erupt* or *explode*. For the Coeur d'Alene language, another Salish tongue from farther east, I found an introductory guide with words in simple sentences like *"Hui, tmiyiple'ent khwe'lish"* ("Please, describe the mountain") and *"Uuqwn khwa ni'syolalqw"* ("The forest is green"), but the accompanying cassette tape—recorded, said the label on the plastic case, in 1975—was torn in two. Now no one can listen for the pronunciation of these unfamiliar sound clusters spelled out in the text: *Eelish*, mountain. *E'l'lish*, hill.

So then I turned to Yakama. Like Salish, it's an agglutinating language, meaning that morphemes, little units of sound-as-meaning, are clumped together into longer words. Virginia Beavert, an elderly woman whose non-Anglo name is Tuxámshish, includes in her Sahaptin dictionary a verb, *láwilat*, meaning "to smoke or steam; to erupt." Reading farther, I learned that *-hlá* is something called an agentive suffix, implying personhood when it's attached as the last syllable to a place name. Loowit; Lawelatla.

But things get even better than that. Many words beginning with *lá-* are related to fire: *lámkw* is a verb (it smokes), *lámkwt* is the noun (smoke or steam). *Láp'ulp'ul* are hot ashes—you can see in the word the principle of repetition to make the plural. (Really, when would one see a single ash? Rarely, rarely, I think, and so *p'ulp'ul* would slip easily off the tongue.) And so these conjugations and inflections illuminate a grammar that isn't positional but rather phonemic—the tiny dental spit of a *t* seems to indicate noun-itude, while the curve of the lips into *w* hints at verbation. In a CD recording you can still hear Tuxámshish, the lexicographer herself, speaking: *"lapaashki lap'ulp'ul"*—literally, "are cooling off, the hot ashes." Then, *láwilaylak* (shine into)—she says that word, too, an easier mouthful of sound to imitate.

Of course, not all words beginning with *lá-* have to do with fire or smoke. What am I to make of *látk'i* (to look) or *látk'in* (to look at)? Do the eyes blaze with attention, I wonder, or is this some fluke of sound that signifies nothing? *Lux* (flame) and *luxlux* (shiny or gleaming)—I think these must carry the spark of an echo from *lá-*, but the typographical mirror they hold up to Latin's *lux* is nothing other than accident, and across this planet's great, capacious curve I am almost certainly the only soul—this very moment in summer—typing these musings and smiling at the coincidence.

Our second day here, three of us followed a doctoral student named Elise into the bright sunlight of the Pumice Plain. She monitors the nesting birds who've chosen this place to try to raise a brood or two. Elise is tiny—shorter than my five feet, four inches—but she walks with speed and stamina. And she was a terrific guide, preparing us each time for what we would see, pointing to each intimate, hidden point on the landscape where birds of the air are raising their still-flightless young.

In a low draw we tried to see the nest holding two nighthawk chicks, but it was nearly invisible, just a scrape in the grass and pumice stones. Nighthawks I know from prairie country, where they startle up from the fence lines when I ride past on my bicycle, their white wing patches like late-winter snow somehow shaded in the crooked angle of their flight. Like a killdeer, the mother flapped conspicuously (*Oh, I'm hurt, look here, look here*) while we tried to ignore her and find the stone-still chicks in the patchy shade cast by the willow. Elise said this is the first year they've found nesting nighthawks, and so far neither weasel nor raven has threatened the chicks. Another prairie bird whose eggs we saw my field guide calls "a pale bird of open ground"—the horned lark. I was constantly surprised to find these open-ground species where just thirty years ago an old-growth forest held its sheltering canopy high overhead. Elise keeps careful tally of each new arrival, recording the changes as they come. How long, I wondered, until the succession of plant life ceases to be open? When will alder and willow, paintbrush and penstemon, shrink in the shade of the trees' return? With her help we found willow flycatchers, hidden so well we had to hold a compact mirror above the nest and look at their reflection. Three days old, Elise said they were, and I looked at the fine line of down along their tiny spines, their two beak-heavy heads laid side by side facing in the same direction.

In the open sun the pebbles of pumice were laced with strawberry plants. Beside a wet seep we saw liverwort and moss. And Derek found a whole patch of tiny ripe berries, so we ate, looping ourselves, if only briefly, into the nutrient web. Later, Elise paused by Willow Springs to show us a clear bend of water in the stream that's otherwise cloudy with volcano sediment, and we all filled our bottles and drank. No filter necessary, said Elise. The water was that pure.

I've eaten thimbleberry, salmonberry, strawberry. I've drunk those cold waters from Willow Springs and marked the spot on my map. I've plunged into Ghost Lake, swum out from the shore and turned onto my back to stare up at the cloudless sky, then gazed toward the nearby slopes of fallen trees, each whitened trunk left where it slammed down in the eruption's shock wave. I've dangled a bright red empty stuff sack from a conifer's new growth, luring hummingbirds that look—with mounting frustration, I imagine—at the vivid, nectarless bloom. And I've put walnut-sized pumice chunks in my pocket, feeling dust rub against fabric with each step I take.

In the afternoon—cloudy this time, the sky like shades of granite—we hike the trail down from Windy Ridge to Spirit Lake to see the drifting rafts of trees that were the old-growth forest Christine remembers. From the ridge top they resemble jags of ice, windblown against the northeast shore. I can imagine them fusing together like the chunks of ice I walked across decades ago in Ohio, when the Hocking River froze over and the town shut down in cold and snow. But when I'm at the water's edge, they're unmistakable as separate forms, sticks slender as my arm floating among larger boles of whole trees.

I find small pieces of pumice and set them on the lake water. How long, I wonder, will each one float? There's almost no wind, but they drift and bob. And when I look out over the water, I see green springing from some of the rafting logs. Some seem to be saplings of conifers, others are alders or the ubiquitous willows; they're all rooted in the horizontal bedding of the blasted trunks. I can't help but think of Whitman again—"uttering joyous leaves of dark green." I remember an interesting snippet of data from yesterday's lecture: in this heart of the blast zone, 70 percent of the new willows are female—slender branches and resilient leaves. Each is the size of a campfire, burning green against the white trunk in today's gray light. Now it's Shakespeare who joins my thoughts: "Sing all a green willow. . . . Sing willow, willow, willow." I sit for more than an hour, listening to what isn't silence, gazing at color as subtle as skin.

I tell myself the story of the blast. There once was a wave three hundred feet high—as high as the tallest, oldest tree rooted beside the blue water. It felled the forest; the downed logs clotted, at first, like platelets forming a scab. When the first helicopters arrived, carrying researchers or rescuers—I'm not sure which— they couldn't even find the lake because ash had settled on the logs atop the water, so that everything looked the same: a dull crust only hours or days old created a facsimile desert on a poisoned lake. Only later did the water bleed through, the wind-drift logs rafting against one shore or another.

So how long until my pumice stones sink? The experiment will have to continue without me, dark settling on the lake while nobody watches, the stars afloat in the night sky. It's time to go.

Only as I'm leaving do I see the ashes.

The size of a campfire's footprint, I think—not a scatter at all. As if some-one had sat there, sinking down into a lap's width of ash. For it's obviously some-one, the bits and shards of bone visible among the finer dust. I've stumbled onto someone's memorial, somebody's open-air grave. Roses, six of them (white and yellow), weighted by a stone—not the ubiquitous pumice, I realize, but some-thing much older, denser, though I don't pick it up for closer inspection. And here is the other rock, a stool where someone sat down for a last moment to-gether. I sit down, too.

Na-nix. In the Bella Coola language, the same word means to mourn for somebody and to forget. Oh, willow, willow, willow. Think of the brevity inher-ent in speech. The full lungs empty out, the sounds flow through the air until the pattern's reverberations dissipate. And yet we're left too with the lithics of lan-guage, the phonemic chips and shards that generations of speakers leave behind in the living system that we call their mother tongue.

Genetically speaking, I'm a dead end. My brother, too, has made the deci-sion: he will not father children. Throughout these months in what I think of as the end of my own biologic summer, turning toward fall, I've been thinking—even when trying not to—of what it means to take oneself out of the gene pool, to forfeit, maybe, that as-if-lettered particularity in the material world's animate utterance.

Last year I scraped the inside of my cheek with a swab and sent it off for anal-ysis to see where my bloodline might have traveled in the long hike out of Africa. The story line delivered seemed far less specific than I would have liked. Some-time between twenty-five and sixteen thousand years ago, my mitochondrial haplogroup lived in the untilled plains and forests that stretched from the Black Sea to the Baltic—the heartland of the Indo-European languages, although the people themselves were there far longer, probably, than the bits of diction we can winnow from prehistory's litter. The brief discussion of my genetic history never mentioned the Americas or my indigenous ancestry.

Language and landscape: the dance with referentiality and abstraction, the thoughts we shape about ourselves and the shadows we cast briefly on the ground. I sometimes find it hard to imagine how old that dance must be, and how many voices must have lifted in song. Is it a line dance, maybe, and my role is now to fall back with the group, hands helping to clap out the rhythm while the head couple twirl once more and move along the line? Have I spun myself in an ecstatic solo, wind-dancing on some overlook above a reflective lake? Singing along all this time, humming when I don't know any of the words, have I been dancing with mountains, dancing with stone?

ANN PANCAKE

Creative Responses to Worlds Unraveling

The Artist in the 21st Century

In 2007 I published a political novel. I'd never intended to write it.

Until I was in my late thirties, I kept my political concerns segregated from my creative writing. Of course, they crept in anyway, but always indirectly and never deliberately. On the face of it, I was an apolitical fiction writer, and I stayed faithful to that segregation for a couple of reasons. For one, I'd accepted the conventional American literary wisdom that explicit politics can ruin literary art, especially fiction, a wisdom I saw confirmed again and again in many of the 1930s social realist novels I read for my dissertation research on class in American literature. But a second reason was more decisive: I simply didn't believe fiction could put a scratch in contemporary social and political problems. What good, I asked myself, was imaginative artistic work in the face of "real world" crises as urgent and overwhelming as the ones we've faced in the last several decades? What was the use of even trying?

So, I continued scrawling away on my short stories (because I'll lose my mind if I'm not writing fiction) while I shuttled my political concerns (because I can't live with myself if I'm idle there) into my academic research and writing, into teaching, into direct activism, and, in 2000, into helping my sister Catherine Pancake make a documentary film about mountaintop removal in our home state of West Virginia.

That's when I got in trouble.

It was July. Catherine and I were running around the southern West Virginia coalfields with a new digital camera, interviewing people suffering from the fallout from mountaintop removal mining, a catastrophic form of strip-mining that blasts up to five hundred feet off the tops of mountains to get at thin seams of coal. On this day, we were with a local woman named Judy Bonds who was working for a brand-new anti-mountaintop removal grassroots organization after she'd been fired from her Pizza Hut job for speaking out against the coal companies. She'd protested after she found her grandson standing in the creek in front of her house holding dead fish in his hands and asking her what had happened. Judy was taking us up a hollow called Seng Creek to meet a family who had recently had severe flash floods caused by a mine directly above their house.

This family, whom I'll call the Reeds, had four children. They showed us the flood damage to their trailer and to their yard, and the oldest son, fourteen years old, told us about being knocked out of his bed by a mine blast. They all talked about how frightened they were that on the mountain behind their house was a slurry impoundment—a large lake that holds wastewater from processing coal—that might crash down on them as a wall of toxic water in the next big rain.

That evening, I found myself in the back of a pickup with three of the Reed children and a couple of cousins, my sister in front with Mr. Reed, bucking up a rough road along a ruined creek toward the mine. As we climbed higher, passing trees that had slid down the sides of the ripped-up hollow, there were bulldozed mounds blocking the road in places, and pools in the creek glittering a metallic green. These tough little barefoot kids told me how proud they were of their daddy's driving and how scared they were of the floods; how they lay in their beds terrified of what might come down off that mine; how they were bound and determined to someday scale the mountain and see what was really up there.

We came to a halt at the foot of a pile of soil and rocks and dead trees, as tall as an eight-story building, which had been dumped over the side of the mountain as the company blew it up in pieces. The kids piled out to scramble over boulders, their agile bodies a surreal anomaly in all desolation. The ten-year-old, Dustin, turned to say to me what the West Virginia Department of Environmental Protection, the governor's office, and even the White House refused to admit: "This is dangerous," Dustin looked in my eyes as he told me. "This is dangerous."

I left Seng Creek altered. The next morning I tried to scribble down as fast as I could all that had happened because I thought it would make a good journalistic piece. At that point, I still didn't believe that fiction would do proper justice to a subject like this one; I even feared the situation might be trivialized by putting it in a fictional form, but then something new happened.

About two weeks after I went up Seng Creek, I heard in my head the voice of a fictional fourteen-year-old who lived under that mountaintop mine. I wrote down about five pages of what he said. I figured it was a short story, but a few days later, the voice of another kid in that family came, and a little while after that, a third voice. About this time, I realized that what I was writing wasn't a short story, but a novel—which I'd never written before, never thought I'd ever write, because I was so bad at plotting. Worse, this was a novel that tackled head-on a complicated and controversial political issue. Both of these realizations scared the writer in me nearly to death.

———

As soon as I let on I was writing a novel about mountaintop removal, my own reservations about political novels were mirrored back. People would ask me why I wasn't writing nonfiction, and by nonfiction they meant the journalistic variety, not creative nonfiction. Some activists seemed put out, as though I were wasting my time. Some writers seemed suspicious, as though I were betraying art. The same question—"Why didn't you make the book nonfiction?"—continues to be one of the most common I get in interviews and during question-and-answer sessions.

I well know there are excellent reasons to be cautious when approaching explicitly political material as a literary artist, and especially as a writer of literary fiction. Nonfiction can directly reflect on ideas, present information, and even advocate for a "side" without violating the promise the genre makes to the reader. Fiction is another story. Treating politics in fiction is hard to carry off without violating the novel or short story's "vivid continuous dream"—John Gardner's term for the spell the best novels cast, a spell too often broken by overtly political works. Of course, fiction can take some liberties—we do have novels of ideas, though they are less popular today than in the past, and there are postmodern experiments that deliberately flout that "vivid continuous dream." But generally speaking, in realist fiction a mere whiff of the didactic or polemic, any glimpse of the work's creator stepping in and directing the reader about how to think or feel, can shatter the world the writer has so painstakingly constructed and unravel the reader's suspension of disbelief.

This is true also of much poetry and certain kinds of creative nonfiction. Integrating into any literary genre the facts, information, and context a political subject often requires is very difficult without undermining the art, and making the job even harder is the reality that contemporary American audiences are less familiar with encountering politics in literature than are audiences in other countries. I can also tell you from personal experience that writing political fiction doesn't make you very popular with commercial publishers. It's no mystery why American fiction writers today are actively discouraged from pulling advocacy politics into their work—except for identity politics, which are a natural match for character-driven fiction and many times aren't recognized as politics. Certainly political literature presents myriad challenges to the writer, and I know there are places in my own novel where I stumbled into exactly the traps I'm pointing out here. But is the fact that such work is challenging a reason to avoid it altogether?

For me, this question became moot when Appalachia—the place where I grew up and where my family goes back seven generations, the place that gives me my stories and language—was being blown up, physically and culturally. The devastation of my place is bald, unambiguous, and impossible to explain away as "natural" or temporary or repairable. It was easy for me to be radicalized. But the truth is, this kind of runaway loss—usually in more subtle and insidious forms—is happening everywhere right now, on the level of the environment, of economics, and of human rights, to name just a few. As artists witness this accelerated unraveling, more and more of them are compelled to treat politics in their art, many for the first time. I know this from my writer and visual artist friends and collaborators, and I know it from my students. As we artists turn more towards these issues, we face hard questions before we even get to how one balances aesthetics and advocacy, the most daunting question perhaps being the one I mentioned at the beginning of this essay: why make art at all? Isn't documentation, the presentation of facts, a more efficient and effective tactic for a writer in crises like these? And isn't direct activism most efficient and effective of all?

After a number of years now of hearing reader responses to my *Strange As This Weather Has Been*, I've finally made peace with my guilt and anxiety about channeling my activist energies into literature. I've at last come to accept that cliché we're told when we're young: you have to trust that your greatest gift is how you are meant to contribute to this life, regardless of what that gift is. As a fiction writer, I will probably reach a smaller audience than a journalist, a scientist, a charismatic public speaker, or a grassroots organizer, but fiction writing is what I do best. I've learned I need to have faith not only in that, but also faith that the journalism, science, speaking, and organizing will be carried out by individuals with those gifts. And once I surrendered to the notion that making literature was what I needed to do, something interesting happened: I started to perceive the unique abilities literature, including fiction, has to educate, move, and transform audiences that are possessed by no other medium, including reportage and documentary.

For example, I believe literature is one of the most powerful antidotes we have to "psychic numbing." It's not easy to actually feel, with our hearts, with our guts, overwhelming abstract problems that don't directly affect us, especially now, with so many catastrophes unfolding around us, and it's tough to sustain compassion for the nameless souls struggling with those catastrophes. But we do have great capacity to empathize with the personal stories of individuals. I once heard Wendell Berry point out that "public suffering means nothing if it isn't understood as compounded of an almost infinite private suffering," and he went on to illustrate this with a quote from André Gide's World War II journals: "thousands of sufferings make a plateau. It's like that bed of nails you can lie down on. But one death, one instance of suffering, one Lear, one Hamlet, is the point of sorrow."[1]

Fiction, creative nonfiction, and poetry do exactly that: they immerse the reader in the personal stories of individual people. In our Information Age, when we can get thousands of facts and sound bites about any subject—and in this way build a bed of nails—literature is one of the few arenas where an individual can actually "live the life" of a person who is a subject of injustice. The reader of a novel or a book-length work of creative nonfiction, for instance, spends hours upon hours vicariously living the lives of other human beings, and such an experience can generate great compassion in the reader. Not even imaginative documentary offers this kind of opportunity for a sustained relationship between audience and subject, both because an audience spends less time with a documentary and because, I would argue, viewing a film requires less effort from its audience than reading literature does. That effort means the reader engages more actively with the art, ultimately arriving at a more intimate and manifold appreciation of the issue the art addresses.

Of course, journalism and documentary, too, present individual stories. But those genres are restricted to the *exterior* worlds of the people interviewed. Novelist Don DeLillo has remarked that one distinction between the fiction writer and the journalist is that the fiction writer can show "the impact of history on interior lives."[2] Creative writing—imaginative writing—gives a writer tremendous freedom to explore and portray the interior terrain of a range of people. My novel, for example, is narrated from six perspectives, so I was able to submerge my readers in the immediate sensual fears, losses, secrets, desires, and loves of characters running the gamut: from a ten-year-old boy obsessed with machines, to a teenaged girl forced to choose between attachment to land and a viable future, to a disabled miner struggling to reconcile his gut knowledge that the mountains are sacred with the dogmatism of a narrow Christianity. If the writer can evoke these interior lives with complexity and compassion, the reader's understanding of social injustice and environmental disaster is dramatically broadened and deepened. Personal stories in literature can wake up and stimulate sleeping and numbed imaginations, reshaping how readers perceive reality and leading them to understand, in a deep organic way, why particular power inequities must be changed.

Also significant when we think about the power of literature for advocacy is that fiction, poetry, and the literary essay can have a much longer shelf life than information or reportage. Literature radiates far beyond a specific time, place, and issue because art embodies truths that are not literal, that are not time- and place-bound. Thus we still read *Grapes of Wrath* when we don't read 1930s newspaper articles about the Dust Bowl, not even those written by Steinbeck. Walter Benjamin, in his essay "The Storyteller," puts it beautifully:

The value of information does not survive the moment in which it was new. It lives only at that moment; it has to surrender to it completely and explain itself to it without losing any time. A story is different. It does not expend itself. It preserves and concentrates its strength and is capable of releasing it even after a long time. . . . It resembles the seeds of grain which have lain for centuries in the chambers of the pyramids shut up air-tight and have retained their germinative power to this day.[3]

Finally, it's essential for us to remember that the transformative properties of literature are not limited to its content. Literature's form, too—its style, structure, figures of speech, tone, mood, formal originality, and experimentation—evoke in readers fresh and profound understandings. Form can be political when it moves an audience to question what seems given. Form can shake up dead paradigms and jolt us into envisioning alternatives. Art's beauty can make an audience yearn for a different kind of reality. And beauty can also simply help heal. As Phil Ochs put it several decades ago, "In such an ugly time, the true protest is beauty."[4]

As I was writing my novel, I didn't give much thought to all those particulars. I wrote it with the conscious aim of just trying to show the truth about the devastation of a place I loved and with the hope of generating compassion for the living beings suffering because of this devastation. If people understood better, I thought, they would help make change. I didn't hold lofty expectations because I knew how limited the audience for literary fiction is, especially literary fiction about Appalachia, but I was compelled to make my own small contribution.

When I started my book in 2000, almost no one outside the coalfields—except hardcore environmentalists—had heard of mountaintop removal. In the thirteen years that have passed since then, the number of people who understand mountaintop removal and are advocating against it has increased beyond anything I'd ever imagined, through the efforts of thousands of residents, activists, scientists, artists, and even a few politicians. Reams of newspaper and magazine articles have been written on the subject, and dozens of documentary films have been made, and several laws and regulations intended to limit mountaintop removal have been proposed, although only a couple have passed.

This takes me back to my story about Seng Creek, the Reed kids, and Judy Bonds, the former Pizza Hut waitress who introduced us to the Reeds. I live in Seattle now, but I try to get back to southern West Virginia at least once a year. In 2008 I was having lunch with some elderly friends of mine there when one, Mary Miller, asked, "How long has it been since you've been up Seng Creek?"

Even though my entire novel was set in an imagined landscape based on that hollow where the Reeds lived, I hadn't actually driven back up in there since 2000, and I told my friend that.

"Well, we got to get you up there," Mary said.

We got up there, or at least as far as we could go. In the years since I'd last seen Seng Creek, the upper part of the hollow had been washed out by a flash flood, just as the Reeds had said it would be. After that, the company had swept in and bought and torn down all the homes. The topography was now altered beyond recognition by fill dirt and giant culverts and non-native grass and two drift mouths for underground mines, and by a sediment pond where the church used to be. Bulldozers worked the steep slopes above our car. I asked where the people we'd interviewed had gone. My friend said the elderly woman I'd based one character on had moved into Charleston with her daughter. And the Reeds? Nobody knew. Finally Mary said, "We got to get out of here before a rock falls on us."

In 2010, two years after that drive up Seng Creek, I got some news about Judy Bonds. In the time since then, she'd won one of the most prestigious awards in the world for environmental activism, the international Goldman Prize, and she'd become known as "the godmother of the anti–mountaintop removal movement." I spent a lot of time with Judy in the early years of the century, and she is one of several women I drew on for the main character Lace in my novel. The news I got was that Judy had been diagnosed with brain cancer. By January of 2011, she was dead at age fifty-eight. Water tests of the creek outside her house— the creek where her grandson held the dead fish—show that it contains poly-acrylamide, a cancer-causing agent used for coal processing.

So, I have witnessed the landscape where my work is set and the people who inspired my characters continue to be destroyed by an injustice my creative work tried to address. And these are just representative episodes in the larger context of the expansion of mountaintop removal in the last decade—at least five hundred mountains blown up, possibly two thousand miles of streams filled with toxic rubble, countless people dead from poisoned air and water. This escalation has continued despite drastically expanded public awareness of mountaintop removal and its fallout, despite great public outcry against it. And just as what happened to Seng Creek and to Judy are only two examples of the larger conflagration in central Appalachia, the Appalachian crisis is just one instance in a larger global context crackling with intensifying life-threatening crises, from global warming to mass extinction to the breakdown of economic systems—all of these documented endlessly, ad nauseam, by the press and others.

Many of us have certainly felt despair about all this, especially about our inefficacy to effect change. I've felt cynicism, at other times apathy; I've felt the impulse to isolate myself, insulate myself. I've wallowed in these states. I've ranted. I've struggled with guilt over my paralysis. Until, finally, this insight broke up that paralysis:

Periods of disintegration most often contain within them profound possibilities for creation, so an era like this one, precisely because of the scale and scope of its dissolution, offers tremendous opportunities for sweeping systemic change. I know we still need truth-telling art. But given our circumstances, I believe we artists must open ourselves wider to how art performs politically *beyond* bearing witness, because I've concluded that the only solution to our current mess is a radical transformation of how people think and perceive and value. In other words, we must have a revolutionizing of people's interiors. And such revolutionizing is exactly what art can do better than anything else at our disposal, aside from spirituality and certain kinds of direct experience which are not as easily available as art.

Take, for instance, literature's power to exercise, develop, and revitalize the imagination, the imaginations of both readers and writers. In our culture imagination is impoverished and misdirected at a time when we desperately need new vision and ideas. The literary arts, especially fiction, make more extensive and sustained demands on a reader's imagination than perhaps any other form of media. Admittedly, the imaginative effort a person must make to read literature means some won't bother to engage with it at all. However, those who are willing to participate can come through the interaction deeply imprinted precisely because they had to engage their imaginations so energetically. And that exercising of the imagination can help readers and writers imagine better in other parts of their lives.

Pushing a little deeper into the relationship between literature and the imagination, I want to point out, too, the way literature—both the reading of it and the writing of it—can reunite an individual's conscious and unconscious. I can't emphasize how imperative I think this reunion is. I would argue that many of our contemporary ills are caused or exacerbated by our culture's rending the conscious from the unconscious, then elevating the conscious—the intellect, rationality—to the complete neglect, if not outright derision, of the unconscious. This is disastrous not only because such psychic amputation cripples people, contributing to feelings of emptiness, insatiability, depression, and anxiety, but also because within that castoff unconscious—in intuition, in dreams—dwell ideas, solutions, and utterly fresh ways of perceiving and understanding that we need urgently in an era of unraveling and transition. I, like all writers, know the power of the unconscious because it's where I've gone for decades for my fiction writing. I know how boundless that realm is, how explosive with energy and light; I know my unconscious is eons ahead of my intellect, worlds larger in vision than my rational mind. This is exactly where we'll find the materials and the fuel for that transformation of psyche I'm talking about. And our very business as artists is trafficking between the conscious and the unconscious; indeed, we are one of the very last groups in this culture who have a sanctioned day-to-day relationship with our unconscious, with our dreams and intuition.

Now I'll crawl even farther out on my limb and, refining this notion of artists' reintegration of the conscious and the unconscious, I'll propose that artists are also translators between the visible and invisible worlds, intermediaries between the profane and the sacred. How is this pertinent to the case I'm making for art's ability to create change in the world? Only by desacralizing the world, over centuries, have we given ourselves permission to destroy it. Conversely, to protect and preserve life we must re-recognize its sacredness, and art helps us do that. Literature re-sacralizes by illuminating the profound within the apparently mundane, by restoring reverence and wonder for the everyday, and by heightening our attentiveness and enlarging our compassion. The magic and transcendence and mystery that characterize true literary art make a piece of literature a microcosm of the wider universe, of the mystery and profundity and transcendence that reside there for those willing to look for it.

Talk of the holy may be off-putting for some, so let's just boil it down to love. Jack Turner, in *The Abstract Wild*,[5] insists that only genuine love of our environment will incite us to save it, and, further, that aside from direct experience, only art can make us fall in love with the world. "Mere concepts and abstractions," like those in science and public policy, "will not do, because love is beyond concepts and abstractions. And yet the problem is one of love." And for those of us who still feel periodically ashamed about not taking more direct action, Turner has this: "We can all drive a spike into a tree, but few can produce visionary fiction or memoirs that transform our beliefs and extend the possibilities of what we might come to love."

Writing these words in 2013, I'm aware of how my confidence that literature matters in the ways I've discussed seems fantastic and romantic. Literature's audience is too small, readers' attention spans are too attenuated, competing media and technologies are too distracting and seductive—I still drift into this skepticism. But I also know that throughout human history the mythmakers, the culture-creators, those who dream forward for their communities, have been the artists. Yes, contemporary culture has trivialized, ghettoized, and marginalized us whenever it hasn't been able to commercialize us, and I fear many of us have internalized this sense of irrelevancy. What I'm suggesting now is that we take ourselves more seriously and make ourselves more relevant.

I believe literature's most pressing political task of all in these times is envisioning alternative future realities. My biggest disappointment with my own political novel is not the missteps where I strayed into polemic or awkwardly integrated information. My biggest disappointment is that my novel does not provide vision beyond the contemporary situation in central Appalachia. I have learned that it's much easier to represent a political situation in literature than it is to propose alternatives—to dream forward—without lapsing into Pollyannaism or cynicism. But I've come to believe that the greatest challenge for many twenty-first-century artists is to create literature that imagines a way forward which is not based in idealism or fantasy, which does not offer dystopia or utopia, but still turns current paradigms on their heads. I now feel charged to make stories that invent more than represent, that dream more than reflect. This is not to say that I have more than glimmers of what such fiction will be, but I carry a burning urgency that it must be done.

NOTES

1. From Berry's talk at the Society of Environmental Journalists' annual conference in Roanoke, Va., 19 October 2008.

2. From Melissa Block's interview with DeLillo, "*Falling Man* Maps Emotional Aftermath of September 11," *All Things Considered*, NPR, 20 June 2007.

3. From Benjamin's *Illuminations*. New York: Schocken Books, 1968.

4. From the liner notes of Ochs's album *Pleasures of the Harbor*, A&M Records, 1967.

5. Tucson: The University of Arizona Press, 1996.

JULIE RIDDLE

Shadow Animals

> In the oldest part of our minds, a thick
> forest stands, inhabited by talking beasts,
> changelings, wild people, and lost children; by
> nightmares, reveries, and profound silences;
> by tricks of shadow and light; by everything
> we once were and never will be again.
>
> —SHERRY SIMPSON, *The Way Winter Comes*

I.

On any afternoon in Stein's grocery store parking lot in Troy, Montana, a truck—American made, four-wheel drive, dented and dirt-streaked, axles riding high—will pull in and park. A young sawyer will jump from the cab. His beard is trimmed neatly or his face is clean shaven; he wears thick-soled leather boots, loose jeans hemmed above the ankles, orange suspenders, and a T-shirt screen-printed on the front with a bull elk in mid-bugle, and on the back with "Got elk?" in large, white letters. (Elk T-shirts are for sale at the Booze N' Bait just up the road. Black bear, mule deer, and moose shirts, too.)

Inside the store, a herd of animals awaits, preserved and mounted above the produce section—spoils from the hunt displayed in the one Troy business that enjoys steady customers. Shoppers peruse heads of lettuce beneath an elk's looming antlers. Mule deer peer down their snouts at human hands squeezing tomatoes and rifling green beans for choice pods. A bighorn sheep, chin-raised and regal, surveys pyramids of apples and oranges. A claw-foot bathtub could nestle comfortably in the moose's dusty rack. Over the years the exhibit has swelled with donations from hunters eager to show off their trophies to the grocery-shopping public. A brass plate engraved with a name and date is tacked to the base of some mounts. Others include a faded snapshot of a hunter grasping the rack of his kill, raising the animal's slack face to the camera moments after the wild thing went down.

Out-of-towners stepping through Stein's automatic doors startle at the parade of dead animals overhead; locals don't bother to look up. During hunting season the rear window of nearly every truck in Lincoln County sports a gun rack bearing at least one rifle. A drive through town during late-autumn twilight will likely include passing three or four men gathered around a truck parked on the side of the road. The men's flannelled arms rest on the truck-bed's rim, and their hungry eyes gaze at antlers jutting from a laid-out carcass. Another man, standing apart, leans against the truck's door, ankles crossed, thumbs slung through belt loops, his mouth weaving the slow spell of story.

A teenage boy will hunt in the misty morning before school and in the brief light after the day's final bell. A high-school date could mean holding hands at the Dome Movie Theater on a Saturday night, or the date could have taken place earlier that afternoon in a truck cab, a girl pressed beside a boy, her legs tucked on each side of the stick shift, the boy's fist knocking her inner thigh as he shoves the stick down, the truck shuddering up steep inclines and easing along rutted logging roads. The couple makes small talk as they scan the woods for a brown rump and flash of white warning tail; a loaded rifle is racked and ready, the warm cab crackling with anticipation of sex and the kill and country music overwhelmed by static on the am radio.

II.

My father spent the summer of 1977 cutting down trees. He was clearing land to build the log house my mother had sketched on graph paper. I was seven years old, and all day until dusk a chainsaw's drone buzzed in my brain and vibrated my bones. My parents had just sold their ownership of a hardware store to pursue my father's frontier dream. We had moved from the city of Butte, Montana, onto twenty-one tree-tangled acres near Troy, a speck of a town in the northwest corner of the state. *Big Sky Country. The Last, Best Place.* My father was finally living the life he had longed for.

My mother had longed to be a wife. She grew up in a time and place when girls were raised to be wives and wives wanted what their husbands wanted. This isn't sacrifice; it's what wives do.

One evening in July, instead of returning to work after dinner, Dad hoisted on his shoulder a large sack he had brought home in a truckload of building supplies. He grabbed a rake leaning against the camp trailer, our temporary home, and handed it to Mom. "Let's go for a walk," he said. Mom, my eight-year-old brother Justin, and I followed him to a faint trail that ran up the hillside behind the camper. Ferns, tall grass, wild daisies, and saplings pricked my bare calves as our single-file footsteps broke a fresh path. At the top of the hill, the trail met an abandoned horse-logging road. Dad turned right and walked until the weeds gave way to a flat stretch of sunbaked clay. He eased the sack from his shoulder, slit it open with his pocketknife, and tipped it. Grains of sand shimmered and formed a pearl-colored pool. Dad drew the rake across the sand, smoothing it into soft furrows—a perfect spot, I thought, for the fairies that lived in the forest. I hadn't seen the fairies yet, but I had seen their slippers that grew in shaded pockets. The elaborate flowers poked from moist duff, delicate and pale purple, half as long as my pinkie finger—just the size for fairy feet. The fairies could use this new ground for their garden, and I would sneak close and spy, as they tended the seeds they had planted, to see the magical, miniature world they would grow.

My father bent on one knee and appraised the sand, then swiveled and studied the length of road that faded into a thicket of woods. He looked hard into the trees, as though discerning a distinct shape emerging from deep shadow. A squirrel nearby scrabbled pine bark and hurled chirped warnings.

"What's the sand for?" Justin asked.

Dad turned and looked up at us. "Animals use this old road as a game trail," he said. "When they pass through here, they'll walk across the sand and we'll be able to see the shape of their footprints and tell what wildlife is in the area, get an idea of how many there are."

"What kind of animals?" I asked.

"Deer, moose, bear. We might see elk if we have a tough winter and they come down from the mountains looking for food."

Deer, moose, bear, elk. Father, mother, son, daughter. We lived where animals lived. We walked where they walked and stood where they stood. I knelt beside Dad and reached out my hand. The sand was warm and fine. I had never seen a deer's hoofprints before. I had never seen a live deer. Did the animals know we were here? Were they watching us right now? I peered into the trees for eyes, bigger than my own, peering back at me from stilled, camouflaged bodies. The thought of animals brushing near, crossing paths with us, made me shiver.

That night, after we climbed into our sleeping bags and Dad extinguished the propane lantern, I listened for telltale sounds drifting from the encroaching woods. There was only the crest and drop of my father's deep, fatigued breaths, the rise and fall of my chest at last slowing to meet his. After I joined him in sleep, a small band of shadow-animals crept from the forest's edge and paused in the darkness of my dreams with ears cocked and nostrils quivering. They moved on with careful steps like measured stitches along the moonlit path spooling through my imagination.

In the morning Justin and I fidgeted through our bowls of cereal, then raced up the hill to the sand. Animals! When Dad caught up with us he identified the curved Vs of deer hooves—big and small, mother and fawn. We looked closer. Were those bear prints? Relief outweighed my disappointment when Dad said the indentation of pads and claws belonged to our curious dog.

Evidence of animals began to appear everywhere. To-and-fro tracks across the sand, piles of poop Dad called "sign" on the logging road. I guessed a mound of brown pellets had been left by a rabbit, but Dad said no, a deer. The sign was shiny and dark, proof that a doe had passed through a short while before. With August came the splat of seed-speckled bear sign, the aftermath of hours spent foraging for berries. I would quicken my step and stick close to Dad.

As my family cleared brush or hauled firewood, my father pointed out hollows of flattened grass where deer had slept shielded beneath branches, and trunks where bucks had scraped the late-summer velvet from their antlers. He fingered coarse brown hairs clinging to bark where bears had rubbed their bodies, and traced gashed aspen where they had swiped their claws; he boot-scuffed the belly of a fallen log, spongy with rot, which had been rolled from its earth-nestled trough by a hungry bear hunting for grubs.

So many mysteries, so many clues, so much to discover, interpret, guess, and wonder.

III.

In October my family moved from the camp trailer into our just-dried concrete basement, where we would live for the next three years. At its center was a double-barrel stove my father had welded from steel drums. Justin and I slept again in the bunk bed my parents had pulled from storage and set up near the stove that Dad stoked each night with hunks of split larch as long as his arm. Lying on the top bunk, I could reach and just touch the foil-coated insulation tucked between the joists overhead. At bedtime, in a bulb's dim light, I studied growing fingers of dark red wet that had begun to seep across the silver foil and stain the clean wood joists. Each night the scents of raw earth, fresh wood, and a strange new odor mingled and hovered above me as my parents' murmurs and the snap of flames and falling embers soothed me to a disturbed sleep.

Outside, frost feathered the basement's slim windows, and sharp stars needled hard but could not pierce the canopy of trees surrounding our underground home. Their low-swooping branches harbored the shadow-animals that had bedded down for the night: sleek bodies curled tight, breathing shallow, and braced for danger.

IV.

My once-peaceful sleep had fallen prey to nightmares when my family lived in Butte, where my parents had co-owned Plaza OK Hardware from 1973 to 1977. Butte, in southwest Montana, boasted the Berkeley Pit, the largest open-pit copper mine in the country. The record of Butte's storied past as a mining boomtown shows the industry was still going strong in the 1970s. Our hardware store did a brisk business. All day long my father helped customers select just the right lawn mower, power drill, chainsaw, or ladder. He ordered merchandise, stocked shelves, and scanned for shoplifters from the smoky-windowed office overlooking the store. He worked seven days a week with a day-and-a-half off every other weekend. He was gone when Justin and I woke in the morning and returned home as we slept. Mom helped out at the store, alternating three days one week, two days the next. She balanced the books, placed ads, clerked, cleaned toilets. My brother and I attended daycare when she had to work, our caregivers changing a few times during those years, based on their availability and whether Justin and I were in school.

After Mom dropped us at the daycare we attended when Justin was six and I was five, a shadow fell when a man would appear and kneel beside me. The man— the husband of the lady who ran the daycare—would smile and praise my pretty blonde hair, finger the hem of my dress. "Is it new? What's your dolly's name?" The first time I asked the lady permission to use the bathroom, she nodded at her husband. He took hold of my hand and led me to a door at the end of a long hall. But instead of releasing me and retreating he came in, too—he came in that first time, and from then on—the door clicking closed behind him. On the other side of that shut door and back down that long hall, just off the entryway, was the room where we ate snacks while seated in small plastic chairs backed in a line against the walls. A picture window overlooked the spare front yard where girls and boys swarmed a swing set and slide, the glass muting the clamor of high-pitched voices, my brother's somewhere among them.

The yard was rimmed by a chain-link fence with a latched metal gate that swung open smoothly when my mother brushed through to collect us, buckle us in the back seat of our car, deliver us home to dinner and play, then tuck us into bed, where Justin and I made steeples with our hands and closed our eyes while reciting with her the prayer she had taught us: *I believe in God above, I believe in Jesus' love, I believe that I must be, kind and gentle, Lord, like thee. Amen.* We felt her soft kiss on our foreheads, and then the room went black, and later a slash of light cut the black when Dad looked in after returning home from work.

When the man's hands would at last release me and he reached for the bathroom doorknob, his boots would pause and turn, and he would say that he'd kill my brother if I told. I didn't tell. The unspeakable words hooked my innards like barbs, wormed deep and began slicing, slowly, skinward. My body became a fluent interpreter of memories my mind refused to raise. Once, at the home of one of my mother's friends, I wet my pants while sitting on her sofa. I was five years old—old enough to know better—but the promise of shame, my mother's embarrassment, and my brother's finger-pointing ridicule could not trump my newfound fear of using a stranger's bathroom. I began sleepwalking—staring vacantly at my parents as they watched late-night TV, stacking bars of soap in the bathroom. Once, I split my toe open on a metal stake as my father and brother slept in a living-room-pitched tent.

Moving to the woods disrupted these nightly prowls; I realize now that the camp trailer and then the basement cramped with our belongings penned my restless body. The stifled terror began to manifest in my mind. Many nights, in that camper, that basement, I lay in bed with my eyes locked open, limbs rigid and numbed by heart-slamming fantasies playing in my unblinking brain. In some scenes I was the pinned recipient, in others the grinning inflictor. At last I would sleep, then wake in the morning wrapped in a residue of fear: fear of the sadistic movies trapped in my head, fear of an invading second self that somehow conjured cruel worlds and delighted in pain, a predator self that stalked me through childhood, clawed my heels, and whiskered the nape of my neck, its panting breath searing my tense skin, urging me into a suppressed, desperate drive to escape that other frightening, frightened self.

V.

By the fifth grade I carried a clear understanding that certain wild animals were to be admired, respected, and—from late October through sundown the Sunday after Thanksgiving—shot. The antlers my father displayed in our log house rivaled the grocery story's exhibit. On our living-room walls hung the select remains of mule deer, white-tailed deer, antelope, and elk. Small, smooth prongs protruded from bits of leather-capped skull. Furred heads bore generous, nubby racks. Animals marched down the center loft-support beam and surrounded crisscrossed snowshoes tacked high on the room's west wall. In the evenings we read *Reader's Digest* or played checkers or visited with company beneath the blank gaze of glass eyes shining in the lamplight.

Dad's collection grew to include the snowy pelt of a mountain goat, a black bear paralyzed in mid-charge, a badger with bared fangs and grasping claws, and a javelina head. (The javelina's beady-eyed glare first greeted me one morning when I had stayed home sick from school and padded downstairs in search of cough drops. The head sat in a box my father had left on the loft steps. Of all the creatures in our home, our dog was the only one that jumped at my sore-throated shriek.) Dad also displayed Justin's deer and elk antlers, after he began hunting at age twelve. The less impressive antlers from their hunts Dad nailed to an exterior wall of the garage.

VI.

Daniel Owens hunted and fished, and he bashed bodies on the Troy Trojans football field, just like his older brothers. The Owens boys wore Wrangler jeans, leather belts with large silver buckles, and cowboy hats. Their boot heels scuffed our high school's waxed hallways. But unlike his boisterous brothers, who drove big trucks and pursued girls in sport, Daniel was quiet and shy, keeping company with a small group of upperclassmen, fellow football players who had taken him under their wing.

Daniel's sophomore year, his friends goaded him into asking Janie Miller to prom. She was taller and one year older. A photographer shot the couple as they posed in front of a construction-paper moon and tinfoil stars, their awkward embrace arranged just so; Janie with her salon-styled ringlets and blue satin dress, Daniel with his ruddy, freckled cheeks and the black tuxedo he had rented from a catalog at Kootenai Drug.

The spring of Daniel's junior year, he died in his bedroom from a gunshot to the head. The police ruled his death a suicide, but my stunned friends said it had to have been a terrible accident. This was Daniel, soft-spoken and kind, the aw-shucks guy with gentle brown eyes and a constant half-smile that made him look as though he had just noticed a telling detail the rest of us had missed.

VII.

The locals in northwest Montana betrayed a casualness toward killing that, to citified outsiders, came off as quintessential Louis L'Amour, or backwoods crass, or downright cruel. Tourists snapped cameras at the grocery store's trophy mounts and no doubt slid the pictures into albums alongside photos of their summer treks to Glacier Park. Family relations from Detroit or St. Louis or Chicago, on rare visits to Troy, shook their heads and uttered remarks of disbelief at the sight of bearded men with foot-long Bowie knives strapped to their hips and trucks with antlers wired to their grilles. California retirees moved to our community for the fresh air and slow pace, endured a couple of carcass-riddled hunting seasons and bitter winters, and retreated south. These brief witnesses to our way of life returned to their far-off homes and must have told entertaining stories of jarring scenes, disdained our supposed ignorance, dismissed our code from a comfortable distance.

But what about those who could not leave? What about the damaged, the different, the vulnerable—lost girls, hesitant boys, compliant wives—bound to place by fathers and husbands, the providers who headed their homes? What choices were open to these resident aliens living in a land where strength reigned, where livelihoods depended upon killing animals, where communal embrace and personal worth were awarded to those who demonstrated the desire to take aim and pull the trigger?

VIII.

Justin was an eager hunting apprentice. As a boy he took aim at squirrels and birds with a slingshot, then a pellet gun. (Mom couldn't abide the bird killing and told him he'd have to eat every robin, woodpecker, or crow he killed. So, he stopped shooting birds. Or maybe he still shot them, but abandoned the yard for deep forest, away from Mom's watchful eye.) He shot stray cats and gophers with a used .22 rifle Dad had bought at a gas station as a father-son fix-up project. Justin graduated to wild game after he passed his hunter safety course and Dad outfitted him with a Ruger .243 rifle.

When my parents were dating, my mother became an eager hunting apprentice, too. She was a petite junior majoring in English at the University of Colorado–Boulder; my father attended gunsmith school at the Colorado School of Trades, in Denver. On nighttime dates, Mom sometimes held a spotlight while Dad shot rats at the city dump. ("That's when I knew she was the girl for me," he joked whenever they told their "how we met" story. "I did it all to please you, baby," she would say.) They hunted jackrabbits at a deserted ranch, pursuing the darting animals by truck. One time, after firing and reloading, Mom forgot to put the safety on and the jouncing truck triggered the rifle, shattering the passenger-side mirror.

My father graduated with a certificate in gunsmithing in May 1966. In August, just before the start of her senior year, my mother withdrew from college and my parents got married. They had planned to move to Alaska to homestead and had bought a used truck for the trip. But one day in October, while they were still saving money to move, my father returned home to their Denver apartment and announced he was taking the entrance exam to join the Colorado Highway Patrol. "Announced" is the word my mother used when she told me this story a few years ago. She was nuts about him, she said, and would have followed him anywhere. And she was relieved they weren't moving to Alaska.

My father worked as a highway patrolman at a one-person post in Colorado's San Juan Mountains. The remote location was his top choice, and even though he was a rookie he got it; the patrolmen with more seniority didn't want the assignment. A rare car chase would get his blood pumping and break up the routine of the road, but after four years he grew bored and restless, and he craved to test his academy-honed mettle. He hired on with the police department in Tucson, Arizona, but we lived there less than a year—the extreme summer heat and stress of big-city living spurred my father to search for new work, and he led his family to Montana.

On my parents' first deer hunt together when they were just married, my father sighted-in a buck standing on a ridge three hundred yards distant and fired, his aim dead-on, piercing just above the heart to send the buck toppling downslope. Mom cried while he gutted the animal. On another hunt, it was Mom's turn. My father situated her with a rifle on a large, flat rock overlooking a ravine, leaving her with instructions: "If anything with horns comes through here, shoot it." He climbed downhill and hiked slowly through the ravine to flush deer her way. Dad was thrilled when a shot rang out; he scrambled back to the lookout site and found her, seated and shaking on the rock. "What happened?" he asked. Two bucks had appeared and Mom had sighted one through her scope, just as he had showed her, drawing the animal's big brown eyes and long lashes near enough to brush. She didn't want to kill the beautiful animal, but she didn't want to disappoint her husband, so she shut her eyes, aimed by chance (perhaps raising the rifle barrel a few inches), and pressed the trigger.

From then on Mom sat beside Dad on occasional daytime hunting drives, but she did not hunt. She did not like the bleeding and gutting, the blood and guts.

IX.

My sleepwalking resumed when I was ten and we moved from the basement into the wide-open space of the log house's unfinished main floor and loft, where for the first time I had my own bedroom. One night a dream my mother had gone missing drove me from my bed and downstairs, across the living room's rough subfloor and cool kitchen linoleum to the front door. (My mother, who slept the sleep of a wary doe, woke as the deadbolt turned.) My semiconscious body recorded my search through touch and sound: chilled steel of bars embedded in the front porch to scrape muddy boots, dew-slick grass, distant cries my own. Behind the house, the sting of metal shielding the tractor's mowing blade, the gouge of sharp bark where my father chopped wood, rounding the front deck to the low rumble of river. As I raced past the front porch my body snagged in sudden limbs—my mother's grasping, gathering arms that yanked me off course and pulled me to her chest, her heart pounding as wild and frightened as my own.

She led me to bed and tucked me in, and maybe she sat by my side for a while, watching to ensure that I would stay. In the morning she told the story of my nighttime escape, and I recalled my dream and the panic of my mother gone—she had vanished without a good-bye kiss or promise of return. I recalled, too, my muted cries and the press of cold, then wet, then sharp; the purl of water over rocks; a grasp of arms. The relief I felt at the story's resolution was as much for finding my mother as it was for having been found.

X.

After each successful hunt, Dad would back the truck into our open-faced garage, slip a gambrel between the deer's hind legs, and winch the body with a hook and chain slung over a rafter. Every year, as autumn hardened to winter, a skinned deer dangled upside-down in the garage to age. The body hung for a week, hoofless and headless, striated slabs of white fat and plumb muscle, taut tendon and glistening bone. When I squeezed past the carcass to get to the truck, my coat sometimes brushed filmy membrane bristled with remnant hairs, and I breathed the thick odor of cold, subdued blood.

To save money on butchering, my parents often quartered the deer themselves. Dad would back the truck bed under the hanging carcass, and with a sharpened butcher knife he cut it in two below the ribcage, the severed front half of the deer dropping into the bed to be driven to the front door. My mother, in preparation, cleared the dining table of its decorative centerpiece and cloth, exposing a long scar chewed into the thick alder tabletop by a handsaw when my father, bent on completing a project, once used the table as a sawhorse. She pulled two hefty leaves from storage (they appeared twice a year, for hosting Thanksgiving dinner and cutting up deer), extended the table to a long oval, and spread plastic sheeting over the surface. The first time Dad slung half of a deer on the table its stout legs buckled and everything—the carcass and tabletop, bone saw and butcher knife—crashed to the floor, delaying my parents' inaugural operation while Dad reinforced the table's brace plates and reassembled the work station.

Beneath the glow of a pendant lamp my mother followed my father's instructions to grip haunches or hocks as he sawed down the spine from the neck to the bottom of the rib cage, splitting the chest in two. He brought in the deer's rear half and sawed the pelvis into separate hindquarters, then packed the quarters in coolers and discarded the plastic sheeting while Mom washed the tools and her hands in hot, soapy water in the kitchen sink. She lifted the table leaves and returned them to storage, closed the table, unfurled over the scarred tabletop her decorative cloth (seasonal fabric she had chosen from bolts at Ben Franklin), and then repositioned her centerpiece—a potted ivy, or a kerosene lamp, or a vase with a philodendron cutting she was nursing to root—to make the scene once again invitingly domestic save for the lingering, primal odor of chilled muscle and stilled blood that had been ushered indoors and warmed.

My parents delivered the quartered deer to a meat market in town, and ten days later they brought the animal back in tidy packages wrapped in white paper marked with letters denoting the contents. Mom stacked the steaks, roasts, burger, and cheese smokies in the freezer.

Deer were plentiful where we lived; a good-sized mule deer fed our family for one winter. Elk were plentiful, too, but harder to come by, since they hid in the brush at high elevations. My father shot two elk in northwest Montana, my brother, one; each fed our family for three years. Mom adapted the recipes handed down from her Midwestern roots, substituting venison for store-bought beef; she liked cooking with deer and elk burger because the meat, when seasoned, took on the taste and texture of hamburger. Her wild-game casseroles and stews and soups bore the hallmarks of traditional comfort fare.

When Dad and Justin shot the antelope crowding Montana's east plains, or rabbit, grouse, or duck, Mom scouted for new recipes that claimed to make the meat moist, tender, and flavorful. She whipped up crock-pot rabbit stew, marinated and simmered duck breasts, and, one lamentable winter, canned antelope. These tastes and textures were stringy and strange on my tongue, but I cleaned my plate because we did not waste food.

XI.

The first time I was cornered in that daycare bathroom in Butte—a little girl used to indulge a grown man's sick delights—my emotional self separated from my body like a hot-air balloon untethered from ax-chopped ropes. I floated high above the scene that played out far below, the man now a shadow, the girl a stranger. When the bathroom door opened, I floated down the daycare's long hallway and out the front door, followed that little girl home, hovered above her as she lay rigid in her bed and as she sleepwalked, too, and I trailed her through the coming days that turned into months and years.

But then came this saving grace: After my family moved to the woods, I found ways to feel. As my brother and I explored the land, wisps of moss brushed my cheeks, stiff pine needles poked my fingertips, my palms grazed rough bark and brittle lichen and got sticky and stained with gummy pitch. The heels of my hands pressed down on sharp stone, raising contours I could trace, a connection to the land embedded on my body.

When I walked into the insistent press of the river that fronted our property, winter's runoff bit my calves, and when I waded deeper into dark, swirling pools, I forced myself to sit and soak. Icy water chilled my skin and muscle, blood and bone, seeped down deep and numbed organs and nerves, then merged with my already numb core. At that moment—for a moment—I felt something like relief, outside and inside connected and united, my separated self restored.

In summer Justin and I floated the river, our bodies draped across inner tubes, tennis shoes protecting our feet, our torsos stiff with life jackets. Toward the end of our float lay a large logjam caught in a deep bend—root-ripped trees swept up in springtime floods, the mass growing and shifting each season. Just before the logjam, the river's bobbing rapids funneled into glassy sheets that gathered speed and plunged beneath the mangled trees, the impact spewing froth. Each time the logjam came into view, our arms turned to paddles and we rowed with all our might to cut an exit from the quickening current to the slow side of the river. Justin was stronger and could pull himself away from danger. I was weaker, but if I began paddling early enough, most times I could beat the current. Sometimes the water won and slammed my tube into the logjam, forcing me to fight back—to lash out and shove and grab and kick—my scraped arms and bruised legs accepting pain, pouring all of my energy and will into escape. And in the struggle to free myself I released swallowed rage.

XII.

When I was twelve, my father got a job as a deputy with the Lincoln County Sheriff's Department. He brought his work home in the stories he told during dinner, sharing the highlights of his shift with relaxed detachment—until Mom would cut him off with a sharp "Doug!" when details turned alarming. He would meet her intercession with an irritated "What?" He was catching us up on his day— what was wrong with that? Most times he spoke the sentences Mom had implored him to hold back. He was, after all, telling a story, and stories must have endings. A woman bit off another woman's ear in a fight. A bar owner had been strangled with a telephone cord, probably by her son, who coveted her coin collection. One man had stabbed another in a bar, the act so swift and covert that witnesses only saw their fellow drinker slump inexplicably to the floor.

At the family dinner table my father transformed violence into evening anecdote, and at bedtime I recorded his stories in a small diary my grandparents had given me, its mottled green jacket adorned with gilded lettering and an engraved lock, its pages allotting just three short lines for each day. My father's dinnertime stories earned the same attention as Justin and me playing spies after school and our truck breaking down while hauling firewood. The diary kept my father's stories contained and safely distant, reduced them to bite-size pieces I could swallow and keep down, allowed me to meet his eye during dinner, ask questions and comment, merit my seat at the table.

My father eventually transitioned from the job of deputy to being the department's evidence technician. He photographed accident and crime scenes, collected and cataloged evidence, testified in trials, and sometimes hauled bodies to the crime lab in Missoula. One evening, when he had worked late and missed dinner, I met him as he stepped through the front door with a bundle of sheets in his arms. Without taking off his coat, he began draping the sheets over the basement stairwell railing like a housewife hanging laundry on her backyard line. Dad was all business as he arranged the dingy white cloth splotched with crimson darkening to deep rust.

"What happened?" I asked. "Who died? How'd he kill her?" Dad smoothed the sheets and absentmindedly answered my questions until Mom rounded the kitchen corner to welcome him home.

"Doug!" she wailed, intoning his name over three syllables. "What are you doing?"

"Hanging these to dry," he said, glancing up as he completed his task.

Mom's hands curled and found her hips. "I will not have bloody sheets in our house, Doug. Not around the kids."

Dad gripped the railing with both hands. "Well I am *not* driving these things twenty-four miles back to the evidence room tonight. They can hang here until morning."

He glared at her and she glared back, defending the fresh line she had drawn between the intruding outdoors and the harbor of home while I monitored their faces and stole peeks at the stained sheets. Finally Dad shook his head. "Alright," he sighed, "I'll take 'em to the basement." He scooped up the sheets and stomped down the steps, slamming the door on my chance to record the end of his story.

Such victories were rare for my mother. Sometimes the sound of her crying woke me at night. I would tiptoe through the dark and find her at the top of the stairway that led to Justin's and my bedrooms. She sat with head bowed, spine hunched, bare feet resting on the steps Dad had hewn from thick logs and secured with steel bolts. I would sit beside her, slip my hand in hers, and hold on as she released grief in strained gasps, eyes squeezed tight against tears that slid down her cheeks and splashed on her bathrobe. Long minutes would pass and then she would whisper, "He won't listen," or "He doesn't care how I feel," or "It's always about him." I knew "he" was Dad, but she did not say what he had or hadn't done.

I would tuck my nightgown under my feet and we'd press close as the cooling house relaxed around us, the refrigerator motor stuttering off, floorboards ticking, embers settling in the woodstove. In time her tense body softened, her breath evened, her tears slowed and then stopped. After a few minutes more Mom would squeeze my hand and say, "You go on back to bed, hon. I'm okay."

"Are you sure?"

"Yes. Now go to bed, it's late." Her hushed voice had grown firm, the wounded wife finding strength as authoritative mother.

I would pad to my room and climb in bed, wait for her careful footsteps retreating down the stairs—then wait for my feet to warm and sleep to settle—my eyes closed against the dark.

XIII.

Like my mother, I did not desire to hunt. My parents didn't push me; my brother, when setting out his gear for an upcoming hunt, would challenge me, much as he would when he'd hold an opened tin of sardines to my nose and insist I eat one, then call me a sissy and demand to know why I refused.

I sometimes rode along on weekend drives in search of deer, but I can't recall witnessing an animal being shot. Whenever my father and brother returned home victorious from a hunt, they would sit at the dinner table to warm up and rest before heading back out to tend to the deer. Mom and I would take our seats at the table and listen as they recounted their adventures. I heard so many hunting stories across fifteen years—stories told by my father and brother, stories told by their friends—that I could imagine the scene as though I'd been there myself: the crack of rifle fire, a deer rearing and dropping—or bolting into the brush, a blood-spotted trail betraying its final flight. I could see the men tracking the animal, finishing off the creature if its flanks still heaved, dragging the body to the truck (by the horns if a buck, a rope around the neck if a doe), skinning the animal to cool the meat, the truck bed dipping under the hefted weight.

This is what I could *not* conjure: scope-drawn brown eyes and long lashes, taking steady aim at an animal and squeezing a trigger, slowed running and ragged breathing, last breaths and warm stillness, methodical gutting, knives and hands bloodied, the sweet fatigue of hard-won success. Hunting, to me, was long rides with my family over dirt roads; falling asleep with my feet tucked next to the heat vent, my head lolling on the nearest down-coated shoulder; rousing, disoriented, at dusk as the truck lurched into reverse when my father turned it around and aimed its headlights for home.

Why didn't I want to kill animals? I had no words to tell my brother, or myself, that I knew what it was to be stalked and caught, that I knew the lure of the chase and the gratification of dominance. My body strained with the whimper of the hunted *and* the impulse of the hunter—and fought to suppress the terror each invoked. And so, somehow, live animals and killed animals coexisted in my child's mind, and in between dwelled their suffering that had become my own—suffering that lay at the bottom of a fathomless gulf.

XIV.

Children learn early the rules they must follow to remain within their family's circle. The rules I tried to follow were these: (1) We each must work to help build the house and meet basic necessities. (2) My father bore the burden of building the house and putting food on the table; my behavior must not distract him from his duties or his pastimes of hunting, shooting, and hiking. (3) No whining, no blaming, no sulking.

When the abuse began, I became afraid of losing the approval and acceptance of my parents, who were my only source of safety. But I also became afraid of the paralyzing night fantasies that grabbed me again and again, afraid of bathrooms, afraid of the dark. After the log house was finished enough for my family to move to the main floor, I grew afraid of the basement that had been our home but subsequently was filled with the foreign shapes and dark spaces of my father's gun shop, deep storage shelves, clothes hanging on rods and draped with sheets, and the wood room. When I had to venture to the basement for chores—to stack firewood, stoke the stove, or sweep bark—I would ask someone to go with me. In the afternoons after school, while my parents were at work, I asked Justin. He would refuse ("Geez, you big baby, it's a stupid basement"), or he would come as far as the doorway and wait, then switch off the lights and tear upstairs, leaving me screaming and fumbling for safety. Once in a rare while he would stand at the door and stew until I had raced through my task or his patience gave out. When my parents were home I knew better than to bother my father, but I could ask my mother. She would set aside her sewing scissors or the checkbook, and sit on the stairway's bottom step and talk to me while I worked out of sight. Her patient voice found me, flowed around me like an easy current; the sureness of my voice responding to hers was a surprise, a relief, a courage-lifting sound.

But then came the night—I would have been eleven or twelve—when I had to take a shower in the cinder-block stall in the basement. My father had built the shower for us to use until our upstairs bathrooms were finished. I don't remember why I had to take a shower that night; a parent's order was reason enough. At the time, my father's friend Dave, a fellow cop and hunting buddy, was visiting from Colorado. When I approached Mom at her sewing machine and asked her to come sit on the bottom step, she glanced at Dad and Dave catching up at the dinner table and pulled the pins clamped in her mouth.

"No, Julie, not tonight," she said.

"Mom, pleeeeeze, please come wait for me."

"I said no. Now, you go on and take your shower."

I made it to the stairwell's bottom step and sat down, drew my knees under my chin and hugged my legs. Bursts of deep laughter punctuated the stories being swapped overhead. How I adored Dave. Dark-haired, handsome Dave, bachelor Dave, who kept horses and gave me rides when we visited, and showed me how to groom the looming, antsy animals. Dave, who dated rodeo queens and said yes to the question I always asked him: "Will you wait for me, so we can get married when I grow up?"

Mom's brisk face appeared over the stair rail.

"Julie. Get in the shower."

By then I was crying, my arms clenching my legs. I craned up at her. "Mom, I can't, I can't. Please don't make me."

When her face didn't soften, panic set in and snapped the brakes on my mouth. My pleas gathered speed, hurtled headlong into blubbering and shuddering and begging desperation, my crying careening out of control—and Dave was up there at the table, hearing my monumental meltdown.

Chair legs scraped linoleum and the light fell dark as my father's frame filled the head of the stairs. "Knock off the malarkey, Julie. You get down there and get in that shower. Now." His words kept time with his index finger jabbing toward the basement's closed door at the base of the steps. My father's final judgment ended my appeals.

Hot water pelted my quivering body. How long was a convincing shower? A few minutes should do. I did not soap up or shampoo my hair. A wet head should be evidence enough, and shampoo burned open eyes. I pulled back the plastic curtain a few inches and peered around the basement, my vigilance blurred by tears and coursing water. There was the double-barrel stove my father had welded from steel drums, and the stacked wood he had split to keep us warm. There was the spot where the bunk bed once stood, where my brother and I had slept. The thick joists overhead had grayed from air and time and heat, but the strips of foil between the joists still shone in the bald light. The stains above the bed, the seeping fingers of dark red, had dried long ago and turned black.

That first summer we lived in the woods, my father had identified hoof prints in the sand and brown pellets he called sign. He had pointed out hollows of matted grass and claw-scuffed trees, and he had named the animals that paused on our property and moved on: deer, moose, bear, elk. That autumn, when we moved into the basement and the overhead stains appeared, I asked my father what the wet red was. "Animal blood," he said, used to glue plywood, liquefied and leaking in the stove's radiating heat. In a single sentence he stripped the mystery down to certain words carrying practical information. "Oh," I said, and that was that. Now I knew what my father knew. This knowledge left me unsettled, but I could not tell him so. I had sensed, from his matter-of-fact explanation and tone, that he would have said there was no reason to be afraid of the things we see and can name.

I did not reveal my fear of the blood, and I never spoke of the fairies that I had once thought lived in the woods. Each spring I saw new flower-slippers the fairies could have worn, but the small plot of sand my father had put down never did produce a garden.

XV.

Dispatch called my father to Daniel's home the night he died. A few evenings later, I approached my father in his basement gun shop. I was eighteen at the time, far removed from that child who had hoped fairies were real, but still I hoped to glean consoling facts to share with my suffering friends, who believed Daniel had died by chance, and to ease my own grieving, too.

My father stood beneath a halo of fluorescent light, hunched over a vise, drawing a flat file across a braced rifle stock.

"Dad? Some of my friends think Daniel's death was an accident."

My father's body didn't register my presence, my interrupting voice, my loaded question framed as fact. The file gripped in his firm hand continued its steady scrape of steel on wood, and in that long, quiet space hope sprouted. Maybe my father would give me a maybe. Maybe this time he would answer with words that carried a fissure of uncertainty, words offering glimmers of softer possibilities.

My father's hand stilled. He stood up and studied me. He looked strangely old against the backdrop of gray concrete, his face lined and shadowed in the stark lamplight. He exhaled a slow sigh, as he did on long hikes when he paused to shift the heavy pack on his back. "Julie," he said, "it's impossible for anyone to accidentally put the barrel of a shotgun in his mouth and pull the trigger." He held my eyes a moment more, searching for any traces of lingering maybes, then turned to the stock and resumed filing.

My father's brief words allowed no room for doubt. The truth of Daniel's death settled in my chest, where it lodged and across time disappeared by degrees, silted over by silence, hidden from my friends.

Some nights, while lying in bed after I had written in my diary and switched off the light, I thought about Daniel. I pictured him easing his bedroom door shut, drawing down the window shade, maneuvering the long shotgun barrel into his mouth (a smooth, simple motion in my imagination), the cold metal choking his throat. And then he did what any Troy boy would do when aiming a gun at a flesh-and-blood target: He pulled the trigger and did not flinch.

XVI.

I think my friends knew, deep down, that Daniel had killed himself. But facing the truth of how he died would have led to facing the truth of why, and few of us—if any—had seen possible warning signs. The members of our community recognized suffering in animals and remedied their distress. In dire situations, men bore the mantle of taking decisive action, both to end an animal's pain and for practicality's sake: a horse's leg fractured by a hidden gopher hole; a deer hit by a truck, back broken, still breathing; the dog given to my family—a Doberman pinscher we named Shadow, her color shifting from smoke to lavender in certain light, sleek and delicate—falling sick, muscles wasting, nerves trembling, mouth frothing. My father, one day while Justin and I were at school, led Shadow into the woods. He did not tell us how she died. There was no need; we knew.

We recognized physical suffering in humans, too, and tended our own wounds. We did not cry, or we stifled tears, and we took stitches out ourselves. No sense wasting time or gas driving into town, no sense paying a doctor to do a simple task. But we had no communal language for suffering we could not bandage or stitch, and so those whose hurt could not be touched held it in, tamped it down, their bodies absorbing pain until some, like Daniel, sought relief in death. Others released mounting pressure in small measure, alone, at night, when no one else could see. Sometimes light sleepers became accidental witnesses: children woke to their mothers' sorrow; mothers woke to a deadbolt's slide. Hard-working husbands and fathers slept soundly, and did not speak of the visions that rose when they lay down at night and closed their eyes.

XVII.

My father was a skilled hunter who brought home plentiful wild game. My mother prepared nourishing meals that she did her best to make taste good. And I accepted the hot, homemade food heaped on a plate and placed before me. After I had eaten all I was given, my father excused me from the table, releasing me to the evening and then to bed, to the grasp of fantasy and restless sleepwalking, prowling the log house as my family slept, pursued by a predator I could not see, searching for something I could not name or locate, groping toward daylight and the relief of trading invisible terror for the hard truth of the known that ordered our world. In this home my fraught body was provisioned, sheltered by trees and fed by animals my father had felled—his heart's desire, the singular desire he had followed and fulfilled, and in the fulfilling had left his family wanting for nothing. What more could a daughter ask for? What more from these abundant woods could a little girl with pretty blonde hair—or my mother, with her tender heart, or Daniel, with his gentle brown eyes—possibly need?

XVIII.

After graduating from high school in Troy I attended college in Spokane, Washington, a three-hour drive from home. When I finished college I remained in the city, where I lived on my own in a studio apartment and worked a series of temporary jobs. The daily routine and demands of school that helped keep me buoyed had fallen away, as had my social support of friends. I no longer spent summers or holiday breaks at home, and had lost the solace I had found in the Montana woods. The pursuing predator began to close in. Bouts of anxiety compelled me to seek distracting activity; most often I would spend evenings cleaning and reorganizing my already clean and organized apartment. On weekends I woke early and tackled a long list of errands, projects, and plans, and climbed into bed late at night, exhausted. Sometimes, as I watched tv or read, a sudden sadness would rise and I would crumple in tears. Once, a panic attack struck while I was at a café, leaving me rattled and afraid.

My senses had ratcheted to high alert, like those of an animal sensing a hunter's approach. My body felt vulnerable, exposed, stripped of camouflage. An escalating fear drove me to the public library, in search of language that could help me name its source. One of the books I found was on childhood sexual abuse. The opening pages contained a long list detailing the ways survivors can manifest signs of the trauma.

For the first time in my life I recognized myself: my childhood fear of bathrooms; my sleepwalking and persistent fantasies of wielding power over others; the intrusive, recurring images that sprung into my mind during the day. I learned that many survivors of abuse coped, as I had, by becoming emotionally numb, and by being hypervigilant of their environments and hyper-aware of others' needs and moods. The list identified my sense of foreboding about the future—even as a child I felt certain I wouldn't live past the age of thirty—and stated that it was typical to be a perfectionist and an overachiever. I recognized my history of exploitative relationships: a boyfriend, whom I dated for two years, had picked up where the daycare abuser left off. I learned I had let him have his way with me because many survivors of abuse become passive, unable to say no or set appropriate boundaries. I read that it was common to feel a pervasive sense of shame.

Additional listed behaviors seemed to apply to me, but I couldn't absorb any more. I slid the book back on the shelf and left the library. I felt nauseated and confused—I didn't know where to go or what to do. But another sensation had surfaced, too: something akin to when, as a girl, I would wade into the deep pools of the river back home and force myself to sit and soak, the icy water chilling each layer of my body, seeping down and touching my numb core, my separated self, for a moment restored.

One evening, a few weeks after I had moved into my apartment, my father called. I was living alone now, he said, and I should have protection. He recommended buying a .38 Ruger snubnose revolver because it was a good weapon for females—small enough to conceal in a purse but powerful enough to kill a man. He could get the gun at cost; he'd pay half if I could pay half.

On a warm September weekend I drove to Montana to visit my parents. Soon after I arrived Dad stepped from his gun shop, holding a narrow red box with a black phoenix on the lid. Nestled inside was my gun, stubby and gleaming stainless steel. He gave me a shooting lesson before I returned to Spokane.

We had begun shooting targets together when I was in junior high, when I had asked him to teach me to shoot and he agreed, allowing me a point of entry into his world. But the shooting we did back then was for fun; the lesson in our driveway that September day was different. Rather than stapling a small paper target of concentric rings to the wood frame he had built for target practice, he attached a large silhouette of a broad-shouldered man, a black X marking his center chest. Dad handed me a compact box of bullets. Hollow points, he said, ideal for self-defense. A hollow point doesn't pass cleanly through the body, but mushrooms upon impact to damage more tissue and cause more blood loss, to drop an advancing man in his tracks. As I slid the bullets into the gun's cylinder, Dad gave me a pop quiz.

"What's the first rule of self-defense?" he asked.

I was stumped. My father had insisted we lock our doors even though we lived in the sticks. He never sat in a café with his back to the entrance and always chose a booth overlooking the parking lot. When I began driving and left the house for school or my waitressing job or a date, he did not say "Good-bye" or "Drive safe," but would warn, "Watch your backside" or "Don't take any wooden nickels." *Stay alert for danger. Don't let others fool you.*

"Lock your doors?" I guessed.

"No," he said. "The first rule of self-defense is to never let the attacker know you have a weapon."

"How come?"

"The element of surprise is critical. If you're waving a gun around, threatening to shoot, why, it just gives him time to react. He'll probably gamble that you're afraid to use it. What you want to do is keep the gun hidden, and if he advances pull it out and shoot. Don't hesitate, don't warn him, just fire. If he's coming after you, I guarantee he doesn't have your best interests in mind."

My father's job was to bust bad guys, backed by the full authority of the law. He trained new police recruits at the firing range and won trophies at marksman competitions. He was the sniper on the Lincoln County SWAT team because he possessed the skill, the courage, the cool-headed calm to ease his rifle into position, settle his sights on the target, exhale slowly, and choose the precise moment to squeeze the trigger. Threat eliminated.

I had heeded his safety warnings—at the age of five my body had become hardwired to sense the approach of danger, to recognize guile in others. But whenever the long shadow of harm closed in, I left my hands hanging limp at my sides and allowed myself to be snared. I did not fight or cry out for help; I held still and submitted, and in submitting wielded the only weapon I possessed: waiting. Waiting for the attacker to decide if and when the assault would end, waiting to be released, waiting for solitude and the exhale of held breath, for the onset of denial slowing my surging pulse.

As a grown woman newly living alone, I hadn't given safety much thought. (I locked my apartment door at night; what more could I do?) Even though I hadn't asked my father for help, he had wanted to get me a gun. I was touched by his concern. I felt proud that he had struck a deal with me; I was working full time and could pay my share of the cost. I was flattered that he had given me an official shooting lesson and had divulged his first rule of self-defense. But his rule contained a false assumption so smooth it had slipped by us both—that with a gun in my hands I could hold my ground with inherent certitude and strength. Arming me could not alter the fact that we had lived as animals lived: when under attack the powerful could fight back, but the weakened would succumb.

I stashed my new gun in my bedside stand, within easy reach during the night, but it did not provide peace of mind. I had begun to sense the surfacing words that would take decades for me to speak: my father's defense had been misplaced, and his call had come too late.

I wonder, now, what might have been. What if, while growing up in Troy, I could have recognized myself within my family and my community as I had when I stumbled upon that book in Spokane? What if my father, my brother, and the other males empowered in our town could have somehow expressed uncertainty in themselves, awareness of the unseen, a desire to understand the confounding *other*? A subtle gesture, an altered tone, a softening of squared shoulders could have allowed an opening for words. Maybe Daniel would have felt emboldened to reveal a sliver of his pain. Perhaps I might have shared my fear of the animal blood, and then the nighttime terrors that plagued me. My mother might have told her stories at the dinner table, her family leaning in to listen as we did when my father spoke. And he might have been the one who awakened to her crying and sought her out in the dark.

I can only wonder, now, what might have been if words had split the silence and cracked hearts had become known. I couldn't consider such questions back then, or imagine new ways of being: we lived as animals lived, governed by what is, not what if.

Still Hunt

The American Wing of the Metropolitan Museum of Art has an airy, skylit atrium, the recently remodeled Engelhard Sculpture Court, a place overflowing with marble and curious marvels. In one corner, the Vanderbilts' humongous hearth. Over there, glowing Tiffany windows. Catty-corner is an annexed Frank Lloyd Wright living room, transplanted entire from Minnesota. But the main draw, anyone can see, is the café. Short of stopping at a fountain, museumgoers head for the line like animals come to drink. A panini, a Vitamin Water. A few minutes in a chair.

Headed in that direction, people circulate around the room's sculptures, each work an island unto itself. One of them, Edward Kemeys' bronze *Panther and Cubs*, rests on a square pedestal in the southwest corner; on the edge, as cats prefer. A lioness is on her side, partially reclined. Two young panthers—less than eight weeks old, by the look of them, when they'd be about ten pounds—are safe at her chest, between her front and rear legs, in a kind of external womb. Her tongue licks one's nape, while the other cub, its belly against hers, appears about ready to pummel its sibling. Two strikingly large protuberances, one realizes after a while, could only be nipples. I don't distrust Kemeys' eye: no doubt that's what it takes to nurse a cougar.

I decided to spend time with *Panther and Cubs* one Saturday afternoon, because several years ago the cougar was declared officially extinct in the eastern U.S. That the animal remains in our homage to ourselves seemed worthy of some exploration. *Panther and Cubs* was sculpted in 1878, though this particular cast was poured in 1907, the year of the artist's death. "Kemeys was America's first *animalier* (animal sculptor) of significance," reads the brief placard affixed to its pedestal. "He favored the American panther, depicting the animal in varied emotional states, from fierce combativeness to the maternal tenderness exemplified in this group."

Ghost cat, catamount, cougar, puma, panther, painter, and mountain lion:

Puma concolor is one of the most widely known and variously named animals in the so-called New World, with more than forty monikers. But if you want to see the shape or form of this animal, the Met is perhaps your most solid bet, because although about thirty thousand live in the American West, unsurprisingly they're reclusive. Crepuscular. Many people who've spent a fair amount of time in or near "wilds" have never seen one, myself included. I've seen paw prints in the damp sand of an Oregon river, and in the adobe mud tight to a brake of chaparral in California, which would cast a concealing shadow in the moonlight. I've found eviscerated, half-eaten deer, and once I heard a female cougar in heat roaring eerily in an oak and buckeye swale. But I've never laid eyes on one. Odds are, though, I've been *seen*. In the wilds, it may be we who stand out like sculpture.

Standing before Kemeys' rendering, one is impressed by the lioness' size: her hind legs seem impossibly long, but cougars, I've learned, have proportionately the longest legs of all felines. Her tail is as thick as my arm, longer (and surely stronger), with a smooth, rounded tip. The cubs are the size of house cats, but lankier, and they are a little less convincing. The statue's bronze is dark, but in life these cats are tawny all over, *concolor*, and the cubs have spots. Males are about half again as large as females, reaching 120 to 150 pounds, and as many as 200. From incisor to tail, they're about eight feet long.

Edward Kemeys, meanwhile, was described by the writer Hamlin Garland in an 1895 *McClure's Magazine* profile as a "thin but sinewy" man of vernacular speech. Born in Savannah, Georgia, he was raised in Scarsborough on the Hudson River, and in New York City. After serving as a white captain for a black artillery during the Civil War, he worked for several years on a relative's Illinois prairie farm, which had kindled his passion for open space during a visit at age thirteen. But he grew restless and, in 1869, at the age of twenty-six, retreated to New York City in search of something he couldn't quite identify. There, for two dollars a day, he found temporary work as an axman in the engineering corps readying the grounds of Central Park for Frederick Law Olmsted. One day during his lunch break, he watched a German sculptor carve a wolf's head at the Menagerie beside the park's original headquarters, the old Arsenal at 5th Avenue and 64th Street. As he later recounted to Garland, immediately he thought, "I can do that!" He stayed up all night modeling his own lupine visage from wax and, in the morning, made a list of future sculptures: "All wild. Deer fighting panther, wolves fighting buffalo, and that sort."

Three years after his epiphany, Kemeys made his public debut with *Two Hudson Bay Wolves Quarreling over the Carcass of a Deer*, which still snarls in the Philadelphia Zoological Gardens. Flush with this success, he immediately forayed west, traveling in Kansas, Colorado, and Wyoming for fifteen months in 1872 and 1873 to observe and hunt big game. After an accident broke his arm, he was taken in by members of the Omaha tribe and lived in their camp. Native Americans and frontier animals became his lifelong subjects—or as Kemeys put it, "I had struck the trail." He carried along his banjo and picked while sitting on stacks of buffalo skins. Once he was back in New York City, his studio became a veritable museum, full of trophy animals and the sculptures they inspired, or the other way around. He put down skins for rugs and wore Native American garb, as if to channel his subjects, and for the sake of performance.

It would seem important to note that Kemeys' totemic animals were firmly lodged in his imagination before he ever visited the frontier and glimpsed them in "the wild." He prided himself on his "intuitive" understanding of creatures, boasting to Garland, "I could sit down before an animal and *drink him dry*." His self-promotion as self-taught aligned with a dominant American myth of both then and now: literally overnight, as the story goes, he transformed from a day laborer to an artist, and soon to one of national caliber. His affirmation of hunting, which was essential to his accurate renderings, was likewise in vogue and separated him from other artists.

Kemeys had to go west to see big game, not least because by the late 1800s animals like the cougar were already all but extinct in the Northeast. It took well over a century for the Fish and Wildlife Service to declare what had long been manifest. *Puma concolor* is a highly adaptable species—in fact, it has the broadest range of any mammal in the Americas, spanning 110 degrees of latitude from Alaska to Patagonia—but we managed to shoot and trap them out of the East quite quickly: from Delaware in 1790, New Jersey in 1835, Massachusetts by 1858. The tail end came just slightly later in New York: 107 cougars were "bountied" between 1879 and 1890, and the final kill was paid for, upstate, in 1894. The last verified record of a breeding cougar in the Northeast was in Maine in 1938. So Kemeys' cats aren't strictly modeled after eastern cougars, though it's not even clear that eastern cougars were ever their own subspecies. DNA analysis suggests there are just six subspecies, and only one in North America. (The Florida panther, of which about two hundred still exist in the Everglades, isn't genetically unique, either. But it is now isolated.)

After his initial visit to the West, Kemeys made one voyage to Paris, where the *animalier* movement was centered. Critics had coined the term to describe Antoine-Louis Barye, who in the 1830s began exhibiting *Panthera* bronzes modeled on captives in the Jardin des Plantes. Kemeys was to become "the American Barye," although his sculpture, by philosophy but perhaps also skill, would never be as refined. The sculptures of the French *animaliers* were classical and allegorical; Kemeys' work radiates a rough-hewn, frontier American idealism. While in France, Kemeys showed his third major work, *Fight Between Buffalo and Wolves*, in the Salon, but afterward he settled into a lifelong routine, forgoing both Europe and zoos for regular excursions across the Mississippi. "I'd go back to New York and work till I sold something," he explained, "and then—back West again."

Soon his popularity swelled, and in 1885 the Art Institute of Chicago held a special exhibition of his bronzes and sketches titled "Wild Animals and Indians." Today, outside the Institute's doors still sits perhaps Kemeys' best-known work: a sentinel pair of African lions, sculpted for the World's Columbian Exposition in 1893 and now an important symbol of the city. Though these exotics may be his most iconic, for the Exposition Kemeys also produced six American panthers— the cougar was probably second only to the wolf in his personal mythology—as well as a pair each of bison and bears, which guarded the bridges to the "wilderness islands" Olmsted created in the lagoon beside the equally idyllic White City and its stuccoed colonnades, a paragon of civilization. It was a heyday for animal sculpture: Kemeys was lionized for his untutored talent and endemic preoccupations. In *The History of American Sculpture* (1903), the first survey of its kind, sculptor Lorado Taft notes that Kemeys was significant to "the slow unfolding of a national art: he was one of the first to see and appreciate the immediate world around him, to recognize the artistic possibilities of our own land and time."

But that particular land and time, one of discovery and superabundance, was fast transforming. In fact, it was also at the World's Columbian Exposition that the historian Frederick Jackson Turner delivered his famous Frontier Thesis, arguing that westward expansion was key to American identity, while also observing it had come to a close. "In a recent bulletin of the Superintendent of the Census for 1890 appear these significant words," Turner begins. "'Up to and including 1880 the country had a frontier of settlement, but at present the unsettled area has been so broken into by isolated bodies of settlement that there can hardly be said to be a frontier line.'" He narrates the successive waves of colonization that pursued "free land" and other resources, noting how each wave returned its intrepid pathfinders to primitive conditions and so fostered a staunch individualism, "a gate of escape from the bondage of the past." Eventually, "in the crucible of the frontier the immigrants were Americanized, liberated, and fused into a mixed race." The gaps between outposts were sutured by trade and its improved routes, culminating in the railroad. A vigorous nationalism and democracy had resulted. But now America had reached the other sea, and what then?

Kemeys and his panthers seem bound up in the contradiction of Turner's thesis: caught between fine art and animal nature, between big skies and the urban studio, they are both quintessentially American and, from the start, nostalgic. "All going, all going," Kemeys said of his subjects. Just about the time he arrived in the West, it began—from a certain angle, at least in the estimation of Kemeys and his ilk—to look like another kind of zoo, where livestock were fenced in, wildlife fenced or wiped out, and Native Americans murdered, confined, and treated as if they'd evaporated. As wildlife reserves and Indian reservations were conceived, they were established separately: the former a garden outside of time, for visitation only by the genteel (Yellowstone in 1872, Yosemite in 1890); the latter a quarantine under the pretense of assimilation. As Black Elk, the visionary medicine man of the Oglala Lakota, was to say, "the white man has put us in a little island and in other little islands he has put the four-legged beings; and steadily the islands grow smaller. . . ."

Of course, Kemeys himself was a colonial force; his trips to and from the West were a symptom of the trend he decried, just as today many prominent environmentalists jet around the world, justifying the emission of far more than their share of carbon dioxide by the high stakes of the cause. Kemeys was an unabashed hunter, part and parcel with the extermination—as was Audubon, who famously shot, taxidermied, and posed his avians as naturalistically as possible earlier in the century. "Every night," Kemeys said to Garland of his first western excursion, "I had all the animals I could use for dissection and posing. . . . I wanted to go to the very heart of the wilderness, and then came to the mountains! I went all through them. I met mountain animals, I killed them, grizzlies, sheep, wolves. . . ." And cougar. With a metaphor both amorous and violent, he exalts that "I went to the heart's core of our American wilderness, and it yielded up its most carefully guarded secrets to me."

All early sportsmen, who were the nascent environmental movement, are enmeshed in this paradox: they wanted to protect "nature" so they could poach it and renew themselves. The Eden of game was slipping away, and so national movements—spearheaded by organizations like the elite, one-hundred-member-only Boone and Crockett Club—began to regulate, began to fashion a gate for that garden, as it were. In his manner, Kemeys was also forging this gate with his bronze. *Field and Stream*—then the most prominent outdoor magazine—praised Kemeys' efforts to the sky:

> The government at Washington has at its hand the very man who could put into parks and avenues of the Nation's capital what ought to be there—a series of colossal sculptures of American wild animals. These would be a better influence, one is disposed to think, than . . . statues of American statesmen and martial heroes. . . . American wild animals and the country that bore them will presently have become things gone forever.

Implicit in his thought is that our wild animals *are* American statesmen and martial heroes, and that to wage a one-sided war against them, to cut them down, was to engage in a clandestine civil war. An ironic sentiment for a hunting magazine, but such was the transition to a conservation ethos.

Shortly after Kemeys' solo exhibition in Chicago, in 1886 and 1887 he published a serialized account of his first western tour in the new and aptly named *Outing: An Illustrated Monthly Magazine of Recreation*. Its title, "The Sunset Land: A Tale of Rocky Mountain Adventure," is telling: the sun fades in the west, yes, but in the consciousness of the nation, the West was a land of fading, of brilliant but evanescent vitality. Serendipitously, Kemeys' dispatches were in those pages entwined with Teddy Roosevelt's series "Ranch Life and Game Shooting in the West," and Roosevelt, then the president of Boone and Crockett, was thereafter a friend and champion of the artist, promoting him for commissions and purchasing his sculptures.

In "The Sunset Land," Kemeys positions himself as a sportsman who "had always craved the free life of the hunter and explorer" and desired to experience the "pure spring of nature," "that enchanted land," "the wild fastnesses of the Great Desert" of the plains. Guided by a friend who had toured before, he wagoned westward from Fort Leavenworth—no railroad went further—to join a hunting party in western Kansas, where Kemeys felt "more like myself than ever before." They soon continued to "Monument," now Monument Rocks, which Kemeys reveled in and identified with: "Nature, in her wildest forms, has brooded for ages over the grim rock-sculptors which sat enthroned around, the naked plains savage and sere, furrowed by cañons. . . ." For an emerging sculptor, the mesas and arches of the West must have had peculiar pull.

Surely there are embellishments in these memoirs: Kemeys claims to have suffocated a wolf caught in a foothold trap, by biting its jugular, and to have reached out with his hand and caught a wounded pronghorn by the leg as it bounded past—could these things possibly be true? There is the expected bravado, the encounters with the sublime. But for someone who made the excursion in his late twenties there is also unexpected clarity and a pensiveness verging on regret. He passes "countless skulls and bones" to find a living herd; he sees Native sky burials and then comments, "on every side stretched the sweeping plain—their hunting ground from childhood, but now invaded, and with scarce security for their own graves." Though Kemeys calls the Natives "savages" with "coppery cheeks," as was convention, from the start he admires them. When he falls into the Omaha camp after breaking his arm, he comes to respect the tribe profoundly, though he also romanticizes it. "The longer I remained among the Indians, the more I came to appreciate the existence," he wrote. "At no time of my life had I been so free to pursue unmolested the study of my art."

Sparingly he mentions sketching and sculpting; it's not the main action (not for *Outing*'s readers, anyway), but it was ongoing behind the scenes—and hunting *was* integral to Kemeys' process. Early on, he describes painstaking dissection and examination: "My studies, sketches and notes were by this time nearly completed, so far at least as bison were concerned, having devoted my time to skinning and cutting up each portion of their anatomy, till all was firmly fixed upon my memory." Fixed also, we must imagine, in his muscle memory. In a departure from his boisterous, sometimes florid voice, Kemeys describes in clinical terms cutting, with a "keen knife," through the layers of a bison's hump: "it consists of a line of spines extending above the vertebral column at the highest point, for about eighteen inches, dropping abruptly forward, and tapering toward the hind quarters, until it loses itself about one foot in front of the hips." The nineteenth-century hunts are notorious for their waste and brutality, but this unfolding of an animal is an intimacy few experience today. Despite his precise, scientific language, one understands the act would be tender, delicate, raw. The argument is still made in the most rigorous art schools that one cannot draw the human figure without a deep knowledge of anatomy—that, in fact, one is not even capable of seeing what is there without knowing, already, what it is underneath. Undoubtedly Kemeys had the same bodily knowledge of a cougar; undoubtedly he had put his hands inside one.

I found myself pacing around and around the bronze *Panther and Cubs*, slowly, looking for a way in with my hands behind my back. Stalking. That is the particular gravity of sculpture: You have to circle to peer through. Each piece has its own territory, demands its space, and then sometimes invites you closer. This, mainly, is what I saw: The lioness' legs are wider than her cubs' bodies, emphasizing just how much the young would grow in the next year to reach adult size; the soft hammock of her skin between her hind leg and flank; the flared, sharp curves of her hip bone and shoulder blades; the astounding size of the paws, as large as my hand; the grooves for retractable claws; how flat she is, lying on her side; how sleek her body for slipping through brush. Kemeys' marks, like brushstrokes, are generally subtle, but thicker on the lioness' chest and hindquarters. They reminded me of claw marks, as if the artist had thought to mimic the animal with each impression.

Clearly Kemeys understood the patterns of the animal's fur, knew just how her coat would lie. His portrayal of this family suggests he knew that, in a robust year, when kills were plentiful, there would be ample time for grooming, for leisure. Both cubs might survive. The lioness' ears are neither erect nor flattened; she is relaxed. The cubs are sated. She gazes over their heads in that distant, catty way. She seems unknowable—which is how animals should be rendered. You can't look into these eyes; or you can, but you will see only yourself, an imagining of the cat's interior. Otherwise there's shadow and green patina. As I circled the sculpture, the echoes of the cavernous gallery almost reminded me of wind on an alpine slope. But not quite.

Few visitors linger in the sculpture court to appreciate Kemeys' work.

Though once on the artistic frontier, *Panther and Cubs* might seem a bit kitschy these days, either too mystical or too banal, or both, in part because of the proliferation of Western lodge art (and gift shop miniatures). Likely we could create an alternate index to the frontier's disintegration through such knickknack commercialization, as the connections between city industry and prairie life tightened. Kemeys was also complicit in this, collaborating with a Chicago foundry, Winslow Brothers, to produce mail-order statuettes and reliefs, including crouched panthers. In 1884, Julian Hawthorne trumpeted his friend in *Century Magazine*, writing, "The American bear and bison, the cimarron and the elk, the wolf and the 'coon—where will they be a generation hence? Nowhere, save in the possession of those persons who have to-day the opportunity and intelligence to decorate their rooms and parks with Mr. Kemeys's inimitable bronzes." These lines seem as much a sales pitch as a call to action, but the philosophy is plain: If the species could not be preserved, at least their forms could be. And they could be possessed, collected. They could imbue your parlor with wild American charisma.

But just as importantly, *Panther and Cubs* may suffer light glances because the Met overwhelms with its labyrinthian abundance. In the sculpture court, it's the children who seem freshest. Something about the atrium's open space, the diffuse, revivifying light filtering through the pyramidal skylight. Or just kids being kids. If there weren't vigilant attendants on hand, the gallery might quickly become a gym, boys and girls climbing and swinging from all these busts and beasts. *Panther and Cubs* is in similar, familial company then, although juvenile cougars, it should be said, rely on their mothers for just twelve to eighteen months.

Beside the cats in the sculpture court is a rectangular fountain, but on this day the water wasn't flowing. Families from around the world perched on its edge to rest, traced the colorful lines of subway maps, and tossed coins over their shoulders. As I sat there, kids came up to Kemeys' cats and reached out for their tails. "Don't touch," one mother whispered, leading her towhead son away. Another lady stopped, stared for a second, announced, "That's bronze, not granite," and moved on. Then came a girl with brown curls and a red dress of pastel flowers, hearts, and other shapes—startling color, for this marble atmosphere. Her mother lifted her by the armpits above the pedestal, eye level with the felines, and her father looked on with her sleeping brother slung to his chest.

"See," said the woman, "it has two babies."

"Where's the daddy?"

"Dad's not here. Maybe he's out hunting."

The child squirmed. "That's daddy, over there!" she shouted, pointing over my shoulder to the center of the fountain, and we all turned to see a delighted bronze boy, a cherubic spout, hugging a flapping duck he must have caught from the water.

There's no breeding population of cougars within several thousand miles of New York City, and there won't be one anytime soon. To start, it's not so much that mom can't find dad as the other way around: Young male cougars disperse thirty to one hundred miles—and sometimes as far as a thousand miles—but females settle and establish territories, on average, only nine miles from where they're born. They stick close to their homeland, a dynamic known as "philopatry" in animals. So although western cougars consistently do venture east across the Mississippi (I imagine them swimming, pawing through the waves with flattened ears), these pioneers are mostly male. They travel "brush belt" corridors, along rivers and the buffers of train tracks. But finding a mate is likely impossible, and every road crossing is hazardous.

Nonetheless, I might have told the girl in red that "daddy" wasn't far away. He's just off the East Drive of Central Park, at about 76th Street, near the summit of Cedar Hill, which tests the resolve of the city's joggers. There Kemeys situated another cat, *Still Hunt*, on a glittering stone ledge in 1883, the same year he sculpted *Panther and Cubs*. When it was unveiled atop the outcrop in June, the *Chicago Tribune* reported, "Then the young lady with the red parasol said: 'Oh, my!' The gentlemen exclaimed, 'Ah!' and all went round to the drive to look at the statue, while the police dispersed the crowd." Now, on weekends, there's no dispersing the crowd. The Drive is a veritable game trail, as people plod uphill in vibrant Lycra and Spandex, sneakers, and shirts that exclaim, "What does it take? NYC Marathon!" Occasionally a lady strolls past, to or from the Met. Sometimes in fur.

There's a saying, in running, for when someone fades hard in a race: "The bear's jumped on his back." Here, it's the panther. When joggers notice *Still Hunt*, their expression is a twist of exertion and recognition, as if they've been running from this creature a long time, but now, here it is, waiting for them—and this was Kemeys' design. As a curious reader of the *New York Times* wrote in a letter more recently, "sighting it unawares can give you quite a chill." A more typical remark by those with breath to spare is "I've never noticed that before," which is testament to its camouflage and siting, and to our collective hurry.

Still Hunt seems to have crept from the sinuous, quiet thickets of the thirty-six-acre Ramble, which Olmsted fastidiously designed as a "wild garden" to offset the park's grand pastoral vision; though, when I visited, someone was practicing his chip shot just there on a modest patch of grass. The lion sits hunched, its haunches taut, a coil of "fierce combativeness." The catamount seems poised for an attempt at springing all the way back into the modern East. A cougar is said to be able to jump eighteen feet straight into the air, and twenty to forty feet forward, which would be clear across the road—though I suppose it would take a running start. At the same time, its expression seems anxious, nervous, even mournful, as if it wishes simply to slink off or to disappear into the rock, rather than leap.

Or, in Kemeys' own words from a story called "The Legend of the Little Panther: A Tradition of the Seneca Indians," which also appeared in *Outing* (in 1901):

> On a rocky projection which overhung the cave's mouth there crouched a monstrous panther, his limbs all gathered beneath him, his immense quarters trembling with eagerness as he slowly and almost imperceptibly at times lifted his cushioned fore feet. His great tail quivered and twitched with pent-up force, and on the yearning head and neck the cat-like ears slowly laid themselves down.

This portrait bears a remarkable likeness to *Still Hunt*, suggesting the "trembling" animation the bronze had for Kemeys, even years after he cast it.

Originally just placed on the ledge, *Still Hunt* was permanently affixed and re-patinated in 1935, three years before the last breeding cougar in the Northeast was recorded in Maine. There it sat, seemingly tense but peaceful, until 1973, when its tail was broken off and stolen. I wonder if that curled fragment is still around, mounted on a mantel like a trophy or buried in the leaf litter nearby, a rare bone for a dog to unearth. Fifteen years later the tail was replaced, and you can trace the faint edge of the repair as if it were a scar from a fight. Already the new tail's round tip has been worn golden and smooth by the oil of passing fingers.

Of course, in Central Park the habitat that could support a cougar is merely intimated in the likes of the Ramble and its counterpart, the equally rock-strewn, Adirondack-inspired Ravine at the park's northern end, where only humans are now feared. Hunters may have bagged the last eastern cougar, but habitat destruction had as large a hand in their demise. Panthers just don't do well in tight conditions. As the East was cleared by untold axmen, habitat was fragmented and white-tailed deer populations crashed for lack of forage. (Now that the East has reforested without big predators, deer populations have exploded.) A cougar needs to kill a deer every ten to fourteen days, which is in part why it needs giant tracts of unadulterated space, its own game reserve. All of Manhattan—where 1.5 million people live—is just 22.7 square miles: room enough, maybe, for just one cougar. (For comparison, Frederick Jackson Turner cited the frontier as at "the margin of that settlement which has a density of two or more [people] to the square mile.") Each night while out on patrol, these big cats walk the equivalent of a full loop around Central Park's drive, over six miles; but this is part of a much larger territorial circuit that often takes weeks to complete. Meanwhile, an estimated 425 to 850 square miles of uninterrupted landscape are necessary for the existence of a viable population of panthers—though less if corridors allow cats to travel between these areas and exchange their genes.

Still, there remains room, so there is still possibility: Road density surveys predict there are almost thirty thousand square miles—an area about the size of Maine—still suitable for apex predators like cougars and wolves in the Northeast, including over four thousand square miles in the Adirondacks. One seasoned cougar biologist, Paul Beier, tantalizingly suggested to the *Times* in 2002 that cougars "will eventually get to New Jersey, or at least close." They'll trickle down gradually from Canada and in from the West. In 2011, on a Connecticut highway, a lone male was run over after it padded eighteen hundred isolated miles from South Dakota, by far the longest journey by a cougar ever recorded. Its DNA traced it to a subpopulation of cougars in the Black Hills, and its movement was confirmed by matching fur and scat samples found in Minnesota, Wisconsin, and New York.

In other words, the frontier for mountain lions is our populated spaces, our suburban tracts. Fittingly, some of the corridors they might use to move east are the same trails by which the nation expanded westward: great and small rivers and, later, that steel river, the incursive railroad. Cats are literally using the seams by which they were eliminated to try to repopulate the East, though the journey is arduous, a real long shot. But the panthers' continuing existence might signal that some "frontier" hasn't disappeared, that by certain rubrics the frontier could even return to the East in places, though the odds are slim. Or maybe the cats' forays and persistence suggest that the frontier, and thus its erasure, were a kind of myth all along.

The eminent environmental historian William Cronon, in his essay "Revisiting the Vanishing Frontier: The Legacy of Frederick Jackson Turner," argues that the Frontier Thesis "expresses some of the deepest myths and longings many Americans still feel about their experience," though Turner's idea quickly fell by the critical wayside. Surveying the work of others, Cronon notes that Turner's poetic narrative overlooked the breadth of colonial forces at work in westward expansion and perpetuated the marginalization of minorities by idealizing their experiences—or simply ignoring them. The thesis also underestimated the potent role of the federal government, business, and cities, which in truth established the establishment on the frontier long before the frontier was said to dissolve.

Even beyond those flaws, Turner himself soon became aware of the essential limitation of his thesis: it was predestined to fade into the sunset. By declaring the close of the frontier in the instant he spelled out its importance, Turner gave his theory a rather short lifespan. American democracy would have to be steered by some other force and, in 1910, he admitted the frontier had become "subordinate in influence to general social forces." He proposed a new grand narrative for American history based on the idea of geographically distinct "sections," arguing that these regions—bioregions, I think we could call them—would compete against each other for resources. In our age, when California, the Northwest, the East, the Midwest, and the South often seem at odds, Turner's lesser-known Sectional Thesis remains compelling, though it may be cultural differences—determined only in part by resources, or the lack of them (water, public lands, tech companies, slavery)—that sustain these tensions.

Yet Cronon observes that one way of salvaging the Frontier Thesis is to reimagine the frontier as a "contact zone," an area or region "where people of different cultures struggle with each other for control of resources and political power." In this model, what was a moving line of irreversible change—a frontier sweeping across the country over time, trailing democracy and/or acting like a prairie fire, with animals and Natives running before its flame—is replaced by shifting territories of cultural exchange, always unequal. These zones might wax or wane, but they are porous, not unidirectional.

As Cronon argues, "we must be careful to avoid embracing frontiers that somehow 'close,'" and we should think about environmental history not as a one-way movement "from free to occupied land" but rather on a spectrum of "abundance to scarcity"—which is a matter of context and value. One culture's abundance is another's scarcity, as the eastern hunter's buffalo hides (the furs that Kemeys carried home to adorn and authenticate his studio floors) were for Natives, who depended on the "endless" herds. Today a rural county's notion of abundance might be land free of cougars, while for the more bourgeois "environmental" set, a free land of abundance might mean a healthy cougar population and the possibility, if remote, of seeing one. Reinterpreted in this light, as Cronon says, "The vanishing frontier no longer needs to vanish."

A museum is likewise a frontier, if we think of it as a "contact zone." Twenty years ago, the anthropologist James Clifford extended this idea to our vaunted, often intimidating halls of cultural capital, borrowing the term from language scholar Mary Louise Pratt, who defined a contact zone as "the space of colonial encounters, the space in which peoples geographically and historically separated come into contact with each other and establish ongoing relations." Under this vision, the imperialist museum is decentralized and those artists and cultures "on display" in its collections become participants, partners in a dialogue. There is lopsided power, always, but also reciprocity—at minimum each party benefits through "mutual exploitation." In the best of cases, the curators and those represented sit together so that communities are truly represented, in the democratic sense, and able to tell their own story. There is genuine interaction and, one hopes, ultimately mutual admiration. Of course, this ideal can't extend to Kemeys' animals, which cannot speak or sit at the table.

A work of art such as a sculpture is an important contact zone as well, and here at the Met visitors like me step into the atrium. As we encounter and gaze upon an *objet*, we make contact with a body—a cultural body, a body politic, a personal body of work—beyond ourselves; there is refraction of meaning and the chance for recognition, for conversation. As I stand in the sculpture hall before *Panther and Cubs*, the layers of its embodied history unfold: Kemeys', the cougar's, Native Americans' and the atrocities they've suffered—all of which the sculpture represents complexly. And one's own history unfolds, as well, a response that, for many museumgoers, is the most automatic and authentic, though it may be associative and passing: Suddenly I want to tell those around me, the other visitors and you, about how I am the only one in my immediate family never to have seen one of these creatures. I was tying my shoelaces in the car when one bounded across the road into tall, dry grass.

What's wonderful about *Still Hunt* is that you can lay not only eyes on this cougar, but hands. *Do touch* is in the wind. You can reach out and brush your fingers across the cat's flank, make contact in the most fundamental and sometimes most crucial sense. The oil-burnished tail of this panther is a testament to this impulse and its gratification. Not at first, though: You hesitate upon seeing *Still Hunt*. Something in the form spurs an instinctual reaction, like a branch might be mistaken for a snake on a sidewalk. Also, you have to scramble up the rock ledge. But then, feeling the chill of the metal, its curves, one finally empathizes with the sculptor's art. Feels his hands.

We would appear to need more of these contact zones, but in fact they're all around us if we choose to recognize them, to interpret them this way. Consider the brushy corridors cougars and other liminal creatures navigate: some are rich ecotones, greenways for disparate species; others are simply places where kids and adults alike can still veer to interface with or imagine something "wild," which is to say quite feral, within a city. Brownfields, abandonments, untended riparian banks. Manhattan's Central Park, though the pinnacle of manicured, remains a frontier: There you can encounter the strange and elemental, something raw, such as a red-tailed hawk (although, potentially one with a name) bearing down on a squirrel. Once in a decade, a coyote creeps through a tunnel and finds its way there, and the media goes wild. From a cultural perspective, moreover, New York City is the greatest of all contact zones. Languages and ideas travel its underground corridors the way cats slink through brush belts.

Some experts have described proximal and distal ways of knowing, which indeed, we can ultimately interpret as close to or away from the body. "The distance between *distal* and *proximal* thinking is an old one in philosophy, physics and psychology," says the lauded organizations scholar Robert Cooper. "Distal thinking refers to effects and outcomes, the 'finished' things or objects of thought and action; proximal thinking, to process and event, to carriers or mediators of things or objects. For the distal thinker, the destination is more important than the journey; for the proximal thinker, to travel is better than to arrive."

Though we can walk right up to the cat sculpture in the Met, it is a distal object, apart from us, pedestaled, cordoned off, explained by a placard: "Kemeys was. . . ." *Panther and Cubs* has come to its final resting place, it seems. Museums suffer from this affliction of stasis, though in recent years—in an effort to stay relevant alongside the virtual—most have made a conspicuous effort to become more interactive and communal. But *Still Hunt* is proximal, with no guards in sight. Touching this sculpture, we dwell less on its definitive meaning, which is contested, than in its making and environment (a simulacrum of cougar habitat, with a golfer standing by). *Still Hunt* seems to travel as the seasons change around it, or as we stumble upon it from different directions. The cat fades into the foliage in summer, seems to grow bolder, hungrier, come winter. By dusk, a streetlamp casts an orange glow on its humped, muscular shoulders—a sun that never fades. When it rains, the loop of *Still Hunt*'s tail gathers water, holding a crescent puddle with sunken leaves and the reflections of those who scramble up the rock.

The notion of a frontier that dwindles until it disappears, leaving only civilization in its wake, rests firmly in the realm of the distal; the revision of that idea as a shifting, permeable contact zone partakes of the proximal. I would wager that Kemeys, in his own time, was a relatively proximal thinker, an adventurer never satisfied, as artists must be if they're to endure. "There is fascination in exploration which I have ever found it impossible to resist," he wrote of his travels in "The Sunset Land." As his deft hands shaped a recollection, a contour, of his western excursions to pour as bronze, one imagines that this, too, was active exploration, not a foregone conclusion in service of a national movement. The form and surface of an animal was a landscape to be studied and mapped, but not conquered—even if Kemeys wanted to do so. Each bronze was cast, "and then— back West again." If we interpret his bronzes only as monuments, that view says as much about us—our current tastes, our own memorialization and diminishment of animals—as it does about him.

On the best of days, we live in the proximal: our perceptions are a contact zone minute by minute. Our perceptions of the panther, which has been eliminated from two-thirds of its historic range in the Americas, are no exception. Like wolves, they have been utterly vilified, but we are beginning to see them otherwise. Kemeys' familial depiction in *Panther and Cubs* shows that, over a century ago, he understood them as social, not evil or only tenacious. The crouched cat of *Still Hunt* is similarly ambiguous, neither fierce nor frightened. Even "The Legend of the Little Panther," Kemeys' retelling of a Seneca myth in *Outing*, may be instructive on this point. I can't say if Kemeys' version is reliable ethnography; it may be tampered with dramatically, or tweaked just a little as all stories are. Seen only in the most obvious light, it again casts Native Americans as savages, but I find the tale hopeful in at least one particular way.

In the legend, the wife of a pacifist Seneca chief glimpses, in a dream, the "monstrous panther" that seems a model for *Still Hunt*. Afterward, she bears a boy who is bloodthirsty, fulfilling her desire for a son and future chief "as savage as a panther." Her wish was the tribe's at large: a preoccupation with returning to glory through bloodshed. Little Panther does lead the tribe into war, but heedlessly, and the people are slowly ruined; eventually, though, he is killed by his namesake—a panther—in "a lonely gully by a cave," thus sparing the Seneca further "decimation." "So runs the legend," Kemeys concludes without interpretation, which seems a respectful gesture. Clearly the cougar and Native Americans are deeply aligned for him, informed by myth, and we might see *Still Hunt* to some degree as an embodiment of Native America's limbo: a delicate position for any animal, any work of art, to occupy. But what strikes me about this curious and complicated legend is that though the panther is construed as "savage" by the people in the story, the tale slyly debunks that notion. The cat turns out to be a savior, ending the rule of an overzealous, harmful man. The "monstrous" panther proves merciful, even as it kills, while human nature is needlessly brutal. This interpretation is, once again, a moral projection onto a speechless animal, but nonetheless it may be a useful parable for our times.

When totemic animals are depicted these days, often they seem confined, at least to me. They're statues not to themselves, but to the commercial interests of Pixar or some other corporate dime. Or they're mediated, stuffy, in some other way, like another pair of local cougars—those in the Museum of Natural History, whose dusty skins are wrapped around forms in a Grand Canyon diorama, though this form of contact has its merits. But *Still Hunt* breathes more easily in situ. It is its own creature: sometimes severe, sometimes sympathetic. Dogs with keen eyesight are known to bark maliciously at the bronze. Perched atop its low cut of Manhattan schist, which glitters with mica, the sculpture reminds me that once we painted animals on rock walls. It reminds me also that Kemeys was once compelled to spend weeks carving into a soft cliff a relief of a buffalo hunt he had witnessed among the Omaha tribe, as he recounts in "The Sunset Land." Freed of a pedestal and any pet-tag interpretation, *Still Hunt* silently asks questions of those who walk or run by: *How does your body react to this form? What is lost if this form no longer exists?*

As I crouched off to the side to scribble a few notes, two boys and their mother walked up Central Park Drive, looking tired. Whole Foods bags from Columbus Circle—a fair distance away—dangled in their hands. They glanced up and stopped in their tracks.

"Whoa," one boy said. "Grr."

"You want to climb up there?" she asked. "I'll take your picture."

They did, and they draped their lithe bodies over the panther, raised their arms, and, after some encouragement, smiled for their mother's magenta phone.

REFERENCES

Clifford, James. *Routes: Travels and Translation in the Late Twentieth Century.* Cambridge, Mass.: Harvard University Press, 1997.

Cooper, Robert. "Systems and Organizations: Distal and Proximal Thinking." *Systems Practice* 5.4 (1992).

Cronon, William. "Revisiting the Vanishing Frontier: The Legacy of Frederick Jackson Turner." *The Western Historical Quarterly* 18.2 (1987).

"Edward Kemeys." *Field and Stream* 9.2 (1904).

Garland, Hamlin. "Edward Kemeys: A Sculpture of Frontier Life and Wild Animals." *McClure's Magazine* 5.2 (1895).

Harden, Blaine. "Deer Draw Cougars Ever Eastward." *The New York Times.* 12 November 2002.

Hawthorne, Julian. "American Wild Animals in Art: With Illustrations from the Sculptures of Edward Kemeys." *The Century* 28.2 (1884).

Kemeys, Edward. "The Legend of the Little Panther: A Tradition of the Seneca Indians." *Outing* 37.4 (1901).

Kemeys, Edward. "The Sunset Land: A Tale of Rocky Mountain Adventure," parts 1–4, 8. *Outing* 10 (1886).

Neihardt, John G. *Black Elk Speaks: The Complete Edition.* Lincoln: University of Nebraska Press, 2014.

Pratt, Mary Louise. *Imperial Eyes: Travel Writing and Transculturation.* London: Routledge, 1992.

"Still Hunt." *The Chicago Tribune.* 13 June 1883.

Taft, Lorado. *The History of American Sculpture.* New York: Macmillan Co., 1903.

Turner, Frederick Jackson. "The Significance of the Frontier in American History." *The Frontier in American History.* New York: Henry Holt & Co., 1920.

SEAN P. SMITH

The Slow and Tender
Death of Cockroaches

In my beginning is my end.

—T. S. ELIOT, "East Coker"

I always find them alone. Laid on their backs and clawing at the ceiling, like they were still falling from a too-high place. I find them on the shelf next to the dish-ware. On the floor, by the rubbish bin in the corner. Between electric burners on the stove. I watch them die, and I wonder if they're missing someone.

Roaches are everyone's favorite enemy. We can all hate them together. Maybe the cockroach can be the new mascot for the twenty-first century, since it's something that everyone can finally agree on.

What is it about roaches? What makes most of the human race recoil in hor-ror and snatch a tissue to squidge them out? (Or a broom, depending on the kind of roach. There are approximately four-and-a-half thousand candidates.) Maybe it's because they scuttle about like an oil slick on legs, gross as all hell. Or that the wretched things are sentient, way more than other bugs, and they always seem to see you coming and beat a well-timed and tactical retreat. I've spent min-utes chasing the same roach, behind the jars of nuts and dried fruit, in and out of drawers and around the sponge next to the sink, until its final taunting dash across the counter into a crack in the wall. Then, after I spend all that time chas-ing them with intent to murder, they just appear out of nowhere, cast themselves on their backs, and decide to die. Alone.

Cockroaches are "them," the ultimate Other for whom we unreservedly nur-ture a deep and violent loathing. Ours is a conscionable hate: no one except the Buddhists will tell you not to kill them.

There is nothing new about this. Pliny the Elder, likely echoing an estab-lished sentiment two thousand years ago, urged that when discovered cock-roaches be summarily put to death. Over the years, they became a handy meta-phor for dictators to apply to society's undesirables, stoking public fears in order to expedite their often violent removal. And I definitely wanted them *out* of my kitchen.

My apartment in Cape Town is the first home I've shared with roaches. They were here before us, of that I'm almost certain—I keep a clean kitchen, but my building is getting on in years, so various fissures in the plaster and tile seem to have availed access for a sizeable colony.

To be honest, I'm scared of roaches. The first time I spotted one on the countertop, I definitely jumped and probably emitted a minor noise of distress before lunging for a paper towel and proceeding with the execution. (It's a grim process. You scoop them up and then squeeze, progressively harder, until you feel the thorax explode in an almost-audible *pop*.) My fear is not particularly rational; there is no great and insidious history behind my relationship to cockroaches. The first occasion I remember even seeing one was as a teenager, on a trip to Texas, when out one night I noticed small lizards dashing around the pavement and occasionally scampering across my sandaled feet. I pointed them out to my friend, who smiled sympathetically and then let me in on some cold, hard truths—such as, lizards don't have six legs. (It was around this time I also realized I needed glasses.)

But those were American cockroaches, enormous brutes that can grow up to about two knuckles' length. In Cape Town, some brief entomological research yielded that I have German cockroaches (or rather they have my kitchen). These don't grow much bigger than a fingernail. And they, along with every other kind of roach, are just about harmless.

Most species of cockroach live in tropical or subtropical forests and carry on like other insects, but about thirty types cohabitate with humans, and it's likely they've been doing so forever, so to speak. Human history is dwarfed by the supreme longevity of the cockroach. Their first ancestors appeared about three hundred million years ago, with "modern" roaches fanning out into every corner of the Pangaean supercontinent by around 150 million BCE. Most of us have heard about, if not experienced, how damned difficult it is to kill roaches. Yes, some can live up to a week without a head, go a month without food, endure forty-five minutes without air—but try surviving three mass extinctions, including the Permian, in which a whopping 96 percent of all life on earth died out, even as roaches were still in their childhood. As with the tardigrade, the microscopic "water bear" and hardiest animal on the planet, evolution struck the jackpot with the cockroach.

The ancient human relationship with roaches has in fact been quite fruitful. Roaches eat just about anything, and in the case of those species that started hanging around human beings, "anything" comprised a whole lot of waste and grime that was better off in a roach's belly than mucking up a human dwelling.

For most of human history, cockroaches were more of a highly discreet cleaning staff than they were pests. They came out after dark, munched whatever crumbs and scraps were scattered about, and retired before anyone woke up. Quite contrary to popular belief, roaches do not carry diseases internally and are actually fastidiously clean in their habits, frequently—not unlike cats—grooming themselves. In truth, roaches seem to have a fairly low opinion of *us*, and have been observed undertaking their cleaning regimen immediately after touching a human.

Cockroaches probably ran into ancestors of the modern-day human pretty early, finding the dwellings of nomadic apes to be particularly rich foraging grounds, so in their own way they've observed the evolution of this strange, curiously frail bipedal. Hominids (that's us) began to walk upright somewhere in eastern Africa a very long time ago. With some disputed estimates looking back as far as seven million years, we know for sure that Lucy, that famous *Australopithecus* discovered in Ethiopia in the 1970s, was strolling about comfortably some 3.2 million years ago. Lucy was still notably simian, both in countenance and in the way her long fingers hung down past her knees; not until about two million years ago did the first human-ish hominid appear on the scene.

We might recognize *Homo erectus* as a very-great-grandparent by its looks, but it was also the first hominid to act decidedly human in its marked inability to stay in one place. Across 1.8 million swashbuckling years, *H. erectus* spread from eastern Africa all the way to modern-day Indonesia. Along the way they made use of controlled fire and primitive tools, lived in organized social bands, and spoke a very basic language. *H. erectus* is the longest-lived hominid to date and actually coexisted with modern human beings for more than half our tenure as a species.

Looking back through the sheaves of evolutionary history, one is increasingly overcome by the feeling that life is nothing more than an endless game of roulette. One can almost hear the little ball whir by as it traverses an infinite possibility of slots before finally coming to rest on a number: a species, the result of a million-and-one unsuccessful bids for existence, cashes out its winnings and makes a go of it. The cockroach won big. The hominid—well, I suppose we should always hope it's too soon to be sure, but our line has already come extraordinarily close to being terminated.

Seventy thousand years ago, *H. erectus* disappeared. Likely as not there will always be debates about exactly why, but its extinction was more or less coterminous with another event, the Toba eruption. Lake Toba in present-day Sumatra is the biggest lake in Indonesia—100 km long, 30 km wide, about 500 m deep—and is also the gaping crater of one of the largest known volcanic eruptions on earth. The explosion was gargantuan. It was one hundred times larger than the well-documented 1815 eruption of Mount Tambora on the Indonesian island of

Sumbawa. That blast killed an estimated one hundred thousand people on impact—and at least that many more died in the following year of volcanic winter, popularly called the "Year Without a Summer," when worldwide temperatures plummeted, crops failed, and famines ensued. The far more catastrophic Toba event delivered a volcanic winter—in which ash disperses into the atmosphere and clouds the sun—that lasted anywhere from six to ten pummeling years and initiated a thousand-year-long cooling effect. And if history has anything to teach us, it's that climate is synonymous with the death or survival of life.

Homo sapiens had already been kicking around for about one hundred and thirty thousand years at the time of the Toba eruption. Cockroaches pulled through just fine—after those three mass extinctions, Toba was a mere hiccup—but H. sapiens fared so poorly that contemporary geneticists estimate only two to ten thousand individuals were left straggling along worldwide. In other words, we avoided extinction by whatever skin Toba didn't scrape off our teeth; all seven billion of us are descended from those sturdy individuals who kept their heads up and bore a decade of darkness.

Casting our nets back into the mists of unrecorded history is a continual act of sketching constellations out of prophecy and conjecture, somewhat legitimized by the latest in scientific technology that will reveal itself as hopelessly antique with the passing of another few years. We cannot absolutely verify this speculative cause-and-effect about Toba, but the eruption of a supervolcano makes it a lot easier to draw conclusions than the slower, more mitigated dwindling-out of one of our even more recent relatives, Homo neanderthalensis.

The cartoonish image of Neanderthals as ogre-ish, dull-witted cavemen has turned out to be far off the mark. Recent research has revealed a cousin close to H. sapiens in genetics, coeval or perhaps more sophisticated in employing technology, and leading a highly developed social and ritualistic life. Neanderthals also conceived something very like religion—probably before modern humans. Numerous excavations across Europe and the Middle East have revealed that Neanderthals intentionally buried their dead and, some anthropologists think, bestowed such artifacts of affection as flowers upon the corpses of the deceased. If the more closely studied history of H. sapiens is at all instructive, careful arrangement and deliberate burial of a body mark a sacred regard for death, and possibly a belief in or conception of an afterlife. What astonishes is that the earliest discovered Neanderthal burial sites in Krapina, Croatia, antedate any discovered H. sapiens burials by thirty thousand years.

We have a tendency to view ourselves as evolution's apotheosis: the be-all, the end-all, the very raison d'être of life itself. This belief is reflected in the Biblical creation myth: in Genesis, God's final act was to fashion a creature in His own image. God told the first man (because apparently women were second class from the very beginning) to go forth and multiply, allowed him to name all the plants and animals, and instructed him to rule over them and to subdue the earth. The whole of Creation was generated for man to exploit according to his whim.

This has proven fairly prophetic, at least concerning the past ten thousand or so years. But we would be fools to think we are masters of the whole of nature. The earth is more than four billion years old; we are a speck on the eyelash of the whole body of this planet's life, and we are not so utterly unique as we may wish; the Neanderthal, before going extinct, was keeping pace with the development of *H. sapiens*, and there is no reason to think they were cognitively inferior—especially if they were the first to invent God. We are not the only of our kind; *H. erectus* vanished rather recently in evolutionary terms, and *H. floresiensis*, the hobbit-hominid native to the Indonesian island of Flores, disappeared even later. Our genealogy continues to grow richer: in 2015 a kind of ossuary discovered in a cave in South Africa yielded a previously unknown species of hominid, *H. naledi*. Yet we are not impregnable: the last time a supervolcano erupted, we lost at least one of our hominid cousins, and humans themselves almost died out. Neither are we the most successful: remember the cockroach.

I climb Table Mountain when I need to think. It looms over Cape Town, a sweeping horizontal escarpment of ancient sandstone often wreathed in mystical swaths of cloud. The mountain is as old as cockroaches. I take one of the less-frequented tracks on the Atlantic seaboard, zig-zagging across the slopes behind Camps Bay before veering up a precipitous ravine carved out by eons of trickling water. The trail, when there is one, wanders in and out of the still-extant stream, and on a hot day I take off my pack and plunge my face into hands full of cupped water. The ravine ends in a small cleft, over which the stream plunges a few meters and where I have to climb a short section of rock to get to the top of the mountain.

Table Mountain has no true summit, but is instead an undulating series of plateaus and small valleys coasting down the middle of the Cape peninsula. I have never been anywhere else like it on earth. From the ravine I emerge, alone, onto a gentle slope populated by a herd of sandstone boulders, all weathered into vivified shapes like a new and nearly animate genus of rough-skinned organisms. They seem to hunker, silently snuffling, in the thick and uncompromising snarl of foliage called *fynbos*, through which I find the narrow, oft-hidden trail. Seeing fynbos for the first time is what walking on another planet must be like. The fabulous geometry of leaf and bitter thorn, the pugnacious shocks of color and earthy commingling with the soil, the vast, fantastical variety of living matter— quite literally I am walking through one of the rarest ecosystems in existence.

With over nine thousand distinct species, fynbos is one of the most diversified of the world's six floral kingdoms. Yet the plants grow only in a small crescent of rugged coast along the southwestern tip of Africa: some fifteen hundred species are found on Table Mountain alone, and nearly double that number on the entire peninsula, making the mountain and its environs home to the richest floral bio-diversity on the planet.

I am briefly at ease among the fynbos. The wind whispers through tendril and weird flower; I see ocean to the west, south, and east; there is the slight gur-gle of water and the gentle hum of crickets. I walk for a while and hear the splash-ing dollop of a shy frog. In a fold of the earth, between phantasmagoric flora and rugged sandstone, I see how little the millennia have changed this land so long home to *H. sapiens*. Then I crest a small rise, see that between ocean and mountain there is city, realize I am suspended above the same wave of urban development that has overtaken every continent. I am but scarcely secluded in a bastion of wil-derness, the likes of which is rapidly disappearing all around the world.

In the city, I walk among ghosts of the vanished forests. On the mountain, I visit specters of the living past.

Dozens of species of fynbos have already gone extinct; dozens more are criti-cally endangered. Many of the rarest types are found only within a cordon of sev-eral square kilometers, leading one local biologist to call Cape Town the floral "extinction capital of the world." Endemism is the blessing of the Western Cape's delightful oddity, but with so many variations of life found nowhere else in the world, the blessing has become a kind of curse that even a vast national park cannot undo. The perhaps-appropriately-named Table Mountain ghost frog, a Jurassic-era amphibian whose last shared ancestor with other frog species lived some one hundred fifty million years ago, is found in only a few ravines of the eastern-facing slope. Its numbers are rapidly declining, and it shares a bleak prognosis along with most of the world's other amphibians.

Of all the animals, amphibians are in the greatest crisis. A full third of all re-corded species are endangered, more than half in stark decline. Frogs, toads, sal-amanders, and newts are all extremely susceptible to pollution of the air and wa-ter; add widespread habitat loss and now-common fungal diseases, and many if not most of their ranks will become part of the lost, unreclaimable diversity of the earth's past.

And we all know not just amphibians are endangered. The list of extinct spe-cies—hundreds and hundreds lost in just the past century—stretches on; the list of creatures flirting with extinction runs much longer. Tigers, pandas, snow leopards, and orangutans—all of them universally adored icons of nature—each number fewer than eight thousand individuals worldwide. Plants and animals are vanishing—not just species, but the sum total: according to one assessment of vertebral organisms over the past forty years, the aggregate of life forms on earth has been halved. In another forty years, researchers deem, the ocean will no longer have enough fish to feed us. At the current rate of depletion, within the span of a few generations some 75 percent of known plant and animal species will be gone.

The last time this many species disappeared over the brief span of a few centuries was sixty-five million years ago, when the dinosaurs' fossil record runs suddenly cold. That was the most recent of the earth's five great extinctions; the day you read this probably falls somewhere in the middle of the sixth. People, in subduing the earth, have set in motion the extermination of most of the world's life forms.

I'm not of the opinion that we can save them—or rather, that we *will* save them. As E. O. Wilson noted in the *New York Times* this past March, the preservation of most ailing species is still manageable. But the bulk of humanity's governments would have to abandon profiteering, and instead focus on protecting what swaths of wilderness still remain with the same vigilance they maintain in protecting the solvency of international banks. Wealthy countries would have to reach further than last year's Paris agreement to reduce carbon emissions, investing heavily in their own alternative energy development, and subsidizing the efforts of emerging economy countries with unprecedented generosity. Aggressive governments would have to deescalate, with global military budgets scaled back and the billions of bloodstained dollars redirected to cleaning up the filth steadily consuming rivers and oceans. Agriculture too ought to be overhauled, subsidized even more heavily to ease the transition to less toxic fertilizers, public campaigns undertaken to shift some cultures away from consuming meat seven days a week. And the fingers of multinational corporations must be pried from governmental necks, with new environmental technologies applauded instead of quashed as a threat to the coffers.

I like fairy tales. But I don't believe in this one.

I do not descend Table Mountain the same way I come up. I slither over moss-covered rocks in Skeleton Gorge, sweat the long, hot track down Kasteelspoort, or punish my knees on the most popular trail, Platteklip. Especially on a weekend, Platteklip Gorge draws enough characters to distract me from the masochistic descent. I hear accents from every continent, nearly enough languages to match, and I see faces and bodies in all colors, ages, shapes. In the summer, a man often sits by the trail playing a wooden xylophone for tips. He does well, a healthy crumple of green and yellow bills atop a pile of coins collecting before him. Warm, earthy notes echo between the walls of the gorge; "I think it soothes the people," he told me once.

We all have enough in common to be soothed by such music. Every person hiking past the man playing the xylophone is related to those same few thousand individuals who survived after the Toba eruption seventy thousand years ago. We're all *Homo sapiens*, and we share the same fate.

As biodiversity declines, the commingling and diversification of the human race is beggaring precedent. The world's largest cities are as heterogeneous as the faces I see slogging up Platteklip, and getting more so by the day despite a global rise in demagoguery striving to prevent it. In 2015, one million people dared to cross the Mediterranean Sea in whatever craft was just barely watertight; thousands died, but most are in Europe trying to make a life. Some governments offer to take them in; others erect fences and dispatch riot police to keep them at bay.

Migrants are the latest undesirables to receive that pejorative moniker "cockroach," but if these people do resemble the age-old insect it's in their insuperable determination to survive. After braving a tempestuous sea only to be denied border crossings, legions have circled entire countries on foot to reach Europe's north, where the economy is stronger and there is a better chance of securing asylum. It is the biggest migration in Europe since World War II.

And that is just Europe. Everywhere, humanity is unbound and moving: To epicenters of commerce, like São Paulo, Lagos, Shanghai. To neighboring countries, where jobs are more plentiful. Or, within the same country, to the city from the village. Entire cultures are dissolving under the strain of war and poverty, migrating and re-forming into something new. It has never happened like this before. We stand at the cusp of great change.

Some say this change will kill us, or that various intervening forces will undo us. The death of much plant and animal life is certain to have dire consequences that no scientific prescience can truly forecast. The oceans, for instance, provide about a quarter of all humanity with its primary source of protein. Honeybees, crucial to the pollination of even those crops grown on massive factory farms, are dying out for as-yet-unknown reasons. Or our demise could result from the effects of a changing climate, which seem to become more identifiable and nefarious with each passing year. Storms are increasing in severity, droughts are becoming fiercer and longer, temperatures are plummeting or soaring, rising sea levels are drowning islands and will, eventually, overcome some of the world's most populous cities.

And if none of that does it, we might just get around to a proper nuclear war.

Maybe *Homo sapiens* are just now hitting their stride, or maybe we're nearing the end of our run. The long-term planetary consequences would, in actuality, be marginal. We'd be giving ourselves wholly to solipsism by thinking that just because the human race is threatened, the world is going to end. The planet has survived more than four billion wringing, trying, life-demolishing years, those five mass extinctions, meteorites and volcanoes and diseases and famines and wars, and still life carries on. The world has been destroyed and remade again and again; we're just perched on the edge of another transition.

No matter what else we do to the planet, though, I am highly skeptical that we'll manage to finish off the cockroach. In no small irony, one of the least desirable creatures seems to be one of the few we'll be left with. Do we hate them because, deep down, we know they will take our place?

This idea really isn't so far-fetched. In just four hundred million years, insects have quietly come to represent about nine-tenths of all life forms on earth. They are rife in every environment except where the temperature is perpetually below freezing, and are probably pleased as punch that overall global temperatures are increasing. Also worth noting: the cockroach is but one of many (and by no means the most fortified) kinds of insect that can withstand significant levels of radiation.

Dare we ask, then, if humans have a monopoly on intelligence? Elephants, octopuses, chimpanzees, and dolphins all possess advanced reasoning, memory, and communication skills (none of which saved the Chinese river dolphin, declared extinct in 2010), yet we seem to be the only species building skyscrapers and writing books. But remember: before Neanderthals died out they seem to have possessed the same—or at times accelerated—capacities for symbolic thought and cultural production. If they had persisted, mightn't they have risen to the same stature as H. sapiens, with comparable prowess in technology and destruction? Would other intelligent animals not do so, given time?

At this point, there isn't time for any other animals but insects. Advanced insect intelligence would look very different from what we regard as our own. Bees are among the smartest (despite their current proclivity for dying in vast numbers): whereas the first hominids likely communicated through varied tonal grunts, bees use a system of dances and the dispensation of odors—a kind of perfumed, whole-body sign language—to organize themselves for singular tasks involving thousands of individuals. (A swarm of bees handily demonstrates that vast numbers can be swiftly marshaled without the internet.) Can we imaginatively expound on what such systems could look like given another million years of development? Another ten million?

This concept has in fact already been elegantly explored by Hayao Miyazaki in his 1984 film *Nausicaä of the Valley of the Wind*, where in a post-apocalyptic future relict human populations must learn to coexist with a race of intelligent, dinosaur-sized insects that has supplanted humans as the planet's dominant species. Predictably, it takes the humans a long time to realize that the insects are not massive, dumb brutes; rather, they just communicate differently and have a unique set of priorities. Likewise, we can also hypothesize that maybe dolphins just didn't *want* skyscrapers, but as long as intelligence remains defined by a fetishized will to power, the question is immaterial: dolphins will go extinct, unless through some stunning ingenuity they find a way to hang on, like the humans in Miyazaki's future.

So do we mourn the world's passing? Earth does not need the dolphin. Nor most certainly does Earth need me, or need you. Life on this planet did not blossom in some primordial pool (or fall from an interstellar asteroid) to embark on a 3.8-billion-year journey just to express *us*, a species we deem "conscious." Life exists for its own unfathomable purposes, and will continue to do so long after we're gone.

And we'll go before insects. We will not have any stake in what becomes of them; maybe after our own extinction, insects will far surpass our capacity for metaphysical thought, or maybe they will carry on as they always have, without skyscrapers and books. The odd truth is that life is impervious to all assessments of value, abiding by two rules alone: it does not remain the same, and it continues. Therefore it cannot be mine to hold vigil over a cockroach's death, slowly waving my arms in some kind of interspecies solidarity. For a quarter-billion years cockroaches have lain down and died for reasons of their own, and not because I cleaned the kitchen. These are not the meek, yet they may well inherit the Earth; they are far more ancient and gentle stewards of the planet than we will ever be.

We will weep when the dolphin goes extinct; we will mourn the last tiger and the last panda. We are delivering ourselves into a world of cockroaches and rats and feral dogs. But from no matter what perceived nadir, the world will move forward. Life will adapt, continue to grow and change itself, to try on new outfits, experiment with new fads. Humans, too, may go out of fashion—but life, in its perpetually re-processing, always-expanding self, will survive.

ANDREW MENARD

All Lines of Order

The Boquillas Trail is located in a remote corner of Big Bend National Park in Texas. It begins with several long steps sloping gently upward, followed by a number of shorter, steeper steps which veer out of sight to the left. The gravelly sand of each step is held in place by a half-buried log, and the very first log separates the trail itself from the cracked blacktop of a small parking lot—creating a kind of artificial threshold or boundary, something people have to step *over* to begin their walk. Several years ago, when my wife and I followed the trail up and over a limestone ridge speckled with the plump, delicately joined pads of prickly pears, we barely gave the steps a second thought.

A map of the park shows that the Boquillas Trail is fairly short—less than one and a half miles round-trip. No one will be reminded of Mao's celebrated dictum that even the longest journey begins with a single step. But walking the trail with my finger beforehand, seeing it double back occasionally to negotiate the slippery contours of the limestone ridge, I couldn't help noticing that its relatively brief and labyrinthine route mimicked the many small bends in the Rio Grande River that are part of the larger bend the park is named for. Mathematicians have long been aware that landforms can remain symmetrical across a wide range of scales—a phenomenon known as self-similarity. But I'd never actually *experienced* this phenomenon until Ruth and I climbed to the rocky crest of the trail and slowly wound our way down to the section of the Rio Grande that cut its way through Boquillas Canyon below. It was as if my feet were able to draw a line from the trail to anywhere. "We are lined with eyes, we see with our feet," Emerson once said.

Toward the bottom of the trail, as we were walking single file, Ruth stopped so suddenly that I had to grab her shoulder for a moment to steady myself—my lofty geographic reverie brought brusquely back down to earth. But a moment later I saw why she had stopped, and why she was looking so steadily at a rock about waist-high, seared and bare in the glaring sunlight.

The rock itself was nothing special—no different from all the others we'd passed on our way down, no different from the slanted cliffs that lined the other side of the river, no different from the landscape that stretched for miles in every direction. But loosely scattered across its flat, exposed surface was a shiny collection of bead-and-wire animals. And next to them was a clear plastic cup holding a couple of wrinkled dollars. Though we were used to seeing displays like this on the streets of New York, where vendors routinely sell everything from hand-wrought jewelry to kitchy portraits of Marilyn Monroe, stumbling onto one here seemed kind of weird. The very incongruity of it prompted a closer look—each of us reaching for one of the colorful animals.

Mine was a roadrunner, about three inches tall, with a head and tail feathers made of wire-strung brown and yellow beads, a body made of bare copper wire interlaced like a French braid, and everything else—neck, legs, and feet—made of wire wrapped like an electric coil. The effect seemed very deliberate and concise. The legs in particular made me wonder if the animal had been created quickly, with rapid weaving and winding motions, either out of habit or from a more magical effort to match the roadrunner's own speed. But I was most intrigued by the artistry and imagination that had gone into it, the apparent desire to entice with something more than a simple, easy-to-recognize shape.

Again Ruth was a step ahead of me. Turning the animal she was holding this way and that, examining it from every angle, missing nothing, she said that it reminded her of Calder's wiry sculptures. I could see what she meant. Even without all the materials he liked to use—leather, cardboard, rhinestones, bottle caps, pipe cleaners, rubber tubing—the colorful javelina she was balancing in the palm of her hand provoked the same frisky, off-kilter associations as one of his lions or leopards. When she put it back on the rock, next to the other animals, and began moving all of them around, playing with them, she said that it made her think of the Calder circus on display at the Whitney. Looking at the roadrunner still balanced in my own hand, I found myself imagining one of Chuck Jones's zanier cartoons—Beep, beep!

Of course, none of this answered the question of what the animals were doing on the rock in the first place. Or who had put them there. Or why someone would trust people not to take the money that was already in the cup or expect them to add a few bills of their own if they wanted to keep one of the pieces. Despite our inclination to play with the animals, the situation was kind of unnerving—not at all the way things worked on the streets of New York, where everything was face-to-face, intimate and negotiable. So, feeling a little confused, we left everything where it was and looked ahead to see where the trail was about to lead us.

That was when we noticed a slender, solitary, dark-haired man, mounted bareback on a white horse, quietly watching us from a relatively flat area on the other side of the Rio Grande. There was nothing threatening or aggressive about his gaze. If anything, he seemed rather hesitant, ready to flee, and it occurred to us that we hadn't seen him sooner because he'd concealed himself within a nearby tamarisk thicket until we stopped to examine the beaded animals. Unknowingly, we'd brought him out of hiding.

Only then did we realize that, whether we cared or not, this section of the Rio Grande had to be seen as a border as well as a beautiful stretch of scenery. What did it matter that the border was just a penciled line down the center of a river which endlessly shifted course? Though clearly porous—indeed, an informal, off-the-books example of NAFTA—the line that divided us from the man across the river, the distance that separated us, was in some sense absolute. As even the most arbitrary or imaginary lines can be sometimes.

Self-interest has always shaped the United States's use of lines, especially as the nation moved farther and farther west, first securing, then erasing one boundary after another. The lowest of land grabs tend to provoke the loftiest rhetoric—yet another example of the "singular accord between super-celestial ideas and subterranean behavior" that made Montaigne so angry and disappointed—and Americans regularly invoked what the Declaration of Independence had famously called "the Laws of Nature and of Nature's God." In 1802, hoping to settle the question of who owned the Mississippi River, Sen. James Ross of Pennsylvania argued that "From the very position of our country, from its geographical shape, from motives of complete independence, the command of the navigation of the river ought to be in our hands." Three years later, after the Louisiana Purchase was ratified, a Massachusetts state representative named Joseph Chandler said the Mississippi River was just the beginning "of our anticipating hopes"— envisioning a future in which "our boundaries shall be those which Nature has formed for a great, powerful, and free State."

How right he was. When Congress started looking past Louisiana to Texas, a special commission concluded that the entire territory of Texas was just an inward extension of the coastline that had been part of the Louisiana Purchase— making it part of the United States, not Mexico. Nor did there seem to be any limit to this geographical version of the divine right of kings. In 1829, with the urge to annex Texas making the United States more and more antagonistic to Mexico, the *Nashville Republican* not only said that the Rio Grande had been "designated by the hand of Heaven, as a boundary between two great nations of dissimilar pursuits," but went on to claim that "On this side of the Rio Grande, the country is seasonable, fertile, and every way desirable to the people of the United

States. On the other side the lands are unproductive, crops cannot be matured without irrigation; in short they are entirely calculated for a lazy, pastoral, mining people like the Mexicans."

Nineteenth-century Americans would never abandon their belief that the line separating the United States and Mexico had simply been discovered, not imposed—proof of God's hand rather than their own. Even something as straight and unvarying as the boundary between Mexico and New Mexico supposedly followed the lay of the land. After a Lt. William Emory surveyed this boundary in 1854, his official report included two etchings: "Near View of the Initial Point of the Boundary Line on Parallel 31°20′ Looking South along the Meridian" and "View from the Initial Point of Boundary Line on Parallel 31°20′ Looking North along the Meridian." Emory claimed that the boundary existed in "a neutral region, having peculiar characteristics so different as to stamp upon vegetable and animal life features of its own." He also considered it "fortunate that two nations, which differ so much in laws, religion, customs, and physical wants, should be separated by lines, marking great features in physical geography." Yet the most obvious feature of the two etchings—one looking north to the United States, the other south to Mexico—is that they both show a flat, nondescript section of the Chihuahuan Desert which stretches all the way from central Mexico to the southern part of New Mexico. Literary historian Kris Fresonke has pointed out that one could reverse the etchings' captions and never know the difference.

Difference was something Ruth and I seemed to discover with every step—the trail fluctuating from moment to moment and switchback to switchback as it snaked down the side of the ridge. When we'd stopped to examine the beaded animals, the tops of the limestone cliffs on the Mexican side of Boquillas Canyon appeared to be just above eye level. But this led us to underestimate how far the trail still had to drop—and the lower we went, the higher the opposite cliffs rose. By the time we reached the bottom, they towered over us—the nearest section curving overhead like a huge dome, its sheared, almost smooth, and shadowless face a lovely ecru color, looking very small-grained in the harsh sunlight.

Pausing a moment to admire the scene head-on, we were struck by how effortlessly its geology turned beauty into a force of nature. The bottom half of the dome was a series of layers. The layers varied in thickness—suggesting they'd been deposited over different intervals of time—but all slanted uniformly downward from right to left, like a cake that had been sharply tilted instead of squashed, the lowest layers diving beneath the river. By contrast, the upper half of the dome was rather jagged and tumbled-looking, an almost chaotic swirl of rock, as if it lacked the skewed harmony and wisdom of the older strata and was still waiting to settle down. Certainly the upper half seemed more likely to crumble and send down a rock slide, even though the area was unusually free of loose or fallen boulders and nothing suggested that Boquillas Canyon had ever reverberated with the hard crackle of skidding rocks. Nature had been both sly and generous with the scene, and the overall effect was stunning.

Just *how* nature had created this effect—the earthly deus ex machina at work behind the deceptively hardened design of the canyon walls—forced us to think bigger than this particular scene. The dome-like cliff on the Mexican side was matched by the somewhat more rounded ridge we'd descended on the American side, with both walls rising to about twelve hundred feet above the river while ranging more than twenty miles to the east in a tight sequence of sharp and sweeping bends that either narrowed the space between them or pushed them apart. Like a plastic ant farm that allows people to see how ants diligently construct their tunnels and nests, the canyon was basically a visual cross-section of how it had been made by the river.

Ostensibly, the Rio Grande had just cut its way down, year after year, century after century, the abrasive power of water slowly hollowing out terrain that had been stationary for millions of years. Americans of Lt. Emory's day would have added that the actual course of the river merely followed a line separating good land from bad—evidence of the eventual difference between a good nation and a bad one. But the angled, layered walls of the canyon told a different story. In fact, the entire region had changed a great deal over time. Above all, the region had been lifted and folded by an east-to-west compression of the earth's crust— meaning that the river itself had remained stationary, kept to its own level, while the land rose higher and higher, forcing the river to meander east or west, north or south, depending on the kinds of rock it had to cut through. Any differences between the two sides of the Rio Grande had been *created* by the river rather than codified or confirmed by it.

On the other hand, none of these differences have ever amounted to much, and even now the similarities between the two sides far outweigh any disparities. Both sides of the Rio Grande's banks have been taken over by tamarisk bushes and river cane—neither native to the area, and both considered so invasive that the two countries work together from time to time to burn them off. In fact, the United States and Mexico have collaborated for many years in the region. When Franklin Roosevelt created Big Bend National Park in 1944, he told Ávila Camacho, his Mexican counterpart, "I do not believe that this undertaking in the Big Bend will be complete until the entire park in this region on both sides of the Rio Grande forms one great international park." Though implementing this plan took another fifty years, Big Bend is now matched by the Parque Nacional Cañón de Santa Elena, just across the Rio Grande from the western side of the park, and by the Área Natural Protegida Maderas del Carmen, just across the river from its eastern side. The layered dome of rock Ruth and I stopped to look at is part of the Maderas del Carmen preserve, which stretches the entire length of Boquillas Canyon on the Mexican side.

The sheer walls of Boquillas Canyon mean that not much of it is accessible on foot. Still, Ruth and I wanted to see what we could, so we headed along the gently sloping bank of the Rio Grande as far as the trail would take us.

At first we were surprised by how wide the bank was, since we could see far enough ahead to tell that it gave out pretty abruptly—imitating, on a horizontal plane, the way the rocky dome slanted into the river vertically. But our sense of surprise quickly gave way to a feeling of delight. For we found that we kept shifting our eyes from the vertical cliffs to the horizontal bank—first looking up, then looking down—as if the canyon were one of those gestalt puzzles in which you see either a vase or two profiles face-to-face, but never both at the same time. Only in the near distance, where the bank disappeared, did everything merge.

Because it was still early spring, the Rio Grande was moving low and slow, in no rush to reach the Gulf of Mexico. Choosing to walk even slower than the river, we discovered that many sections of its bank were covered with loose pebbles, many others with an uneasy mixture of sand and pebbles, and one in particular with a peculiar series of small, grass-tufted mounds that resembled Maya Lin's sculpture *Wave Field*. Slowing even more, we picked up a few of the scoured pebbles—graded bigger toward the cliffs, smaller toward the river—relishing the hard, punctuated sound they made as we walked over them.

At one point we stopped completely, the sun on our faces, a breeze at our backs. All around us, tamarisk bushes sought the water's edge and river cane grew in great green swaths. The cliffs to our right opened up a view of the canyon, the cliffs to our left closed it down. The river ran green in some places, brown in others. Occasionally the dry, resinous scent of creosote wafted down like a branch drifting in the vaporous, earthy stream of river smells. Feeling lulled by the sound of the river, and sheltered by the cliffs on either side, I experienced one of those intense, exhilarating moments that have often crystallized my relationship to nature.

Nature is remarkably specific. Anyone familiar with the Southwest, for instance, can tell right away that none of the so-called spaghetti westerns were ever shot in Utah, Colorado, Nevada, Arizona, New Mexico, or Texas. Likewise, anyone familiar with Southern California knows that all those movies from the 1930s and '40s that supposedly took place in Africa or South America were really shot in the white sands of the Mojave just east of Los Angeles or among the dry, rolling, oak-studded hills just north of it. However, I'd say that our strongest and most sympathetic experiences of nature are usually specific to a particular moment as well as a particular place, and more often than not they're unique. Did Wordsworth really mean his heart leapt *every time* he beheld a rainbow? Did Wallace Stevens place more than *one jar* on a Tennessee hill? Better to say that each turned a moment into a quality or an eternity.

Many of my own moments resulted from seeing something familiar in a new light—one of the first being the time I stood waist-deep in the swirling white backwash of a heavy surf, my ears popping, my nose dripping salt water, my hands shielding my eyes against the sun setting over the crest of a wave, and realized that even though I'd spent most of my childhood in the Pacific Ocean, I would forever remember that moment as one of the happiest of my life. It was as if everything I'd experienced while snorkeling, scuba diving, tide-pooling, body-surfing, or simply hanging out on the fine-grained muddy beaches of the Pacific had instantly been invested with a strange and overwhelming joy. Wittgenstein might say it was an extreme version of learning how to appreciate what we already know.

Still, I've been equally struck by the *un*familiarity of a situation or place—and that's basically what happened at Big Bend, where everything I'd been taking note of in bits and pieces suddenly fell into place and became whole. Though different from my adolescent epiphany, the shift in perspective was equally astonishing. All at once I felt that I was seeing the relationship *between* things, not just the things themselves, as if mere words had been replaced by a grammar. Features that had earlier seemed somewhat random or chaotic now seemed necessary. Rocks lay where they lay for a reason. River cane took root where it did for a reason. Even the most residual or peripheral aspects of the scene fit a pattern—part of what *made* it a pattern in the first place.

Clearly, I had awakened to a new and wonderful world. I was alert. I was conscious. And because we've become so accustomed to the need for *self-consciousness*—think of how obsessed Thoreau was with the state of being asleep or awake—the heightened awareness of my senses gave me nearly as much pleasure as the beautiful stretch of river I was beginning to make sense of. One of the reasons I mistrust the sublime, at least as Kant memorably defined it in the *Critique of Judgment*, is that it resists "the interests of the senses." Of course, Kant meant something very specific by this, defining the sublime as an expression of the mind's capacity to imagine limitlessness. But the concept has played an iffy, often reactionary role in American history. Manifest Destiny in particular trafficked in the rhetoric of the sublime, deliberately slanting the idea of limitlessness to mean that a nation which had barely moved west of the Mississippi could lay claim to an entire continent—if not in person, then "by map" alone. In the 1820s, an anonymous article reprinted in the *North American Review* declared that "Americans are far from being pleased with the irregular figure which the Republic exhibits upon the map. This and that corner of the continent must be *bought* (or conquered if it cannot be bought) in order to give a more handsome sweep to their periphery." These were not the sentiments of someone interested in his senses. If Lt. Emory had relied on his senses in the Chihuahuan Desert— really *looked* at the land before him, really measured it by eye rather than his sextant—he wouldn't have claimed there was some sort of natural or providential boundary between the United States and Mexico, and then identified that supposedly God-given boundary with the abstract lines of latitude and longitude that circled the globe. Parallel 31°20´, indeed!

All of this came to mind when the rising and falling sounds of a song again reminded us that the Rio Grande was a river to be looked at but not crossed—yet another gestalt of sorts that had us toggling back and forth between scenery and politics, the United States and Mexico. For perched on a large rock across the river were three men singing *Cielito Lindo* over and over again—though just the first verse and the refrain, each four lines long:

> De la Sierra Morena,
> Cielita lindo, vienen bajando,
> Un par de ojitos negros,
> Cielito lindo, de contrabando.

> *Ay, ay, ay, ay,*
> *Canta y no llores,*
> *Porque cantando se alegran,*
> *Cielito lindo, los corazones.*

At first the men seemed to be serenading us and a few other tourists wandering through the canyon. But *they* were clearly on their side of the river and *we* were clearly on ours, so even when their singing appeared to have the incidental, background quality of birdsong, there was almost a taunting edge to it—as if to prove that the border cut both ways. The same thing was true of the way they sometimes gestured with their hands, effectively beckoning us and needling us at the same time. Even the song itself was fraught, since it's said to be about a young woman rescued from a bandit stronghold in Spain:

> From the Sierra Morena,
> Pretty little darling, are coming down,
> A pair of black eyes,
> Pretty little heaven, which are contraband.

Ay, ay, ay, ay,
Sing and don't cry,
Because singing brightens up,
Pretty little darling, the hearts.

What made this situation especially strange was that unlike the man on the white horse, the men standing on the rock didn't seem to be selling anything. We didn't see anything laid out on the river bank and nobody was holding anything up. Nor did they indicate they might be holding something back, waiting for one of us to show an interest of some sort. The only thing that seemed to explain their presence was that they were *there*. And from our side of the river, you couldn't even tell *how* they'd gotten there, since the rock was just an eccentrically eroded portion of the cliffs and didn't offer any obvious means of reaching it.

Maybe the sheer obscurity of the situation—the question of what the men were doing there in the first place and what they might want—explained why several of the people ahead of us on the trail started acting a little nervous. None of them stood stock still or bolted back up the trail. But three or four moved away from the river's edge as they passed the men, angling back only after they'd opened up a comfortable gap, and one couple put even more distance between themselves and the men as they returned, nearly hugging the cliffs at times. It occurred to me they might feel as threatened by an unaccustomed urge to be watchful as by the men themselves. Not everyone is used to keeping their eyes peeled like New Yorkers. But I wasn't surprised to cross paths with a ranger a little later who said he'd gotten several complaints about the men and was about to investigate.

On our way back up the trail, Ruth and I decided to buy a few of the beaded animals after all. We found them just as we'd left them on the rock—still waiting for a playful hand to animate them, perhaps, but something worth looking at once we got back to New York and a tangible reminder of the line we'd crossed when we stopped to look at them in the first place.

While selecting the ones we wanted, we noticed that the man on the horse was watching us again. To signal him, to let him know we were paying for the animals, we held the plastic cup in a slow, silent movie kind of way and exaggerated our gestures as we put the money in. A little later, looking back from above, we watched him slowly splash across the river, work his way up the trail until he reached the rock, lean over from the horse's back to pick up our money without taking the money that was already there, then return without a second glance to the other side. For some reason I was reminded of a scene in *Chinatown*—the one where Jack Nicholson is squatting down in what's supposed to be a dry riverbed, waiting for a young Mexican American boy who may know why there's a small pool of water there. When the boy shows up, riding a large white horse, he says very softly, very matter-of-factly, that the water "goes in different parts of the river. Every night a different part." Then he jerks the horse's head around and leaves without a backward glance.

I've often wondered whether we would have encountered the men selling the beaded animals and singing *Cielito Lindo* if a small border crossing in Big Bend—just two or three miles upriver from the Boquillas Trail, and officially named the Boquillas Crossing Point of Entry—hadn't been closed at the time.

The crossing point is very low-key: just a dirt road, a parking lot, and a few buildings. And it's only for pedestrians in any case, since people make their way back and forth across the Rio Grande on a small flat bottomed boat. But the crossing is more important than it might seem at first. Among other things, the village of Boquillas del Carmen lies just uphill from the river, and the village is known for its restaurants, embroidered bags, and, yes, beaded animals. When the crossing closed in 2002—one of the many ancillary responses to 9/11—American tourists stopped coming, the village's economy tanked, and a number of people left. I can easily believe that those who stayed felt they had little choice but to lay out their wares for the tourists who still visited the Boquillas Trail—even if the need to keep their distance forced them to trust the very people who'd closed the border in the first place. That some might also want to taunt those people is hardly surprising.

Happily, the Boquillas crossing reopened in 2013, after a lengthy study by Customs and Border Protection concluded it would be useful and safe. Despite all those who opposed the move, the agency found that "the establishment of the Boquillas border crossing is consistent with the designation of the area as a region of binational interest and that the Boquillas border crossing is needed to fill the long stretch of border between Presidio and Del Rio where there is currently no authorized international border crossing." There's even a hint that closing the border had been counterproductive, since the study also specified that an "enhanced security focus at the border crossing" generally "discouraged illegal activity in the vicinity" rather than making it easier. Jane Jacobs had pointed to something similar in *The Death and Life of Great American Cities* when she said that crowds and neighborhood businesses—with their "constant succession of eyes"—were the key to safe sidewalks in New York.

But here's the most interesting thing about the study: it wasn't prompted by fears of a hostile border. Instead it had an *environmental* focus that turned the entire issue of Big Bend's southern boundary into a good neighbor policy. Contrary to Sen. Ross, Joseph Chandler, Lt. Emory, and all the others who had misused natural law over the years, the opening paragraph of the Customs and Border Protection decision read: "In 2010, the Presidents of the United States and Mexico issued a joint statement supporting the designation of a region of protected areas on both sides of the Rio Grande, including Big Bend National Park, as a region of binational interest. In support of this, CBP began working with the National Park Service to establish a border crossing to allow authorized travel between the areas in the United States and Mexico."

For some reason Mexican and American authorities waited until 2015 to celebrate the reopening. But in early April—nearly four years to the day Ruth and I visited the park—they held a joint ceremony, first on one side of the border, then on the other, bridging a river the United States still calls the Rio Grande and Mexico still calls the Rio Bravo. According to a *Houston Chronicle* article, the double ceremony included comments by Secretary of the Interior Sally Jewell, U.S. Ambassador to Mexico Earl Wayne, and Mexico's Minister of Environment and Natural Resources Juan José Guerra Abud. Secretary Jewell emphasized that the Big Bend/ Rio Bravo region is one of the most bio-diverse in the world, and that "butterflies, reptiles, flowers, plants, birds . . . don't know of this artificial boundary." Ambassador Wayne echoed these sentiments when he declared, "The park is a symbol for what the border can be—a place that brings us together, not one that divides us."

So here I sit, admiring my crafty roadrunner, knowing that when Ruth and I bought it we crossed a line that no flesh-and-blood roadrunner would ever recognize. Needless to say, the most important line between a good and a bad country is always the one that lies *within* a country's borders, not the one separating it from any other country. I later discovered that even the NPS website for Big Bend cautions that, like the pair of black eyes in *Cielito Lindo*, anything not sold in Boquillas del Carmen or the park's camp stores is "considered contraband." But contraband is the language of nations, not nature, and one of the things that sets a good country apart from a bad one these days is its attitude toward nature. Because the Mexican border has become such a contentious issue, far too many people now believe that nature needs to be secured rather than preserved. And yet, as the Customs and Border Protection study showed, when things are seen in a less fearful light, an appreciation for nature encourages the United States and Mexico to *share* their border instead of constantly fighting over it. If various factors have hardened the boundary between us from time to time, nature has always been a way of softening it again. In the eyes of nature, even where the two countries diverge or come into conflict, we are more like a gestalt than anything else—not antipodes, not antonyms, but different sides of the same thing. To slightly amend a phrase Pascal made famous: Nature is an infinite sphere, whose center is everywhere and whose circumference is nowhere. No lines at all.

JASON MOLESKY

Coal, Natural Gas, "Other Material," and Whiskey

Hydrofracturing Country, USA

Late December, 2016: Winter dark brings monstrous things from hiding.

This time of year, my parents' yard used to be silent. Now, as I stand among their bare dogwoods, I can feel the industrial hum in the ridges of my skull. It builds from the edge of the dairy farm just across the road, where floodlights blast a bluish, alien glow over a sentry booth, a security gate, and a barbed-wire perimeter fence slashing along the rise.

Three years ago these georgic acres, like so many others in southwestern Pennsylvania, were transformed into the site of a hydrofracturing operation that extracts methane (natural gas) from deep underground shales. The official name of this site, printed on a sign along the road, is Gotham City. It occupies a knoll four hundred feet from my parents' bedroom.

During the early stages, the disruption was more aggressive. My parents tell of the rattling in their bones, clouds of toxic sand, constant diesel traffic. Not long after all this started, my father got his first nosebleed. My mother's symptoms, more severe, presented later, after the drilling rig and pumping trucks had given way to a small compressor station and a cluster of condensate tanks. Even with this modest footprint, the compressor's engines sound throughout the valley. Every conversation, every laugh, is underlain by an implacable droning. Indoors, your senses adapt temporarily and you cease hearing it. Then the noise returns, and you remember that you're being slowly poisoned.

My wife and I sit on the porch ringed by holiday garland. Two heavy trucks boom past on the winding farm road, causing our dog to cower. In a few days, we will leave this place. We'll take the turnpike back to New Jersey, where I'm a graduate student in literature and Kate's drafting her first novel. Having the freedom to escape the blight and toxicity carries such guilt that for a moment I am seized by a vision—Gotham burning, the perimeter fence a fiery wreck, the detonator flashing in my hand. A vain, dreadful fantasy, and I shiver it away.

The stars yield to Gotham's floodlights. The droning goes on and on until its nuances and variations emerge, coming to seem almost beautiful—a postmodern dirge, a threnody for Washington County, Pennsylvania, my ancestral home.

My mother's grandfather, Francis, went into the mines like his father before him. He was twelve years old and smoked nothing but Camels. Initially he looked after the mules and led wagon teams from the pit. Later he dug coal with pick, shovel, and blasting powder, then trained as an underground shop mechanic—a relatively safe and enviable position.

Francis was twenty-one when he married Anne, sixteen. The couple made their first home in Cokeburg, a prototypical coal town built around the mine and the associated coke works. The company dumped its slag and slate in the middle of town, forming a great mound of gray-black rock that separated the bosses' stately brick homes from the rows and rows of duplexes where Anne and the other wives reared the next generation of working bodies. No one hung the laundry outside. Anne would often wake to find her small garden patinated by soot. She would squint up at the hills, at the fields and pastures. When her rage grew too frightful, she sang hymns.

Finally, World War II brought a coal boom. A series of strikes resulted in higher wages, and in 1949 Anne and Francis purchased an acre of land a mile away, next to a dairy farm in the village of Scenery Hill. The property wasn't as dear as it might have been, since most of it lay on a steep incline with a view of Cokeburg's slate dump. But the acre was theirs. "Landowners" became a word no longer hateful. Anne planted dogwoods and silver maples to improve the sightlines, and Francis started work on the basement foundation, laying block, hammering floor joists. The well he dug in the back yard produced pure, delicious water, the best they had ever known.

For nearly a decade, they and their three sons lived in the home's foundation while Francis completed the first floor. Not until near the end of his life were they able to add the second floor they had always envisioned—a task that relatives maintain finally killed him.

My parents bought the house when Anne passed, and my father—another handy, parsimonious coal miner—renovated it, from bones to eyelashes, for the next four years. He and my paternal grandfather—a retired miner himself—did the skilled labor, while my brother and I lugged cement and shingles, lumber and bricks, power drills and come-alongs and cold lemonade. We built an attached garage from the foundation up, demolished and rebuilt the basement, replaced Anne's sun porch with a vaulted entry, paved the driveway, added a rear deck, changed out Francis's jackleg electrical work, and tackled the many other projects Dad kept dreaming up.

The jobs had to be squeezed into nights and vacations, because Dad was logging sixty- and seventy-hour weeks as a shift foreman at the mine. He had busted his ass since age twelve saving money to put himself through engineering school at Penn State, and even earned his master's at WVU, yet two decades after entering the mines he still found himself underground, laboring in darkness just as his father had done. If he couldn't build upon his father's life in the way he had intended, he would turn his energies on the house.

All the sweat and sawdust seem to have effected an alchemy. A year after completing the work, Dad was promoted to the coal company's engineering office.

He, my mother, and my two younger siblings moved into the house the summer I left for college. For me, the house in Scenery Hill is a repository not so much of my own memories, but of my family's aspirations, the area's history, something larger and more encompassing than myself—but a place that nonetheless has produced my *self* by inflecting my thoughts and feelings in ways I will never quite master.

I worked through college as an underground coal miner, intending at first to make it a career. Mining was simply what a man did. In the darkness I became adept at splicing anaconda cables and replacing the teeth of cutting heads. But as time passed and I read about mercury rain, labor movements, and literary history, I discovered that writing and scholarship, too, are forms of mining, and that through them one can go deeper, and differently, than the elevator shaft allows.

This essay goes below the ground—not exactly as I did while mining coal, but in much the same communal spirit—to explore how hydrofracturing in places like Scenery Hill extracts much more than just natural gas. Toward this end, I draw strongly on my family's experiences in southwestern Pennsylvania, and on the region's broader history.

I also use evidence from contemporary journalism and scientific research. Some of these sources are cited in-text, and all can be found in the endnotes that follow the essay. In my view, the great majority of the controversy that now trails hydrofracturing research has been manufactured by the industry and its handmaidens in the usual manner. From the Kettering Institute's cooked studies of leaded gasoline and zinc-mill pollution, to the "merchants of doubt" who have more recently cast miasmas over inconvenient truths, this time-tested strategy—dodge, shift, occlude—may be the most reasonable course for capitalist industry, but it is also indecent, mendacious, and cruel. If my sources seem to evince a bias, it's not for the right or the left, but for the strange truths on and under the ground, and for all we blithely refuse to see.

———————

That same December night where this essay began, just after I bring the dog indoors my parents give to Kate and me twin decks of playing cards. The reverse side of each black card is embossed in shimmering, meretricious red with the word COAL and the state symbol of Pennsylvania, the keystone.

"The founder of the feast," my father says. "Coal." He smiles with a sort of ironic pride. In the next room, A Christmas Carol with George C. Scott is playing.

We're sitting at Anne's kitchen table. The oven, cabinets, and counters are also those she used. Sometimes the effect is comforting, but tonight it feels uncanny and bizarre.

"They were handing them out at a holiday function," Dad says, gesturing to the cards. "I figured I'd had enough of the real thing. Twenty-two years underground, wasn't it, hon?"

Mom sips from a bottle of water. Like many people in hydrofracturing areas, she no longer trusts the well. "Twenty-two years," she sighs. "I'll take engineering for you any day."

"It's not terrible," Dad says.

"Not terrible?" she says amiably. "Compared to the mine?"

"Yeah," he says, "I'd say it's an upgrade. It does have indoor plumbing."

This draws from us laughter and groans. Even our dog, with her eager eyes and lolling tongue, looks to be in on the fun.

Then the dying cat, Topaz—cancer of the leg, metastasized—caterwauls from the basement bathroom, and we remember when and where we are.

My parents have lined that bathroom with newspaper and old blankets to turn it into a makeshift hospice through the holidays. The idea is that my younger siblings, who grew up with Topaz but now live out of state, should get the chance to say goodbye.

"Poor little guy," says Mom. "If it weren't for that darn vaccine . . ."

According to Topaz's vet, the cancer sprang from a reaction to a now-discontinued vaccine. Mom has informed Kate and me of this diagnosis at least five times. She says this nearly every time the cat comes up in conversation, and quite possibly it represents the true account. Either way, as with so much else, she needs to believe in it.

When Gotham began operations in 2013, I hoped that my parents would sell the property and move. But how do you leave a home like this one? A home whose every board and brick you measured, sawed, hammered, drilled, loathed, loved, swore at, and confessed to? One where your grandmother's lilacs still bloom? How could you bring yourself to sell a home so imbued with your own being, one that has come to hold the narrative of your life?

I now know these are gratuitous questions. My parents will never be able to sell the house. Even if they somehow managed to find a buyer, most banks won't grant mortgages for homes so close to hydrofracturing operations. The danger of industrial accidents, methane explosions, and well-water contamination is simply too high. Actuaries deem such mortgages unacceptable risks.

In 2016, the character of the U.S. electricity-generation system changed. Natural gas (methane) capped a decade of incredible growth by surpassing coal to become the nation's top source of electric power. Despite the benefits coal has brought to my family—and to civilization—there's no denying that it has become a monstrous anachronism in the twenty-first century. Unfortunately, replacing coal with another fossil fuel only reiterates the same problems in different guises: generating electricity with hydrofractured natural gas is no better than using coal, and in some ways it is more dangerous.

At first glance, natural gas would seem to merit the enthusiasm policymakers have shown for it. Relative to coal-fired power plants, natural gas plants reduce carbon emissions (CO_2) by 40 to 50 percent per unit of electricity. They also generate a small fraction of coal's air and water pollution. When we limit our analysis to the grisly smokestacks, natural gas looks like a relative panacea. But if we also consider the other components of an energy system—i.e., the way that a fuel is extracted, transported, and sold—the apparent advantages of natural gas quickly evaporate.

With respect to the climate, for example, methane is a hugely potent greenhouse gas, and the amount of it leaking from pipelines and other infrastructure is enough to cancel out the greenhouse-related benefits of the lower carbon emissions. Methane decomposes from the atmosphere faster than carbon dioxide, but for the short time it's present, it packs a much stronger punch. A given amount of methane causes eighty-four times more warming than an equal amount of CO_2 over a twenty-year period, and twenty-eight times more over a century. With current leak rates of 3 to 7 percent of total volume, a new natural gas power plant with a fifty-year operational life will generate *more* warming than a similar coal plant for up to ninety years. Partisans of gas often tout anti-leak measures, but the most optimistic targets put forward by the Obama administration, were they somehow enforced, would only reduce emissions by less than half. Even in the best case, then, methane leakage alone nullifies most, if not all, of the climatic advantage natural gas ostensibly holds over coal in the short-to-medium term—a period climatologists judge critical for avoiding runaway, self-sustaining climate change.

Crucially, natural gas doesn't displace just coal on the electrical grid; it also displaces zero-emissions energy. Cheap gas pouring from shale reserves has already shuttered nuclear plants around the country. Research indicates that, in the absence of a robust carbon tax, natural gas will also delay wind and solar energy in most markets for decades. Because gas financially strangles clean energy in a way that coal cannot, many projections show that a strong turn to natural gas power will actually *increase* long-term U.S. carbon emissions. Far from being a bridge to sustainability, a natural gas energy system locks society into a future of high greenhouse emissions and all but guarantees catastrophic global warming.

Some supporters of gas, such as Jay Apt of Carnegie Mellon, admit that it offers no real climate benefits relative to coal, yet still argue for its use on the grounds of environmental health. And indeed, studies show that metro areas begin to enjoy cleaner air and water, fewer illnesses, and increased longevity the moment their electric utility changes from coal to natural gas. Move into hydrofracturing country, though, and questions of pollution grow more muddled—by benzene, toluene, ethylbenzene, and xylene (BTEX); formaldehyde, methanol, ethylene glycol, naphthalene, hydrogen sulfide, volatile organic compounds (VOCs); and sundry other toxins that shale drillers release into local ecosystems with impunity. Along with the slow violence of bad air and water, residents also face the threat of more immediate catastrophes. When a well pad exploded not far from Scenery Hill in 2014, killing a worker, forcing evacuations, and starting a noxious fire that burned for four days, the company in question remediated the issue by sending its "neighbors" a certificate for a free large pie at Bobtown Pizza.

The health impacts of living near a hydrofracturing operation are well-documented: greater incidences of asthma, allergies, muscles aches, fatigue, nausea, joint stiffness, headaches, rashes, lesions, unexplained hair loss, weakened bones, and other ailments. Emerging studies have strongly linked the practice to reproductive and fetal health problems, such as low sperm counts, infertility, miscarriage, stillbirth, birth defects, and low birth weights. Researchers also expect to see elevated rates of cancer. The number of Americans potentially affected could be as high as 15.3 million—the number estimated by the *Wall Street Journal* to live within one mile of a gas well drilled since 2000. And because few citizens of hydrofracturing country derive any material benefits for their suffering, direct symptoms also seem to engender a sense of helplessness and injustice that intensifies other public health crises, such as addiction and suicide.

Taken collectively, the health impacts of natural gas power are probably no worse than those of coal, but they are more localized. Pollution from coal power plants affects everyone, while the impacts of hydrofracturing fall most heavily on those living near the well pads. In this bizarre scenario, rural people like my parents are made to imbibe poisons so that the rest of us can enjoy better health and cleaner environments. Naturally, such unequal fallout distribution bodes poorly for the health of the body politic as well.

To be clear, I am not arguing that coal should regain preeminence. Any well-informed, reasonable person will agree that renewable energy, fostered by public investment, offers the only way forward. And toward this end we must acknowledge that those who claim hydrofractured natural gas to be a viable bridge to anything other than a toxic dystopia are either mistaken or lying.

Overall, natural gas has gained traction over coal not for "green" reasons, but because it promises greater profits, not least for the big banks that arrange the financing. The upfront costs of new drilling—eight million dollars per well in 2018, according to the *Oil and Gas Journal*—means that hydrofracturing has more to do with Goldman Sachs than with Daniel Plainview. Paltry regulation makes compliance costs minimal, and once shale wells are drilled and fractured, they don't require much labor outside of roving security guards. The field workers they do use are, for the most part, non-union, nomadic, and precarious, consisting of itinerant contractors who follow the rigs like carnival operators. From a capital perspective, unaffiliated transients hold distinct advantages over locals: they are cheaper, more tractable, and almost certain never to strike. A pipeline, needless to say, multiplies these gains, eliminating labor costs even further while ensuring that a steady supply of product almost always arrives on schedule.

The shift to natural gas has nothing to do with the climate, the environment, or public health, and indeed it benefits none of these. Rather, powerbrokers are moving the United States to a natural gas energy system for the oldest reason in civilized affairs: it very efficiently funnels profits, well-being, and control over resources to the financial elite at the expense of the rural poor.

Seven thousand feet beneath my parents' house, the Marcellus Shale lies like a great buried chalkboard, eighty feet thick and a hundred miles wide. The Marcellus runs from the Finger Lakes of New York to the Blue Ridge Mountains of Virginia, underlying most of Pennsylvania, West Virginia, and eastern Ohio. This formation holds one of the richest deposits of natural gas in the world.

Until about a decade ago, the gas was unrecoverable. Then technical advances made the hydrofracturing of deep shales feasible, and production in Pennsylvania exploded—immediately. No health studies, no water-quality assessments, no moratoria. The mood was comparable to that of a seedy bar just before closing time: a desperate concupiscence, a drunken abandon.

The U.S. Energy Information Administration reports that in 2008, just before the boom began in earnest, Pennsylvania produced 198 billion cubic feet of natural gas. This was a relatively modest amount, good for fifteenth place nationally. In 2017, the state produced twenty-eight times that volume, 5.46 trillion cubic feet (more than 5 trillion of which came from fracturing in the Marcellus). Data from FracTracker Alliance shows that 11,006 shale wells were drilled in Pennsylvania during these nine years, an average of more than three wells per day. Pennsylvania now produces more natural gas than any state but Texas. Based on figures from the CIA *World Factbook*, if Pennsylvania were to become an independent country—Methania, perhaps—it would rank seventh in the world in natural gas production, coming in just below China.

Thanks to the hydrofracturing of shale reserves—the Marcellus as well as the Bakken in North Dakota, the Barnett, Eagle Ford, and Permian in Texas, the Niobrara in Colorado, and many others—the United States is now the world's leading producer of both oil and natural gas. That is to say, over the last decade or so, fueled by hydrofracturing, we quietly became a petro-state.

There was little public debate or reflection about this epochal shift in energy policy. The elected leaders of a nation of morphine addicts, suddenly discovering a cheaper method for cultivating the opium poppy, would not question whether it was advisable to do so. They would plant immediately, and everywhere possible. They would exempt morphine production from regulatory oversight, particularly if they happened to have strong ties to leading poppy-seed companies. We should not be surprised that this sort of reflexive plunge is precisely what happened as regards the hydrofracturing industry in the United States of the naughts.

Donald Trump gave the keynote address at the Shale Insight conference in Pittsburgh in September 2016: "I think probably no other business has been affected by regulation [more] than your business," he told the assembled energy executives. "Federal regulations remain a major restriction to shale production." This simply could not be further from the truth. Hydrofracturing on private and state land, where 90 percent of wells are located, has received exemptions from nearly all federal environmental legislation. This regulatory gap, one of the most baffling and egregious imaginable, is the legacy of Dick Cheney, whose former employer, Halliburton, pioneered proto-fracturing technologies as early as 1949 and remains the unquestioned industry leader.

Cheney chaired the 2005 Energy Task Force, which inserted into that year's Energy Policy Act the so-called "Halliburton Loophole," a series of now-infamous amendments, each only a few lines long, that works to effectively prohibit the EPA from regulating hydrofracturing. Before anyone outside the Dallas Petroleum Club knew what hydrofracturing was, the federal water-protection statutes that would have imposed checks on its unimpeded growth were quietly eviscerated. Just as Cheney did during the second Iraq War, he relied on absent intelligence and ordered a crippling preemptive strike against the American people.

One of these amendments, in a single sentence, exempts hydrofracturing from the Safe Drinking Water Act: "The term 'underground injection' excludes ... fluids or propping agents (other than diesel fuels) pursuant to hydraulic fracturing operations." This is a paragon of efficiency and temerity, an expertly struck lance to the eye. Another amendment even more adroitly captures the quintessential hilarity of hydrofracturing: it requires the federal government to consider noxious fracking fluids, millions of gallons of which are injected into each well, as "other material" rather than as "pollutants," thereby exempting hydrofracturing from all major parts of the Clean Water Act. (Other amendments, pertaining to rainwater runoff and related matters, take care of the rest.) Such sinister misappellation suggests an extraordinary talent for satire; Vonnegut, even Swift, could have done no better.

Like any artist's work, though, Cheney's is hardly sui generis. He surely took inspiration, for example, from a 1990 amendment that exempts individual oil and gas wells from the Clean Air Act. Its brilliance lies in the decision to leave large processing facilities and regional compressors under the Act's jurisdiction, allowing the industry to claim that it is being sufficiently regulated. Meanwhile, clusters of gas wells spanning entire counties, which collectively emit far more air pollution than any single facility, remain beyond federal oversight.

Thanks to Cheney's ability to build on the achievements of his predecessors in startlingly original ways, Pennsylvania stands at the vanguard of the nation's transformation into an oil and gas colony. We should recognize his genius by awarding him a prize commensurate with his enduring influence on American culture. The Pulitzer Prize in Poetry, awarded for "The Halliburton Loophole," could potentially do the job.

In the heart of the Marcellus, more than a mile underground, the temperature approaches 165 degrees Fahrenheit. One can hardly fathom such heat, pressure, and darkness. This is primeval chaos, the roiling deep—a domain that artists and seers have always delighted in chronicling.

The deep is the realm of betrayal, parricide, and cannibalism. Goya has Saturn devouring his children there. Milton's Sin is perpetually eaten by her half-born offspring at the gates of Hell. Dante reserves the ninth and final circle for traitors, two of whom, Cain and Ptolemy (son of Abubus), killed close relatives. More recently, we have H. G. Wells's tunnel-dwelling Morlocks making meals of their distant relations, the Eloi; and Cormac McCarthy's *The Road*, featuring half-butchered humans kept alive in a root cellar to preserve their meat.

High-volume slickwater horizontal hydrofracturing continues this rich cultural tradition: it is a betrayal of the present and the future, an act of cannibalism perpetrated deep beneath the surface against family members now alive and those yet to be born.

Methane results from the decomposition of tiny sea creatures that died some four hundred million years ago. Their corpses sank to the bottom of an inland sea, where they were entombed in mud. Over eons, the mud hardened into shale, and the corpses within decayed anaerobically to form bubbles of methane gas. Hydrofracturing works by drilling down into the shale and systematically cracking it with high-pressure jets of fracking fluid. This forces the methane out of the shale and into the well's production tube, which conducts it to the surface for distribution.

The process begins with the requisite gas leases. In return for the right to drill, companies offer royalties of 15 to 20 percent (around seven figures in the first year for a group of wells like Gotham's). Then they sweeten the deal with a signing bonus of up to eight thousand dollars per acre, as Peter Kelly-Detwiler describes in the 2013 *Forbes* article "Shale Leases: Promised Land." Since few rural landowners can refuse the industry's money, leasing is usually a simple affair. But some parcels of land, such as my parents' acre, are deeded as split estates, meaning that one party owns the land, while another owns the mineral rights to the underground resources. A drilling company that has contracted with the mineral owner can encroach upon, use, and modify the land in any way deemed "reasonably necessary" to developing the gas. Surface owners receive nothing; if they object to their land being turned into a heavy industrial zone, they have no legal recourse. My parents' plot is small and steep enough that it has so far remained intact, but many people have seen their land overtaken, rousing disgust, bewilderment, and fury.

When the papers have been signed, geologists and logisticians select the optimal site for the well pad, usually about five acres. The plot is cleared, graded, covered with gravel, and surrounded by a barbed-wire perimeter fence. A sentry booth is installed near the compound's gate. Gravel driveways and access roads are built, and an impoundment pit is dug to hold toxic waste. To safeguard aquifers, the pit is lined with a layer of woven, reinforced thirty-mil polyethylene— or, in more prosaic terms: we rely on a tarp half as thick as a dime to protect everything in the area from being poisoned.

Next the drilling rig arrives, a towering derrick with steel joists and girders in reds and yellows, an abstract sculpture ten stories high planted in the midst of pastures. It typically remains onsite for six to twelve weeks (and sometimes longer), drilling almost constantly. The earth shakes, the noise is enormous. At night the rig becomes an imperial ziggurat, bright with spotlights, hissing smoke and lording over the hillocks, rumbling like Jonathan Edwards' Angry God.

Operators first drill vertically into the earth for more than a mile, using a sequence of three or four progressively harder and smaller drill bits. A rotating column of steel pipe drives the bit, and also acts as a conduit for the viscous fluid that provides lubrication and clears away drill cuttings. At fixed intervals, usually every thirty feet, drilling pauses so that this column—the drill string—can be extended at the surface with a fresh length of pipe, allowing the bit to plunge deeper.

When the bit approaches the gas-imbued shale, operators transition to a wondrous technique that David Blackmon of *Forbes* recently called "a marvel of engineering and scientific innovation"—horizontal drilling. Technicians use computer imagery, telemetry sensors, and a specialized hydraulic bit to guide the drill string (which, though steel, is relatively flexible at this length) through a gradual arc called the "bend," so that when it enters the Marcellus it is nearly horizontal. On that course, drilling continues through the shale layer for as many as three miles, radically increasing the well's extraction radius.

With the well finished, the rig is moved a few meters away, where operators drill yet another well, this one curving off in a different direction. At sites completed before 2016 or so, four to eight such wells were typically drilled on any given well pad. But plunging natural gas prices have since inspired drillers to evolve more efficient methods. As of 2018, the most advanced Marcellus operations have received state permits to drill *forty wells* from a single pad, an extraordinary concentration of risk—and royalties. (Gotham City, drilled in 2013, comprises four wells, all aptly named after a violent billionaire—Bruce Wayne A 1H, Bruce Wayne A 3H, Bruce Wayne A 5H, and Bruce Wayne B 7H.) When all drilling is complete, operators break down the rig and remove it to the next pad—and the next, and the next, with no end in sight.

As the boreholes are being drilled—or, rarely, just after they are finished—operators line them with steel tubing, called casing, which they cement into place. Near the surface, multiple layers of casing and cement are installed, purportedly to sequester the area's groundwater. According to Pennsylvania state inspectors, however, 6 to 7 percent of well casings generally fail within the first year. And because wells lose structural integrity as they age, some scientists estimate that 40 to 60 percent of casings will fail within thirty years and nearly all will fail within a few centuries. Clearly, operators do not case their wells to protect the environment over the long term; they case their wells to protect *their wells* over the short period of prime gas production. Long after the drilling is over, danger remains buried like a subtle, insidious land mine.

The casing that lines the horizontal section of the well, deep in the shale layer, is called the production casing. Once it is in place, operators fill it with tubes of small charges designed to perforate metal. At eight charges per foot (the industry average), a three-mile-long horizontal spur requires some 126,000 charges. This is a military-industrial sortie taking place beneath forests and houses. On cue, the charges explode. They are typically arranged in a spiral pattern, and each one blasts a bullet-size hole through the production casing, opening it to the shale.

At this point, finally, high-volume slickwater hydrofracturing can commence. A parade of water trucks begins roaring past homes on the narrow, sinuous rural roads at any and all hours. Over approximately two weeks, diesel-powered pumping stations inject four to ten million gallons of slick-water (fracking fluid) into each well at incredible pressures. Slickwater consists of 98 percent freshwater, 1 percent sand, and 1 percent noxious chemicals that the federal government sees as "other material." To get a sense of how toxic these chemicals are, consider—as Abraham Lustgarten reports in *Scientific American*—that a nurse in Colorado suffered multiple organ failure after stripping the protective clothing from a rig-worker who had been splashed with some of them during a spill. Sixty thousand gallons of "other material" are used in each well; the precise blend depends on conditions, but frequent ingredients include benzene and other BTEX chemicals, boric acid, sulfuric acid, 2-butoxyethanol, lye, phenols, lead, diesel fuel, kerosene, and dozens of other carcinogens, mutagens, and endocrine disruptors—along with many undisclosed compounds legally classified as "proprietary trade secrets" (for example, "Flo Stop P," "ZetaFlow," and "EXP-F0173–11"), the toxicities of which remain officially unknown. In a further insult to environmental health, the slickwater, unbelievably, is often mixed onsite, throwing clouds of silica and powdered chemicals into the air. My parents say it was "like a sandstorm."

Injected slickwater races down the borehole and into the horizontal spur, where it shoots through the spiraling holes in the casing. Each jet punches the shale with enormous force, cracking the rock. What results from this concentrated assault is an endlessly branching network of fissures, which the sand and other proppants in the slickwater hold open so that the methane can flow more easily out of the shale and into the well. The slickwater, lately imbued with the radioactivity of the bedrock, remains for the most part beneath the ground under enormous pressure, stewing, reacting with itself, seeking avenues of release.

The portion of slickwater compelled by pressure to come back up the well with the first frenzy of gas—perhaps 20 percent of the total used, or more than a million gallons—is shunted to a nearby impoundment pit where, in the best case, it rests atop folds of wafer-thin plastic. There it becomes known as "produced water." Some operators reuse this to fracture other wells, but after a few more runs it is slated for "permanent" disposal. Trucks arrive. They are marked "Residual Waste," a phrase that exactly encapsulates how area residents feel they are treated by the drilling companies. The trucks ferry the sludge to so-called deep injection wells, where machines pump it several miles underground, into bedrock deemed porous enough to retain—forever—billions of gallons of radioactive poisons. Deep injection wells, however, have leaked. They have also caused earthquakes, which in turn likely increase the rates at which they fail—yet another toxic cycle.

The pad's successfully fractured well is capped with a wellhead, a stout mass of valves and pipes. In the industry this structure is known as a Christmas tree, for it is of that size and usually painted green. Condensate tanks built to look like silos are also brought to the site; these will store complex hydrocarbons, the raw materials of plastics that rise with the methane. Other specialized components—for example, compressors like the one that drones constantly outside my parents' home—are likewise hauled in to filter the gas and prepare it for transport. When the well has been linked to a pipeline, the valves atop the well are opened—in industry-speak, the Christmas tree is "lit up"—and production begins.

Gas output from shale wells peaks immediately—a gushing oil well offers a fair analogy. After one year, a well's daily output has generally fallen to 30 percent of the initial rate; after two years, 20 percent; after four years, 10 percent; after eight years, 5 percent. Royalty payments plunge accordingly.

Shale wells are expected to keep producing, at lower and lower rates, for twenty to thirty years, during which period they may be re-fractured three or four times. To maintain supply, new wells must be constantly drilled. "We'll have a million new oil and gas wells drilled over the next few decades in the U.S.," Robert Jackson of Duke University told the *Wall Street Journal* in 2013. "One to two million new gas wells. Those are the projections," said the director Josh Fox on *Democracy Now!* If our natural gas use continues as predicted, these estimates are terrifyingly credible, representing the delirium by which we are consciously planning to lay waste to entire regions of the country and bury beneath them trillions of gallons of sludge. In an age of increasing water scarcity, a natural gas electricity system will permanently convert vast amounts of freshwater into toxic underground rivers. Now and forever, this stygian poison will seethe through the modified geology of Pennsylvania in complex, unpredictable ways, imperiling aquifers for the rest of time. By this marvelous process operators write the epic of hydrofracturing, line by line, well by well, indelibly into the earth.

All the while, the small dairy farm that hosts Gotham City goes quietly about its business. The farming proceeds as if the well pad that infuses it with capital—and much else—were simply not there. Dairy cattle graze and water in the shadows of Gotham's condensate tanks. Right alongside the perimeter fence, fields of hay and corn undulate dreamily.

Most hydrofracturing operations in the state are located on farms just like this one. These farms sell their products to processing facilities and regional distributors. They also supply locally sourced, "farm-fresh" ingredients to restaurants and grocery stores throughout Pennsylvania and neighboring states, reaching metro areas from Cleveland to New York City. No regulatory agency requires a packaging label that would inform consumers as to whether their food originates on farms that host hydrofracturing sites or are located dangerously near them. Perhaps the health impacts of fracturing are not as localized as some might wish to think.

In a sense, we are all living in Scenery Hill, in my parents' home.

Late in September of 2015, Mom's energy levels plummeted. Rashes rose all over her body, accompanied by headaches, nausea, and vomiting. Dad's occasional nosebleeds had stopped, but Mom's symptoms only grew worse. Around All Saints' Day, her thick, wavy hair began to fall out. Her joints grew stiff, some mornings she could hardly turn her head to look at the clock, and soon she had to give up her job as a clerical assistant at the physical therapy clinic. She had enough trouble just getting out of bed, making chamomile tea, turning the pages of her Bible. By mid-November she was spending nights in the recliner with Topaz because she couldn't climb the stairs.

The doctors were at a loss. She had a clean medical history and a healthy weight; she had always exercised; she didn't drink or smoke. Her GP initially diagnosed her with a urinary tract infection. Next, an ER physician thought she was having an allergic reaction of some sort. One specialist said she had an autoimmune problem; another said mild sepsis. Mom visited rheumatologists, allergists, internists, and others; ultimately, they threw up their hands.

Finally she asked one of the specialists if the hydrofracturing operation four hundred feet from her bedroom might have something to do with it. She told him she had mostly stopped drinking the well water a year earlier (after hearing about potential dangers), but still used it for tea, coffee, and everything else, including her then-frequent baths. The specialist seemed surprised at the proximity of the drilling, but assured her that there was no cause for worry. "Certainly," he said, "the proper regulations would have been put into place." Most likely her symptoms stemmed from an "unnamed virus."

Slowly, in the first months of 2016, Mom started to improve. No one has any idea why. In March of that year, she managed to dance with me at Kate's and my wedding. Around April Fool's Day, she returned to her job, having missed half a year of work.

The specialist congratulated her. "Looks like you're one of the lucky ones who fight off the virus," he said.

Mom's much better now, three years after her first symptoms, with a full head of hair and a sprightly manner. But her illness, whatever its cause, seems to have exacted a lasting toll. To look at her face, you'd think she might be forty. But as she takes the stairs, the tendons in her forearm strain as she grips the bannister, and her footfalls resound in careful pairs: tock—tock, tock—tock.

She doesn't like to talk about the illness, perhaps out of kindness to us. "Who knows?" she'll say. "I guess it must have been one heck of a virus." When I was little and asked her unanswerable questions that the myths used to satisfy—*Why is there a world? Why is there water? Why is there evil?*—she'd tell me that I should put them on my list to ask God when I got to heaven.

We'll probably never know whether an exotic, inscrutable virus hobbled my mother for half a year, or whether Gotham City itself is the responsible virus. We do know, however, that when she got sick, Pennsylvania's Act 13—the industry-written bill passed in 2012 to "modernize" state oil and gas regulations—did not require drilling sites to report chemical spills and other toxic events to nearby residents. (The act makes a callous geographical distinction in this regard, as it has always compelled accident reportage for city water systems.) That Mom's symptoms mirror those cropping up across hydrofracturing country could be simple coincidence, of course; Occam's razor does not always apply. Still, the possibility of an unreported chemical accident, along with her daily exposure to high baseline contamination, would seem to make her chiropractor's vague diagnosis the simplest and best one: "Your system is screaming 'toxicity,'" he said.

The Pennsylvania Supreme Court has since abrogated the industry's right to toxic silence, forcing drillers to report new contamination to residents. The Court has also struck down other repressive elements of Act 13, such as the draconian zoning rules that had prohibited communities from banning hydrofracturing. Even so, it's no secret that gas executives hold the reins of state government: an analysis of public records by Common Cause shows that the gas lobby spent more than seventy million dollars garnering influence in Pennsylvania between 2007 and 2016. Along with its lax regulation, Pennsylvania remains the only major energy-producing state that levies no extraction tax (officially "severance tax") on natural gas. And so it happens that as the shale boom raged, the state balanced its budget at the expense of its flagship universities, Pitt and Penn State, which have become, according to *U.S. News and World Report*, the first and third most expensive public colleges in the nation for in-state students. (Two other Pennsylvania schools are in the top ten.)

Many residents have taken to calling the state's Department of Environmental Protection (DEP) the DGP, for "Department of Gas Protection," while others joke that DEP actually signifies the agency's apparent motto, "Drill Everywhere, Please."

The nonprofit *Public Herald* reports that the Pennsylvania DEP received more than 4,100 complaints of water contamination near hydrofracturing sites from 2004 to 2016, but suppressed them out of concern that, in the words of a DEP lawyer, they might "cause alarm." Moreover, though the number of complaints increased along with the growing number of shale gas wells, the DEP pronounced

93 percent of such complaints "unrelated to oil and gas drilling." Among these are a complaint regarding a site fifteen miles from Scenery Hill: the DEP's report reads, "Complainant noticed an odor to water about a year ago after sludge pond [toxic waste impoundment pit] was put in above her. Son has been getting sick and having liver problems, dog has died and neighbor's 2 dogs and horses have died. Dogs and son had/have arsenic in urine. . . . Sample results do not indicate that there was any impact to the well water from gas drilling operations." To be sure, the DEP has many committed employees. The root of the problem lies not with them, but with the legislators who accept industry money to impede the department's mission.

Political voice has become a commodity, and like most people directly impacted by hydrofracturing, my parents are in no position to buy. The noise, the air pollution, the strange illnesses, the *Who knows? Who cares?* attitude toward the aquifer that supplies their well water—love it or leave it, as someone once hollered. Like a colonizing empire, drilling companies are capable of imposing themselves—and do so. When my father walked to Gotham to ask about noise mitigation (after he and my mother had been awakened before dawn one Sunday), the site manager offered to have him arrested.

There are more than fifty well pads within five miles of my parents' home, each with between four and twelve wells. The landscapes I remember have become dreamscapes. Aside from Gotham City, one sees signs for well pads called Hulk, Wolverine, Iron Man, Captain Jack Sparrow, Zorro, and Captain USA. Other pads include Captain Planet, Captain Planet 2, Wiggin Out, Three Musketeers, Mad Dog 20/20, and Bovinator—an apt name no matter what it may signify. Then there are the fairy tale pads: Mama Bear, Papa Bear, Baby Bear, Golden Goose, and Rumpelstiltskin. The story of Rumpelstiltskin, of course, tells of a magical creature new to the area who offers to spin hay and straw into gold—but at the price of your firstborn son.

Washington County, where Scenery Hill is located, exemplifies two pervasive features of contemporary rural America, hydrofracturing and opioid addiction, having more of both than any other county in the state and rivaling any county in the nation. With more than seventeen hundred shale wells drilled since 2008, there are few hills left from which one cannot espy a hydrofracturing operation. If fatal overdoses remain slightly less ubiquitous than well pads, this is only because most of the former are discovered in time to be reversed.

That the onset of the shale boom neatly coincides with the drastic upswing in the tendency of the county's people to dose themselves fatally with powerful opioids would seem to throw a monkey wrench of substantial size into the gas industry's claims, blaring from billboards and television screen across the county, that hydrofracturing represents the glorious return of industrial pride to these shadowlands. Hydrofracturing has created some jobs—mostly in hospitality, hotel construction, and auxiliary industries such as pipefitting and trucking—though not nearly as many as claimed by the gas industry and its familiar, the government. The *Columbus Dispatch* reports that the four Ohio counties with the most shale gas permits actually *lost* local employment between 2007 and 2013, at the height of their boom. Gas-related job figures in Pennsylvania often look rosier, but only because the state's Department of Labor, for more than five years, attributed *every single job* in broad industries like trucking and construction to the presence of the gas industry—effectively claiming that all FedEx drivers and stone masons owed their livelihoods to Marcellus drilling. This practice went on until the summer of 2015, when investigations by NPR StateImpact and other groups brought it to light. (The state's job figures likely remain inflated, though not as grossly.)

The unpleasant truth is that Main Streets are still boarded-up and passed over, and most of the Marcellus region looks as senescent now as it did before shale drilling began. The lion's share of the economic benefit hydrofracturing has brought to Washington County accrues to a few large landowners in the form of royalty checks, while smaller landowners who hold mineral rights are placated with mortgage money and silenced by standard nondisclosure clauses.

As for the parallels between fracturing and overdoses, obviously correlation is not causation, and laid-off steelworkers are far from the only ones shooting up. But hydrofracturing, in addition to its litany of more direct insults to residents' health, casts a certain pall. As Governor Andrew Cuomo of New York said before banning the practice in his state, "I've never had anyone say to me, 'I believe fracking is great.' . . . What I get is, 'I have no alternative but fracking.'" People feel trapped—and *are* trapped: well pads four hundred feet from homes reinforce the already prevalent sense of a boot on the neck. Drilling companies call themselves "good neighbors," but nearly all residents see them for the overlords they are, and recognize that Washington County has again become an extraction colony—only this time without the good local jobs of the unionized coal era. Powerless and made to feel so, without control over the rhythms of their day-to-day lives, many are driven to act (and vote) in ways that outsiders might find inexplicable.

Recent debates on the toxic style of populism raging through much of hydrofracturing country tend to overlook the actual toxicity, but the chemical and psychological fallout of having one's community transformed into an energy sacrifice zone surely contributes to the declining life expectancies and political grievances lately observed among many working-class rural Americans.

The vice-president of regulatory affairs for a large Texas-based gas company operating in Washington County issued a public apology in 2016 for comments he made during a closed-door meeting, the contents of which were leaked to the Pittsburgh press: "To be frank," he told stakeholders, companies like his avoid drilling near "big houses" whose residents may have the resources to be a hindrance, preferring to operate in economically depressed, poorly educated areas instead. This part of the speech, he insisted, was merely "an attempt to inject dry sarcasm." The data, however, suggest that he wasn't joking. A study by the Frac-Tracker Alliance found that, of the 779 shale wells drilled between 2010 and 2014 in the three Pennsylvania counties just northeast of Washington County, only two wells are located in census tracts with median home values of $200,000 or more.

Another of the company's executives recently boasted about the ex-military psychological operations officers on his staff. "We have several former psy-ops folks that work for us," he said, as reported in the *Pittsburgh Post-Gazette*, "[and] having that understanding of psy-ops in the Army and in the Middle East has applied very helpfully here for us in Pennsylvania." On the surface of things, soft counterinsurgency tactics like industry-sponsored community picnics seem harmless enough. But threats of arrest, like the one issued to my father, are already accompanying the free hotdogs and "Why Natural Gas?" brochures. Meanwhile, in 2010, leaked emails revealed that the Pennsylvania Department of Homeland Security had compiled terrorism dossiers on local groups opposed to Marcellus drilling, then secretly forwarded them to energy companies, lobbying firms, and private security contractors. Although the agency's director resigned during the ensuing scandal, there is little reason to believe that such collusion has stopped. One gas executive whose company was involved in the effort insisted that "we are dealing with an insurgency."

If his assessment seems hyperbolic at present, that may be because he is paid to think in terms of the future. The pace of shale operations in Pennsylvania slackened somewhat during 2015 and 2016 in response to a glutted market, but even those years set state production records, and new drilling has since rebounded. Thirty rigs are now operating in Pennsylvania, and the long-term outlook remains as chilling as ever. The industry organ *Energy in Depth* declared Pennsylvania's record-breaking 2017 shale gas output "simply incredible." Ongoing projections for 2018 are just as high. If no laws restrict or discourage the practice, drilling in the Marcellus will continue for decades, and the same applies to presently more active fields like the Permian in Texas.

Tens of thousands of new shale wells are in planning nationwide, along with scores of new natural gas power plants and a mass of pipelines and supporting infrastructure. If these projects and others like them are completed, their inertial force will commit the U.S. to a natural gas electricity system for the next half century, if not longer. As hydrofracturing expands, the damage it wreaks will intensify. An energy plan that begins with natural gas pipelines and export terminals necessarily ends with the sea walls and border fortresses of a hot, dry, desperate planet. If we keep to the insane path that's been laid out for us, the battle for hearts and minds is likely just getting started.

The "insurgency" referred to by gas executives, if it ever materializes, would not be the first to conduct operations in southwestern Pennsylvania. Historically, Washington County is best known as the nexus of the so-called Whiskey Rebellion of the early 1790s. Contrary to the popular view—or what still exists of it—this insurrection was not about vulgar frontiersmen too pigheaded to pay taxes on their booze. Instead, it erupted after Alexander Hamilton and the banker Robert Morris extorted war bonds from farmers in western Pennsylvania and transferred them to wealthy elites, whom they judged could make more productive uses of the capital. This episode is notable not only for its audacity, but also because it set the pattern of extractive class violence that recurs throughout the region's history like a choral refrain, conditioning life in coal towns from the mid-1800s well into the 1940s, and rearing its hydra head once more in the gas fields today.

During the Revolution, our cash-strapped Congress resorted to paying soldiers and farmers in bonds that they could use to settle property taxes after the war. Hamilton and Morris loathed this tax policy because their economic theory held that, for the United States to develop, capital must flow from agricultural lands into finance and industry. As long as farmers held the war bonds, they would be insulated from the market, and the economy would remain stagnant. And so Morris, who controlled Pennsylvania's finances, stopped accepting the bonds as tax payments. Farmers then had to earn money to pay their taxes—exactly his plan. Toward this end, the farmers sold their now-useless war bonds to speculators—at a fraction of face value.

Four hundred financiers soon held 96 percent of Pennsylvania's war debt, and Hamilton seized the opportunity. As Treasury Secretary, he persuaded Congress to honor the bonds at full face value, plus 6 percent interest. To raise the money, Congress (under Hamilton's guidance), levied a steep excise tax on whiskey, the chief agricultural product of western Pennsylvania. By careful design, then, the tax fell most heavily on the same swindled farmers; those who, in Hamilton's theory, had to suffer so that the nation—that is, the dynamism of finance capital—could be free to prosper.

The farmers did not take kindly to Morris and Hamilton's plan. They tarred and feathered tax collectors, raised a militia nine thousand strong, and marched on Pittsburgh—the site of the nearest armory—singing of secession and Robespierre.

Hamilton, ever the skilled publicist, was the one who named this uprising the Whiskey Rebellion, but a better name would surely be the War Bond Revolt.

Faced with a threat to the new nation's sovereignty, President Washington set off with a large army toward Washington County—ironically enough, the first to designate itself in his honor. As his troops approached, the outgunned militiamen dispersed into the hills and slunk back to their farms, compelled to accept, for the good of the metropolitan economy, a system of expropriation more humiliating than the official colonization they had just cast off.

Former militiamen who lived near Scenery Hill—then called Springtown, apparently for its excellent freshwater springs—would surely have fulminated against Morris and his ilk at a new inn and tavern about a mile from what is now my parents' home. The Century Inn would remain open until 2015, making it at that time the oldest continuously operating hotel on the National Road. During my youth it was a nice restaurant known for having hosted many historic figures, reputedly including Washington himself. And on the tavern wall, in a frame near the hearth, hung a remarkable object: the only surviving flag used in the Whiskey Rebellion.

During the summer of 2015, just before my mother fell ill, the Century Inn was destroyed in a midnight electrical fire that left only its stone frontispiece intact. The Inn's owner, a local art collector, lived in its upper floors. Leaving her paintings and jewelry to burn, she escaped that night carrying only the flag—an eagle on a field of navy, compassed by a block of thirteen white stars. As she stood holding it on the lawn, if she had squinted against the flames, she could have seen two brilliantly lit drilling rigs mounted on the hills—impassive, looming, eerily beautiful.

Hydrofracturing devastates rural bodies and communities in the Marcellus and other shale regions, and threatens to render many more places uninhabitable by ensuring climate chaos. Like the opioid crisis, though, hydrofracturing is, first of all, a symptom. Dealing with it requires us to look beyond the surface manifestations, terrible as these are, to the deeper roots that have taken hold in the substrata of our society. From Hamilton to Halliburton, from the early national period to the transnational present, capital and government have worked together to extract wealth from rural Pennsylvanians, whom they have tried to disparage, variously, as "white Indians," "Communist agitators," and "terrorist insurgents." Their allies in the media and academe have always justified these violent expropriations by invoking fantasies of economic dynamism and national freedom, most recently "energy independence" through "clean-burning natural gas." The new populist backlash against these institutions has often shown itself incoherent, self-defeating, and misdirected to the point of cruelty, but one cannot say that it is wholly naïve about the long arcs of history.

Instead of identifying the new populists only by their worst impulses, and embracing the tradition of slander, we would do better to end the toxic cycle and begin a different conversation. Whatever our views, we all feel and know—have long felt and known—that there is nothing free or dynamic about being held in throe to investment banks and fossil capitalists who (let's call it what it is) have sunk to the decadent phase of simple plunder. They want to sell us inhumane natural gas infrastructure—and then, as the seas rise, enormous dikes patrolled at the border by armed drones.

We can certainly build public renewable energy instead. But first we have to renew our faith in each other, fellow citizens of a diverse country, whose promise as a people has not yet flagged.

REFERENCES

Adams, Mikaila. "Cabot Plans 85 Wells in Marcellus Shale in 2018." *Oil and Gas Journal*, 23 February 2018. https://www.ogj.com/articles/2018/02/cabot-plans-85-wells-in -marcellus-shale-in-2018.html.

Alvarez, Ramón A., Stephen W. Pacala, James J. Winebrake, William L. Chameides, and Steven P. Hamburg. "Greater Focus Needed on Methane Leakage from Natural Gas Infrastructure." *Proceedings of the National Academy of Sciences* 109, no. 17 (24 April 2012): 6435–40. https://doi.org/10.1073/pnas.1202407109.

Apt, Jay. "The Other Reason to Shift Away from Coal: Air Pollution That Kills Thousands Every Year." *The Conversation*, 6 June 2017. http://theconversation.com/the-other -reason-to-shift-away-from-coal-air-pollution-that-kills-thousands-every-year-78874.

Bernstein, Lenny. "The Heroin Epidemic's Toll: One County, 70 Minutes, Eight Overdoses." *Washington Post*, 23 August 2015. https://www.washingtonpost.com/national /health-science/the-heroin-epidemics-toll-one-county-70-minutes-eight-overdoses /2015/08/23/f616215e-48bc-11e5-846d-02792f854297_story.html.

Blackmon, David. "Horizontal Drilling: A Technological Marvel Ignored." *Forbes*, 28 January 2013. https://www.forbes.com/sites/davidblackmon/2013/01/28/horizontal -drilling-a-technological-marvel-ignored/.

Cato, Jason. "Owner of Washington County's Century Inn Vows to Rebuild after Fire." *Pittsburgh Tribune-Review*, 19 August 2015. https://triblive.com/news/washington /8942457-74/inn-harrington-century.

Central Intelligence Agency. "Country Comparison—Natural Gas Production." *The World Fact-book*. Accessed 9 September 2018. https://www.cia.gov/library/publications /the-world-factbook/rankorder/2249rank.html.

Compendium of Scientific, Medical, and Media Findings Demonstrating Risks and Harms of Fracking (Unconventional Gas and Oil Extraction). New York: Concerned Health Professionals of New York; Physicians for Social Responsibility, 2018. http://concerned healthny.org/compendium/.

Cusick, Marie. "Gas Exec Apologizes for Suggesting Range Resources Avoids Rich Neighborhoods." *NPR StateImpact: Pennsylvania*. 22 April 2016. https://stateimpact.npr.org /pennsylvania/2016/04/22/gas-exec-apologizes-for-suggesting-range-resources-avoids -rich-neighborhoods/.

Davenport, Coral. "Donald Trump, in Pittsburgh, Pledges to Boost Both Coal and Gas." *New York Times*, 21 December 2017. https://www.nytimes.com/2016/09/23/us/politics /donald-trump-fracking.html.

Doman, Linda, and Ari Kahan. "United States Remains the World's Top Producer of Petroleum and Natural Gas Hydrocarbons." U.S. Energy Information Administration, 21 May 2018. https://www.eia.gov/todayinenergy/detail.php?id=36292.

"Fracking: So Where's the Economic Boom That Was Promised?" *Columbus Dispatch*, 28 January 2014. http://www.dispatch.com/article/20140128/NEWS/301289852.

Free Pass for Oil and Gas: Oil and Gas Industry Exemptions. Washington, D.C.: Environmental Working Group, 2009. https://www.ewg.org/research/free-pass-oil-and-gas/oil-and -gas-industry-exemptions.

Friedman, Jordan. "10 Colleges with the Highest Tuition for In-State Students." *U.S. News & World Report*, 3 May 2016. https://www.usnews.com/education/best-colleges/the -short-list-college/articles/2016-05-03/10-colleges-with-the-highest-tuition-for-in -state-students.

Gold, Russell, and Tom McGinty. "Energy Boom Puts Wells in America's Backyards." *Wall Street Journal*, 26 October 2013. https://www.wsj.com/articles/energy-boom-puts-wells -in-america8217s-backyards-1382756256.

Hogeland, William. *The Whiskey Rebellion*. New York: Simon and Schuster, 2010.

Hopey, Don. "Drillers Using Counterinsurgency Experts." *Pittsburgh Post-Gazette*, 13 November 2011. http://www.post-gazette.com/news/environment/2011/11/13/Drillers -using-counterinsurgency-experts/stories/201111130191.

Ingraffea, Anthony R. *Fluid Migration Mechanisms Due to Faulty Well Design and/or Construction: An Overview and Recent Experiences in the Pennsylvania Marcellus Shale Play*. Oakland, Calif.: Physicians, Scientists, and Engineers for Healthy Energy, 2012. https://www .psehealthyenergy.org/our-work/publications/archive/fluid-migration-mechanisms -due-to-faulty-well-design-andor-construction-an-overview-and-recent-experiences -in-the-pennsylvania-marcellus-play/.

Jacobs, Nicole. "Pennsylvania's 2017 Shale Gas Production Was Off the Charts." *Energy in Depth*, 19 March 2018. https://www.energyindepth.org/pennsylvanias-2017-shale-gas -production-was-off-the-charts/.

Jalbert, Kirk. "Environmental Justice, Failing PA's Oil and Gas Communities." *FracTracker Alliance*, n.d. Accessed 9 September 2018. https://www.fractracker.org/2016/06/pa -environmental-justice/.

"Jobs: How Pennsylvania Counts Its Gas Workers." *NPR StateImpact: Pennsylvania*, 2016. https://stateimpact.npr.org/pennsylvania/tag/jobs/.

"Josh Fox on Gasland Part 2, the Fracking-Earthquake Link, and the Natural Gas Industry's Use of PSYOPs." *Democracy Now!* 12 July 2013. http://www.democracynow.org /2013/7/12/josh_fox_on_gasland_part_2.

Kaplan, Thomas. "Citing Health Risks, Cuomo Bans Fracking in New York State." *New York Times*, 21 December 2017. https://www.nytimes.com/2014/12/18/nyregion/cuomo -to-ban-fracking-in-new-york-state-citing-health-risks.html.

Kelly-Detwiler, Peter. "Shale Leases: Promised Land." *Forbes*, 3 January 2013. https://www .forbes.com/sites/peterdetwiler/2013/01/03/shale-leases-promised-land/.

Ladlee, James R. "Natural Gas Production Decline Curve and Royalty Estimation." Penn State Marcellus Center for Outreach and Research, n.d. Accessed 15 September 2018. https://extension.psu.edu/natural-gas-production-decline-curve-and-royalty -estimation.

Lustgarten, Abrahm. "Drill for Natural Gas, Pollute Water." *Scientific American*, 17 November 2008. https://www.scientificamerican.com/article/drill-for-natural-gas-pollute -water/.

———. "Injection Wells: The Poison Beneath Us." *ProPublica*, 21 June 2012. https://www
.propublica.org/article/injection-wells-the-poison-beneath-us.

"Marcellus Money." Philadelphia: Common Cause and Conservation Voters of Pennsylvania, 2016. http://marcellusmoney.org/.

Mooney, Chris, and Brady Dennis. "Obama Administration Announces Historic New
Regulations for Methane Emissions from Oil and Gas." *Washington Post*, 12 May 2016.
https://www.washingtonpost.com/news/energy-environment/wp/2016/05/12
/obama-administration-announces-historic-new-regulations-for-methane-emissions
-from-oil-and-gas/.

"Oil and Gas Activity in Pennsylvania." FracTracker Alliance, n.d. Accessed 10 September
2018. https://www.fractracker.org/map/us/pennsylvania/.

Phillips, Susan. "PA Supreme Court Rules with Environmentalists over Remaining Issues
in Act 13." *NPR StateImpact: Pennsylvania*, 28 September 2016. https://stateimpact.npr
.org/pennsylvania/2016/09/28/pa-supreme-court-rules-with-environmentalists-over
-remaining-issues-in-act-13/.

Schlanger, Zoë. "Chevron Gives Residents Near Fracking Explosion Free Pizza." *Newsweek*,
19 February 2014. https://www.newsweek.com/chevron-gives-residents-near-fracking
-explosion-free-pizza-229491.

Shearer, Christine, John Bistline, Mason Inman, and Steven J. Davis. "The Effect of Natural
Gas Supply on U.S. Renewable Energy and CO2 Emissions." *Environmental Research Letters* 9, no. 9 (24 September 2014). https://doi.org/10.1088/1748-9326/9/9/094008.

Stoll, Steven. *Ramp Hollow: The Ordeal of Appalachia*. New York: Hill and Wang, 2017.

Troutman, Melissa A., Joshua B. Pribanic, and Sierra Shamer. "Hidden Data Suggests
Fracking Created Widespread, Systemic Impact in Pennsylvania." *Public Herald*, 23 January 2017. http://publicherald.org/hidden-data-suggests-fracking-created-widespread
-systemic-impact-in-pennsylvania/

U.S. Energy Information Administration. "Electricity Data Browser—Net Generation for
All Sectors." n.d. Accessed 9 September 2018. https://www.eia.gov/electricity/data
/browser/.

———. "Pennsylvania Natural Gas Gross Withdrawals and Production." n.d. Accessed 10
September 2018. https://www.eia.gov/dnav/ng/ng_prod_sum_dc_spa_mmcf_a.htm.

Wang, Marian. "Pa. Homeland Security Head Resigns amid Controversy over Tracking of
Activists." *ProPublica*, 1 October 2010. https://www.propublica.org/article/pa.
-homeland-security-head-resigns-amid-controversy-over-tracking-of-activi.

"Wells Drilled by County—Report Viewer." DEP Office of Oil and Gas Management, 2018.
http://www.depreportingservices.state.pa.us/ReportServer/Pages/ReportViewer.aspx?
/Oil_Gas/Wells_Drilled_By_County.

SUSANNE PAOLA ANTONETTA

Commensals

Theme and Variations

> Humans, who make up .01 percent of the biomass
> of the earth, have destroyed 83 percent of the
> wild mammals in it, and half of all the plants.
>
> —YINON M. BAR-ON, Rob Phillips, and Ron Milo, "The
> Biomass Distribution on Earth," *Proceedings of the National
> Academy of Sciences of the United States of America*, May 2018

We didn't want to kill them.

We'd come to feel we understood them: they had not just their rituals but their recreations. One night they ate seventy-five dried hot peppers I'd stored in the basement. They had the sense to leave the hottest ones, the chiles de árbol, but they downed the guajillos, pasillas, anchos, goats' horns, and left just-ripped packages and some seeds. The rats had been in our house three months when this happened, and we understood this eating as the kind of punctuation mark you stick in your life after too much repetition. An interior burn, to beat ennui. Boredom can call for a little suffering, even a little heat.

The rats lived in our walls and the crawlspace above our bedroom, so at night—when rats are most active—we lived in something like a surround-sound carnival, the cheap kind, with small rides squealing and groaning and loud but unintelligible barkers. The rat man we called said rats are too smart for catch-and-release. They'll remember anywhere warm with food, he said. And they're burrowers, they love walls: warm, sheltered, the right amount of freedom.

They arrived with the equinox, just before my birthday. These rats, we came to think, had a sense of occasion. It was like them to act on transitional days, ceremonial days.

The rat man, Tod, was young, probably twenty, with a tan uniform that struck me as fur-like (though I might have been biased that way) and slicked-back hair. He told us we had twelve rats, an oddly precise figure given that he did not see them all, but we accepted it on the grounds that these rats would live in the context of a meaningful number. One day Tod leaned into the crawlspace, then came down and held a dead rat in our faces, caught in some kind of exterminator pincers. It lay on its side, lids locked and tail slack, mouth open in the shape of a sigh. "It's not a roof rat," he said, as I screamed a little. "It's a Norway rat." We had assumed: under roofs, roof rats. These rats really do come from Norway, he said, and I wondered why they couldn't find their way back to that place.

Rats are one of a handful of species that thrive along with humans and have proliferated beyond any natural order. They crest along on our surf, if you can imagine surf as homes and garbage. We give them food, warmth, breeding space, and lots of stuff to shred for their nests. They belong to a lucky group called *commensal species*, those whom human lives accidentally favor. The root of the word means to share a table or dine together, which we did with our rats that scrabbled through the wall alongside our dining table. Meals became, at times, almost cozy, our dinnertime clanking and passing, their scritching and swooping, as if we played at this survival game together. And in fact (I learned), rats live in family groups and rarely interact with rats beyond those, as many modern humans can hardly name their neighbors. Our kinship is true.

Other commensals are deer, coyotes, raccoons, and some bacteria.

Few wild species have the fortune of commensals. Overall, we've scalped this planet of its biomass, flattening it in the wild to about a sixth of what it was. I read about this in an article published in the *Proceedings of the National Academy of Sciences*, by authors who complain that science does too little weighing. Many people believe humans will have to colonize other planets—maybe leave this one altogether—to survive. This is science fiction that's rewritten itself in our dreamings, as science-fact, or perhaps, science-hope. We have a problem, and this feels like an answer. We are 7.6 billion and growing, and the number's impossible, especially with warming weather—our climate each year becomes subject to more disasters and fewer crops. The Arctic's melting, and city towers will scrape the bellies of ships. To stay in place in these cities, we'll need to be afloat, wood-cupped.

The fact is, we can't survive without the biomass we've destroyed and are destroying. People from Tesla's Elon Musk to physicist Stephen Hawking have pleaded for colonizing, and Hawking before his death became obsessed with the idea. First he said we had one thousand years to flee the planet, but then as warming accelerated he changed the number to one hundred. As Hawking phrased it, "To stay risks being annihilated." Likely we'll start with Mars or the moon. Pioneers will build enclosed dwellings, great bubbles, to hold our atmosphere. Each bubble pumped to life with gasses, like carnival balloons. It won't be easy.

The number of rats our symbiosis creates has become out of control, a "ratpocalypse," which the *New Republic* claims we are on the verge of. People in some cities, such as Chicago, spread rat birth control powder on their streets, tapping it into their apartments on their heels. Rats thrive on disruption. If you could walk through an untouched forest, you would not see rats. They'd need landslides, flooding—something to toss things around, create burrow space and dead organic matter. Humans represent continuous disruption: we are always plowing and reaping, tearing down and rebuilding, even blowing up. Two healthy rats left alone to breed (no pause, no predators) can in three years lead to a rat population of half a billion: twelve years breeding, and every human on the planet would be twinned to his or her or their own rat. All sprung from one rodent Adam and Eve. Then which species would overwhelm the other? Rats begin breeding at four weeks, gestate for three weeks, and deliver six to twelve pups, thumb-sized and blind, misshapen as tubers, and a hairless and intestinal pink—which in a month will breed, and so on, and so on. I'd have to say: advantage, rat.

Wild rats aren't our only symbionts—we've bred others, lab rats. My university has science, so I must walk past labs where these white rats crouch in daytime, then chitter and pace at night: spectral ovals. I don't know where they're kept, because my school doesn't want anyone to know; from time to time people in ski masks break into these labs, pulling up the little wire doors. The ovals pour down from the cages, drops of cream hustling toward the exits. The ski masks know these rats, infused with disease, lumpy and sick, can't survive. It's a gesture, as it is when you look in a mirror and curl your hair with a finger, suck cheeks in through your teeth, to look good to an imagined person you desire, but there is only you.

Most medical rats are Wistars, a bio-engineered rat. Rats resemble humans physiologically, they have malleable genes, and they live only a few years, so you can follow disease progression to the end. Here is the marketing language for the basic Wistar: "Ideal For general multipurpose model, infectious disease research, safety and efficacy testing, aging, surgical model" [error and awkwardness theirs]. It is also cancerous, developing spontaneous tumors. There are hybrids of hybrids: the Wistar Furth, bred to get leukemia, will also get renal failure and grand mal seizures. Wistar Kyoto is hypertensive. And so on.

Wistars can cost anywhere from fifteen dollars to more than one hundred dollars per rat, though they do go on sale. You buy them from an online store, exactly as you'd buy from Amazon; you click on the rats you've selected and put them in your cart, and when you have enough rats, you proceed to checkout. Live rats are shipped using a method called "Sew Easy," and I admit I haven't looked into this, enjoying my mental pictures too much: an apron with pockets swollen with rat, a patchwork quilt (maybe the popular Double Wedding Ring, the inter-locked circles), each square thick, and moving.

Wistar rats were initially developed for anatomy instruction by Dr. Caspar Wistar, who in 1892 founded his self-named institute in Philadelphia. When the Wistar Institute opened, it housed dead humans: dried or skeletal or preserved with injections of wax. Wistar had no idea the Institute would become a rat-womb, though probably he did realize his name contains the word "rats," spelled backwards. (And contains the word "star," which in its own way is relevant.) Milton Greenman, who helped create Wistars, called them a "living analogue to the pure chemicals" used in experiments to get accurate, reproducible results. Identical drips and systems, expressed in small body after small body. Other lab rats exist, but most descend from Wistars. The rat types are called *strains* or *models*. They're bred to be docile, and specially handled when young in what the sales material calls a "gentling process," so they won't bite.

Lab mice were the first creatures given human brain cells, a type of cell called *glial* (like happiness, like a song), extracted from fetal tissue and injected into pups. In the mouse brains the glial cells reproduced beyond any imagining—three hundred thousand glial cells became twelve million, formed into a type of glials called *astrocytes*. These are beautiful, and look like thready and vulnerable stars. Astrocytes drape their tendrils over neurons and speed up and intensify signals between them. As the pups grew, their brains became encased in an astrocyte net, like each mind had a Milky Way sunk over it. "We could see the human cells taking over the whole space," said a researcher named Steve Goldman, one of the first to do this, who sounded a bit stunned. "It seemed like the mouse [cells] were fleeing to the margins."

After mice, rats were infused with human brain cells, on the idea that rats were *already* more intelligent than mice, so let's see what happens. It's a kind of reasoning that feels very human, chasing bad logic into acts for no purpose, like admiring your own face through eyes you can only pretend are not your own. These mixed-brain creatures are called *brain surrogates* or *chimeras*, generally *chimeras*, the ancient word for creatures stitched together out of different parts. Yes, these lab mice and lab rats are far smarter than normal rodents. They learn much faster, and they remember, and become little whizzes at running mazes and the like. Chimeric mice memories, reports one researcher who tested them with electric shocks, exceed normal mice memories by four times.

In another experiment mice and rats had miniature human brains—each brain the size of a lentil, grown in a lab from stem cells—placed in their craniums, at the side of their own brains, hooking in, like parasites. Researchers did this to see how long such organoids could survive in the brain, but with the side interest of seeing how these cells, too, might stimulate intelligence. Each implant had bored above it a transparent, lentil-sized window. These lentils intermeshed with rodent neurons, but did not make the creatures any smarter. The human parasite died in a few months.

We have no idea if the chimeras have human self-awareness, understand their cage as cage, their fate the same as the mouse next door who got his brain opened and body shredded last Tuesday. It is possible, according a piece by seventeen ethicists in the science journal *Nature*, that the chimeras will become sentient, will develop "advanced cognitive capacities." The *Nature* authors suggest it may be most humane to keep the chimeras in a functional coma throughout their lab lives, so they don't have a chance to think. Or perhaps just destroy the enhanced mice faster than the normal ones, or even not destroy them but rehome them after testing, if alive. Researchers should act according to *their diverse sensitivities*, in the authors' words. My scientist friend, Thor, recalls that one chimera researcher promised to immediately kill any mouse who began displaying humanlike awareness. Thor wrote to me: "I had this image of injected mice in a little doll house being watched by white-coated humans and as soon as one of the mice picked up a little toy tool and started to use it, he would immediately be snatched up and murdered."

Like the rats in our walls, colonizers will have to create new recreations and rituals. Special days like arrival days, days to acknowledge that at one time a place burned too hot. Animals will escape and go feral, as they do, and plants will go weedy, as hybrids do. (You can't trust their seed, which reverts to the less desirable parent genes.) And humans who are born and come of age in colonies will forget we humans made it all. As Bar-On, et al., point out, they'll take 83 percent of what they have and waste it away.

A scientist named Adam Ozimek writing in *Forbes* argues against planet colonizing, calling it absurdly hard, and not necessary. Finally, I think as I start reading, someone believes we can make it here. But no—his thought is building biodomes for us under the oceans to flee to. Those ship bellies our moons. Marslings and moonlings and oceanlings, as we are Earthlings. Coyly we use the diminutive.

I imagine all the creatures we might want to bring with us. For good outcomes we'd hybridize like mad, maybe a bouncing chicken adjusted for new gravity. We'd pack to leave and place the strains of cows and goats and poultry into our little carts. And what if we're someday able to expand throughout the galaxy? Would we lose 83 percent of that, Milky Way erased to a little smear?

Instead of worrying as I should, I think of words. The *mass* of biomass, or body mass, comes from an Anglo-Saxon word meaning *lump*. The word *commensal* has a root meaning *meal* or, more accurately, *table*. And though priests will tell you *Mass* also comes from this word for table (Mass as communion, food), it does not: it comes from Latin *missus*, parent also to *missive* and *message*, meaning to send away.

If we leave this planet I imagine many of the mice and rats in labs will make their own escape. Knocking down and/or clawing open their cages. Rats practice dominance, so I expect they'll have it out: the strength of the darker ones, the intelligence—but docility—of lighter. Or they'll cross-breed. They'll have their desires and their habits, and they'll have imagination. Fat, rich: the new apex predator.

We might bring some of the Wistars with us. (We might consider that rats don't forget.) We might make a plan to come back to our Earth-home when it cools. We might then learn our planet is something other than what we thought: we misunderstood, or our understanding has been all this time tenuous and limited.

We imagined Earth was ours. Our children will have grown up with this story, and our children's children: the dome-less air, the houses you could build anywhere as long as you shaved the land free. But our blank homes won't count, just the walls will, new cities of many brains, lovingly crocheted with consciousness. The rats making their own real little tools. We have pushed the rats out of our home's borders, and now they will push us out of theirs. I doubt we will be their commensals. How many billions of them then? How many homes, empty to our eyes, but in-between, full and seething? Oh, we will dine with them again, sealed off, off from those living edges.

—*for Bruce*

CAMILLE T. DUNGY

Is All Writing Environmental Writing?

We are in the midst of the planet's sixth great extinction, in a time where we are seeing the direct effects of radical global climate change via more frequent and ferocious storms, hotter drier years accompanied by more devastating wildfires, snow where there didn't used to be snow, and less snow where permafrost used to be a given. Yet some people prefer to maintain categories for what counts as environmental writing and what is historical writing or social criticism or biography and so on. I can't compartmentalize my attentions. If an author chooses *not* to engage with what we often call the natural world, that very disengagement makes a statement about the author's relationship with her environment; even indifference to the environment directly affects the world about which a writer might purport to be indifferent. We live in a time when making decisions about how we construct the products and actions of our daily lives—whether or not to buy plastic water bottles and drinking straws, or cosmetics with microbeads that make our skin glow—means making decisions about being complicit in compromising the Earth's ecosystems.

What we decide matters in literature is connected to what we decide will matter for our history, for our pedagogy, for our culture. What we do and do not value in our art reveals what we do and do not value in our times. What we leave *off* the page often speaks as loudly as what we include.

I could choose among several paths walking from school to my childhood home in the Southern California hills. Route One was the most direct as the crow flies. It involved the fewest inclines but required a precarious scrabble down a pathless embankment to get to the greenbelt attached to the cul-de-sac where we lived. Route Two involved an initial ascent, then a level walk along the street where Jeff Blumenthal kenneled the Dobermans he often sicced on my sister and me. Running from the dogs was complicated by the steep stairs leading down to the greenbelt that separated our streets; this should have been the easiest way home, but we avoided it whenever we could. Route Three had no dogs, no stairs, no embankments, and no greenbelts, but it was significantly longer, ending with a climb up a three-block road that had *hill* in its name.

We also had a fourth option. We could climb beyond Jeff Blumenthal's cul-de-sac and into the foothills that backed both his house and ours. In the hills, we walked along drainage canals and animal paths, avoiding our suburban streets and the heavily irrigated strips of park dividing them. We climbed down, finally, over chaparral shrubs and scraggily anti-erosion landscaping, directly into our own back yard. Our parents didn't like us to take this route because we sometimes ran into coyotes or rattlesnakes, but I preferred the risk of the improbable encounter with a rattlesnake to the surety of Jeff Blumenthal's Dobermans. On that little-traveled path, I was free from the tensions of my built environment. I could be like the landscape in the hills beyond our house—a little wild and moderately protected.

Aggressively trained Dobermans, sun-lazy rattlesnakes, green turf in a desert, and ice plant clusters to keep serrated foothills from sliding over newly constructed neighborhoods represented the thin divide between the natural world and our built environments. When one world impinged upon the other, my daily life was directly affected.

When I began to write, words and images sourced from my childhood's landscape became part of what and how I wrote:

> LANGUAGE
> Silence is one part of speech, the war cry
> of wind down a mountain pass another.
> A stranger's voice echoing through lonely
> valleys, a lover's voice rising so close
> it's your own tongue: these are keys to cipher,
> the way the high hawk's key unlocks the throat
> of the sky and the coyote's yip knocks
> it shut, the way the aspens' bells conform
> to the breeze while the rapids' drums define
> resistance. Sage speaks with one voice, pinyon
> with another. Rock, wind her hand, water
> her brush, spells and then scatters her demands.
> Some notes tear and pebble our paths. Some notes
> gather: the bank we map our lives around.*

---

* From *What to Eat, What to Drink, What to Leave for Poison* (Red Hen Press, 2006).

"Language" was the first poem in my first book. This seems as right a decision about order as I've ever made.

Environment is a set of circumstances as mundane as the choice of paths we take to get home. When I lived in Iowa City for my final years of high school, our main routes home—in a car now, because we lived eight miles from school—involved either the interstate and a major thoroughfare, or the back roads that led through farmland and patches of prairie.

On recent visits to the Midwest I've driven through ghost landscapes—less prairie, less farmland. Memory overlaid my vision, inscribing alternative realities onto the present, making me aware of where I was within the context of where I have been.

Isn't this one of the things we do when we sit down to write? We decide how to describe what we are compelled to describe. Even while moving through vast cities like LA or Chicago, by being attuned to a world that is more than simply human I can't help but think of what might have been there before we privileged our own interests: commerce and industry, asphalt and glass. In this way we can apprehend what might have disappeared and what still lives alongside us, biding time—ginkgoes, catfish, the rivers, crickets.

Looking out my office windows where I live now in Northern Colorado, I see the foothills of the Rocky Mountains on most days, and the actual Rockies on really clear ones. People in Fort Collins navigate by those mountains—which are to the west, and so, except on about five overcast days a year, you always know just where you are. The mountains are a constant guide. Consider how different this topographical navigation is from an orientation based on your proximity to a particular building, to a particular street—South of Houston, or SoHo, for instance—or navigation by some other man-made landmark—east of Central Park. Here I'm using references from New York City, the environment of my husband's youth; for him, thinking to navigate by nonhuman landmarks took a little time. Similarly, "Two streets down from the Waffle House," we might have said in the Virginia town where I once lived, or "Just after the entrance to the college," or, "We're the house with the blue trim. If you reach the Church of Life, you've gone too far." In such urban environments, it might be difficult to remember that you are, in fact, *in* an "environment," given that we've come to think of the terms *environment* and *nature* as referring to someplace wild and nonhuman, more akin to the foothills of my childhood than to the cul-de-sacs terraced into their sides. But that line of reasoning slides us toward the compartmentalization I resist. Our environments are always both human and other than human.

————

I feel an affinity for what ecologists call ecotones, areas at the margins between one zone and another—like the tidal zone where beach and ocean overlap, or the treed and grassy band where forest becomes meadow—spaces that are often robustly productive and alive. These are overlaps rich with possibility and also, often, danger. The margins of one biologically robust area and another are sometimes called conflict zones, because the clash between one way of living on the Earth and another can be violent and charged. They are spaces that reward study, revealing diverse possibilities for what it might mean to be alive.

Writing takes off for me when I stop separating human experiences from the realities of the greater-than-human world. A poem that at first seems to have everything to do with some so-called environmental concern might end up being about some human condition, or I might begin a poem thinking about some human concern and end up writing something that's chock full of natural imagery. The connection I feel to experiences that are beyond my own, beyond simply the human, causes me to fuzz the lines.

In a radical and radicalizing way, these fuzzed lines bring me face to face with the fragility of the Holocene—or, more precisely, the destructiveness of the Anthropocene. To build an age around the concerns of one species is to ignore the delicate balance required in any ecotone. When one way of living on the Earth takes priority, the overlaps that support a healthy system of exchange collapse. Without that exchange, one path becomes the only path, and so whatever dangers were inherent on that one route cannot be avoided, because whatever possibilities were available on the others can no longer be revealed. I do not want such a limiting set of circumstances for my writing or for the literature of our time. I certainly don't want such a limiting set of circumstances for my world.

In 2009, when *Black Nature: Four Centuries of African American Nature Poetry* was published, one of the most remarkable statements the book made was that black people could write with an empathetic eye toward the natural world. In the general public perception of black writers, the idea that we can write out of a deep connection to the environment—and have done so for at least four centuries— came, and I think still comes, as a shock.

As the editor of *Black Nature*, I was able to make the anthology a complete project by expanding the presentation of how people write about the environment. Not all the poems in the anthology are of the rapturous *I walk out into nature and find myself* ilk, though such poems *are* there. The history of African Americans in this country complicates their ability and/or desire to write of a rapturous idealized connection to the natural world—as when I have driven over the Tallahatchee River and had my knowledge of history, of the murder of Emmett Till, make it impossible for me to view those often-quite-scenic waters in a purely appreciative manner. And so, many of the poems in the collection do not fall in line with the praise school of nature poetry but, instead, reveal complicated—often deadly—relationships. The authors of these works mix their visions of landscapes and animals into investigations of history, economics, resource extraction, and other very human and deeply perilous concerns.

In complicating or "de-pristining"—I'm patenting that word—my environmental imagination, I engage with what has come to be called *ecopoetics*, connecting topics we often understand to be the provenance of nature poetry with topics about our current and past human lives. In doing so, ecopoetics has expanded the parameters of who is writing environmental work, and how. This mode of creating and understanding poetry is expanding our ideas about the very nature of what constitutes environmental writing.

Writers exploring ecopoetics ask themselves questions such as these: How does climate change affect our poetics? How do we write about resource extraction, agribusiness, endangered bird species, the removals of indigenous peoples, suburban sprawl, the lynching of blacks, or the precarious condition of gray wolves and the ecosystems dependent upon them? Our contemporary understanding of ecopoetics takes into account the ways human-centered thinking reflects on, and is reflected in, what we write. And, contemporary ecopoetics questions the efficacy of valuing one physical presentation of animated matter over another, because narratives about place and about life contribute to our orientation in, and our interpretation of, that place and that life.

All of our positions on the planet are precarious at this moment in history, and attentive writers work to articulate why this is the case—including many writers of color who were already engaging in this mode of writing long before the ecopoetics movement took off. (Works by Alice Dunbar Nelson, Lucille Clifton, Claude McKay, Anne Spencer, Sterling Brown, June Jordan, Evie Shockley, Sean Hill, and Ed Roberson spring immediately to mind.) But only as the ecopoetics movement gained traction has such de-pristined writing finally been identified as environmental writing and, therefore, begun to be seen in a new light.

Without giving myself license to believe that all writing is environmental writing, I could very likely assign expansive poems—including many of those anthologized in *Black Nature*—to just about any category other than that of a nature poem. But to separate the importance of human interactions with the nonhuman world from the importance of cultural and political considerations would be to limit the scope of such poems entirely. This is particularly true given that the black body has so frequently been rendered "animalistic" and "wild" in the most dangerously degrading and limiting senses of those terms.

According to what Jeff Blumenthal yelled at us as he commanded the attacks, he sicced his dogs on us because we were black girls and, in his mind, beneath him. Hearing all the names he assigned to my body, so many of them intended to limit my potential, I quickly learned the danger of categorical labels. Never mind all the things Jeff Blumenthal and my sister and I might have had in common; our differences were enough to cause him to be indifferent toward our safety. He was hostile toward our presence in a space he considered his own. So, walking the easy path home from school was often nearly impossible.

The history of human divisions is often constituted of stories about one set of people being hostile toward the presence of others. An ideology that would demand the exclusion or subjugation of whole populations of human beings is an ideology quick to assume positions of superiority over all that is perceived to be different. If you can construct a narrative that turns a human into a beast in order to justify the degradation of that human, how much easier must it be to dismiss the needs of a black bear, a crayfish, a banyan? The values we place on lives that are not our own are reflected in the stories we tell ourselves—and in which aspects of these stories resonate with us. To separate the concerns of the human world (politics, history, commerce) from those of the many life forms with which humans share this planet strikes me as disastrous hubris and folly. We live in community with all the other lives on Earth, whether we acknowledge this or not. When we write about our lives, we ought to do so with an awareness of the other lives we encounter as we move through the world. I choose to honor these lives with attention and compassion.

J. D. HO

Rebellions of the Body, Creations of the Mind

Fourteen doctors puzzled over my symptoms before a fifteenth finally presented the results of an eight-hundred-dollar allergy test explaining my seven years of debilitating digestive issues. I stopped eating everything on the list—basil, oranges, raspberries, artichokes, asparagus, mustard, melon, oregano, papayas, plums, yeast—and I improved. At that time, I anticipated neither the extent of the illness nor the ways it would weave through my existence, influencing what I read and wrote about, and even how I lived my life. But over the years, the allergies have grown so numerous that I can't even recite the full list for those who inquire. No doctor has ever diagnosed the underlying cause. In my lesser moments, I rage against my allergies, feeling persecuted by my own body. In better moments, I'm more philosophical. I wonder what utility allergies have in life. I wonder at their mystery, their connection to the universe.

Allergies have given me a fraught relationship with food, and, as any illness would, they make me identify with others like me. My favorite co-sufferer is Charles Darwin, who shared not only many of my symptoms but also many of my passions. I like to think of Darwin's entire life in connection with food, because he brought his scientific brain to something seemingly unrelated, as if he sensed that the rebellions of his body might, in fact, have deep connections to the ideas in his mind.

Upon Darwin's return to England from his expedition to the Galápagos Islands, South America, and Australia, he suffered from digestive issues (including pain and frequent vomiting) that plagued him for most of the rest of his life, forcing him to remain at home writing—instead of voyaging, socializing, or lecturing. Darwin assiduously recorded his symptoms, documenting his digestive system from input to output. He was a man interested in process, doing what his nature dictated, observing and recording the mystery of his own body. He took a wide range of medicines to no avail; the only relief came from a popular Victorian treatment known as the water cure, which seemed to help. Water cures, offered at spas with supposedly curative water, involved cold baths, wet sheets, and a strict diet. I often feel as Darwin did about his water-cure diet, which forbade, as he complained in a letter to his sister in 1849, "sugar, butter, spices, bacon, or anything good." In the years since his death, doctors and scholars have speculated over what was wrong with Darwin, presenting evidence for Chagas disease, irritable bowel syndrome, hereditary cyclical vomiting syndrome, Ménière's disease, Crohn's disease, anxiety, stress, depression, hypochondria, lactose intolerance, and plain old food allergies. We will probably never know the exact cause of Darwin's troubles, but we know that, for Darwin, food was more than sustenance. It was by turns antagonist, science, pleasure, work, and impetus for creativity.

Food shaped his entire life.

The arrival of my allergies coincided with the central dividing event in my life: leaving my warm Hawaiian island home for college in northwest Massachusetts, where my nostrils and eyelids froze shut when I walked outside in January. Long before I knew about my allergies, food was a rich and diverse part of my childhood. I grew up with so many fruit trees in my yard—papayas, oranges, lychees, tangerines—that I could always walk outside to get something to eat. The idea that food should grow right outside my window has remained with me. Perhaps because of the contrast between my home state and my adopted state, I became obsessed with trying to be part of the new place. I have worked on organic farms, eaten carrots right from the earth, cooked vegan food with New England hippies, and even tried to harvest my own amaranth by beating the stalks on a sheet in the driveway. I've been a gastronomer in the sense that I have loved growing and knowing my food, which has made it easier to accommodate my allergies.

During my freshman year I took a botany class to expand my plant knowledge, but, struggling to function in a new climate and to digest things I did not yet know I was allergic to, I also struggled academically. My botany professor probably thought I was the student least likely to use what little I'd learned, but I've carried botany with me through years of farming, hiking, working in botanical gardens and nurseries, and tending my own garden. When I was diagnosed with allergies, botany helped me navigate the aisles of supermarkets, because genetic relationships were a good predictor of additional allergies. An allergy to mustard meant allergies (mild to severe) to other members of that family: cabbage, kale, bok choy. I had to figure out what was related to what. Is turkey in the same family as chicken? Is a sardine a herring? Illness expanded a whole branch of my knowledge: phylogeny, hierarchy, genetics—the substance of Darwin's breakthroughs, his science, and his life. Illness made me think of how every living thing in the world is related to every other living thing.

Darwin, too, was a foodie in college. Diana Noyce writes in *Gastronomica* (Summer 2012) that while a student at Cambridge Darwin belonged to a club dedicated to deviating from the standard British fare of pork and beef. He ate squirrels, owls, hawks—anything he could hunt down. Later, on the HMS *Beagle*, as he voyaged around the world, he sampled iguanas, jaguars, armadillos, agoutis (supposedly his favorite), pumas, bizcachas, and many other species, including countless types of marine life. Darwin once accidentally ate a rare Patagonian ostrich he'd been seeking for his scientific collection. "Fortunately," he wrote in *The Voyage of the* Beagle (1839), "the head, neck, legs, wings, many of the larger feathers, and a large part of the skin had been preserved; and from these a very nearly perfect specimen has been put together." I can imagine him in the cramped quarters of the ship, painstakingly cleaning, preserving, and labeling the remnants of his meal, licking his fingers as he did so.

In his *Autobiography*, Darwin described the *Beagle* voyage as the most important event in his life. It shaped his thoughts not only on the journey but also after he returned home and became seriously and constantly ill. In England, illness forced him to think about food much of the time, often in a negative way. He likely remembered with pleasure the animals he'd studied and consumed on his voyage, when he'd literally absorbed the diversity of life into his body. In addition to thinking about finch beaks and seeds, Darwin turned the lens upon himself—and I would go so far as to suggest that Darwin's own eating influenced his ideas about natural selection, that his food difficulties made him look at every living thing and ask: What feeds you? What made you? What will you become? How does the outside world course through your body? How does life change forms before our eyes?

Food gives rise to ideas.

Darwin was interested in how the food we eat shapes us in body and behavior. He not only *ate* the animals he encountered on his travels, he observed what *they* ate. As he documented in *Voyage*, he "opened the stomachs of several [lizards] and found them full of vegetable fibres and leaves of different trees, especially of an acacia. In the upper region they live chiefly on the acid and astringent berries of the guayavita. . . . These lizards, when cooked, yield a white meat, which is liked by those whose stomachs soar above all prejudices." Darwin formed a complete chain between himself and these almost inedible berries. He noted a transformation within the lizard, the great utility of the guayavita in creating delicious meat; he, in turn, became something different by eating the lizard. Somewhere in that chain is evidence.

Here is the evidence of my body: produce treated with many pesticides (strawberries, bananas) leads to vomiting; factory-farmed animals cause stomachaches; fatty meat, even some chicken, makes my gallbladder rebel; eggplants set my hands on fire; highly processed foods can be literally hard to swallow, and they wreak havoc on my digestive system when they make it there; as mentioned, my allergies often occur in plant and animal families; some foods cause lesions; most restaurants and absolutely all bakeries are off limits.

About ten years after my initial allergy test, I began to be sick after every meal again. My doctor reran my tests. She told me I had become allergic to legumes (including soy), dairy products, eggs, and sugar—in addition to the long list I'd already been living with. For weeks after the test, I stood in the aisles of supermarkets and literally cried. I became acutely aware of the lack of diversity in modern agriculture and most grocery stores. Further, the doctor told me not to overdo the things I *could* eat because if I ate them more than a few times a week I might become allergic to *them* as well. I had to learn to eat meat after being vegetarian or vegan since I was a small child. Now, whenever I look at any food, I think about whether I can tolerate it—a habit Darwin probably shared, a habit born of long-term allergies and of constantly thinking about food, because deviation from my diet has such drastic consequences.

Darwin repeatedly cataloged connections between food and the bodies of the animals he studied, and his stream of data began to take on a new shape. For instance, a sloth-like creature's teeth "indicate, by their simple structure, that [sloths] lived on vegetable food, and probably on the leaves and small twigs of trees." Later, describing a bird, he wrote that its "muscular gizzard [is] adapted for vegetable food." And Darwin connected the relationship between body and food consumed to bigger ideas brewing in his mind when he famously noted the beaks of the Galápagos finches: "Seeing this gradation and diversity of structure in one small, intimately related group of birds, one might really fancy that from an original paucity of birds in this archipelago, one species had been taken and modified for different ends." Food determines the purpose of a life, a being's place in the world. If the finches of the Galápagos have bodies that dictate what they eat, couldn't it also be true that my body dictates what I eat and what niche I fill in the universe?

Darwin did not confine his observations to nonhuman animals. He repeatedly noted that the place where *people* live dictates diet as well. In Tierra del Fuego, "with the exception of a few berries, chiefly of a dwarf arbutus, the natives eat no vegetable food besides this fungus [*Cytarria darwinii*]. . . . I believe, Tierra del Fuego is the only country in the world where a cryptogamic plant affords a staple article of food." He observed that the indigenous peoples near Buenos Aires ate a great deal of salt, and he hypothesized that this was due to their primarily vegetarian diet. In contrast, the Spanish Gauchos, who subsisted on meat, did not consume salt in huge quantities. The Gauchos, who led an outdoor life herding cattle, ate what their lifestyle and environment both provided and demanded.

Darwin's travels let him see firsthand the relationship between our bodies and our diets. The food available in a place shapes the body, behavior, and identity. The body also, in some ways, determines what we eat. It is reasonable, then, to take this food/body connection further, to suggest that our bodies contribute to how we think, and that, by association, food shapes thought.

Darwin carried these observations and connections with him to England, where he sat down to write. As he documented everything he ate, he must have wondered how he was being shaped by his environment, and why his body seemed ill-suited to English food. He must have wondered what purpose his illness served beyond tethering him to the writing desk. Food, and his troubles with it, became directly connected to his creative process, which was a significant component of his science.

Darwin had long been on my radar because of my interest in the history of science, but I never felt a personal connection to his ideas until a 2015 article in the *Biological Journal of the Linnean Society* brought up Darwin's digestive issues and allergies. "Darwin Diagnosed?" suggested that he was, in fact, lactose intolerant, a condition not understood during his time. On the *Beagle* voyage, Darwin likely consumed few dairy products, which could have caused greater sensitivity when he resumed his dairy habits; upon his return to England, béchamel sauce spelled disaster. The authors of the article, Anthony Campbell and Stephanie Matthews, take their hypothesis further, noting that the presence of lactase, the enzyme that digests lactose, is an evolutionary marvel, a "niche construction" (and one that developed independently in different parts of the world), because many humans keep it long after they need it as infants, and thus are able to digest milk as adults.

Darwin's hypothesized illness dovetails with his own intellectual endeavors, almost as though a lack of lactase wrote a message on his cells, telling him to consider evolution: the ways change happens in humans and in the landscape, how we shape the landscape, and how it shapes us. This collision of ideas—allergies and evolution—continues to be relevant and to raise vital questions: If some bodies developed persistent lactase in response to the advent of animal husbandry and dairying, will we change again in this time of a warming planet? Will the human body adapt to extreme weather and the accompanying changes in food? Even if we don't become genetically different, will we become like the wetland ibises Darwin observed in the desert, making do with scorpions? Will we eat bitter desert fruits and cactus leaves? What will our new diet turn us into?

Seasonal allergies are worsening as a result of longer growing seasons and drastic swings in weather. Food allergies are also on the rise and, I hypothesize, for many of the same reasons: allergies are a phenomenon intensified by the modern world, the industrial revolution, urban living, and climate change—in other words, human activity. Climate change is already affecting agriculture, especially crops such as coffee and grapes. At some point, we will all lose not only coffee and grapes, but many other foods as well.

My allergies mean that I am an early adapter, used to nostalgia for foods I can no longer have.

The *Beagle* voyage brought home to Darwin the beauty and delicacy of the relationships among plants, animals, humans, and the environment. He noted that the place where each creature lives is unique, life-sustaining, and interwoven with existences we may never understand. Darwin wrote,

> The number of living creatures of all Orders, whose existence intimately depends on the kelp, is wonderful. . . . Amidst the leaves of this plant numerous species of fish live, which nowhere else could find food or shelter; with their destruction the many cormorants and other fishing birds, the otters, seals, and porpoises, would soon perish also; and lastly, the Fuegian savage, the miserable lord of this miserable land, would . . . perhaps cease to exist.

When Darwin ate lizards, he ate everything the lizards had eaten, including the water and the minerals the guayavita berries had absorbed. Our existence depends upon a vast network, one Darwin attempted to see and understand. Something from every bit of soil, water, and air that goes into producing my food ends up in my body, causing reverberations deep in my cells. I seek to understand the human relationship with food, the mystery of it, its future, its past, how we'll manage to grow what we need when the weather becomes our enemy; Darwin anticipated these questions, though he may not have anticipated the exact nature of climate change and the challenges it would cause for food production.

Darwin's illness spurred his creative thought about animals and food, evolutionary relationships, and niches. My own illness makes me ask: What is my body fighting? What is in this food—or what happened to this food—that causes me to react?

An allergy is the body's response to something it sees as hostile or foreign.

The word comes from the Greek *allos*, "other." A common view is that allergies are the body overreacting to things it doesn't really need to worry about, but as Dina Fine Maron reported in *Scientific American* in 2013, allergies could have an evolutionary function: preparing the body for responding to real dangers (e.g., snake venom), and therefore increasing the likelihood of survival. This idea applies to less apparent dangers too: pollen, mold, and pollution, substances sure to fill our human future in increasing amounts. The downside of this system is that even if it often saves lives, it sometimes causes death by overreacting.

A friend of mine, who also suffers from a long list of allergies, says she and I are canaries, harbingers of the future, chirping into the darkness. We are bioindicators, showing that much of our food has become poisonous, even if not everyone has been affected yet. But I think allergies may be both the result of *and* a preparation for climate change. My friend and I are prepared for the world ahead because we think so much about food, and we are willing to eat anything to which we are not allergic—including snails, crickets, and weeds.

If allergies are a reaction to the "other," I wonder: If I see through the eyes of my food, if I place myself in *its* existence, will it decrease my allergies? If I have knowledge beyond a label that says organic and free range, if I have empathy, if I understand the purpose of a life and all its connections big and small, if I understand what is harming bees and other pollinators . . . will I understand what is harming me?

With the onset of my allergies, I began to grow my own food in earnest and with diversity as a priority—lamb's lettuce, elderberries, cardoons, and many other uncommon plants—in order not to eat particular foods too frequently and thereby develop sensitivities to them. I forage in the woods for mulberries, pawpaws, pecker-fretted apples, and sandy pears. Allergies have impelled me to turn my small plot of land into a menagerie (from the word *ménage*, meaning "household," and that is how I think of it). I plant things that provide food for me and for the bees, birds, foxes, mice, bears, coyotes, groundhogs, squirrels, crayfish, and anything else passing through. I have begun the project of making my food a part of my existence and my body, weaving my life and my mind into the place where I live. By eating of the place, I absorb its spirit. My body forms cells out of the ground I walk on. I eat what's here: dandelion, chicory, daylily, hostas, rose of Sharon, burdock, opuntia cactus—all without a hitch.

I struggle through winter if I don't put enough by. I pay attention to the seasons, to locations of trees and when they fruit. I wander the woods by my house. I wander the fields, eye level with the bees, sometimes with the ants. I walk in the tracks of the foxes, bears, and coyotes, who have eaten from the cherries before I have. I see their scat filled with cherry pits and marvel that we eat the same things. Eating what they eat, I wonder if I understand them, if I can imagine their lives, inner and outer, their fears, their comforts. What do I want if I am the fox? If I am the bee? Food is no longer *other*, but me. I draw connections between myself and the dirt, the air, the rain. Things return to their source. I watch the squirrels eat the hickory nuts, and then I eat the squirrels, consuming the hickory nuts they've digested, just as Darwin ate the guayavita transformed into lizard's flesh.

My mind asks; it goes in all directions. What is the purpose of my life? What is the message written in my cells and on the simplest molecules that feed me? It is this: allergies are a way to investigate each component of the food that sustains us; they are woven into the intricate web that binds us to the tiniest beings, to invisible organisms in the soil, to particulates in the air. If we don't consider these things as part of ourselves and take note of how the world around us is changing, the patterns of survival and adaptation Darwin observed will no longer keep pace with the world we have made and are making. As Darwin observed, with his way of perceiving food as part of a chain of connected changes, the loss of one key species in the kelp forest could also mean the loss of the entire system.

DAWNE SHAND

Remorse

The first time I saw the Cahaba lilies bloom, I fell into the river fully clothed, like a Baptist. I had come home to my parents' farm near Selma, Alabama, having traveled a thousand miles south with an eleven-month-old in tow, with such high hopes of writing about this backwater river I'd grown up near. All I had seen of the wildflowers were grainy sepia-tone photos published in an out-of-print booklet: "Cahaba: A Gift for Generations, A Series of Historical Essays Revealing the Cahaba River Past, Present, and Future." Printed in the late 1990s by the Cahaba River Society, it was too big to be called a magazine, too thin to be an anthology, and with every page resembling a mad person's scrapbook. Despite the visual chaos, it was thick with fascinating details: Cretaceous-era marine fossils tumbled from the river's chalky banks; the basin's array of fish, freshwater mussels, and snails rivaled, per mile, the diversity of the Amazon River and the Mekong Delta; political intrigue in the 1970s had sunk the Cahaba's chance at inclusion into the National Wild and Scenic River system.

Most bewildering and exciting to me were the lilies. Photographs showed them shooting high above the water and growing thickly like hedges. The plant had once grown on all the Southeast's rivers that crossed the geological fall line of the Appalachian Mountains, but dams had eradicated most of these habitats. The Cahaba's shoal beds were the flower's last great stand. Something so lovely hiding in such close proximity to roads I traveled often . . . it just seemed so improbable.

At the time of this first exposure I was grotesquely nauseated and pregnant, so I'd had to wait another year and a half before I could return to see the spectacle for myself. In May 2005 I followed a college van through a former paper-company forest in central Alabama and into the three-year-old Cahaba National Wildlife Refuge with much anticipation. I left the patched county byway, turned onto a new slag road cutting through woods, and parked by the Judson College vehicle. Near the lot, the trees parted to reveal a low bank, maybe eight feet high. A belt of rocks like a tumbled sidewalk, tilting and jutting across the river's width, interrupted the current, which frothed and made a racket. Rooted in the rocks' crevices were immense bouquets, and I clambered down to see the moon-white blossoms rising waist-high above the water. Their green stalks, tall as small children, held trumpet-shaped flowers.

The professor had named this annual outing "Sitting with the Lilies," but the college girls had no such meditative intent. They leapt across the river as if walking on water were an everyday occurrence, crossed to the opposite bank, and made their way to a tall rock ledge. I watched as each gave a loud yell when she jumped in deep water. After marveling that in the middle of a moving river were these enormous wildflowers, I moved toward the group—but misjudged a step and found myself waist-deep in the river. So I plunged in, floated on my back, and gloried in the sky's all-encompassing blue. A coddling warmth suspended me, and the sense of being enveloped in a world so lovely and unknown swept me away. I wanted to embrace the whole overlooked wilderness—the freckled girls with their sweet manners, the raucous children I'd seen arrive on the back of a pick-up truck, the men in their camouflage clothing with their neoprene chairs fishing above us. The fact that rarity upon rarity, botanical and animal—of small things once thought lost or just discovered—existed within the roots and range of this hidden corner of rural Alabama seemed miraculous.

So, I'd fallen in the Cahaba, swum it, canoed sections of it, and seine-fished it—all with the goal of writing a book about this peculiarity, one of the longest major rivers in the U.S. without a significant dam impediment. I had imagined traveling from the headwaters down those 180 river miles, swimming with the river's madtoms and iridescent darters, sunning with turtles on pale sandbars, watching light shift through Spanish moss over cypress swamps. The Southeast's imperiled aquatic biodiversity was an important science story. It could have been structured to follow a familiar, much-loved lament—the miraculous creation of these rivers, their destruction, the hope for their resurrection.

What first lessened the Cahaba's innocence and implicated me was a family revelation: my grandfather served as a volunteer deputy sheriff in Dallas County during the voting rights movement. I first learned of his involvement in the "water posse" through a story about the region's worst flood, which inundated the region for seventeen days, its high water mark in Selma still unsurpassed.

"During the flood of '61," one of my uncles said to me, "Pawpaw went out on the Cahaba rescuing people."

The uncle was sitting with me and my parents in their den, bouncing my baby daughter on his knee and telling stories about the river to an audience. He couldn't help laughing halfway through this story, and his shoulders literally jumped up and down, a gesture that reminded me of the father he was remembering.

"Scared a black man so badly that he and his pig got out of the boat and swam to shore," he said.

Only later did I realize how hard it would be to explain our response. My grandfather was a hapless outdoorsman, so him being in a fishing boat on a flood-swollen and dangerous Cahaba seemed absurd. But I had the feeling we were laughing at the sight of a black man fording the flood waters with his pig. Our humor cut to the bone.

My uncle had helped arrange for me a canoe trip with his younger brother, Shot. The two of us were planning to see the Cahaba's emptiest corridor, which passed a section where Mother's family had once lived. My uncle left after extracting a promise from me to ask Shot for more stories about that flood.

Days later, Shot's friend and I picked him up outside Selma's city limit. Shot was leaning on a bridge's guard rail, holding a vinyl lunch bag and wearing his signature outfit, Liberty-brand overalls, a white tee shirt, and sandals. I opened the truck door and he said, "Get in the back," and then, "Hello. How are you, dear?"

Before the truck could make its U-turn on the empty highway, Shot started telling us about a dying alligator he found on just such a road: "I said to myself, that's the kind of thing I need at work."

His friend and I laughed as the truck bounced over quilted, ragged asphalt. I had forgotten how the details of everyday experience, here, became epic.

With the alligator in the truck bed, Shot arrived at the factory, walked in, and immediately asked old James at the front desk—"country as grits and white as sour cream"—for a contractor-size garbage bag.

"James said, 'What you want it for?' He was already skeptical," Shot said, then explained how he took James's reluctantly offered plastic bag outside, stuffed the alligator in it, and carried it inside the plant.

"We're sitting around the break room and I've got it stowed under my chair. James asks, 'What you got in there?' So I put my hand in. It's dead by now, the jaw is slack. I put my hand beneath the jaw so when I pulled it out the mouth dropped wide open."

Shot dropped into a whisper.

"I put that dead gator in his face." He paused, then said "Boy!" with his volume higher, "He called me everything but my mother's son." James had toppled over in his chair but came up cursing.

We passed lined fields of young, green cotton plants before turning onto a creviced red clay road that looked more like a path to a rabbit hole than a canoe put-in, which it wasn't anyway—just a ramp beneath the short Suttle bridge that was itself barely visible. The truck's carriage scraped along, the hitch making a frightening racket as its cargo bounced over the badly washed-out path. We backed up to the water's edge; Shot's friend left after he'd steadied the boat and helped push us off.

Once on the river, I started to row as though it was good exercise. Shot asked me not to: he preferred the quiet.

"You can hear more that way," he said.

So we drifted down the ribbon-narrow, tree-shaded river as the early sun caught a few wisps of lingering fog. We took in sounds—a mechanical whir on a nearby farm, water's drip over soapstone ledges, a cow's thrash through brush. Shot pointed out unusual trees: Catawbas with their orchid-shaped white flowers, a flood-felled cypress lying with its roots still gripping the moist banks and its limbs as tall as the surrounding trees. We passed a sandbar—wide, pale, and inviting—at an elbow of the river. Then, we found ourselves in a section where the river was cutting through one meander and forming a shorter, narrower chute straight ahead. The main current, however, was continuing in its older path with a velocity that threatened to entangle us in flood debris.

"Row, row, row," Shot shouted.

The river was entrancing one minute and frightening the next. We had to work to round a tree-topped island with a steep sandbar. Dozens of turtles scuttled down the bank, flinging white clouds behind as they dove into the river. I caught a glimpse of their oval forms swimming beneath us. Shot powered the boat away from the overhanging thicket of limbs and vines until the river turned placid.

"Your brother said to ask you about the flood of '61." I glanced back, expecting Shot to tell another family tale, simultaneously entertaining and mildly disturbing, about my grandfather's flood rescue. But Shot didn't respond for a few moments.

"Yeah, he and Jim Clark were fishing buddies. That's when Daddy was a deputy sheriff. They went out to rescue families. They'd probably been drinking a little bit. Got to an old black lady's house; she came out and said, 'Thank God you're here.' And Jim Clark said, 'God my ass. Jim Clark's here to save you.'"

In '61, Jim Clark was a local sheriff who had yet to step onto the national stage as the face of white intransigence and violence in Selma. That my grandfather was "deputized" in Clark's posse I had not known until this moment.

I didn't know what to say. Uncle Shot didn't add anything as we floated downstream.

The sound of chiding kingfishers followed us. Swallows darted out from behind their nesting cavities, which pockmarked a steep vermillion embankment.

We stopped for lunch at the juncture of Oakmulgee Creek, beneath a moss-covered cypress tree stranded in sand. We could not have been more alone there, on a little-noticed river carving up a destitute region.

I think he could tell, as he unpacked his lunch bag, that the revelation about my grandfather was weighing on me.

He said, "Guy at work asked me, what provisions was I taking on this trip? I said: fruit, water, granola. He said, 'That's not river food. You need pork rinds and beer.' I told him he was a half-wit that went double or nothing with God and lost."

I laughed. But eventually, I came back to the subject that had derailed me.

"Was Pawpaw on the bridge with Jim Clark?" I asked, tentatively.

He paused.

"Probably, but I'm not for sure." He offered few words, but these began to dissipate, for me, the silence that enveloped any discussion about my family's witness of the voting rights movement. Our trip ended my first month on the Cahaba. I left with my own unsettling story.

Over the next two years, I came to understand the river's true complications. The 16th Street Baptist Church bombing had been planned along this river, by a KKK break-off called "The Cahaba Group." Once, I had gone to their meeting place outside Birmingham. There wasn't much to see: a small impoundment that pooled the city's drinking water. A broken-down fish ladder. Winter-dormant trees hanging on to brittle brown leaves. A short waterfall. The steep hillside hid the spot from anyone driving by on the surrounding interstates, highways, and byways that were overhead. I wasn't alone, yet none of us felt comfortable there. I left the planning site, which had no marker. This history was a side note that served no organization's purpose—not the water board, not the city, and not the river's conservation group.

My research bifurcated: on one side, the hard science of how the Cahaba's ecosystem functioned; on the other, the question of how the white community responded to demands for equal citizenship and then covered their tracks. And this entangled me so much so that I began to believe I had to return and see the most inaccessible of the river's flowering rock beds, Hargrove Shoals. An aerial photograph of it showed an enormous stretch of lilies, so blanketed in blossoms that it resembled an elaborate, mile-long casket. Seeing this photo before I left Alabama in 2005 made me anxious that I had missed a crucial experience of the Cahaba. I hoped seeing it might provide something like balance to what I knew so far.

In May 2007, I caught up with the Cahaba River Society mid-river as its organizers shepherded dozens of inexperienced paddlers along a waterway enduring a hundred-year drought. Because the portage was physically challenging even when the water level was running high, field trips went infrequently to Hargrove Shoals. That day, rocks resembling cuspids rose sharply above the surface. The group's field director, Dr. Randy Haddock, was acting the part of crossing guard, finding a rivulet through the rock maw on the first shoal bed for canoes to squeeze through. Mine, however, was wider than the others. A grinding crunch forced me to climb out, then pull the canoe while walking through shallow water coursing over slick, uneven terrain. I put my hand out to a boulder, hoping to steady myself, but slipped. A colony of snail shells, scraped from the rock as I fell, clattered. I glanced up to see Randy's horrified face.

The lilies were the showiest of the refuge's imperiled things, but not the rarest. Whorled river snails, flat pebblesnails, cylindrical lioplax—their footholds on a few rocks here and in an adjoining stream added to the tally of endemics that made the river basin's snail population one of the continent's most diverse. After passing through this first obstacle, the group paddled another half mile before climbing out, grasping each canoe's rim, and pulling the vessels over Caffee Creek shoals. Below the water's surface, submerged boulders were wrapped by burgundy vines with minuscule pink blossoms. Water willow and its tiny, white-and-purple-streaked slipper blooms grew alongside the taller lilies.

Then we paddled slow water as the river made a wide bend through the Oakmulgee Ranger District of the Talladega National Forest. Hargrove Shoals presented first as a low fence stretching to both shores. As we pulled closer, water pathways appeared to wind between huge bouquets. The paddlers found flat rocks first for mooring, then for picnicking. I climbed out and walked along the shoals' scoured surfaces.

The flowering stretched as far as I could see, but the haze blurred any distinction between air and plant. The lilies wouldn't emit their earthy, honeyed fragrance till later in the day, when their pollinators became active. Near me, the stalks stood wall-thick around a large, flat chert. I lay down, feeling encompassed and hidden, and put my ear to the sun-warmed rock. The current drowned out all the sounds from above. In that moment, this obscure place seemed otherworldly.

In his 1767 book *Travels*, William Bartram wrote that "nothing in vegetable nature was more pleasing than the odoriferous *Pancratium fluitans*,* which alone possesses the little rocky islets which just appear above the water." Bartram's descriptions of the southeastern United States, from North Carolina to Alabama, mesmerized European writers. *Travels* inspired the Romantic poets: Coleridge

---

* In 1836 John LeConte corrected Bartram's failure to provide a Latin description to accompany *Pancratium fluitans*, making LeConte the official scientific discoverer of the lily he named *Hymenocallis coronaria*.

with his famous fragment *Kubla Khan*, Wordsworth, and Chateaubriand. In the poets' minds Bartram conjured the idea of the New World as a Garden of Eden, a paradise where man does not yet know remorse.

From a rock dais, Randy offered glass vials for collecting and tasting lily nectar. For the urbane of Birmingham, Alabama, this outing provided an opportunity to drink in the lilies before discussing the Cahaba's ecological status and the city's destruction of its headwaters. Then he explained the parasitic spawning relationship between mussels and fish to a group that, in the battles over development ordinances, might be persuaded by flowers and reason. One hundred and thirty-one types of fish were swimming in the Cahaba; sixty-four rare and imperiled plants and animals, of which thirteen were endemic only to this basin, made the refuge one of North America's eight "freshwater hotspots" of aquatic biodiversity. These quantifications were to conservationists what William Bartram's Edenic descriptions in his *Travels* had been for the eighteenth-century poets—signs of something unspoiled by man.

Transcendent love of place had created the political will to set aside large and difficult-to-access wilderness areas, like the one I was leaving. I knew the tradition, articulated by Ralph Waldo Emerson, of experiencing deeply personal and revelatory moments in these natural environments. I came here as the individual seeking insight and found Hargrove Shoals to be astonishing. Few were ever going to see it; the refuge itself, with its single dirt path, couldn't handle many trekkers. But the experience had failed to make me a less unruly narrator.

In October 2007, I turned in a book manuscript to a Southern university press. I had written a series of loosely linked essays about exploring the natural history of the Cahaba and the surrounding region. Like the booklet that inspired the project, my manuscript was chock-full of living things: endemic prairie wildflowers; symbolic plantings at the entrances to slave cemeteries in the Black Belt; flame-colored fish. Quotes from Transcendentalists appeared next to statistics on biodiversity. I meandered at odd moments to ask why Southern landscapes seldom appeared in the body of American nature writing. To the acquiring editor, I turned in a mess, written in the leftover moments of days spent running after a toddler, but I hoped the review process would shape it. Worse first books had been published.

In its final chapter, I did take one significant, and probably ill-conceived, detour away from the Cahaba. During my May visits in both 2005 and 2007, an admission by a former state trooper to shooting a Civil Rights–era protester, Jimmie Lee Jackson, captivated the region. Jackson's death had inspired the first voting rights march.

On 18 February 1965, the twenty-six-year-old Jackson attended a night-time civil rights meeting with his mother, Viola Jackson, and his grandfather, Cager Lee, at a church on the town square of Marion. Protestors gathered in the AME Church because the activist James Orange had been arrested. Rumors swirled that he might be lynched. Approximately five hundred people gathered to walk the length of the city block, along the town's main square. As they left the church, they were met by Alabama's state troopers, Sheriff Clark, and a few members of his posse, as well as some neighbors and bystanders. Someone shot out the streetlights; a melee ensued. Jackson's grandfather and mother fled to a building behind the church, Mack's Cafe, where troopers cudgeled them. Jackson went to help them and was shot at close range by Fowler. He died eight days later.

No images survived from the night, because newspaper reporters were also attacked and their cameras destroyed. Jackson's death gave protesters the idea of marching his body on a funeral bier to George Wallace in Montgomery. Marion, thirty dirt-road miles from Selma, was too far off, making Selma, with its paved highway, a more feasible starting point for a march on the state capital. What ensued on the Edmund Pettus Bridge in Selma relegated Marion, and Jackson's death, to a side note in the larger history of the 1960s' Civil Rights movement.

The *Anniston Star* first broke the news on 6 March 2005 that James Bonard Fowler—now a seventy-year-old farmer in Geneva, Alabama—was claiming his role in the Black Belt's voting rights' history. Fowler told the investigating journalist, John Fleming, that he watched tv documentaries describe the murder of Jimmie Lee Jackson as a defining moment for the Civil Rights movement. Fowler balked: he fired in self-defense. The *Anniston Star* quotes Fowler as saying,

> He was trying to kill me and I have no doubt in my mind that, under the emotional situation of the time, if he would have gotten complete control of my pistol that he would have killed me or shot me. That's why my conscience is clear. But on the tv on documentaries you watch, they say that Jimmie Lee was murdered by an Alabama state trooper.

James Bonard Fowler seemed to speak from a position of hearing himself unnamed but held responsible.

No mainstream news outlets outside Alabama picked up on the story of Fowler's confession in 2005. Two months after the news broke, I read about it in the Marion paper while standing in line to buy a Coke at a convenience store after a hot day on the Cahaba—strange happenstance in the internet age.

In May 2007, Michael Jackson, the first black district attorney to be elected in the state of Alabama—he came to office in 2005, three months before Fowler's confession—empaneled a mixed-race grand jury and got a guilty verdict. While I was home to see Hargrove Shoals, James Fowler appeared at the Marion courthouse to be booked by Jimmie Lee Jackson's cousin—deputy sheriff Carlton

Hogue. This might have been construed as a heroic story. Instead, I had the feeling it was being met with a wish to avoid old wounds.

My knowledge of Fowler's admission in 2005 and his indictment in 2007 coincided with my lily trips, which was thin plot. But I had observed, by asking questions about Clark's posse, that people in this region had discussed their experiences of the Civil Rights movement only as private asides. The 2007 grand jury indictment made people begin to talk openly about the decade—harrowingly, but nonetheless out loud for everyone to hear. A trial and the possibility of others made public a conversation about this region's complicated legacy.

So, I ended my manuscript by talking about a murder trial yet to get underway because, I reasoned, a story about a river can meander.

I waited for editorial feedback as the 2008 presidential election came to an end. During then-senator Barack Obama's campaign, he came to Selma to celebrate the anniversary of the voting rights marches. There, he said, "Don't tell me I don't have a claim on Selma, Alabama. Don't tell me I'm not coming home when I come to Selma, Alabama." I thought about my grandfather's role in the moment the future president referenced, but wasn't sure what to make of the information. Selma had again become part of the nation's political dialogue, but so had the term "post-racial." At the time, the phrase seemed to mean we no longer had to discuss race, that avoiding the issue of whiteness as a racial profile was a strategic choice. And this made me wonder if the opposition to the voting rights movement had somehow become a dated topic.

In an Ipswich, Massachusetts, coffee shop surrounded by images of the world's most daunting peaks, clam diggers and database editors stood in line for affogato, cappuccino, and chai. As I used hijacked wi-fi during those twice-weekly preschool reprieves, my internet searching provided little useful information about Clark or his posse. Newspapers, reporting on past anniversaries of the voting rights marches, referred to his men as "unemployed vigilantes." Clark continued to sit for interviews until his death in 2007, but no one I knew of had spoken on the record about participation in the posse. I was unsure of what to make of Jim Clark's connection to Browns, Alabama, where he owned eighty acres, where my father's parents began their dairy farm—and where I was born. I hadn't yet pieced together the fact that Clark recruited his horse-mounted posse from his acquaintances—the cattle farmers of Browns and its surroundings.

In April 2008, the editor emailed to say the comments from the first blind reviewer were good enough. We could work with them. Then a photocopied letter arrived days later. The plain white page included no attribution, no letterhead, no date. It was four short paragraphs that filled two-thirds of the page.

"I feel sorry for Dawne," the note began. "Her glass is half-empty."

The reviewer, a self-declared daughter of the Deep South whose glass was half-full, thought certain of my landscape descriptions were of modest quality, but I had missed the signs of the region's regeneration. And as for Jackson's murder trial, she wrote: "Officer Fowler, the retired law officer and Vietnam veteran, wounded Jimmie Lee in the line of duty assigned him by the Governor of Alabama."

When the time arrived for the editor to talk with me by phone, my outrage had reduced to a nervous simmer. I sat with earnest resolve, pen and paper in hand, prepared to refute these comments.

"One of your sources called me," the editor began. "He said he hoped we would have nothing to do with this publication."

Immediately, I had that awful raised-hackle sensation, as if being threatened. "Who?" I asked defensively.

She refused to name him. One complaint of his in particular disconcerted her: he was disappointed I hadn't been more willing to learn from him.

Confused, I stammered something about respect for my sources, then tried to refocus the conversation on the reviewer's comments, which lay before me.

"This review—it's an evaluation of the work's promotional value for the reviewer's organization, isn't it," I said, as this was how I had dismissed the critique.

But the editor needed the financial support for the book she imagined. She, along with the blind reviewer and the unnamed source, wanted a book about the beauty of the Cahaba River, one that would inspire a nascent conservation movement for an important waterway facing very serious environmental degradation.

"You've overlooked a rare plant, Golden Club, which has been sustained by a group of ladies from Birmingham all these years," she added. True, I didn't know what she was talking about, but then she added a line I did understand in its entirety: "The black community is not involved in the state's conservation movement. They just take turtles out of the river to eat. And these are an endangered species," she said.

I countered with a fact that seemed unassailable: "The 16th Street Church bombing was planned along that river by a paramilitary arm of the KKK who called themselves 'The Cahaba Group.' That's not separable from this river's narrative."

When she didn't want to give credence to this coincidence, I shifted the conversation to the state trooper, James Fowler, since the note complained I had not interviewed him: "As I wrote in my email—Fowler has flaunted his crime, shown no remorse. Not to say he shouldn't be treated as a complex subject, but he has bragged about the shooting. He shot a second black man in his custody. He attacked his white superior officer, which finally got him fired. He has a record of drug arrest in Southeast Asia. Why is a daughter of the Black Belt coming to his defense?"

"You're writing like a Yankee," the editor said as the conversation came to an end.

From my office window, I noticed the lights on the drawbridge over the Merrimack had turned on as fog from the Atlantic surrounded it. The editor offered a few more recommendations for what to do with material that began on a river and ended with an ongoing murder trial. "Our Civil Rights story has been published. And the story about your grandfather being part of Clark's posse—that's something you should write and share with your daughter."

Stunned at the death of a first book project I'd hung much hope on, I sat fuming. The two anonymous sources seemed to have a powerful stake in what stories would be told about the region. The suddenness of the editor's change in position, from "we can work with these comments" to "drop all references to the Sixties," made me think I had endangered her publishing future.

To everyone who asked, "How's your book?" I said I'd been banned. This helped cover the weedy disappointment which grew out of that phone conversation. If I had been unsure before about how to handle my material, the conversation unmoored me. My overwrought prose hadn't helped, but neither was it the real fuel behind the provocative reaction the manuscript received. I had placed Jim Clark and his posse, which symbolized Alabama's infamy, into the Cahaba's garden of biodiversity—a sinless state. The phone call was a warning: Asking questions about the white community's response to the Civil Rights movement represented dangerous territory.

These were not the insights I expected to have blossom when I first fell into the Cahaba, although their slow and excruciating arrival often resonated with Uncle Shot's admonition about being quiet: "You can hear more that way."

I could have ignored the flood story: "Pawpaw went out on the Cahaba rescuing people." Silence was an option. The Jackson trial and the "Cahaba Group" lived in the public domain, but Clark's posse existed only as a caricature. With the members unnamed and forgotten, my connection could have been severed. Still, instead of burying my grandfather's belonging, I pursued it. At times, the effort left me deeply unsure of what to feel about him—revulsion, empathy, love?

Once, a brief rest in a conceptual jail cell clarified that difficulty. I found this room within the National Voting Rights Museum and Institute on the Selmont side of the Edmund Pettus Bridge in July 2012.

As I left my parents' house for the museum, my mother offered my grandfather's four-pronged metal cane, because I had badly sprained my ankle days earlier. Its offering came after a moment of hesitation, as if she wasn't sure I would be careful enough with this, the one thing of his she kept. After a stroke paralyzed his left side and robbed him of clear speech, he relied on it.

"Drive safe," she said.

Getting out of the car and going into the new museum building, I leaned heavily on the geriatric cane. I bought my ticket and limped through a curated story I knew well, but was still surprised to see names, new to me, in the exhibit on "Foot Soldiers" of the movement. The naming of local people and their contributions was the purpose of the initiative. Never had I found, however, my grandfather's name in any archive or book or museum, although his fishing buddy, Jim Clark, was omnipresent. I could even hear Clark's voice being broadcast in a hallway.

Toward the end of my circuit I entered a room, narrow as its doorway, that had walls lined by metal bars. Inside it were a prison cot, a water bucket, and a urinal. With my ankle throbbing, I sat on the blue pillow-ticking mattress, closed my eyes, and leaned my head against the back wall. The cane's handle rested comfortably in my hand. Outside the mock cell looped a video of the former sheriff, Jim Clark, being interviewed late in his life. Someone was arguing with Clark and said heatedly, "You didn't see us as human." Clark, offended, said, "That's not what happened."

Behind the bars, monochrome prints papered the walls, including photographs of young people standing in long lines outside the Dallas County Courthouse. Behind my back was an enlarged mug shot of a serious, confident young man. Hanging on the bars was a framed photograph of a man in a fedora being led away by two white uniformed men. Nowhere did a face betray fury. The collage created an eerie sense of calm and resolution.

I looked at the stainless steel urinal. On its top, a small placard excerpted a sixteen-year-old's memory of being jailed in Selma: Clark had told the students in the cell, "You niggers act like cows and dogs, that's the way we're going to treat you." The young man recalled watching the interrogation of another jailed teenager. Clark asked that person's name, and he replied, "Joseph T. Smitherman," which was also the name of the city's white mayor at that time. Clark must have assumed Smitherman was provoking him, because he sat the youth on a block of ice and beat him in their cell. The narrative ended with the child's witness of hearing a local minister convince the sheriff that the teenager wasn't lying.

As I sat in that brightly lit, confining space, these torture tactics were hard to take in. Like an electric charge, anger jolted me. Because I was tired and in physical pain, the unexpected surge of emotion came as a surprise. I couldn't tell what my instincts wanted to fight as the cane I held became my weapon. Sitting there holding my grandfather's legacy, I had the urge to strike something. In that moment, I felt indicted by that room.

Unsettled, I hobbled out of the museum to my rental car. By the parking lot, a spray-painted mural on the garage-bay doors of a storage unit depicted President Obama and the White House with this caption: "Hands That Picked Cotton Picked a President!" Towering overhead, an interstate-size billboard offered a twenty-thousand-dollar reward for information about the 2012 theft of a Nathan Bedford Forrest statue; someone had no compunction about wanting back the likeness of the Ku Klux Klan's first Grand Imperial Wizard.

I pulled out of the parking lot and decided to drive to the house my grandparents built. Two decades had passed since I followed the county roads through Selmont. The first traffic light was at the intersection where the attack on unarmed protesters happened.

"You know, I was in the first car stopped on Highway 80 that Sunday," my uncle had said to me, quietly, the afternoon he told us about the 1961 flood. On 4 March 1965, he was a nineteen-year-old college student driving home from Montgomery with neighbors. State troopers halted traffic on the east side of the Edmund Pettus; from a car, he had watched the protestors crest the bridge.

"I'll never forget, a cloud of tear gas cleared, and there was our neighbor on a white horse holding a bull whip," he said, shaking his head. "You never know when you'll witness something important."

Cars now pass a highway sign welcoming travelers to this National Historic Trail, an All-American Scenic Byway. Near the intersection, the old movie theater had reopened as an evangelical church. Its two screens—one for black tastes, one for white, although no sign had demarcated them in my lifetime—had closed four years earlier after its manager was murdered in the parking lot. I turned left by the Selma Curb Market, covered with wall-size images and hand-painted words: bait, groceries, cold beverages. On its side wall, deer grazed and quail took flight.

From my passing car, Selmont looked forlorn: the convenience store, which used to sell us Coke slushies and loose candy thirty years ago, was abandoned. At the shuttered battery plant, tall pines trellised the unused water tower. The pink cinderblock house, the only marker for a left turn along the hedgerows and fields, was still there, was still pale pink. When my grandparents moved to the opposite end of the county from where we had lived in Marion Junction, the drive seemed long and the directions hard to follow; I remember listing them for my mother to prove I could arrive here by myself. That I could still find this path made me feel that same excitement I felt as a kid coming out here.

Questioning my family about my grandfather's involvement with Clark's posse yielded thin slivers of memory, but the tentativeness of the inquiries was mine alone. I was my grandfather's first grandchild. He kept my kindergarten photo in his wallet until he died in August 1997. I adored him, but knew little of his life.

I stopped my car where their former property began. On either side of the dirt road were curved gateways made of sandstone brick, each with an open double arch between two pediments. My grandfather had them built to mark his property line—house on one side, a field for growing peas on the other— although an unpaved public road cut through it. His tastes always ran toward pomp.

The house stood exactly as I remembered it, a well-sited brick ranch with a carport on two wooded acres. When I knew my grandparents best, they had achieved a foothold here in middle-class security. When I was a child, every crossing of the Edmund Pettus Bridge meant we were getting close to this home, full of aunts and uncles, their spouses and my cousins, and every visit felt like an adventure. For all the hardships, and there were many, my aunts and uncles had been cared for in a way that carried them to their own economic stability, marital stability, and advanced education. I too had been neatly pressed, well-schooled, and loved—given the parameters which, for better or for worse, have bound my hands as I've tried unknotting Walter Braxton Barnes's role at the height of the Civil Rights movement.

ROBIN PATTEN

The Carcass Chronicle

We found the elk's carcass in the morning, just downhill from the pasture fence where she lay sprawled across an iced-over stream. *Carcass* is a harsh word for that once-graceful animal, a cow elk whose small head and hooves made me think she'd only lived a few years. Her eyes were still liquid and soft, looking upwards to the sky. Below that stare, a gaping hole in her neck held a pool of blood large enough to ripple in the cold breeze. Her hide was half gone, ribs exposed, but her head was untouched, those eyes seeming to watch, making her more elk than carcass.

The wolves had brought her down the night before, first when she tried to jump the fence behind the cabin and failed to clear the top rail, breaking the pole clean through. The snap of wood only twenty yards from where I lay reading in bed had caught my attention. Setting the book down, turning off the music playing on the nightstand, I listened in the quiet. A sound seemed to come from outside, a stirring of something in the night so soft it was like a dreamed presence. The cat didn't notice anything and went back to purring. I went back to my book.

The fallen elk had risen to move through the dark, away from the place where her body had printed the snow, where red splashed across white. With wolves on her and blood streaming, she had gotten up, staggered from behind the cabin, through the ice of the creek, and across the small dirt road that goes to the barn. There she met the pasture fence. That obstacle finished the hunt, and she died on the other side, the wolves ending the struggle as she made that last leap, the snow holding the story to be read the next morning.

Wolves commonly kill elk where I live, on the edge of Yellowstone National Park. It's the natural way of things in the greater community of life. Yet this death occurred only a short distance from where I rested peacefully in bed with quiet music and purring cat, a death revealed as the morning sun warmed the valley— the beauty of the natural world entwined in torn flesh and staring eyes. What rises in the face of events so natural yet so severe is not so much an emotion as a stillness, an abrupt pause in what we know as life.

Later, considering that soft sound drifting through the dark as the elk's life was torn from her, a thought came. Perhaps this is how death moves: muffled, unseen, inevitably closing in—like creatures pushing softly through snow in the night.

We needed to move the carcass, so the ranch hand wrapped a chain around her neck and hauled the dead elk off with the bulldozer. Blood streamed from her mouth as the chain tightened and the roaring machine dragged off the limp body that bounced and bobbed as it slid down the gravel road and out of sight. Removing the elk bothered me, for wolves had brought her down and wolves should feed on her carcass. That her last move happened behind a smoke-belching bulldozer bothered me more, seeming so wrong for this animal who had spent her life in high meadows and mountains. But the move was a necessity: buildings all around, dogs running loose, horses in that pasture. She would now lie where scavengers could reach her, beyond constant human activity.

Two days after the elk's death, I walked out to the front pasture, across the white field where last summer's Timothy grass swayed golden over the snow, down through pine woods, through a secluded meadow, and out to the forest edge not far from the river. I found the bulldozer tracks coming in from the other direction; they took me to the carcass. I wanted to know if the wolves had found their prey.

With the bulldozer's blade, the ranch hand had pushed the carcass away from the trail along the woods, shoving the elk to her final resting place atop a snow pile, head lolling down the pile's front, rigid legs sticking off the back. And yes, a wolf had been there, pressing hand-size paw prints into the snow, almost up to the elk's remains. Almost. No canine tracks at the body, the carcass looking little different from the morning that the elk died. The wolf had only come within ten feet.

Another elk had also come, fresh cloven prints so close to the carcass that the living elk could have put its nose on the body, smelling wolf and human and death. Curious? Mourning? It seems an elk would avoid this site and its scents.

Wolf passing up meat, an elk exploring its kindred's demise: there was mystery here, a story unfolding. And so I returned the next day, and the next, in what became a daily journey, a time of reflection, observation, notes taken in a small black book with fingers stiffened by winter chill, written while standing under a long-dead tree. That old pine became part of the day, part of the narrative, marking the site and offering protection from the wind. And a perch for the ravens.

Ravens go to roost at the end of the day, leaving a carcass to the quiet of evening. For a few days, evening was when I visited the site and found only the wind swinging through the forest, a muted chorus of rustling branches and creaking trunks rising from the swaying trees. Tracks showed the presence of those who came and went from the crumpled body. In that last diminishing light of day was a sense of creatures watching, though I had no way of knowing whose eyes were on me: fox, coyote, eagle, marten. All felt alive, standing there next to death.

The ravens went unseen until I changed the timing of my visit, journeying to the site mid-morning, four days after the elk died. A handful of big black birds hunkered on the carcass, vigorously pecking and pulling at the flesh. I slipped closer. A bald eagle lifted into flight, abandoning its meal at my approach. The ravens followed, departing as one, sifting into the trees. An intricate pattern marked the snow around the carcass, entwined toe and talon prints, a mosaic of the birds' activities as they danced around the bounty of meat.

Morning visits became my norm, part of the rhythm of the carcass day: canines at night, birds in light, ravens and eagles feeding until late afternoon, me appearing mid-morning and sometimes evening as well. Ravens and eagles abandoned the carcass in my presence, gray jays and the occasional magpie jumping on the torn flesh as the big birds lifted off, those smaller birds making use of the time when I was there. This was the general pattern over the following weeks, though with shifts in species and numbers, witnessed yet not always understood.

In the first few days of morning visitations, I'd arrive to find an average corvid cohort of eight to ten ravens. Then a recruitment call went out; the raven numbers grew.

The call happened on a bright, crisp morning, the air sound-carryingly clear. Perched in a lodgepole pine close to the carcass, a raven started calling, a chuckle followed by a long, musical bark: "Hah! Hah! . . . Hah! . . . Hah!" The bird jerked forward with feathers ruffling at the force of each sound.

Something about that call—its unfamiliarity, its penetrating persistence and intensity—caught my imagination, piqued my interest. What *was* that raven saying? I returned home, started searching academic papers, websites, and bird books for clues to the meaning of this unique vocalization. And there it was, right on my shelf, in a book I hadn't looked at for years: Bernd Heinrich's *Ravens in Winter*. It seems that raven in the pine had been "yelling."

In the 1980s, ravens captured the attention of Heinrich, who noticed that after a raven or two discovered a carcass, they would often loudly announce their find, and other ravens would come to the meat. Wanting to understand why ravens would advertise their food rather than keep it to themselves, Heinrich dragged cow guts, dead beaver, and other grisly remains into the woods, going out in freezing pre-dawn temperatures to get to an observation point before the birds arrived. Eventually, he determined that nonbreeding vagrant ravens "yell" to gather a group and control a carcass against dominant resident ravens. This is not about sharing. It's a way to get *some* food in the face of a territorial dominant.

Yet, the yell is more than a call to gather a group of anonymous carcass-controllers. Each raven has its own voice, with unique acoustic qualities. Ravens are familiar with the calls of other vagrant ravens that inhabit the same general region and so can identify which one is yelling, then choose whether or not to join the feeding frenzy, coming to the call of social allies.* The gang that congregates on a carcass is thus a gathering of familiars.

On that cold, clear morning, with the elk less than a week dead, the raven's yell had echoed across the sage flats and into the forest. The following day, around twenty ravens gathered, almost three times the number who'd been ripping at the carcass the morning before. They were a close-knit group—feeding together in a mob, lifting as one from the bloody remains when I approached, dancing synchronously through the sky. They seemed in continuous conversation, voicing their raven thoughts and concerns, yelling, crawking, calling, cooing, and squawking during squabbles. I watched those ravens conversing within their complex and structured avian society, communicating in ways humans are only just beginning to understand. I watched and wondered what convoluted ideas were in those sounds, given that a simple "Hah! Hah!" can convey a story.

And they watched me, that great flock of black birds. Even as I watched this process, I was being watched—the observer now observed.

They scrutinized me from the beginning. That day when I heard the raven yell, rather than simply removing themselves to the surrounding forest as I approached, a few ravens remained behind, circling just overhead as the others disappeared into the trees. One paused in a hover, looking down with arched neck. I returned its gaze, looking skyward at that bird with its curled, gray feet the only break in the black, its impenetrable ebony eyes staring down, reducing the human below to nothing but a wisp of a question. I felt I was being judged. Then the raven tipped a wing and was off into the woods. Released from scrutiny, I called as it departed, "Cra-a-awck!"

After my first few visits, the ravens began announcing my arrival whenever I walked toward the carcass, a black shape sweeping past with a rush of wings and a loud cry as the old dead pine came into view, the call jerking my attention to that moment, even as the bird brought my presence to the attention of the flock. The raven's racketing cry shifted my focus, that feathered creature sailing toward

---

* Szipl, Georgine, et al., "With whom to dine? Ravens' responses to food-associated calls depend on individual characteristics of the caller." *Animal Behaviour* 99.0 (January 2015): 33–42.

the dead elk pulling my awareness out of the comfortable dominion of home that I'd just left. On reaching the carcass, I would find the ravens already lifted, milling about in the surrounding trees. As I examined the carcass, three or four would fly from the sheltering woods to the opening where the elk lay, to circle overhead, keep track of my movements, follow me as I stepped back to stand under the pine and scratch out notes or simply to look up through the craggy, bare branches, watching them watching me. Always, at least one would stall mid-flight, floating ten feet overhead, fluttering wings twisting the air into a rustling whirlpool, neck arched, staring down, stilling me with a stare.

Yet I did not keep silent. An urge to participate drew out my feeble *crawks* and *croos*, though I feared I might be saying something untoward. My voice went out in an attempt to communicate acknowledgment, a human cry into an expanded community.

Eleven days after the kill: a shift, a change. On that gray, still morning, the raven group scattered, leaving behind only disjunct calls echoing in oppressive air. Ravens drifted about, separating, moving near and far, high in the sky, shifting erratically through the pines. A bald eagle stared down from a high perch above the carcass before rising to soar out of sight, followed by a second that had been on the remains. The pile of bone and flesh lay empty, deserted by pecking beak and tearing talon.

Tension in the air, a throb. Standing in my habitual spot under the pine, I noted: *A different feel . . . Now a big raven has perched nearby.* Jet-black eyes rested hard on me, seeming to question my presence, then abruptly the bird took off, disappearing in a feathered squall of sound. Ravens were strewn about—sporadic calls, no groups. Then quiet. A breeze, a tree whisper, a river murmur.

Walking home by a different route, I crossed the dirt road to the ranch where a burly raven stood alone, exactly in the middle of the road, calling, calling. "*Crawk, crawk! . . . Crawk!*"

On day twelve I arrived to silence. *They are GONE*—the words scrawled in my notebook. The ravens were gone. Gone. No birds called from the site, no ravens, eagles, magpies. Nothing. Fox and coyote tracks, but only one set of jay tracks. No creatures, only eerie silence and the carcass—now a mere rack of ribs flecked with flesh, head thrown back half hidden by snow, hind legs still connected at the pelvis but pointing toward opposite ends of the earth.

A raven call wafted in from a far distance. Another. The group had disbanded, dispersed to other parts, the carcass apparently reduced to a state that no longer made it worth feeding en masse. And so—the floating calls of the day before, the taut air, all stretched to the point of breaking, of breaking up. The beginning of the end of this carcass gathering—though it remains a mystery why other bird species departed as well. The ravens had discussed and determined this stage the previous day, through sounds and perhaps in other ways that I felt in the tension, but didn't understand.

And that big raven proclaiming *something* from the middle of the road, with his ringing "*Crawck, crawck, crawck.*" Just what? "Off! Off! We're off to other places!" Or, my romantic sentiments chime in, "Farewell! Farewell! Farewell, lady who stands by the Tree!"

What messages lie in raven calls? Academic articles and Heinrich's books can illuminate the "yell." Other sounds, cries, and behaviors are more obscure, floating past like a foreign language. And not just ravens had been talking around the carcass during those days. Eagles voiced their thoughts, a trill drifting through the forest, or a high-pitched call—so frail for such a mighty bird—floating down from the sky. Jays and magpies tossed out their notes. Unheard, the canines also conversed, their pee stains marking the snow.

On leaving the cabin and walking down to the carcass, for a moment I stepped out of human society and away from machines, removing myself from our material and ideological constructions, immersing in that swirl of another society's communication. I had become a visitor to a different culture, surrounded by foreign dialogue and discussion, skimming the edge of a dance beyond everyday life.

A solitary raven flew over the ranch. I watched, pausing as I put my things into the car. A town day. No time to walk the well-packed path across the snowy field, down through the small meadow, along the forest edge looking for tracks, noting bird calls, arriving at the carcass, watching, listening, sensing. A town day. No time for the note-taking, the thoughtfulness that comes with daily observation of death reincarnated into raven, eagle, fox, coyote, wolf.

The raven arced black against the winter-gray sky, headed in the carcass's direction. A single call dropped down from the heights, the only sound in my world as I stood motionless by the open car door.

This thing—this decaying, decomposing, scavenged, dismembered, disemboweled, rotting-fleshed, once-graceful, now-tendon/bone/guts disintegrating into something other, this heap of decay surrounded by vibrant beings functioning in an ancient rhythm, a dance engrained in all cells and part of who we are, who we should be—this *carcass* had captured my attention.

I got into the car and drove toward urban noise and stores and traffic, though not without another glance toward the heavens. But the raven had slipped out of sight, leaving the sky empty.

———

They are GONE, I had written, stunned at the raven crowd's departure. But not *all* the ravens were gone. Energy remained to be harvested from that sprawled carcass with one hoof dangling off the snow pile, bare ribs arcing, snow-covered skull grinning. Sustenance remained for bird and canine: bits of hide, bone, tendon, even flesh. In the days that followed, a few ravens remained, harvesting that last bit of death, perhaps the territorial ravens who'd been crowded out by the mob. They perched in the old pine tree, black shapes in the dead branches above, sometimes *crawk*ing, other times silent, their eyes on me. They continued to monitor my stay, watching, checking, discussing things until I departed, leaving them to their meal.

Solstice day, when light is precious and limited. My cold fingers recorded a shaky note: *Raven has landed in the Tree above me.* The massive bird peered down with a curious cock of his head. A conversation started with another bird in the woods. *Crawck! Coor-ra-ack!*, the bird above me called. Answering *crawcks*. The talk carried on. And on. Back and forth the birds conversed, from woods to pine, pine to woods. Occasionally, during pauses, I clucked or crawcked softly up at the raven, who would throw me a glance, then resume chatting with the other raven in the forest. Was I their topic? That odd creature at the base of the tree, that human who persisted in visiting, but never took anything from the carcass.

A spell of silence settled in. In that penetrating stillness, the raven above stared directly down at me, locked my eyes with his look, and told me something—softly, in a tone that wasn't meant to carry to the other bird in the forest. That big old raven conveyed his thoughts in crooing notes that held the percussive quality of rolling wooden beads, a resonating sound beyond music, beyond voice. I quietly clucked back, unable to imitate anything like that vocalized beauty—but I wanted to answer. Twice more he spoke, looking directly at me. Gentle and soft, the ebony bird gifted me a message.

I heard that bird. I heard them all—all those creatures, plant and animal alike, by listening with more than my ears, attuned in a way that left me balanced on the brink of understanding something inexplicable and timeless, yet close, as if seeing another world by looking through gauze.

The raven lifted, flew into the woods to join the others. After the black form had merged with the forest, gone from sight, I packed away pen and notebook and walked into the day, carrying wonder and a bit of sorrow. Would that I could have fallen over the brink.

Almost two weeks after the kill, the wolves returned: a pair who walked side by side, their tracks leading without deviation to the carcass. They stayed for only a short time, eating a minimal amount, mostly from the elk's head. This they flipped upside down, stripping the jawbones clean, leaving two bony arches lined with dark brown teeth, the middle molars ground down almost to nothing. Those stained and worn teeth meant the elk was old.

The elk's small size had led me to believe she was young. Wolves normally take the old, the weak, the sick, promoting healthy populations. Harboring a sense of guilt, I had thought this elk's death a fluke: that in her naïve youth she had spooked in the wrong direction, and our fences—our human constructions—had created barriers that allowed the wolves to take her down. Her teeth, tarnished and ground by many years of grazing, countered that narrative, showing me the predator-prey cycle pulsed as it should. Wolves are beasts of balance in the natural world; the great canines stir the land, driving forward natural dynamics and rhythms of life and death. And if the wolves hadn't taken her, then winter might have killed her off, that season which culls the old, the weak, the sick, as sharply as wolves' teeth but more slowly.

For their own reasons, for whatever motives that drive the great canines' meanderings, the wolves left after this reappearance, day after day going by without a sign of their passing. A question floated in their wake: would they return again for this beast they had killed?

Walking shoulder-to-shoulder, leaving parallel tracks in that undeviating path toward their kill, they came back. For three nights they fed, tearing at what remained of the elk. Along with the ongoing work of other scavengers, they reduced her down further, ripping the carcass into pieces, into something other than animal: a leg lying over here, a scapula over there, the pelvis removed altogether.

Other than animal. I could not forget there once *was* an animal. From the beginning, from the moment the carcass was pushed into that ungraceful sprawl across the snowbank, it held reminders of a living elk inhabiting a material body.

First, it was her hooves sticking out from the snowbank, suspended in air. Despite her age, they were unscratched, healthy-looking—as if they had many more miles to cover before death should have come and sent them uselessly pointing skyward. Those cloven feet remained clean and untouched until birds started using them as a perch, coating them with creamy-gray streaks, after which the hooves no longer seemed to whisper *We should be on the ground . . .*

Early on, as scavengers excavated her gut cavity, her droppings appeared, fully formed black pellets scattered across flesh, across snow, food completely digested spewing from her split entrails. These were remnants of her grazing days when she pulled energy from the grass, the sustenance that allowed her to walk, lift a hoof and scratch her ear, call to her herd-mates. To live.

Then the wolves exposed her palate, her mouth's hard upper plate, leaving it clean, untouched, pink-pearly flesh still covering the bone. As she grazed, she had torn the grass with lips and lower teeth pressed against that hard palate, for elk have no upper front teeth. Before the wolves hunted her down, she had been pawing through snow to graze on the remains of last summer's grass, using that palate, drawing that energy, producing those pellets. Now, her grazing was done, the grass that she had turned to flesh now feeding others.

Her eyes. On a day near the end, when wind blasted snow horizontally through the trees and all seemed set in motion, I arrived to find that the wolves had shifted the carcass, exposing the head that had been buried in snow for a time. The skull's resurrection provided another reminder: dark holes stared skyward, eyes completely gone, pecked away so cleanly that a red rim of flesh encircled the gaping socket, like a bloodshot border to a deep-brown eyeball. She gazed at me just as she had the day she died, elk again, not carcass decomposing and scattered.

Elk.

Even as the dead elk scrutinized me, the wind hurled itself against the woods, the sagebrush, me. Snow whipped past us all, whirling, incessant movement encompassing the world—except for that old cow elk who was utter stillness, the complete stillness of beyond. Her eyes looked at me, her leg bone stretched behind, the last remaining hoof rested on the snow. Unmoving.

The material transformation was obvious and understood. But the ancient question rose for me with every reminder of past life: what of the elk that lived within the flesh and bone, the animal who ate her food, had her young, sensed her surroundings? What of the spirit that lingered in those liquid brown eyes that first morning, or the departed spark of life haunting those flesh-rimmed sockets?

That day when she stared at me from beyond the threshold of life was violent and lashing, everything chaotically moving, reducing me to a small speck amidst wildness, engulfed in a wind that was a beast of its own. In the ground blizzard a raven arrived, a single black specter floating low over the bones like a ghost in the blowing snow, there and gone. Then only the fierce wind, stirring all things—except those creatures beyond such worldly forces.

The quiet of aftermath settled in on the morning following the windstorm, snow gently drifting down, covering what little remained of the carcass—a short section of ribs curving above the white. A few bird tracks circled the protruding bones. Nothing more. Only an unbroken cloak of crystals, and the drawn-out ending of the life of one elk.

Two ravens sat in the old pine watching, restless, then gone, leaving an emptiness in the dead branches. I did not stay long, feeling a new sadness, an oddly different sense of loss. For weeks, more than a month, a timeless series of days, I'd taken that walk down to a crumbling corpse where life was enriched. My visits were drawing to an end that did not feel complete. I stood for a moment under the pine's branches, beneath the birds, then made my way back home.

I returned the next day, to stand again under that old pine, to once more take out the notebook and pen, to write of the only things present—which felt like nothing:

> Silence. No ravens, no calls, no birds. It is done.
>
> A fox has been here, chewing. Only a fox, tiny little prints and a packed-down place in the snow where s/he lay chewing on the bones, getting the last of the flesh and tendons and marrow.
>
> No ravens. No wind.
>
> It feels deserted . . .

"It feels deserted." An odd feeling.

Deserted by what?

Something intangible wove through that time at the carcass. In the quiet of those last days, what slipped away were the overt signs of a deeper place, hints of a world outside of our ordinary lives.

The carcass site had become a thin place.

A thin place occurs where the veil between our known, visible world and another realm—the invisible world, the eternal, the "other"—diminishes, allowing a sense of what lies beyond our everyday existence.

Holy and sublime sites inspire the term "thin place," locations such as the island of Iona off the west coast of Scotland, a destination for spiritual seekers. I once spent a few months on Iona, and after my time there I came to believe that Iona is no closer to another realm than any other wild, rugged island. But over the centuries, human history has transformed it into a recognized spiritual setting, so people arrive on that particular island with a heightened awareness that creates an openness, a broadening of the senses that allows the layers to peel back. Perception grows to allow a glimpse of a broader realm, yet one seen through gauze, as if standing on the brink. And then Iona is experienced as a thin place.

Take that same awareness and openness to another island—or a forest glade, a remote valley, a distant summit with views stretching beyond horizons—and watch, listen for long enough, take time for contemplation, and perhaps the layers will peel away. A thin place may thus not be so much a place as an awareness, the term *place* becoming our geographic grounding of an experience that is not material, our anchor to what we can understand.

Compare a carcass site to the holy island of Iona or the glory of a high mountaintop? Call a small clearing holding a rotten, eaten corpse a place of stretching to a further awareness?

Yes.

In that little meadow nestled against the forest, a carcass whispered simultaneously of past living and death's closeness. In that place, a life crossed boundaries as death transformed into energy and other beings, the greater-than-human community dancing around her remains, connected by threads beyond human ken. Ravens held their gatherings, spoke of things, set things in motion that lie outside our knowing. Wolves came and went, according to their own rhythm. Eagles, coyotes, fox, and marten shared space, taking what they could from what remained. And always the surrounds, animate and alive with the murmuring of non-animal voices—river, forest, and wind. This was a place outside of our everyday doings: the tangible stretching out into the unknown, an empty eye-socket calling, *remember*.

The carcass existed alongside yet also beyond ordinary material reality, existed within another space. The layers peeled back to reveal something so close, something only thinly veiled, a thin place where a lone human could walk into an expanded way of sensing, a changed awareness.

When only a bit of rib remained, when the ravens had departed and the trees stood so still, what had deserted the place were the many cues that pricked my senses, creating the awareness, building connections, allowing for a different way of experiencing the place around me. But the thinness remained, perceived if the open awareness stayed as well.

For two weeks after that silent still day in the storm's wake, I abandoned the visits. Then, one quiet, contemplative day, I again made the walk across the field, through the meadow, along the forest, to the place. A raven stood silhouetted against the sky in a dead tree, facing the river in a spot where other ravens had perched before. Another raven balanced on the last bits of the carcass, ignoring me while pecking at a leg bone that canines had dug from the snow. Peck, peck, peck—nothing sumptuous left to tear at.

I'd hesitated to return, expecting that feeling of desertion, as if the chronicle had come to a close. The raven on the far tree spoke otherwise. The raven at the carcass drummed like a heartbeat. A breeze set the trees to talking. The story continued to unfold, there at the heap of bones.

It is done, I wrote on that day of desertion, knowing better. For I can walk away—I could never have been present—and the story will carry on, long after the elk bones are scattered and turned to dust.

PART THREE
2017–2020
SOHAM
PATEL

As a new assistant editor to *The Georgia Review* in 2018, I was energized by Doug Carlson's avid commitment to environmental writing. As a writer, thinker, and editor, I've always felt environmental justice is social justice, which is in line with my commitment to open up spaces for writers who aren't normally heard, especially as part of the nature writing conversation. The pieces in this section approach eco-writing in new forms, take on received notions of idyllic subjectivity, and speak truth to the social injustice of the Anthropocene.

Whereas *This Impermanent Earth* begins at the confluence of Stanley Lindbergh's and Stephen Corey's magazine, it chronicles the end of Corey's twenty-two-year career as editor and the beginning of Gerald Maa's tenure. Maa shares a commitment to invest in diverse conversations around nature writing. In this new life, new season, and new gathering of original voices, he also understands the value of a polymorphous and inclusive perspective on what eco-writing can be. These new pieces all draw from physical and human sciences through collage, poetics defense, reflective pedagogy, and field writing—multigenre approaches to environmental writing.

Susan Cerulean speaks to us from an Earth "afflicted by our species" in an essay titled "I Have Been Assigned a Single Bird." Central to the essay is her father, who she has moved to a facility near her house because of his dementia. Introspection on the challenges of caring for elders informs her activism safeguarding besieged shorebirds near her home on the north Florida coast. The competing urgencies of caring for her father during his illness, finding "a single oystercatcher brooding her eggs on the sand," and delivering talks about wildlife advocacy amass, reformulating her relation to the collapse of environmental boundaries that destabilize our lives and relationships.

For nearly a decade now, Aimee Nezhukumatathil has been defiantly unflinching in the face of the racist impulse toward cultural homogenization that has defined the lyric voice in contemporary poetry. Her poem "In Praise of My Manicure," which appeared in the Summer 2017 issue of *The Georgia Review*, underscores this impulse and serves as a potent backdrop to her contemporary work as an essayist. In the poem, she describes how a snake's heart "can slide up and down the length of its body / when it needs to." This shifting heart is an excellent metaphor for the ways in which poetry and activism interact. In the brief essay presented here, Nezhukumatathil deepens her thesis, urging biodiversity, urging us to call up our childhood wonder, to use it to engage not only with immediacy but also with scientific studies and the names of animals. Her engagement and attention act as a proclamation of solidarity, not just that we are animals but also that we know animals.

In his essay "Etymology, Ecology, and Ecopoetics" poet and critic Tyrone Williams uses the evolution of pronouns and gender as a jumping-off point to explore how the notion of environmentalism without a serious consideration of "environmental racism" overlooks how central racial oppression is to the unfair and exploitative use of resources. Williams explores the lineage of the terms "ecological," "environment," and "poetics" as an attempt toward a reconstruction of language in a vulnerable, at-risk world. He applies his theory by way of demonstration in a close reading and analysis of several ongoing contemporary ecopoetic projects.

Such a project is the one undertaken by Craig Santos Perez, who has set out to build a "creative pathway toward environmental literacy." In the essay presented here, Perez documents his ten-year journey developing a university course on the topic of ecopoetry, guiding readers through his weathering of semesters with his students at the University of Hawai'i, Manoa. Perez includes public engagement components in his curriculum by inviting his students to work with the communities around them. He sees this strategy as "a powerful way for students to actualize their desire to 'do something' about environmental justice and climate crisis, as well as to think creatively about how poetry can make an impact in the world as a form of literary eco-activism." Perez concludes with an appendix that surveys the course's reading lists, key terms, and units so that the essay can also serve as a pedagogical tool that will surely become essential reading for both environmental writing and creative writing pedagogy.

In "Do Migrants Dream Of Blue Barrels?," Raquel Gutiérrez considers the border, those coming from the southern side of it, in a ride-along with two volunteers from the organization Humane Borders/Fronteras Compasivas. The organization maintains water stations in the Sonoran desert where so many migrants die each year. Gutiérrez lives at the periphery of the first and third world. "The border and the imprint of migrants' death that is left in its hinterlands animates most experiences I have in the nature that surrounds it," Gutiérrez writes. These two competing landscapes push them to interrogate their own privilege as a U.S. student within a suprastructure that directly reproduces the tragic climate refugee crises.

Brenda Iijima, whose work had already been in conversation with recent material presented in *The Georgia Review*, is the author of this anthology's last essay, "Who We Are as Floral, Faunal, Mineral Beings." In this work, Iijima makes use of essay and collage to reflect on her own ecopoetical practice of meditation as a path toward dissolving the term "human." This dissolution requires a continued "rethinking how it is that we are actually many beings moving through time and space together, collectively responding to our environment changes how we negotiate personhood altogether."

Iijima was moved by *The Georgia Review*'s Winter 2017 art folio, which featured the work of Toshihiko Mitsuya, a Japanese sculptor whose primary media is aluminum foil. One of the installations, *Aluminum Garden*, is composed of 180 intricate aluminum garden plant sculptures. Mitsuya calls the sculptures "structural studies of plants." Mitsuya's work inspired Iijima to write a poem of more than two hundred lines, "The Pallysodoe," published in the June 2019 issue of the *Brooklyn Rail*. Mitsuya's creations thus became part of a poem that calls out the United States' brutal history, that celebrates communitarian spirit, and that interrogates the exploitative dangers surrounding the Dakota Access Pipeline, whose purpose is to move crude oil underground to provide fuel to us as consumers. In the essay concluding this book, the poet continues to render the themes and techniques that began in her response to Mitsuya. A poet sees a sculpture, then writes a poem. The writing of this poem turns into an essay. These paths reaffirm the notion that eco-writing lives in the exciting intersection of art, policy, and science.

This anthology's final chapter is a gathering of writing published in *The Georgia Review* between 2019 and 2020. I hope this section enacts the idea of network and body: the way Iijima connected to Mitsuya's aluminum garden, the way we are humans surrounded by oceans, the ways our bodies erode like shorelines and our elders and snakeskins. Despite the evolving form and field, eco-writing continues to collapse the categories both between humans and between human and nonhuman while continuing to contest the discourses that exclude or silence.

SUSAN CERULEAN

I Have Been Assigned the Single Bird

Our bodies return our bones to the Earth in many ways. For some, strokes and hemorrhages ricochet like internal lightning inside the brain, or through the heart and arteries. Such was my father's fate, and for him, those strokes led to dementia and a long decline. It fell to me and my husband, Jeff, to care for that sweet man during the last five years of his life. As many people do, we struggled to reconcile the minutiae of the bedside with our full-time work, with three sons to raise, and with the urgent call to speak and act on behalf of our climate and the besieged wildlife of Florida.

The writer Bill Kittredge once said, "I dream of the single-hearted heaven that is the coherent self." In the face of dementia, a coherent life for any of us seemed out of the question. Jeff and I knew that if we took Dad into our home, the chaos dismantling his brain and body would overwhelm us. So we rented a room for him in an assisted-living facility only a mile away, and there we saw to his care.

One afternoon, during the second September of my father's stay in the nursing home, I stood near his bed and pressed my forehead against the window. Through the glass, I could hear the muffled calls of cardinals and red-eyed vireos. I did not open the windows, for the late summer air steamed like a thick, hot pudding.

When we first moved Dad into that room, the emerald light filtering through the windows had reminded me of swimming underwater in a warm river. It wasn't really so bad, like you might fear kudzu-mediated sunlight could be. But as time passed I noticed that many of the tall pines around the nursing home were dying under the weight of the vines swarming their living canopies. I saw that those smothering lianas were like the tangles and plaques in my father's brain, that both kudzu and Alzheimer's replace a vibrant living place—a brain once full of inborn competence and memories of long-gone houses and long-grown children—dissolve those things in super slow motion, replacing them with loss. Dad's drugs, the Namenda and the Aricept, were like winter frost in the forest. For a time, they would keep the plaques in his brain at bay. But link by link, the invasive vines weighted that scaffold of mature trees with blankets of biomass. I could still make out the biggest magnolia, setting its red fall fruit, but I didn't know if it would survive until freezing December nights slashed the tough kudzu back to its knees.

Taking care of my father seemed like a constructive thing to do, a reasonable contribution to our family, a bow to the man who had raised me up. My desire to care for him came from some instinctual place in my body, not from reason or duty alone. It was the right thing to do. Maybe I thought with enough resources and kindness, I could raise him up from Alzheimer's as I had raised my son from a baby to a man. But this was a dementia of my own, to think that I could change the course of this disease.

And I had yet to answer the question: How does the tending of one dying old man—his protracted dying—stack up against the urgencies of the world? Perhaps it was something about trying to fix or mend what is close at hand, those whom we are most closely related to and deeply love. Maybe, I thought, through this impossible task, I would learn the language of tending the world.

Now I'd be in charge of everything. Or so it felt. I was about to learn how to be with my father's dementia, which would have only one possible outcome, and at the same time, continue to search for a path out of the cultural dementia afflicting the Earth.

During the time we cared for my father, I began to volunteer as a steward of wild shorebirds on several islands along the north Florida coast. Two or three times a month between March and August, I'd slide my kayak down the concrete ramp at Ten Foot Hole in Apalachicola. I'd tidy my lines, floating in the backwater basin between a double row of house boats, sailboats, party boats, deep-sea fishing boats. I came to know them like I did each home on our street in town. Some of the sailors and anglers recognized me, too. I liked to imagine I was becoming part of the place, the background, not on a first-name basis, but worth a nod, not a startle. The fisherfolk might not have known where I was going, what my job was, but I felt as if I were a moving piece of the working waterfront. Not a tourist.

My territory was a teardrop of sand just south of the Apalachicola bridge, where I was to locate and keep track of any nesting birds. Most likely candidates were least terns, black skimmers, certain small plovers, or American oystercatchers. I'd line up the prow of my boat with the red channel markers, adjusting for the tide and the river's wide current. Then, I pushed my shoulders into my double-bladed paddle, also aligning with a mindset that might make me as much a part of the scenery on my upcoming bird survey as I was among the people of the boat ramp. That was my goal. Otherwise, as I entered the birds' nesting ground, I would be perceived as a threat. I imagined fading into quiet, becoming background, being benign. *I am a simple being, only passing through. I have a familiar aspect, and trajectory. Don't be afraid, not of me.* I cloaked myself in that mantra.

Very quickly I found a single oystercatcher brooding her eggs on the sand. Over her long orange dagger of a bill, through scarlet-rimmed eyes, she had been tracking my approach long before I saw her. Her eye saw my paddle slicing the quiet waters of the boat ramp, watched my path unfolding, even before I myself had ascertained the mood of the wind. Never should I think that my eyes are brighter and more alert than hers, she who has sifted into this landscape every day of her life, and every day of the lives of her kind, for millions of years. From that long perspective she watched me from her nest scrape on the sand, three eggs burning into her belly through her brood patch, ready to spring off the nest and expose her eggs to the sun in order to draw my eye from the shingle of beach that was home. Her job was to watch for danger, and our human selves are a grave danger to everything wild and vulnerable on the planet.

I didn't know the Earth was afflicted by our species until I was well into my twenties. All I wanted to do was submerge myself in the delight of it, and I did: the Atlantic Ocean, cold and dark and irresistible. Piles of autumn leaves: scarlet, orange, cadmium yellow. Canoe expeditions through the pitcher-plant bogs of the Okefenokee Swamp, and the chill of the Suwannee River's springs. I took those wild places, and the reliable turn of the seasons, for granted. Excesses of winter simply meant a pair of snow days; of summer, a brief wave of heat. There was no reason to imagine the seasons would ever lose the structure they offered my life. The natural world was mine to dwell upon, and I did. But now I understand that all of the ways the Florida coast and its islands are being diminished are symptoms of our culture's commitment to infinite growth.

In the 1950s and '60s, when I was a child, we knew little about chronic diseases of the mind, body, and spirit; what we did know we kept to ourselves. Cancer was the big C, depression had no name at all, and the word *alcoholism* was seldom used. So when Alzheimer's came creeping into my father's brain, our family had had a lifetime's training in not naming—and not really knowing—what was going on, not just illness, but also the shame that comes with it, and the helpless, hidden sorrow. We couldn't have named, at that time, its emotional potency.

Alzheimer's, Pick's, Lewy Body, Parkinson's: these are not the natural result of aging, but are specific, identifiable diseases of the brain. Most dementing illnesses do their damage gradually. As they progress, the affected person loses intellect, abstract thinking, judgment, and memory, and eventually descends into complete disorder and oblivion. The word *dementia* comes from the Latin *demens*, meaning madness, or the irreversible deterioration of the intellectual properties of the brain. *De* (undoing) plus *mens* (the mind). That's dementia.

The Earth is the brain and the body into which we were born. In some nearly parallel way, we face not only a crisis in numbers of people diagnosed with dementia; as a culture, we are stricken with this disease and its attending violence. For why else would we knowingly destroy the planet that sustains our very lives? Our Western economic and political systems, all the ways we personally consume, and give over our power to corporations and oligarchs—those are the illnesses that are killing our planet. When you have the physical disease, you experience it alone. But this dementia is cultural.

What is our part, what can each one of us do, to alter the trajectory we ride? How can we bring healing to this world? My deepest desire regarding both my father's illness and the Earth's biosphere was to save, to rescue, to ensure continuance, and for many years, I thought I could.

I learned this conviction from my father, who cultivated in his children an earnest commitment to repair the broken world, beginning with what ailed our own family. One Friday, a teacher planning day (meaning our mother had to work in her classroom, but we four kids were home from school), Dad prepared a ceremonial lunch to enlist our support. He set the maple dining-room table with placemats and the brown glazed soup bowls we rarely used. He served us lentil soup, good bread on a cutting board, and a fragrant wedge of cheddar. Everything about that meal was unusual, especially Mom's empty chair.

"Kids, we need to do more to help your mother," he said, carefully slicing the cheese. We did not understand what weighed on her so heavily, nor did he, but we knew she was in a dark place. He hoped it would relieve her if we contributed more to the running of the household. To me and Bobbie, he assigned the family's laundry, and we agreed to try. But our mother's depression, fueled by alcohol, was not fixable with detergent and an ironing board, and certainly not by her children; that wasn't something we could understand yet. What Dad knew was that something was deeply wrong in our home. Something was wrong with our mother.

Now I realize that something is deeply wrong with our Mother.

Despite growing up alongside my mother's chronic illness—was it depression or alcoholism, or the latter an attempt to medicate the first?—still I'd emerged into young adulthood with a remarkably optimistic belief in rescuing things. I thought we could save the world, or my adopted state of Florida, at least. I'd been hired as a wildlife biologist in 1984 as part of the state wildlife agency's new Nongame Wildlife Program. Unlike today, the 1980s were heady times for an energetic person who wanted to advocate for wildlife. There were many of us, and we were encouraged in our work, never attacked. We believed in good science and a stewardship ethic, and our chain of command did not hold us back or muzzle us. Governor Bob Graham listened intently to the great conservation leaders of the time, and in successive sessions, the Florida legislature (Democrats and Republicans working together!) not only funded the Nongame Wildlife program, but also established water quality standards, addressed wetlands protection, required local governments to start planning how to handle Florida's explosive growth, and set in motion what for many years was the nation's most successful land-acquisition program.

Diagnosis of Florida's ills seemed simple. Identify the trends. Take them one at a time, figure out what's causing the problem. Repair what's wrong.

Take the Florida black bear.

In the 1980s, black bears, though classified as a threatened species, were still hunted in Florida. It was rare back then to see one. You could ride along Highway 319 from the Ochlockonee River Bridge to the FSU Marine Lab and maybe one year, maybe twenty years after you started hoping and watching, you'd spot something larger than a dog, with longer legs than you could believe. It would lope across the highway in front of your car and you would turn to your companions and try to find words to describe the thrilling quality of the animal, like no bear you'd ever seen sleeping at the Tallahassee Junior Museum, or in a zoo. Most of all you'd notice the athletic stretch of its limbs, so clearly built for pacing the many square miles of its huge home range.

Once in a while, I would attend meetings of the agency's appointed commissioners, and felt both frightened and fascinated by the bear hunters who came to advocate for their sport. They didn't suit up like the staff bureaucrats, or the wealthy landowners and corporate businessmen on the commission. They wore camouflage pants, leather boots, and caps pulled low over their eyes. I saw more than one scratch his spine against a post, as if he were a bear and the post a tree. If you squinted your eyes, you could imagine the hunters as forest animals. They seemed of an earlier time in Florida, when this land was an open frontier, and everything—land and wildlife alike—was up for trapping or shooting, skinning, and eating. I simply couldn't believe that anyone wanted to shoot a bear for sport. And yet, they did. I also knew those hunters and I shared the same love of wild woods.

In 1994, bear hunting was closed statewide: science, and perhaps reason, or even morality, prevailed. The bear hunters were forced back into their forest camps and inholdings, and to silence their guns. Bears began to bounce back.

So saving wild things seemed concretely doable, if not easy, at least if the problem was hunting a threatened species for sport. I'd yet to learn that there was so much more we'd have to address, beyond stopping the shooting. The deaths of birds and other wild animals I'd witnessed were usually single, and after the fact. A cardinal killed after impacting a window. Hawks and owls reduced to feathered mop heads on the side of the road. Once, a snowy egret shot and roasted over a bonfire by some children in Perry, Florida. I'd yet to face the underlying cause of my state's diminishing wildlife: rampant overdevelopment and habitat loss. And maybe worse, the concomitant warming of our climate.

I had worked for Florida's wildlife agency and several conservation groups before that for nearly twenty years, and by any measure, wildlife and natural landscapes were still losing ground.

"Here's the thing," said my husband, Jeff, an oceanographer and biogeo-chemist by training. "There's really only one issue that is driving all the rest and that's climate change."

I protested. "How could there be anything worse for wildlife than habitat loss?" Bulldozers and asphalt trucks had seemed like more than enough to contend with.

Scientists had known that the climate had been changing for some years by that time. But it wasn't reported much in the news, and to me, it was a new and unthinkably enormous concept. I began to really digest what none of us wanted to be true: that beginning in the eighteenth century, as humans began to burn coal and gas and oil to fuel economic growth, the amount of carbon in the atmosphere accumulated at an ever-accelerating pace. That the product of our industrial respiration, millions of years' worth of carbon stored beneath the earth as fossil fuel, had been spiking in the atmosphere and now was spoiling our nest.

On our frequent outings along the Big Bend coastline south and east of Tallahassee, I studied the forests fingering into the Gulf—cabbage palm, slash pine, red cedar, live oak, yaupon holly—rising from the needles of salt marsh. A pattern of dead and dying trees intermixed with those still living caught my eye.

"Our coastline, these forested marshes, might actually be at the leading edge of climate change in Florida," said Jeff. Because of our area's low elevation, sea-level low, and its extremely gentle slope, a warming Gulf of Mexico was forcing saltwater intrusion and murdering our coastal forests.

"What do you see?" I asked my father on a short, dim winter's solstice eve. It had been eight years since his diagnosis, four years since he'd come to live near us in Tallahassee.

"A bright light glowing," he said. I could discern no source of illumination save the desk lamp between us.

His dreams were what we had left between us. They grew ever more fragmentary in the reporting but sufficed to let me know where his unconscious was taking him.

"I dreamed . . ." said Dad. His voice strengthened. "I dreamed I was walking down Hamilton Avenue." That was the street in Glen Rock, New Jersey, where my father had lived with his family as a boy.

"How old were you in the dream?" I asked.

"Seventeen."

"Who else was there?"

"My mother and Billy Joe Francis," he said. Many times during Dad's last months, he asked me if I remembered Billy Francis. I came to think of Billy as one of Dad's angels, though I knew only the barest facts about him, from Dad and his brother, my Uncle Don.

Dad said that Billy was known as Hot Dog Francis, because his father ran a local delicatessen. Billy was an only child; he enlisted in the army during World War II at age twenty. Not long after, he died, not on a European battlefield, but in a Miami hospital of malaria. He came home in a box just as dead as if a bullet had killed him. Dad wrote a four-page letter of condolence to Billy's heartbroken parents. Now Billy Joe Francis was at Dad's side, keeping my father company deep into the wakeful night.

My father's room had grown dense with his stasis, with his enforced stillness in chair or bed. His lungs and throat sometimes filled with phlegm, which he would clear by coughing. The pothos plant in the corner had ranged and curled to fill the space between the window and his bed. It presided over a filing cabinet whose only function now was to hold up the plant, his radio, and sometimes, at night, his glasses. I would bring fruit to occupy myself when I visited, slicing apples, a navel orange, a pint of strawberries into a glass bowl. "Who's here in the room with us now?" he asked. He'd been reporting visits from his father and mother to our caregivers. "No one, Dad, it's just you and me."

But that wasn't his experience. His eyes startled open wide.

"Huh?" He leaned forward in his chair, uncrossed his knees, and stared into the empty corner of the room. His bare shins protruded from the soft gray of his sweatpants.

"Oh, okay," he said, confidently, nodding his head. "Yes."

He turned back to me with a report.

"That was your grandma," he said. "Didn't you see her standing at the door? She was waving at me, but I wasn't completely sure what I was supposed to do. Do you think she was telling me to stay, or to come with her?"

Candace McKibben, a dear friend and hospice minister, had told me what

Dad was experiencing weren't hallucinations, but "thin places," life moments when a person senses a connection with something far beyond the ordinary realms.

"The dying are most often visited by their mothers," she confirmed. How much sense it made that the woman whose body was our gateway into the physical world might be once again present as we take our final breaths.

On a visit to the bird-nesting island, I experienced another kind of a thin place. I had made my way around the tiny landscape with my spotting scope over my shoulder and my binoculars around my neck, moving slowly, keeping count of all the birds I saw. On earlier visits, I'd seen pairs of oystercatchers slipping around like shadows, so I looked for them in particular. Just as soon as my eyes keyed in on the shape of a large ebony bird sitting on the sand, it startled away. How fearsome I was to that parent, with my spider-like tripod and upright slow-moving stance. Imagine if the only way we could protect our newly born was to draw the predator away with our own bodies and our own voices, implying *there's no nest, no chicks, no eggs, keep your eye on me, let me draw you far away from what I am trying to bring into the world.*

I fixed in my mind where I first spotted the bird and stepped carefully over the sand to a nest between a broken bit of plastic bucket and a certain white morning glory blossom.

And there they were: three eggs marbled brown and black, as fragile and unlikely as snowflakes on the sand. An extra-high tide could so easily wash them away. A crow or a large gull could devour them. Or if all went well, this line of oystercatchers might continue another generation.

Away I went, on and around the island. Eventually, I found three nests spaced the length of a football field from one another, creating a nearly equilateral triangle of nest points, as far apart as the dry land could serve.

From an egg in the last of the nests, I saw the tip of the bill of an oystercatcher chick, meeting the salt air for the very first time. At first, I thought the hole meant that the egg must be damaged. Had ants punctured it, or was the eggshell thinned and then fractured by the weight of the parents' bodies? But no: there at the center of the hole, a tiny bill, a new rare life.

I was awash in gratitude and awe. Though I wasn't welcome to watch, I knew the full hatch of that chick, its first tumble onto the sand, would be as miraculous and sacred as the birth of any other species on earth, life crossing between the worlds.

In the end, my father's death was a similar crossing. A final virus commandeered his lungs, and with it the illness came that would end his life. Those last few days, although his body labored, my dad didn't appear to be in pain. The nurse gave me possession of the liquid morphine to administer as I felt it was needed. We sang to him, stroked his face and his hands. As he took one last breath, his lids flew open, and one final glance of his gray eyes swept our faces. I saw his body ensouled, and then I saw his corpse, spirit gone. Now he no longer was. Like an eggshell, his physical frame was left behind for us to oil, and wrap in cloth, and bury in the ground. His soul, like the dark chick, had fled. I stepped from the room to call my son. His grandpa, my father, was dead.

It's difficult to advocate for something if you don't know how it is faring. If people or beings can't tell you with their voices how they are and what they truly need, how else are we to understand how to help? Even though I was not an expert counter of birds, no one outdid me in my passion and love for them. But counting was important, too.

I took part in my first Christmas Bird Count, in South Carolina's Aiken State Park, in 1976. I remember garlands of American robins in the trees and cold approaching frostbite on my feet. My job thirty-five years later was exactly the same: to find and tally as many kinds of birds as possible in a single day on my assigned territory. It's supposed to be a census, but of birds, not people. On today's Christmas Bird Count—the 115th consecutive event—we were among seventy-two thousand citizen scientists observing the numbers of wintering wild birds.

I inherited my territories on Cape San Blas and St. Vincent from a petite, supremely businesslike birder named Barbara Stedman. In 2009, when I met Barbara, she'd already been keeping tabs along this stretch of North Florida coast for more than thirty years. While Barbara and thousands of other citizen scientists have been watching, their data show us that since 1967 absolute numbers of common birds have steeply declined. Some species have nosedived as much as 80 percent, including the northern bobwhite (quail). Many—like evening grosbeaks, meadowlarks, and several kinds of duck—have lost 50 to 70 percent of their population, in just four decades. Those Christmas Bird Count data have been ominously corroborated in "Decline of the North American Avifauna," a September 2019 report in *Science* magazine. In it, the authors point out that extinction begins with loss in abundance of individuals, which profoundly affects ecosystem function. The report finds that since 1970 our continent has suffered population losses of more than twenty million terns and gulls and more than fifteen million sandpipers.

And the losses, they slay me—the bitter fact that 70 percent of shorebirds have been eliminated from the North American landscape since 1973. Whenever I walked on a beach, my mind took refuge in counting—actually, first checking to see if there were enough birds to count. And always, I knew, that what

I observed—say, twelve red knots, eight ruddy turnstones, twenty-five sander-lings—was but a fraction of what should be. But I'd focus on what still lived, not what was lost.

Over time, I allowed my own body and my own senses to listen to what the coast might want to be said directly. I offered myself as a conduit. More and more space in my journal became devoted to the voices of the birds and the sand and the seeds. I fixed my words in my notebooks, just as rare shorebirds lay their foot-prints in the sand, side by side with the paw prints of the endangered red wolf and her pup on St. Vincent Island. I learned to meander, to sniff, to observe, to ex-plore, just like those wolves on the beach. In a relaxed curious state, with steady attention, I could learn to be present. I moved gently so that wild animals would feel safe in my presence. Taken together, maybe our tracks would say, *We were here, and we found it beautiful beyond all imagining, and worth every effort to preserve and protect.*

A red knot hunkered down at the water's edge, a bundle of feather and bone pressed against the sand. We'd been admiring the knots as they moved through north Florida on their migration, five to ten at a time, mostly. They fed vora-ciously, plunging their bills over and over into the wet sand at the water's edge, reminding me of a host of paper-doll birds, so alike was one to the next. But this one had been stopped short in her unimaginably long travels (at least six nonstop days and nights of flight) from the high Arctic to the tip of South America. She had been unable to find and gorge on horseshoe crab eggs and other foods that would allow her to recover and regain weight. This bird wasn't going to make it.

Her eyes slitted shut, and her bill opened and closed rhythmically. I crouched at a distance that wouldn't add to her distress, watching her sip the last breaths of air she would ever inhale. Now and again she trembled.

But she was not dying alone.

A sanderling, feisty loner of the winter beach, nestled down in the sand near the knot's head. I'd never seen a sanderling assume such a position, though surely they do when they incubate their own eggs. Then a second red knot took up a post at the rear flank of the downed bird. Two lesser yellowlegs (tall shore-birds uncommon on this beach) moved in, intervening between the small sheet-ing waves of the Gulf and the knot. They tilted their heads sideways, seeming to ascertain the knot's situation, and then simply stood close.

The four vigil birds—only one a conspecific—were companioning the red knot as she died. My human mind ran through its paces. First, as a citizen sci-entist, I thought I should look for identifying color flags or bands, because red knots are so highly endangered. But her feet were tucked under her body, and

I was not going to pick up this bird during her death. That would be extraordinarily disrespectful. Then I wondered for just a moment if we should try to take the bird to a wildlife rehabilitator. Considering the eight bumpy miles we had to travel back to the ramp, and then who knows how far by car to find help—that trauma was out of the question as well. My impulse to rescue was contradicted by the impossibility of capturing and stressing the bird in its final hours.

After a few minutes, I didn't study the bird anymore. I relieved it of my fierce attention and replaced that with love and compassion. The four vigil birds showed me what to do: simply be with. Simply offer tender presence to the incapacitated one. As I sat quietly on the sand, I watched the sun glimmer on the yolky limbs of the yellowlegs. The wind lifted the delicately barred back feathers of the downed and dying knot. The tide continued its rise. We breathed.

"How would you like me to inscribe your book?" I asked the woman across the long folding table. "Is it a gift for someone else, or for you personally?" I had just delivered a talk about advocacy, and now it was time to sell and sign books.

"Just tell me what to do to save Florida," she said. "Just write that down for me."

I have been plotting and working and writing my way toward that question my whole adult life. And yet, Florida and my state's wildlife, the Earth herself—all the things I dearly love and wish I could protect—seem no closer to being "saved" than they were before I began. Perhaps *saving* is the wrong verb.

A man—white, heavyset, dressed in a pumpkin-orange shirt—raised his hand from the back of an auditorium in Clearwater, Florida. There was a logo stitched on his breast pocket, but he stood so far back in the darkened rows of chairs, I couldn't read the words, or the expression on his face. I wondered if he was a heckler or a fan. My talk had been wide-ranging: Standing Rock, climate change, the Trump administration's attacks on the environment, and the need for urgent, radical change.

His question: *What is the single most important thing that every one of us should do right now, given all that confronts us?*

I pulled down deep inside myself for an answer.

What I said: *Don't turn away. Face what threatens the unborn of all species with all of your strength and all of your heart.*

We must watch and work on behalf of the beautiful things, watch them with exquisite attention, praying that their spirits will inform our actions on their behalf, and our own. Bill McKibben, perhaps the most effective and tireless advocate in the U.S. on the issue of climate change, says this: "How do you cope with celebrating a dying world when you think you should be trying to save it? You—

we—are required to bear witness to it. This is one of our jobs. It's as close to religious duty as one could imagine."

One fall day, I searched out the youngest snowy plover chick hatched on the Refuge that season. In her small roving body rested the last chance that year for our landscape to contribute to the continuity of plovers, a single bird begun as an egg laid on this very sand. I'd seen that chick and her parent on an earlier survey one week before, near the outfall of Oyster Creek. Just now, though, the beach seemed empty of everything but trash and more trash. We picked up two enormous loads of plastic bottles and balloons in the green net fish bags we keep for that purpose. We saw no chick. I assumed she had been snatched by gull or ghost crab, vanished like all the others this season into the belly of a predator.

We circled back toward the east, and Little St. George Island, to continue our search. And there she was, flashing across the strand, her tiny body skittering, zigging and zagging, as she snapped at tiny flies. We followed her path with our binoculars, and she led us to a glorious surprise: 150 black terns, paused on their southbound journey to winter on the coast of South America. To my eye, they resembled small ebony sails temporarily furled. Sleek and gray and unexpected on the white of our sand. I'd never seen so many before.

It was a good place for that plover chick, threading through those black terns and a handful of others—least, Caspian, royal, gull-billed—all paused on the outer edge, between their summer and winter lands. I saw many fewer ghost crabs on the evanescent edge; the absence of their swift claws would give the chick a better shot at survival. Still: the last of the chicks, the last of the black terns.

In the 1920s, Arthur Bent described the black tern as the "most widely distributed, the most universally common, and most characteristic summer resident of the sloughs, marshes, and wet meadows of the [Dakota] plains." Since the 1960s, black terns have been declining at the rate of 2 or 3 percent each year. I have seen them only here and on the leading edge of Little St. George, their wings beating while the tips of their toes still touched the Refuge, which was disappearing as well.

As the sun began to angle into the sea, I thought about how our planet and our sun had created this palette during uncounted nightfalls, long before the plovers or I had come to be. Earth has turned in far lonelier eons, without bird or human. I staggered under a gratitude so weighty, I had to sink to my heels, for I had the privilege to share this time with the creatures I loved.

The flaming sun lit up the whole of my face. The wind lifted my hair. I closed my eyes and became simply another breathing presence on the sand. No boundaries.

In our saltwater-and-bones bodies, each one of us loves the birds this much. They companion us at this time on the planet, weavers of air current and nest cup. Their songs were our first music as a species, their call notes the first living patterns on our collective human eardrum. We learned percussion from the woodpecker, to scream from the eagle, and to sing complicated melody from the warbler and the thrush.

Just as our bodies are constructed of the dust of stars, they also carry the memory of a time when our lives were always with the birds, out under the spread of the sky, when we lived without separation.

How is the dementia we are inflicting on our world similar to a dementing illness in a single human brain? In both cases, the afflicted suffer from the paradigm of perpetual growth, the smothering and overexploitation of diversely beautiful and unprotected common resources. In human dementia, the losses are painfully observable. One by one, the beautiful life forces are dissolved. Dancing, laughing, smiling, problem-solving, remembering and imagining, and eventually breathing are all stolen from the individual.

For the Earth, the dementing disease—our system of economic and political dominance—has terminated the Cenozoic era, the time of this planet's maximum flowering and biodiversity, and replaced it with the largest extinction event in sixty-five million years. One million species have been already lost and replaced with a spiraling increase in human biomass. Industrial civilization has induced an apparently unstoppable climate crisis of epic proportions.

In his last years, I did for my father everything that I could, with the full and gathering knowledge of the eventual outcome. I knew he would die and he did. Is our Earth also terminally ill? Does the human-induced pace of species extinction and climate crisis ensure that we will also lose our Mother?

I believe we can redeem our species. As Amitav Ghosh has written, "the derangement of our times is rooted in how we live." That's the difference between my father's illness and the illness of the Earth: the latter is animated by cumulative human actions, guided by legal and economic systems that treat the natural world as property to be exploited, not as an ecological partner. It follows that we can mitigate, to some extent, the damage to climate and biodiversity.

But the work must start now, and it must be swift. The systems of power that have done the damage will not lead, nor should they be allowed. We're on our own, but we are billions.

Octopus

Octopus vulgaris

A dead octopus turns lavender, like the sky over the Aegean just before the stars appear. The only time I've ever held one in my hands, I was on the island of Thasos, in northern Greece. My family and I were nearing the end of a month-long stay where I spent mornings teaching poetry to students from around the world and afternoons snorkeling with my young sons and husband in turquoise-colored coves. One day, our host at the hotel, Tassos (yes, his name was Tassos of Thasos), announced he'd be hunting octopuses that morning. Right away I asked to join him. We usually had fresh calamari about twice a week, and I was eager to come along and see how this delicious appetizer was caught and brought from sea to table. I was especially excited because Tassos was a member of the famed Greek special forces, somewhat akin to the Navy SEALs, and was known around the island for being able to hold his breath underwater for ungodly amounts of time.

Of course, we've all heard about the intelligence of an octopus, but probably each of us won't fully grasp in our lifetimes just *how* smart and sensitive they are. Each arm of an octopus forms an asterisk that we might as well apply to any statement we make now about its intelligence. Its brain lies just behind its eyes in what is really the body, not the head—and each time the octopus devours a snack of crab or cockles, the brain can stretch itself to make room for the esophagus. Octopuses are among the only animals found whooshing and gliding through every single ocean on the planet. They're known to wheel around anywhere from pelagic ripples near a shoreline to six thousand feet below the surface, huddling close to hydrothermal vents in the deep.

Tassos showed up on the beach at the expected time wearing full snorkel gear and brandishing a spear gun. I stayed on the beach with our boys while my husband went into the water with the other faculty and students. By his account, later, everything people said about Tassos—and more—was true. Tassos could free-dive so deep that the others on the hunt completely lost sight of him—including his shadow—even in the sparkling clear sea.

I collected and jumbled smooth white marble pebbles in my pocket while I waited for their return, their spoils, and tried to find bits of sea glass to cheer up my eldest, whose lip was still quivering from the pain of being left behind. I tried to console him that it'd be too cold, too deep, too scary. But this was a mighty injustice, to be left to wander the shore with his mama and little brother—particularly given his love of the hunters' quarry. He had dressed as a cephalopod for Halloween for the previous three years, with, most recently, a blue-ringed octopus costume that I stuffed and stitched together for him, complete with eyes made from pop lights.

The horizontal slit of an octopus's eye is a door that judges us. I am certain it knows we humans are messing up entirely, that in just a matter of decades the oceans will become unswimmable for any of us animals. The octopus pupil stays parallel, steady as a raft in calm waters—even if the octopus cartwheels away in a dance—the pupil never becomes vertical like a cat's. And the skin around this wondrous eye is malleable, with the ability to form "lashes" or whiskers spontaneously for protection if it feels threatened. But even if you make an octopus grow lashes, you can be sure its eye will remain fixed on you—you, a creature whose arms have no neural intelligence or taste sensors, not a single one of the *three hundred* suckers that run down the length of each octopus arm. These suckers contain about ten thousand sensory neurons that detect texture, shape, and, most of all, taste. How marvelous to even have just one sucker on the inside cup of our hands. Just one! For a moment you think the octopus must have something almost like pity for you for your lack.

Once, two researchers at the Seattle Aquarium conducted a test to see if octopuses could tell humans apart. Each day they more frequently approached their eight resident octopuses, with one scientist holding a bristled stick behind his back, to poke the octopuses with, and the other with food. The researchers wore the same blue jumpers and were about the same height, they also changed which side of the tank they approached, but in less than a week, the octopuses could distinguish them correctly. One even aimed its siphon at the researcher with the stick and squirted water at him, and the rest of the octopuses would start moving with something like glee toward the one holding food.

After almost an hour, my husband and the group of ragtag octopus hunters swam back into view. Two of them—my own students—started running toward me, and I knew there could be only one reason why. They were cradling an octopus, bringing it back to their teacher, who had been swooning and hoping to see one for most of the month. *Hold out your hands, hurry!* they yelled, and plop-slopped it into my spread fingers. I could see the octopus starting to blanch pale and pulse lavender in my hands, not at all like the healthy mottled violet and nutty beige-red color I had grown accustomed to seeing in aquariums all my life.

Its three hearts tapped slower and slower, just minutes away from death, but I didn't know it right away.

Instead I focused on its golden eye, how it fixed upon my shape. How its arms wrapped and drooped around my wrist and up my forearm while it took me in, tasted me. In those moments I held it, how many things it might have felt or known about me. Could it sense the love and exhilaration I felt for it or my sheer despair once I realized it was dying in my hands? I only know that I had never been looked at, consumed, or questioned so carefully by another being.

TYRONE WILLIAMS

Etymology, Ecology, and Ecopoetics

I type "ecological racism" into a search engine and one hundred percent of the results are variations on environmental racism.[1] Google does not recognize the phenomenon of ecological racism, which does not mean of course, that it doesn't exist. As an online encyclopedia, Google, no more than Wikipedia, is only as exhaustive as the parameters of its application. If we think of ecological racism as more encompassing than environmental racism—which implies delimited geographical contexts buttressed by legal, economic, cultural, social and, above all, political enforcements—then the very concept of ecological racism becomes explicitly plural, homologous to, for example, the institutionalization of *they* as a pronoun of a singular subject. The queered pronoun *they* does not displace the binarism of he or she; it is an additional marker of sexual orientation and gender identity. So too ecological racism is not a refusal of the concept of environmental racism. Unlike local and regional systems that support environmental racism, national and transnational systems support ecological racism. These modes of racism are thus moments on x/y axes (policies/practices), not discrete phenomena.

Ecological racism's homology with the non-binary *they* is not only due to the fact that both terms can enter the public sphere only as certified concepts by way of institutions[2] but also due to the connection between heteronormativity and the biological essentialism underlying the concept of race.[3] As teachers and students have heard and read repeatedly, race is a social construct of Western anthropology and philosophy and, as such, must be distinguished from older expressions of ethnocentrism that precede the concepts of sexual orientation and race.[4] Of course, like any other metaphysical concept, ethnocentrism has proven to be durable and adaptable despite the widespread propagation of secular Enlightenment and humanist values. The fusion of ethnocentrism with the relatively novel concept of race during the Western Enlightenment gave birth to what later generations would come to call white supremacy and, concomitantly, heteronormativity. The dissemination of these values across the globe, the exportation of Christianity and expropriation of natural and human resources by colonial powers in Portugal, Spain, Belgium, England, and France, proceeded under the sails of the "new" human and physical sciences. The competitive struggles for resources and land on other continents would eventually exhaust the global powers of these national empires even as the rise of industrial capitalism and eugenics in the mid-nineteenth century facilitated the congealing of national interests into rabid nationalisms. And nationalism, along with the ecological racism associated with late capitalism, is the current political, socioeconomic and cultural miasma under which we live. Thus, the movement from nationalism to globalism parallels the shift from environmental racism to ecological racism.[5]

Keeping in mind that this term is plural even as it points to a singular subject, we can see how ecological racism implies the racialization of those heretofore marginalized by class, ethnicity, or sexual orientation. The "blacks" of England, a reference to Pakistani immigrants, do not correspond to the "blacks" of the United States, yet both populations are marginalized as a whole even as individual "exceptions" enter the dominant public spheres of both countries. The racialization of populations once classified as ethnic groups cannot be separated from the advent and consolidation of natural and human resources under global capitalism.[6]

As these permutations of "blacks" demonstrates, globalization also means the distribution and consumption of linguistic tropes across natural and national borders. Facilitated by social media, yet another instrument in the toolbox of capital, new lexicons, colloquial phrases and discrete terms enter the public spheres of developed and developing countries every day. And given the current debasement of the human and physical sciences, the cynical manipulation of public language, in the United States at large, a field like etymology or, more accurately, the values implicit in etymology (source-hunting, the interest in linguistic accuracy and "origins"), can be tempting sources of valorization for those who see themselves as part of a global resistance to resurgent populisms and ecological collapse brought on by, in part, laissez-faire market forces.[7] The implications of the words and phrases we use and do not use, the ease or unease with which we adopt technological and commercial terminologies, absorb or repel "foreign" imports, while central to all poetics and poetry, appears to take on especial urgency for ecopoetics practices.

Here's a minor example, the one that served as my opening move. Although the phrase ecological racism is nonexistent according to the world's most widely used search engines, each separate and individual term brings up hundreds of "hits" when searched alone. "Ecological" and "racism" have a long linguistic history, though "ecology" is much "older," etymologically, than "race."[8] Nonetheless, if I were to use the phrase ecological racism in an essay, I might have to explain it in the body of the text or in a footnote, but I would not have to underline or italicize it since the individual words of the phrase are part of my native language, English. Still, unlike the French compound word I used above—laissez-faire—my phrase, though written in English, is apparently "invisible" in the public sphere. That a foreign-language phrase may have more currency than an English one only underlines the linguistic commonplace that a neologism, compound word or phrase comprised of native language morphemes can be more counter-intuitive and opaque than a foreign-language word or phrase which has become "naturalized" by decades of usage.

Still, whether one should or should not italicize a word or phrase is dependent on both style guides and on social institutions and cultural contexts that are never simple and straightforward. In the *written* English language, one signals the presence of a foreign element, a word or phrase still considered "alien," with the italic font. But because italic itself is usually written in square-cut Gothic letters, it functions as a customs officer, stamping others as "other" with itself, a former other. Yet, as the third word in the second sentence of this paragraph reminds us, italics also serve as a grapheme of stress, emphasis (sans the sardonic implication of its cousins, the scare-quotes). The difference between alien and stress is here, as elsewhere, a matter of citizenship, what word has yet to be, perhaps will never be, naturalized.

For example, the Greek word *oikos*, usually translated as "house, dwelling place, habitation," is a derivative of the Proto-Indo-European (PIE) root *weik-*, a root that can mean to fight, to conquer, to bend or wind, and, as a noun, a social unit or clan "above" the household. Thus, the difference between *oikos* and *weik-*, between the domestic and supra-domestic, may also be understood as a question of citizenship, one always settled by the latter. These examples remind us that in addition to a stressed native word, italics can also indicate the presence of a contemporary (e.g., *shari'a*) or historically remote (*weik-*) "alien" term.

Ecology, whose etymological lineage can be traced back to this Greek-PIE lineage, may be understood then as first and foremost a question of citizenship in a specific environ, who and what belongs and does not. While linguistic citizenship is usually determined by both population and usage, and is thus a matter of historical dates, assimilation, acculturation, and so forth, ecological citizenship is a function of evolutionary adaptations at the cellular/genetic levels to environmental change. A common phrase like "invasive species" captures not only this assumption that the native and alien belong to different environs but also bears the presumption that an ecosystem's organic, interdependent populations are, and should be, stable and, for the most part, unchanging. In short, "invasive species" reveals the way we tend to think of ecology in synchronic frameworks, bracketing its historical dimension.

In other words, ecology, like etymology, is both synchronic and diachronic, comparative and evolutionary. Intertwining as two strands of the multiple helixes comprising human history, ecology and etymology trace mutations and adaptations of extant and extinct environmental systems and discrete words.[9] However, while ecology often presupposes mapping changes in environmental networks from the past to the present in order to hypothesize about future developments, etymology shuttles back and forth between present and past word usages and meanings. While we may be interested in trying to predict, for example, how changes to inorganic matter in a particular ecosystem might affect the prospects for the survival of its native organisms, we typically aren't concerned about what new terms and lexicons might arise from repurposing or recombining the semantic, syntactic or grammatical values of current or anachronistic words. And though linguists often talk about "living" and "dead" languages, our reflex is to recognize this kind of discourse as purely metaphorical. After all, languages aren't "alive" or "dead" in the way that a stalk of corn or red fox may be dead or alive. We may like or dislike the changes in the way words are used or combined as our languages evolve, but we don't usually believe we need them in the way we need food, water, clothing and shelter.

These commonsensical beliefs and assumptions do not necessarily square with current and emerging developments in the human and physical sciences. For example, both linguists and neuroscientists have suggested that it is not clear that *homo sapiens* and its predecessors could have survived various ecological challenges over millennia without the development of languages. Moreover, modern developments in neuroscience, nanotechnologies, psychoanalytic theory, subatomic physics, cosmology, sociology and linguistics trouble the differences between sentience and non-sentience however much Enlightenment values and assumptions determine the knowledges produced by these sciences.[10]

Although the study of word origins and developments would seem to be independent of, if not irrelevant to, the study of the various "kingdoms" of earth (animal, plant, bacteria, etc.), etymology and ecology dovetail as the hidden "theory" that motivates the practice of what is today called ecopoetics. Ecopoetics is obviously not the only field in which the relationship between etymology and ecology may be observed; as I noted above, each term orients the other in any number of the physical and human sciences. The lexicons and glossaries of language systems used to analyze and transcribe ecological systems—local, regional or global—determine the values ascribed to premises and conclusions that are irreducible to, even if arising from, scientific, cultural, historical, and social data.[11] At the same time ecological systems frame the presumptions, values and developments of linguistic practices. As a specific iteration of this etymological/ecological dynamic, ecopoetics is accorded a certain privilege insofar as its varied practices—from narrative/lyric to paratactic, nonlinear, and experimental forms—are thought to correspond to the "roots" or origins, the biochemical interactions and observable macroscopic phenomena, comprising ecological systems. In arguing that etymological as well as ecological concerns orient ecopoetics from "behind" as it were, I am also insisting that the Romantic concept of "correspondences" between the visible and invisible worlds, between subject and object, motivates both representational "nature" poetry as well as experimental ecopoetry.

Although this latent organicism is rarely articulated as such, it underpins the very premise of an aesthetic practice that attaches itself to, or annexes as an index of progressive activism, an *oikos*. Since the practice in question is here a poetics, ecopoetics is literally the making of a house or, more colloquially, keeping house, taking care of a house.[12] The bioethics of stewardship is implicit in the most representational "environmental" writing, which tends to limit the scope of its concerns to discrete phenomena, as well as in the most experimental "ecological" writing, which emphasizes systems analysis. For example, the late Mary Oliver was renowned for her traditional lyric poems about the natural world. The contemporary poet Brenda Iijima has long been involved in the ecopoetics movement, focusing in particular on ecological destruction and the poisoning of the natural environment, a subject that rarely, if ever, appears in Oliver's poetry. Yet, in one of her poems, Mary Oliver's celebration of the goldenrod and critique of human sentience—"And what has consciousness come to anyway, so far, // that is better than these light-filled bodies?" (18)—seems not that dissimilar from this couplet in a Brenda Iijima poem: "Power looms textiles predict cities of sand / where presently stands of trees flourish." (27) For both the traditional lyric poet and the innovative ecopoet, human consciousness and the built world compare unfavorably to the given world of nature.

Ecopoetics may be understood, then, in the parlance of American real estate, as an "addition."[13] Although an explicit concern with terminology concerns only a small percentage of ecopoetics (and an even smaller percentage concerns etymological/ecological dynamics), the question of which word best describes a specific praxis is a question of selecting from a thesaurus, choosing and using, avoiding and discarding, terms, impossible without the field of etymology.[14] Both etymology and ecology may be oriented by pre-cognitive values and ethical concerns that neither term explicitly endorses: one's interest in etymology may be driven by an ur-phoneme or -morpheme fetish refracted through concern for, say, accurate word usage; one's interest in ecology may presuppose the desirability of a stable, if changing, environs. Insofar as these affective motives are "additions" to the objective study of word origins and systems of organic/ inorganic interdependence, ecopoetics exploits the boundary between objective analyses and affective interest.

This ecological/etymological dynamic suggests that ecopoetics is, finally, a domestication of the domestic writ large, a doubling down on the house (earth) as a home (world). As an annex of ecology, ecopoetics replicates its cognitive values (objective analyses) while building an affective add-on.[15] In doing so, ecopoetics marks the site where the apex of dialectics is decapitated and the antagonistic struggle between thesis and antithesis (e.g., nature and culture) cannot be synthesized into a "peaceful" resolution.[16] Thus, ecopoetics distinguishes itself from traditional environmental or "nature" poetry by its anti-pastoralism, a stance which remains antagonistic to the extent it arrests the "third" turn toward sublation. Certain ecopoets and ecocritics accept this inevitable dilemma and simply index the struggle itself. For example, both Joshua Corey and Rob Halpern have argued that the mineral kingdom in general, and the pebble or stone in particular, served as the example par excellence of absolute alterity in the proto-ecopoetry of Muriel Rukeyser, Francis Ponge and George Oppen.[17] Other ecopoets like Brenda Iijima and Jennifer Scappettone attempt to circumvent dialectical thinking by dissolving subjects and objects into an affective imaginary where rage, pleasure, hope, regret, and frustration mark the limits of cognition in the midst of collapsing ecosystems. Nonetheless, circumventing traditional dialectics when thinking the human-human or human-nonhuman encounter is, as a practice, more difficult than one might imagine.

Examples of both kinds of encounters can be seen in what Angela Hume and Samia Rahimtoola call the "queering of ecopoetics," the title of a "cluster" of essays they assembled for a special issue of Interdisciplinary Studies in Literature and the Environment (ISLE). Contributors include critic Sarah Ensor who suggests that the poet William Wordsworth and essayist/fiction writer Samuel Delany model a queer ecopoetics ethos in the ways they confront the problem of physical encounters with the "other."[18] Hume and Rahimtoola situate Ensor's recovery of an ecopoetics predecessor like Wordsworth in opposition to the more radical positions of queer critics Lee Edelman and Jack Halberstam who desire to "dispense[s] with the future altogether" by refusing what they regard as the heteronormative cult of the child. Hume and Rahimtoola reject these positions: "Critiquing the Child as the basic organizing principle behind current political discourse, Lee Edelman vaunts queerness as 'the side of those not "fighting for the children."' ... Edelman draws on Sigmund Freud's concept of the death drive to embrace the queer as a figure of negativity—anti-productive and epistemically unintelligible—who radically rejects 'every realization of futurity.' ... Similarly, Jack Halberstam has suggested that 'queer time' disregards conventional life goals such as stability and longevity to enact velocities of living that unfurl without concern for whatever might come next. . . ." As Hume and Rahimtoola note in their critiques of Halberstam and Edelman, the narrow focus on an acceleration of pleasures insulated by the present winds up endorsing a consumerist ethos, that all too familiar "live-for-today attitude that defines our social and environmental relations."[19] A failure to understand the relation of the consumer[20] and commodity culture to both early and late capitalism can be seen in Ensor's readings of Wordsworth and Delany while Halpern's reading of Oppen explicitly confronts the relationship between an ecopoetics sensibility and mid-twentieth century capitalism.

Ensor is interested in the ethical problem of "contact," in what happens when a human has a physical encounter with the nonhuman, an event which ideally offers another mode of reducing, if not entirely erasing, the subject/object antagonisms that predate capital.[21] Dissatisfied with "ecosexuals" like the queer performance artists Elizabeth Stephens and Annie Sprinkle who unapologetically "make love with the earth . . . shamelessly hug trees, massage the earth with [their] feet, and talk erotically to plants . . . ," Ensor finds potential models for ethical contact elsewhere, in the examples of Wordsworth's 1798 poem, "Nutting," and Delaney's 1999 nonfiction work *Times Square Red, Times Square Blue.* Ensor, interested in what she calls "an ecopoetics of contact," in what it means to almost touch, to almost be touched, sees in these works by writers separated from each other by two centuries, sexual orientation, geography, ethnicity and race a transcendental model for human-nonhuman and human-human haptic encounters that are neither utilitarian or solipsistic. Thus, these encounters between subjects and objects must be serendipitous. Moreover, the subject must linger before its object of interest in a poise of disinterest.[22] Ensor's valorization of one suspended between rest and contact seems to indefinitely defer haptic encounters. But what is presupposed in this pre-haptic dance between menace and flirtation is leisure, having the time to encounter or engage the nonhuman and human "outside" of labor, "outside" of purpose.[23] Consequently, her reading of "Nutting" only illustrates how leisure is the "hidden theory" of her haptic ecopoetics.[24]

Halpern's reading of Oppen's "geological imagination" illustrates the promise and limits of ecopoetics. Halpern sees in Oppen's objectivist poetics, Rukeyser's social realism, and Francis Ponge's "ordinary objects" poetry a kindred recognition of the limits of human temporality when measured against geological temporality. For all three poets, clarity of language is an ethical imperative since it recognizes the limits of human linguistic practices and, by implication, human consciousness vis-à-vis the natural world.[25] However, as Halpern notes, the positive value attributed to clarity reinscribes the familiar dialectics of humanism responsible for the various crises (political, ecological, etc.) all three poets confronted. For Halpern, Oppen's objectivist poetics exemplify this dilemma. On the one hand, Halpern notes that Oppen's "objectivist realism... offers a prophylactic against the metaphysics of speculative realism in our own present time." (46) That is, unlike objecthood philosophies that valorize the nonhuman (e.g., geological temporality) over the human, Oppen keeps his eye on the world humans have built and, just as important, have not built.[26] On the other hand, Oppen's "elaboration of 'clear' and 'obscured' maps readily upon a more familiar dialectic... 'concrete' and 'abstract'" and thus draws "his poetics into the orbit of a commodity logic whereby a thing's most concrete materiality harbors the most abstract social relations." (51) As we have already seen in other ecopoets who come up against the limits of apprehending the natural order, Oppen's objectivist realism must acknowledge that "words bear the burden of impossibly coinciding with phenomena one can never immediately apprehend." (52) And so, "a poem is not a stone and never will be." (53) Angela Hume, co-editor of the collection of essays that includes Halpern's, draws this conclusion from those ontological limits: "While poetry composed in a field is not organic material or life itself, it gets as close to the organic as possible without actually becoming it..." (4). The distance between nature and culture orients the poetics of a modernist like Oppen, a deep image nature poet like Mary Oliver and an ecopoet like Brenda Iijima. And all three derive this nature/culture dialectic from English Romanticism.[27] Organicism, the desire for closing the distance between humans and humans, humans and nonhumans, orients almost all the permutations of ecopoetics, and, as with the Romantics, it is a corollary of anti-humanist, anti-industrialist and, often, anti-capitalist stances. In other words, ecopoetics embraces anti-progress positions that, in the best cases, avoids the trappings of "back to nature" utopianism.

A recent example of a critical, unsentimental ecopoetics is the special collective exhibition "Digital Trash" (Sept.–Dec. 2018). Along with an array of videos and photographs reporting on the physical waste generated by digitization, the exhibit featured a "mine field," as it were, of cellphones below a monitor explaining the tons of waste seeping into the atmosphere due to Google, Microsoft and so on. As Jennifer Scappettone pointed out in a text accompanying her part of the exhibit, *Lament: How the Mine Opened Up*, the resources required for, and waste products from, digital infrastructures and devices are much more environmentally destructive than the oft-maligned use of paper products, a pejorative only because of the refusal to reforest logging sites and encourage "green" paper manufactures. More to the point, the question of human overpopulation, though once thought to be the number one source of ecological destruction, rarely appears now as a concern among eco-activists or ecopoetics.[28]

Scappettone and Iijima are unapologetically polemical and dogmatic in their respective denunciations of ecological destruction, corporate malfeasance and capitalist exploitation. At the same time, they do not spare themselves from their indictments, and in that sense, we read in their works epic and dramatic demonstrations of both the power of institutional domination of the environments in which we live and the resistance to those aligned forces.

Brenda Iijima's *Early Linoleum* frames lyric and narrative poems with "hyper essays" teeming with quotations, paraphrases, and citations as far flung as pop songwriter Jimmy Webb ("MacArthur Park) and philosopher Jacques Derrida, all in the service of "rehabilitating dubious historical accounts that have been buried subcutaneously—to rally around the gendered, administered bodies that ware, and the textual artifice where we arrange edifices of our embodied experiences." (1). For Iijima, citation is less a matter of case law authority than it is an argument from tort law, the presumption, here, of wrongdoing. The legal terminology here does not indicate the subsumption of ethics; rather, it indexes Iijima's recognition that "we pick it, hunt it, gather it, and catalogue it: telemetry and telescope tracking, chips and ankle bracelets." (4) Thus, the hyper essays engage but also parody rationalism. They enjoin an assembly of like-minded artists, critics and philosophers, so that, in many ways, this text performs a battle royal of choirs. This method, long employed by Iijima, preempts the charge of apocalyptic proselytizing to the extent it proposes history as a tug of war between well-armed armies, even if the fiery denunciations of those on her side cannot match the firepower of those on the other side.

Early Linoleum investigates the problems around archeology, geology, property, vegetarianism, misogyny, racism, and more. The glacial burial of metals and minerals and erection of mountains ("Calcium carbonate sediment makes marble/Ice sheets congeal compression colossal/ Buckling folding buckling folding"—25—and "the rocks are alive/Geologically the rock slabs stacked like the islands of Japan/ Convert limestone and dolostones to marble and metadolostones"—32) might tempt one to "translate" the history of the earth's geological developments into a kind of "intelligent design" once mining, for example, opens up the Pandora's Box of silver, iron, and other elements toxic to flora and fauna. Despite our taste for categorizing discrete objects according to lines of descent, these exchanges of elements across the mineral and animal kingdoms reflect our concepts of the vertical limits of private property. Our legal, commercial, and militaristic invocations of mining and fishing rights on the one hand, and the bracketing of air space on the other, lead Iijima to wonder, "is it private property to the molten core?" (6) In her more lyrical, subjective moments, Iijima "explains" her personality in relation to the physical environment: "Acid rain made me irritable/ all of the song birds disappeared." The collapsing of past and future into a present is of course a typical strategy of the prophet whose fleshy weakness is simultaneously spiritual strength—and vice versa: "My little white body fell off a makeshift bridge/ Into the frigid water I fell/I gripped a rock." (19) As in early Susan Howe, antinomianism assumes all kinds of "antisocial" behavior: "I knew the meatballs were hacked meat, sure, no illusion. . . . I begged my mother for avocados and nuts. . . . It was inappropriate to talk to souls . . ." (21). In terms, however, of the development of the United States our folly is summed up in two lines: "Cotton with its thorns, railroad ties, Napa Valley crops // *Then water came* " (126) As historian Mike Davis has pointed out in his studies of the development of the West in general, Los Angeles in particular, the transformation of the desert into green land has had, and will have, devastating consequences for residents, not only the increasingly large and frequent wildfires but also the draining of water resources never designed to sustain large sedentary human populations.

Jennifer Scappettone's *The Republic of Exit 43* covers much of the same geographical territory as not only Iijima's *Early Linoleum* (Massachusetts and New York State) but also an Rodrigo Toscano's *Explosion Rocks Springfield*.[29] As in *Early Linoleum*, *The Republic* is saturated with rage, but while Iijima's book deploys citationality to conjure a community of like-minded individuals (even if some might excuse themselves from the group), Scappettone's book is an over-the-top literary mash-up. The book's subtitle—*Outtakes & Scores from an Archaeology and Pop-Up Opera of the Corporate Dump*—accurately summarizes, without exhausting, its contents. While the black-and-white photographs in *Early Linoleum* largely serve to mark off sections of the book, the predominantly color photographs and overexposed pictures of paper ribbons of text that dominate *The Republic* read like a libretto shredded by Edward Scissorhands. These strips of paper are not just metaphors for the unearthing of metals and minerals long buried under geological strata. They also correspond to the soundbytes, the snippets of information and disinformation, that pass by, over and through our bodies every day of our digital lives. These multicolored Burroughs-esque cut-ups washed in chemical browns, greens and overexposed blues deconstruct the contact ecopoetics of Ensor. For in this context, contact with a poisoned environment is the last thing anyone would want to have. And as the *Digital Trash* exhibition makes clear, we are already too much in "contact" with the miasmas of overproduction.

Featuring a cast of characters from Greek, Roman and Italian myth (Virgil, Orfeu, Sirens and Io), Lewis Carroll (Alice) and a chorus of chemical compounds, industrial tools and machines and corporate CEOs, *The Republic* reads like a lunatic version of American history—that is, exactly like the consequences of American history: "Is it possible to mobilize the disgust provoked by encounter with what has been cast off, to transform a wasteland from an abject repository of undifferentiated filth into an archive?" (99) This sentence is from "Garbage Arcadia" and it serves as one of the questions central to this project. The other, and perhaps more pressing issue, is how an ecopoetics might make sense of the complex of layerings, the yoking together of ancient ruins and modern structures, that define the city- and land-scapes of our lives. Or as Scappettone puts it, "Is it possible to mobilize the disgust provoked by encounter with what has been cast off, to transform a wasteland from an abject repository of undifferentiated filth into an archive? Can one render its contents, negated and amalgamated matter, coherent only in being excluded from the *polis* as stuff and as discourse, legible to the senses?"[30] The immediacy of the pop-up, akin to the Happening, abuts the operatic melodrama of our overscored lives. Thus, the poems in the book function as linguistic analogues of the paper strips—bits and pieces of miscellany, billboard ads, advertisement jingles, clichés, device descriptions, etc.:" *Future-proofed enclave test/* Of Arithmetic—Ambition, Distraction, Uglification/ *Slung in the air/* Two-way voice. In-only voice/ *Bent to wantonness/* Of wire husbandry." (22)

In bringing together the gendered notion of household and farm management with technology—that "wire husbandry"—Scappettone reminds us that the queered pronoun *they* perfectly captures the non-binary post-humanist world. As the old binarisms of Enlightenment humanism (man/woman, nature culture, West/East, etc.) flare up like dying embers, and populism, fundamentalism and fascism retake the world stage, ecopoetics, the nexus of etymology and ecology offers us glimpses into our singular dark future. Because we still live on a single planet, they will have always been the first pronoun of our nonbinary past, present and future.

NOTES

1. However, ecological justice along with climate justice, are recognizable terms, referring to justice for all living entities.

2. For example, the stamp of approval of a dictionary or the publication and ensuing popularity of a book like *The New Jim Crow* facilitate changes in grammar and connections between past and present legal and paralegal practices.

3. Michelle Alexander, *The New Jim Crow*. A twenty-first century term like same-sex, a twentieth-century term like heteronormativity, and a nineteenth century term like homosexuality reflect new value-laden nomenclatures and paradigms for old practices.

4. Ethnocentrism attempts to stabilize group identity amid the amorphous fluidity of human migration and, more broadly, human evolution. It manages bloodlines by sight and hearing, by visible and audible signs of similarity. Outbreaks of violence against the external "stranger" and internal "defector" are symptoms of futility as blood, evolution, the play of recessive and dominant genes, and geological place (?) mock its attempts to contain and expel the alien.

5. Environmental racism, as noted earlier, is a feedback loop of enhanced health risks, job opportunities, educational success, and social relations for certain populations due to zoning policies, industrial interests, and business/governmental collaborations that calibrate profits and revenue streams in relation to potential legal and political complications. Ecological racism measures these same effects within the contexts of national and

transnational economic policies and strategies. Examples of the former is the building of garbage incinerators in or near poor urban communities or situating nuclear power plants near impoverished rural populations. An example of the latter is the use of Somalia's territorial waters in the Indian Ocean as dumping sites for waste from trawlers and freighters owned by companies operating in India, China, Japan, the United States and Russia. This illegal dumping affected the livelihoods of not only Somalis but those of Kenyans and Tanzanians as well. Resistance to this activity was the seed of the infamous Somali pirates that received international media attention in the first years of the twenty-first century.

6. The 2018 book *Perfume Area* connects ecology and etymology in "Helvetica the Perfume" where the "Swiss typeface" is understood to be "far from neutral," the latter assertion a rejoinder to the inventors of the typeface who claimed that it, like the Swiss during the World Wars, was neutral. Thus this piece begins, "Helvetica the Perfume consists only of water. This is, apparently, the scent of nothing." (41) The "scent of nothing" evokes an ecology of global capital as a network of natural nonsites. Thus, as one example, Helvetica refers, etymologically, to the tribes that populated the geographical area of present-day Switzerland. They came into contact with, and were absorbed by, the Romans. This ordinary story of human migration, encounter and assimilation (or conquest) is, writ large, the essence of perfume, which may be subtle but can no more be "neutral" than confined to an "area."

7. During the 2008 economic recession, which threatened the banking industries and housing markets in the United States, several hard-core Republicans and economists insisted that these industries should be allowed to fail since they had been unable to adapt to the emerging dynamics of the free market.

8. Although ecology can be traced back to 1873 when it is first used in a scientific paper, it derives from *oecology*, a "branch of science dealing with the relationship of living things to their environments," coined in German by German zoologist Ernst Haeckel as *Ökologie*, from Greek *oikos* "house, dwelling place, habitation" (from PIE root **weik**- (1) "clan") + -*logia* "study of" (see -**logy**). In use with reference to anti-pollution activities from 1960s. (https://www.etymonline.com/search?q=ecology). Race derives from the sixteenth century Middle French and Italian *razza* ("a tribe or group of people") while racism appears in the early twentieth century.

9. As I show below, language systems are more like ecosystems than single words. However, I'm pairing ecology with etymology in order to argue that ecopoetics shares with traditional environmental poetry a search for origins and an organicist metaphysics.

10. In keeping a language "alive" through spoken and written utterances we do not, of course, endow it with sentience, but sentience is not a requirement for all forms of life. For me, no argument for a broader conception of life is much better than the one Emily Dickinson makes in "My Life Had Stood, A Loaded Gun."

11. "Jargon" is often, if not always, an index of this tendency toward greater and greater accuracy. The use of Greek and Latin terms in, say, botany is merely one example of a general premise. This also applies to prefixes like ec-, con- and com- as well as to suffixes like -ism, -ite, -ist, and so forth.

12. This common definition of poetics as "making," "what is made," can be found in an online Etymology Dictionary (https://www.etymonline.com/search?q=poetics).

13. Just as a house with a new "addition" is thought to increase its selling value, whatever its appraisal by county officials, so too ecopoetics may be understood—with no moral judgment implied—as one of the more recent "market-enhancement" treatments of poetics.

14. Tina Darragh's and Marcella Durand *Deep Eco Pre* is one exception to the rule.

15. Sometimes the cognitive and affective are evoked interchangeably, erasing the dis-

tinction between original and add-on. In Craig Dworkin's *The Pine-Woods Notebook* (2019), the scientific, aesthetic, subjunctive and mythic converge in the commodity ("Aerosols bloom above boreal forests"—22) and natural/spiritual ("A liquid elixir of pine pitch mixed with pitch-pine switches quickens"—32).

16. The brooding pessimism of a Robert Frost has its sources in the failure of cognition to "know" the natural world; the pessimism of ecopoets like Iijima and Scappettone is that that failure, a philosophical one, has only buttressed the exploitation of the natural world for human utility.

17. See, for example, Joshua Corey, "Three Pebbles—Or, the minimal materialisms of late modernism," *jacket2* (https://jacket2.org/article/three-pebbles. I discuss Rob Halpern's analysis of George Oppen as an ecopoet below. Rob Halpern, "'The Idiot Stone': George Oppen's Geological Imagination; Or, Objectivist Realism as Ecopoetics," *Ecopoetics: Essays in the Field*, 42–61.

18. Sarah Ensor, "The Ecopoetics of Contact," *ISLE: Interdisciplinary Studies in Literature and Environment*, Vol. 25, No. 1, 2018

19. "Introduction to Queering Ecopoetics," 3.

20. The "early 15th c." word consumer is defined as "one who squanders or wastes," agent noun from *consume*. In economics, "one who uses up goods or articles, one who destroys the exchangeable value of a commodity by using it" (opposite of *producer*), from 1745." *Online Etymology Dictionary* (https://www.etymonline.com/search?q=consumer

21. Sarah Ensor, "The Ecopoetics of Contact," Queering Ecopoetics, *ISLE*

22. Ensor discusses Delaney's casual cruising for the mere pleasure of looking, of gleaning without pausing, much less stopping to pick up someone.

23. In her reading of Delaney, Ensor passes over the relationship between leisure and work: "However, if *Times Square Red Times Square Blue* teaches us anything, it may be that contact itself is neither good nor bad, neither healthy nor pathological; for Delany, contact is an ethos regardless of its outcome. What his book insists, we might say, is not that contact is good (although sometimes its consequences are) but rather that contact is; his account urges us to acknowledge the ways in which contact shapes the dimensions of our everyday life even (or especially) when it does not resolve itself into a legible end." (46)

24. Ensor misses transitive verbs in the poem, apparently because they signal "purpose." And she misreads Wordsworth coupling of "'Voluptuous" and "restraint" to pre-empt the charge of solipsism against the narrator.

25. As we will see below, the ethos informing Brenda Iijima's ecopoetics is not unlike that of Ponge, Oppen and Ruykeyser.

26. Halpern's critique is informed by the socialist values he shares with Oppen.

27. It is not surprising that ecocriticism emerges in academia as largely revisionist studies of English Romanticism.

28. Not one essay in Hume's and Osborne's anthology of essays, *Ecopoetics: Essays in the Field*, confronts this issue.

29. All three books individually and collectively extend the so-called Rust Belt from Buffalo across the northern border of the United States to its eastern shores.

30. Jennifer Scappettone, "A Garbage Arcadia," *The Republic of Exit 43*, 99.

CRAIG SANTOS PEREZ

Teaching Ecopoetry in a
Time of Climate Change

I arranged ten desks in a circle in preparation for students the first day of my undergraduate poetry workshop. It was fall 2011—my first semester teaching in the English department at the University of Hawai'i, Mānoa. The students filed in, out of breath and sweating. "The AC feels good," one said. "It's 90 degrees outside." I took roll, reviewed the syllabus, and began our first creative-writing exercise: haiku. As I would later learn, that August was the hottest in the history of O'ahu.

Despite the heat, the students kept up with the coursework as we explored sonnets, villanelles, and imagism. By October, the rains came and the island cooled. During one workshop, however, our cell phones beeped with flood warning alerts. Sure enough, by the time our class was over, the campus was drenched. A record number of storms (including "twin hurricanes") made landfall that semester, canceling many classes. Student absences also increased because of illnesses transmitted by the swarms of mosquitoes on campus. Our workshop fell behind, and I had to scrap many of my lesson plans. I was frustrated. And the students seemed to be drowning in stress and a new kind of "eco-anxiety" unrelated to grades, work, tuition, or debt. I knew we were experiencing the impacts of climate change that were prevalent across the Pacific: record heat, extreme drought, increased storms, infectious diseases, ocean warming, rising sea levels. But I didn't discuss it with them. *I didn't know how to.*

After that difficult semester, I couldn't teach creative writing again without addressing the climate crisis. So I proposed to my department's curriculum committee a course on "ecopoetry" that would help students understand the environmental changes around us and give them the opportunity to express their emotions through poetry. Ecopoetry generally refers to poetry about ecology, ecosystems, environmental injustice, animals, agriculture, climate change, water, and even food. It emerged in the 1990s as poets questioned the naturalness of "nature poetry," especially since nature itself was rapidly changing due to global warming and environmental destruction. Even though I had never taught such a course before, I was familiar with and interested in ecopoetry partly because of my own cultural background.

I was born and raised on the western Pacific island of Guam. As a kid, I always played with my cousins in the jungle or at the beach. We were taught, by our grandma mostly, to always act respectfully in nature, because that is where the spirits of our ancestors dwelled. But as I became a teenager, I witnessed how not everyone treats the environment as a sacred place. Guam is a U.S. territory and one-third of our island is occupied by American military bases, which have contaminated our land, air, and water for decades, from the spraying of DDT to the leaking of PFAS into the island's largest reservoir. Indigenous environmental beliefs and ethics, as well as the legacy and ongoing impacts of environmental injustice in Guam, have been major themes and concerns in my poetry.

I have taught Ecopoetry every year since 2012, thanks to strong student registration. A diverse enrollment has reflected the demographics of the state; most of my students have been Hawaiian, Pacific Islander, and Asian American, with a smaller number of White, African American, and Latinx class members. They have been barefoot surfers, skaters, dreadlocked hippies, mountain bikers, fraternity and sorority members, athletes, vegetarians and vegans, and selfproclaimed "nerds." Their majors have ranged from English to Ethnic Studies, psychology to science, hospitality to Hawaiian. Despite these differences, the students have always bonded through their shared love for the islands.

Unfortunately, most students know very little about ecology, environmentalism, or climate change. This is even true of science majors, whose knowledge seems to be more specialized in chemistry or physics. This gap led me to teaching ecopoetry as a creative pathway toward environmental literacy. So instead of reading just poetry, we also read science journalism and ecopoetry essays, as well as watch documentaries and YouTube videos about concepts like nature, ecology, wilderness, environmental justice, the Anthropocene, extinction, and climate change. As they read these contextual sources, I ask them to annotate key words, images, symbols, facts, data, history, or descriptions that will form the foundation for their own poems. To help students organize all this information, I divide the course into weekly units focusing on different themes/concepts, such as "Pastoral," "Solastalgia," "Water," "Trees," "Animals," "Outer Space," "Plastic," "Nuclearism," "Oil," "Wildfires," "Disaster," "Gardens," "Geo-Engineering," "The Anthropocene," and more. I also include themes related to identity, such as "Ecofeminism," "Indigenous Ecopoetics," "Black Ecopoetics," "Queer Ecopoetics," and "Disability Ecopoetics." Along with providing a framework for engaging secondary readings, this organizational structure helps students develop environmental literacy while also priming them to interpret and write their own ecopoetry.

For each unit, I assign ecopoetry related to the theme. We read and discuss the poems in the context of our supplemental materials, focusing on both literary interpretations and craft elements. I highlight how poetry can communicate environmental issues through creative language and expressive form. Moreover, I foreground how poetry can put a human face and emotional experience on abstract natural disaster and climate crises. For example, one poem I teach is a long poem, "Gentle Now, Don't Add to Heartache," by American poet Juliana Spahr. The poem is about how the environment has been degraded and how many species have gone extinct. The students read the poem aloud and can hear the heartache and mourning of the speaker. They can feel the overwhelming loss embodied in the long lists of extinct and endangered species. In terms of course readings, I introduce students to a wide range of poets, forms, and styles. Diversity is an important pedagogical ethic when teaching ecopoetry, because it reflects and honors ecological biodiversity. I have found that the most strategic way to present this is through ecopoetry anthologies, since the anthology form is itself an assemblage (see Appendix A for recommended texts). I supplement these anthologies with my own course reader that features Hawaiian and Pacific Islander ecopoetry. Through close reading an array of ecopoetry, the students develop critical reading and interpretation skills, an understanding of poetic craft and technique, and the recognition of the power of ecopoetry to humanize environmental themes.

Inspired by our reading and discussion, I then prompt the students to write their own original ecopoetry based on the current theme. Through their poems, they can demonstrate their understanding of the theme by incorporating their notes in creative ways, and they can articulate their own personal, emotional, cultural, or political relationships with the topic. We then conduct a conventional poetry workshop so the students can receive constructive feedback on their drafts, after which they revise and ultimately perform their finished poems aloud to the class.

The most memorable part of this course is not actually what happens in the classroom, but the experiences we have outside campus. Several times a semester, I organize class meetings that literally connect students to the environment. Imagine—students are sitting in a circle at Kaimana Beach, a small strip of sand at the end of Waikīkī. We read aloud "Ocean Birth," a stirring poem by Māori writer Robert Sullivan. The sound of waves crashing against the shore punctuate the rhythm of the lines. The trade winds billow the pages of poems in the students' hands. After we discuss the poem, the students find their own spots on the beach to freewrite. Several students stand in the ocean, the water rising to their knees, while they write in their journals. One student, lost in thought, does not notice a large swell approaching until it is too late, and his journal is soaked. We have had class at an arboretum in the valley behind our campus, inspired by the many native and introduced trees there. We have also met at a sustainable farm and community garden, as well as in Honolulu itself for our "urban nature" unit. The poems written from these fieldtrips tended to be the most powerful and vivid work the students produced.

When I first taught this course, several of the more conscientious students asked on the last day of class, "Is it enough to simply read and write ecopoetry?" We concluded it was not enough. As one student poignantly phrased it, "*Ecopoetry inspires us to act.*" The following semester, I began including community and public engagement components, requiring students to attend two community-engaged environmental events throughout the semester (extra credit if they attended more). On the syllabus, I list local environmental organizations they can volunteer with, such as the Surfrider Foundation and the Sierra Club Hawai'i. Over the years, students have attended beach clean-ups, volunteered for farm work days, participated in Earth Day, and attended the Hawai'i Conservation Alliance Conference and the Honolulu Climate Change March. Beyond participating in environmental movements, we also brainstorm ways to engage the public. Students have shared their ecopoetry on social media platforms to educate their friends/followers, submitted their ecopoems to the school newspaper, distributed their poems as broadsides around campus and local coffee shops, and organized ecopoetry readings on and off campus. The most substantial public ecopoetry project we completed was a collaboration with an online magazine, the *Hawai'i Independent*, in 2015. Each week of the semester, the magazine published a selection of student poems, accompanied by my introduction that explained our theme and readings for that week (see Appendix B for a selection of my introductions and a URL for the student poems). Community and public engagement has been a powerful way for students to actualize their desire to "do something" about environmental injustice and climate crisis, as well as to think creatively about how poetry can make an impact in the world as a form of literary eco-activism.

As I write this, I am preparing for my eighth year teaching Ecopoetry. This summer of 2019 was the hottest in history, breaking the record set when I first taught the course. I am rereading the *Hawai'i Sea Level Rise Vulnerability and Adaptation Report*, published by the state in 2017. How will my students confront the data from this report: rising temperatures, increased respiratory and mosquito-borne diseases, extreme drought, collapsing fish populations, more frequent hurricanes and tsunamis, and the extinction of endemic species? How will they cope with the fact that sea-level rise will cause periodic flooding, permanent inundation, and coastal erosion, which will damage more than 6,500 structures, 25,000 acres of nearshore land, 500 Hawaiian cultural sites, and forty miles of major roads and highways—causing over $20 billion in damages? How will they reckon with the projected displacement of over 20,000 residents?

Despite my anxiety, I know our classroom will be a space where we can learn about, confront, and cope with the climate crisis together. We will be inspired by the ecopoetry we will read and the places in Hawai'i we will visit. We will empower ourselves by creatively transforming our thoughts and emotions into ecopoetry. We will participate in the environmental movement, engage the public, cultivate hope, and imagine sustainable futures through our poetry.

Appendix A

The anthology I have most regularly assigned is *The Ecopoetry Anthology* (2013), edited by Ann Fisher-Wirth and Laura-Gray Street. This anthology opens with excellent introductions by the editors and the former U.S. poet laureate Robert Hass, and it includes both historical and contemporary ecopoetry. Other anthologies I have assigned as required or recommended reading are *Black Nature: Four Centuries of African American Nature Poetry* (2009), edited by Camille Dungy; *The Arcadia Project: North American Postmodern Pastoral* (2012), edited by Joshua Corey and G. C. Waldrep; *Big Energy Poets: Ecopoetry Thinks Climate Change* (2017), edited by Amy King and Heidi Lynn Staples; *Ghost Fishing: An Eco-Justice Anthology* (2018), edited by Melissa Tuckey; *Fire and Rain: Ecopoetry of California* (2018), edited by Lucille Lang Day and Ruth Nolan; and *Here: Poems for the Planet* (2019), edited by Elizabeth Coleman.

In terms of scholarly anthologies, I have assigned *Ecopoetry: A Critical Introduction* (2002), edited by Scott Bryson; *Eco Language Reader* (2010), edited by Brenda Iijima; *The Poem's Country: Place and Poetic Practice* (2018), edited by Shara Lessley and Bruce Snider; and *Ecopoetics: Essays in the Field* (2018), edited by Angela Hume and Gillian Osborne. For individual scholarly monographs, I have introduced students to *Sustainable Poetry: Four American Ecopoetics* (1999) by Leonard Scigaj; *This Compost: Ecological Imperatives in American Poetry* (2002) by Jed Rasula; *Greening the Lyre: Environmental Poetics and Ethics* (2002) by David Gilcrest; *Can Poetry Save the Earth: A Field Guide to Nature Poems* (2009) by John Felstiner; *Ecology of Modernism: American Environments and Avant-Garde Poetics* (2015) by Joshua Schuster; *Remainders: American Poetry at Nature's End* (2018) by Margaret Ronda; and *Recomposing Ecopoetics: North American Poetry of the Self-Conscious Anthropocene* (2018) by Lynn Keller.

Appendix B

Below are a few selections and excerpts of my introductions to the collaboration with the *Hawai'i Independent*. For links to the full publications, which include the student poems, please visit craigsantosperez.com/eco-poetics/.

SOLASTALGIA

Discussions about ecopoetics often involve nostalgia. The word itself has a fascinating etymology: from the Greek *algos* (pain, grief, distress) and *nostos* (homecoming). The word further descends from Proto-Indo-European *nes-* (to return safely home), which is cognate with Old Norse nest (food for a journey) and Gothic *ganisan* (to heal).

From the seventeenth to nineteenth centuries, nostalgia was considered a wound and a serious disease afflicting people who had been taken from their homes and families by colonization, war, enslavement, industrialization, and globalization. These massive displacements not only separated peoples from their native countries, but also separated them from the natural environment, since many migrations arced toward urban centers. Climate change has increased this kind of migration.

Another term, *solastalgia* (combining solace, desolation, and nostalgia), speaks to the pain and distress caused when your homeland is destroyed but you are not necessarily displaced. In other words, you yearn for what your home was before it was desecrated by mining, logging, fracking, military testing, or oil spills; it is feeling homesick even when you are still at home. Sadly, solastalgia is becoming more and more common, especially for peoples of color and those in developing countries.

Ecopoetry is one expressive form through which people have addressed the pain, grief, and trauma associated with nostalgia and solastalgia. Two poems that we read and discussed in class were American poet Robert Hass's "The State of the Planet" and Hawaiian poet Brandy Nālani McDougall's "Water Remembers." In these poems, the natural world is longed for because of its association with home, innocence, family, peace, sustenance, and nurturance.

Thus the first poetry prompt for our ecopoetics course was related to nostalgia: students were asked to write about a childhood memory in which they felt connected to nature.

The "pastoral" is another important topic in ecopoetics, referring to a long tradition of poetry about idealized rural life. The pastoral goes back to ancient Greece, with poets like Hesiod and Theocritus, and to Rome, with Virgil, and through the literary renaissances of Italy, Britain, and America. Throughout, the romantic pastoral acted as a criticism of the squalor and poverty of urban and industrial life. The pastoral encouraged a return to nature and rural life as a space of virtue, honest work, reflection, transcendence, and—even—romance.

Of course, anyone who has actually worked on a rural farm knows that it's not all peaceful sheep and idyllic shepherding. Thus, a tradition of the antipastoral also emerged, criticizing pastoral poets for romanticizing rural life, as well as for ignoring the race, class, and gender problems one might find on the farm—or plantation. These problems extend to how the rural landscape is often gendered in the pastoral as well.

Since modernization has removed so many from nature, many poets have imagined and fantasized what it might be like to live back on the farm, the ranch, the homestead, off the grid, et cetera. In class, we discussed one of the more interesting (and problematic) twentieth-century pastoral poems: Allen Ginsberg's "Wales Visitation."

Admittedly, my favorite kind of pastoral is the "necro-pastoral" (see the haunting work of Joyelle McSweeney, who writes both poetry and scholarship about degradation, decay, and contamination). "Necro" comes from the Greek nekros, meaning death or corpse. Imagine a landscape filled with dead bodies, enslaved bodies, diseased bodies, mutilated bodies, worms, rats, cockroaches, rabid animals, decaying trees, polluted rivers, smog, rotting food, ruins, and blazing wildfires. This, too, has a long, changing tradition. Think certain scary fairy tales, the Book of Revelation, Dante's circles of hell, the Gothic, vampires, zombies, apocalypse stories, Halloween, Banksy's Dismaland, for example. The necro-pastoral aims to make us look at death, sin, evil, fear, and destruction so that we might consider our mortality, morality, and ethics. Sometimes fear wakes us up better than romance. Like the pastoral, the necro-pastoral has its own problematic relation to race, class, and gender.

In terms of ecopoetics, the death and destruction caused by climate change has brought the necro-pastoral to the forefront of our imaginations. We are now surrounded by images and stories of the necro-pastoral—from the Tar Sands to industrial slaughterhouses, from raging wildfires in California to massive chemical explosions in China, from the mass die-offs of fish washing ashore on Pacific coasts to the mass migrations of refugees to the shores of Europe. Collapse and catastrophe flood the stream of all our media. Speaking of floods, Hawai'i has experienced quite a few with the onslaught of a series of hurricanes. With all the rainfall, the streets of Waikīkī were recently flooded with more than 500,000 gallons of raw sewage. Waikīkī, often cast as a literary site of the Pacific necro-pastoral, was shut down. So we decided to write poems about Waikīkī, sewage, and shit.

THE OCEAN IN US

The essay "The Ocean in Us" (1998), by Tongan scholar Epeli Hau'ofa, insists that the "sea is as real as you and I, that it shapes the character of this planet, that it is a major source of our sustenance, that it is something that we all share in common wherever we are in Oceania."

Alongside Hau'ofa's essay, we read the poem "Ocean Birth" (2005) by Māori poet Robert Sullivan. This poem is a chant-like ocean pastoral, lyrically calling forth the currents, the sea creatures, the names of Polynesian islands, and the bodies of Pacific Islanders to all sing their songs of birth. The poem ends: "Every wave carries us here— // every song to remind us— / we are skin of the ocean." Hau'ofa and Sullivan represent a Native Pacific perspective on the ocean, in which the ocean is our source, our origin, our common inheritance.

We also read and discussed two texts that speak to a Trans-Pacific perspective. First: "Oceania as Peril and Promise: Towards Theorizing a Worlded Vision of Trans-Pacific Ecopoetics" (2012) by American poet Rob Wilson. This essay foregrounds the ocean as a theoretical network of global flow, "liquid modernity," and "postmodern fluidity," as well as a material network of capitalist shipping lanes and airfreights, military bases and testing sites, and marine territorializations and exclusive economic zones—all routing across the west coast of the American continent, the Pacific Islands, and Asia. Thus, the ocean represents both peril and promise. It is in peril from us through plastic pollution, overfishing, nuclear testing, and warming, but it can also be perilous through rising tides, tsunamis, and hurricanes. The ocean also represents promise in the sense that it offers a vision of "transnational belonging, ecological confederation, and trans-racial solidarity."

Lastly, we read and performed the poem "Pacific Ocean" (2009) by American poet Brenda Hillman. This poem views the Pacific from California, where the poet touches the coastal waters and launches into a meditation on the vastness and complexity of the ocean. As such, the poem flows in fragmented waves and currents of perception, swirling with flotsam and jetsam, memory and information, plastic and prayers, of spice and maritime routes, dreams and drownings. Or, as Hillman puts it: "a fertile dread ... mixed with ecstasy."

Every culture—and even every person—has a different relationship to, and understanding of, the vastness and complexity of the ocean. And even though poets represent the ocean in different ways, it has always been a space and place of deep symbolism and meaning. As Hau'ofa wrote: "The sea is our pathway to each other and to everyone else, the sea is our endless saga, the sea is our most powerful metaphor, the ocean is in us."

THE POETRY OF DISASTER

To me, storms invoke nostalgia. Guam, where I grew up, lies in "Typhoon Alley." I remember a super typhoon so forceful that it broke through shutters and flooded our bedrooms. Our family closed all the doors and slept in the hallway as the storm shook the house.

Guam is also located in the "Ring of Fire," an area of frequent earthquakes and volcanic activity. One of the scariest moments of my life occurred in 1993, when an 8.1 earthquake struck for nearly sixty seconds. My family ran and held each other under a doorway until the earth stopped trembling.

Natural disasters are one of the most prevalent themes in ecopoetics, especially since disasters are occurring with much more frequency and intensity due to climate change. In Nicole Cooley's essay "Poetry of Disaster," she suggests that the poetry of disaster opens up a space for us to gather and grieve, to seek solace and solidarity, to express sympathy and empathy, to educate and raise awareness, and to share our trauma and resilience. Cooley also highlights how the poetry of disaster inspires action, pointing to the Poets for Living Waters project, an example of literary activism responding to the BP Gulf oil disaster.

Indeed, disasters not only inspire poems, but they inspire post-poem literary activism, including publication in mainstream and social media, benefit readings, fundraising anthologies, educational websites, ethnographic/ interview-based poetry projects, and writing workshops for survivors.

We read or heard and discussed several examples of disaster poetry and literary activism: in response to the 2005 Hurricane Katrina, the 2009 tsunami in Samoa, the 2010 Haiti earthquake, 2013's Typhoon Haiyan in the Philippines, the 2015 earthquake in Nepal, and the ongoing Syrian refugee crisis.

CREATION STORIES AND
INDIGENOUS ECOPOETICS

Creation stories are central to indigenous ecopoetics, since they are often encoded with ecological ethics. While native peoples have always looked to our creation stories for guidance and inspiration, many non-native peoples have turned to indigenous stories to address the crisis of climate change.

Indigenous creation stories, and native ecopoetics in general, foreground how the primary themes in native texts express the idea of interconnection and interrelatedness of humans and the non-human world; the centrality of land and water in the conception of indigenous genealogy, identity, and community; and the importance of knowing the indigenous histories of a place. Moreover, native writers often employ creation stories and ecological images, metaphors, and symbols to critique colonial views of nature as an empty, separate object that exists to be exploited for profit. What scholars refer to as "ecological imperialism" includes the displacement of indigenous peoples from ancestral lands; the establishment of plantation, industrial, and chemical agriculture; the development of tourism and urbanism; the contamination from militarism and nuclearism; rapid deforestation and desertification; the extraction of natural resources and indigenous remains; and species extinction and endangerment.

Lastly, indigenous ecopoetics reconnects people to the sacredness of the earth, honors the earth as an ancestor, protests against further environmental degradation, and insists that the earth (and literary representations of the earth) are sites of healing, co-belonging, resistance, and mutual care.

RAQUEL GUTIÉRREZ

Do Migrants Dream
of Blue Barrels?

I live in Tucson. People tell me they love the images they see on my various social media feeds of the mysterious, moonscape desert that surrounds. Many of the friends, acquaintances, and strangers who follow me on social media live along both coasts, so of course it gives me great pleasure to be able to ignite their awe for the uncontainable beauty of the Sonoran desert, even if from afar. For me, being in this desert on any given morning or early evening means giving over to the expansive possibilities of the landscape. It has offered new perspectives when I am stuck on a writing project—to step out into any number of trails and parks and take it all in, whether it's the way the light moves across the shallow valleys of Gates Pass before sunset or the way the temperature surprisingly drops ten degrees when your trail takes you into the shadowy parts sitting below Pima Canyon. The infinity of surprise that lives here is hard to deny.

But as 115–120 degrees Fahrenheit becomes the new normal for Southern Arizona, indicating a climate change that may not be reversible in years to come, there is another thing one cannot deny—any slight carelessness on your part and the desert will kill you. That fact makes itself clear on a recent ride-along outing with Guillermo and Stephen, two volunteers for the regional organization Humane Borders/Fronteras Compasivas. As I climb into their water-replenishment truck, I am told that if we broke down in Arivaca—an hour and fifteen minutes south of Tucson—we would be exposed to the same conditions as the Latinx migrants we are trying to help. I stare dead-eyed behind my Ray-Bans at Guillermo—we would never be exposed to the same conditions as migrants making this trek.

I shake off any doubt that we will be okay. All of us engaging in humanitarian work should have it seared into our minds that we are the lucky ones; after all, we are traveling with over one hundred gallons of water into the harshest topographies in the Southwest. At the worst, we will be sweaty and uncomfortable changing the imaginary flat tire, in my mind's wandering to worry—but we won't die.

I make contact with the privilege I carry into different parts of the valley that blanket the infamous border town Arivaca, though I'm not sure I can ever make peace with it. In this part of the country, the thing you do—if you are somebody's anchor baby, a pedantic gadfly, a broke bourgeois bohemian who cares about justice and human rights and has heated conversations about immigration policy with family members during the holidays, the you who still writes diversity statements for scholarship applications, or eats nopal fries and drinks aged-whiskey cocktails with the liberal latte-sipping NPR listeners in downtown Tucson, where the adobe façades were restored to make it look like you are still in the Old Pueblo—you come and face these incongruent truths, maxing out credit cards to do the thing you do in the name of justice. If there is anything to do with the privilege, it is to risk it. And it will never be enough.

Humane Borders maintains a system of water stations in the Sonoran Desert on routes used by migrants making the perilous journey to the north mostly by foot. Each station has its own name: Green Valley (Pecan Orchard), Elephant Head, Rocky Road, K-9, Cemetery Hill, Soberanes, Mauricio Farah, and Martinez Well.

Getting into the truck at Green Valley, we are promptly driven to the first water station, situated behind a pecan orchard. It looks momentarily out of place and time with its trees lined up tightly, towering above a few acres covered by bright green grass, an indication of the obscene amounts of water it must consume on a daily basis. But I am thankful nonetheless for its place in the landscape and hope it is there to offer some shady respite to the men, women, and children who make the orchard a part of their journey.

As soon as we get to the water station, I quietly gasp at the sight of concrete blocks, a quartet of two-by-four wood planks, and a fifty-five-gallon plastic blue barrel sitting stoutly but bravely above the desiccated arroyo. These objects in any other home-improvement configuration might not inspire such deference, but it is like seeing Stonehenge in real life—or rather seeing these water stations gives me the same feeling as when I saw Stonehenge as a high-school sophomore. That there is so much life beyond the little world you're trying to escape from— we're all trying to leave something behind and go toward something better, and there shouldn't be any guilt or fault in that desire. These water stations are myth come to life, a border fable if you will—friends from back home in Southern California who have come out to the desert to do humanitarian work right in the trenches, a newer ground zero located in the Southwest, see the danger firsthand, see the danger abstracted. This severity. Our national border policies producing the need for these rebel barrels. Suddenly I don the beige mask of humanitarianism, sunburnt pink on my brown skin.

But I don't want this severity to be normalized. My body is here to meet the risk; that is what it is about, right? I will be the distraction so somebody less privileged can make their escape. I will make space in the back seat where I sit, absorbing the bumpy impact over difficult terrain. I don't want to be arrested and face jail time, or a felony mark on my record like Scott Warren (the Arizona State University School of Geographical Sciences and Urban Planning lecturer and volunteer for the advocacy group No More Deaths, who in January 2018 was arrested and charged with harboring and one count of conspiracy, which are felonies. Warren will face a retrial in November and twenty years in prison if convicted of those charges. But all the charges will be dropped—a precedent-setting victory for humanitarian aid workers). I have a deep-seated fear of being arrested. But fears are meant to be conquered, I suppose from the back seat of the SUV. I don't know if I can use this platform so somebody can find the words to say, "there is a problem on the border," and bring them into their privatized space within a place, a city even, uncertain of calling itself a sanctuary. That space may be here right now, or sometime in the near future.

Do migrants dream of healing elixirs photosynthesized with the cancerous UV rays of the sun? Do they spot the plastic gallon bottles situated at the base of the ocotillos that obscure vultures and other carrion birds, perched in wait?

I go to Arivaca for lunch with A one late-winter day. A is a good friend of mine who works with No More Deaths, another gender weirdo who has been this-close to being charged with a felony for illegal transport of immigrants. Through A, I meet other queers who I may have spotted at punk shows in Oakland or Los Angeles or standing in line at the co-op in Brooklyn. Many an anarchist punk has made their way to Tucson to work for No More Deaths—so many that No More Deaths feels like some kind of queer rite of passage into Tucson's radical communities, where any given Friday night there'll be a wild mesh-and-Day-Glo, Bay Area–style dance-party fundraiser for undocumented queer and trans people, or bail funds specifically for queer organizers caught in the crosshairs of draconian border policy. I love A's tales of hooking up with fellow aid workers that came through for the summers only. Sex and No More Deaths had a very plutonian quality—the intensity of the work that took place there inspired a unique eros.

It is still quiet on the shore of the Arivaca lake. Scott Warren hasn't yet been arrested for bringing provisions to migrants stuck in a safe house, when A and I stop at La Gitana Cantina for a quick cold beer. No More Deaths is the necessary intervention, much to the chagrin of Arizona's conservatives. What is the alternative to letting people die in the desert?

A picks me up in their dusty, decade-old dual-cab Toyota two-door truck. We stop at the co-op in Tucson for olives, anchovies, crackers, and kombucha before jumping onto the highway and through the mountain roads that spit us out three miles from the border itself. The town is Wild West tiny with a general store and a saloon jumping colorfully into my sightline. It's too early for a round at La Gitana Cantina, but that doesn't stop the parking lot from being packed at eleven am. A parks in front of the Arivaca Humanitarian Aid office to introduce me to the lovely aid worker whose name shall remain anonymous, who welcomes me in and speaks to me in a familiar Spanish, narrating a day in the life that feels absurd after seeing every other car be a border-patrol truck, and wondering who might be eyeballing A. I buy a tee shirt. And take a few photos of the "people-helping-people border zone" murals that portray a Disneyesque pastoral landscape with desert wildlife hiding behind traffic cones and stop signs.

Living in the borderlands, you count among your friends and neighbors those who want things to be different here. We use our time to stay aware, to be in service. We live here to embody the lesson that everyone should be entitled to improve upon the conditions of their lives. That often means leaving behind a pressure-cooker combination of corrupt governments, violence, and barren lands. Those lessons arrive differently for us. We are people connected to immigrants and migrants in deep and complex matrices—as their children, their lovers, their friends, their bosses, their customers, their neighbors, or if, we are lucky, their students. Some of us will never know that direct experience of movement across harrowing terrain. We will never know the hard choice to begin those journeys. Some of us are in networks of care that rely on a rapid-response strategy to help the most precarious members who have made those choices with funds, warm clothes, or a place to stay after leaving the detention centers that dot the Southern Arizona landscape.

And sometimes, if you're like Francisco "Paco" Cantú, your connection is a complicated relational dyad that will haunt the rest of your days. Cantú spent four years in the Border Patrol and distilled those experiences tracking and arresting border crossers—and the moral injury it produces—in his memoir, The Line Becomes a River (Riverhead, 2018). His book was released to much fanfare, ingratiating him with the liberal media and putting him in the crosshairs of border activists who angrily called him out on several platforms for capitalizing on migrants' deaths for his artmaking. While some of this critique is echoed in Tucson, the reality of our lived days is that to see a border cop with some *toque de mexicanidad* is a quotidian event. And it's time to reckon with why Mexican

Americans, the children and grandchildren of Mexican immigrants, decide to don olive-green pants and green-and-gold-patched white shirts to police Southern Mexican and Central American migrants making the journey north. Why do these inhabitants of Southern Arizona divorce themselves from the recently arrived? What is gained by enacting these distances? What are the proximities they make way for? I struggle with these questions as a way to understand my own kin. I ask more questions.

Why did my Salvadoran immigrant brother fourteen years my senior join the Marines after barely graduating high school? Why did he become a Los Angeles sheriff's deputy? How did we happen to share the same uterus at different times? It's time to unmake the quotidian, to learn from those who have permanently damaged themselves carrying out our draconian and inhumane policies from the inside out. To a more privileged subject, the quotidian brings a sense of doom to all of my other like-minded efforts: voting, calling my senators and representatives, tweeting my outrage, unleashing tiresome tirades to trolls whose worlds seem to get bigger while mine diminishes with activists and scholars dying early deaths.

I am often asked if I know Francisco Cantú—but he's just Paco to me. Paco the well-read, soft-spoken king of the nerds, who brings up Cormac and Anzaldúa in the same breath and will only discuss mezcal-distillation processes if you specifically ask him about them. I am asked if I support the border patrol, because I like his tweets on occasion. *This is Tucson,* I say. *You can't change the past.* In a red state known for denying Mexican American high-school students a chance to learn about their histories by banning ethnic studies curriculum, it means a lot when anyone is willing to step up for the disenfranchised.

You can't change the past and be the ideal advocate in Tucson; there are people who very literally made it impossible for young people to even learn about the past. I don't want to have to build false dichotomies about someone's past against someone else's as a way to defend those pasts. Living with the past is the hardest task to be burdened with day in, day out, seeing the ways tensions improve between Mexican American and Indigenous communities or don't. Harnessing those energies for a solidarity where we center the migrant's plight feels more important to me.

My dad sheepishly admits that the reason he hasn't gone back to the gym in his neighborhood is that he accidentally hit the gas instead of the brake and totaled his minivan by slamming it into a light post in the gym parking lot. It must have been bad, I said. He laughs. At seventy-five he often doesn't give me the backstory to most of his mistakes, and any story is often filled with omissions too painful to remember. I think of the story he shared with me over a crab dinner he splurged on in Fisherman's Wharf after riding the Greyhound all night to San Francisco, where I was living at the time. In the late sixties he had been arrested for working without papers in San Francisco and was placed in custody on a fishing boat in Alameda, California, for a couple of days, cleaning the deck while agents found him a bus to El Paso. This was a time when detention centers meant nothing more than a ride to Ciudad Juárez or Tijuana, while Mexicanos on both sides of the line listened to the San Jose, California, band Los Tigres del Norte sing earnestly about contraband and betrayal in a transnational drug deal between lovers gone wrong. That golden age where you got back on that hill, grassy and lush, and tried it again until you got it right. And he did. My dad got that right.

I start thinking about the ways in which the untraceable is made evident, or how the migrants' journey has been represented to me throughout my life as a reader, a writer, and the Los Angeles–born 1980s child of parents from El Salvador and Mexico—and the one in the here and now, the adult child. In prose, we have writers Rubén Martínez of Los Angeles, who in his 2001 nonfiction book *Crossing Over: A Mexican Family on the Migrant Trail* rode with the Chavez brothers, indigenous members of the Purepecha tribe from the town of Cherán, Michoacán, in search of a better life. But how is a life made better if it means working in the poultry industry in rural Arkansas that will call ICE on you at a moment's notice? Or Reyna Grande rendering firsthand without mincing words the very particular experience of crossing over. People come north because the alternative is death. Their portraits of others or selves desperate to reunite with family in the North, all in various pursuits of better economic stability.

As a reader, these voices have meant finding the language to illustrate the ways migratory traumas continue to haunt families both constituted and torn apart by inhumane border policies. But my parents' migration took place in the late sixties and early seventies—they were essentially crossing an imaginary wall with nary an agent in sight to police such boundaries. Or overstaying their visas as in the case of my mother, who was a nurse in San Salvador. She came to the U.S. fleeing a violent husband. But she stayed in Los Angeles in the early 1970s, dare I say in the innocent heyday of border crossing, on par with episodes of *The Brady Bunch*? Or the golden age of border-law breaking, such as that scene in *Born in East L.A.* where Cheech Marin's Lupe interrupts his own privilege as a Los Angeles–born-and-bred Chicano who finds himself caught in the Kafkaesque bureaucratic nightmare of an unlawful deportation. The climax of the film happens when Lupe, atop one of the many hills throughout the borderscape of Tijuana and San Diego, summons the migrant masses with the elegance of an orchestra conductor to run down the hill, overwhelming two slack-jawed border-patrol agents underestimating the ethnic disempowered other, as per usual.

Back in the truck, I feel myself dolefully assign the landscape its benevolence, something to help muster the belief that what we are doing will make the slightest impact. It is Sunday. Of course we all have the same thought that morning—will we encounter anyone in need of our help?

Do migrants dream of blue barrels in the middle of the emptied ocean floor? Hiding in the brush in this harsh wilderness, dying under the weight of the sun?

In the distance, I stop and listen closely: a purple flag waves intrepidly in the hot summer wind, its color dulled by the daily solar pounding of summer.

After surveying the water station for cleanliness, potability, visibility, and evidence of possible tampering, we move on to the next one in Arivaca proper, Elephant Head. But before heading out of the pecan orchard, Stephen asks Guillermo to stop the truck on the periphery, where he spots empty water bottles and a spectrum of detritus of migrants past. Plastic bottles that are empty but still intact signal recent passage. However, there are also old, discarded backpacks that, like the life they carried inside, have been emptied and are succumbing to the harsh conditions of this merciless desert. They are bits of human evidence that make the area seem anachronistic—to travel by foot in a time saturated by every imaginable technology. This is our refugee crisis.

It is not hard to sense that specter of migrant death nearby or in my third eye. Everything in that mise-en-scène blinks like a neon sign—migrants who came through the shade of the pecan trees more likely than not found their downfall in the washes around Arivaca, eleven miles from the borderline itself.

The border and the imprint of migrants' death that is left in its hinterlands animates most experiences I have in the nature that surrounds it. There's no saguaro I pass or silhouette of a mountain range at sunset that doesn't have the uncanny attached to each of these natural encounters. The beauty of the desert never exists in a vacuum for me, much like art for art's sake. This sentiment is approximated for me in the artwork of my friend Karlito Miller Espinosa, who like me left a coastal metropole for Tucson in 2016. An artist known for his exquisitely executed murals—from New York to Kiev—he started working in more conceptual registers that allowed for a more direct critique of the cultural zeitgeist in which he found himself. His three-dimensional installation pieces centered on cement bricks made from sand and debris collected from sites around southern Arizona borderlands where migrant bodies have been found. *Untitled (Corridor)* (2018) is a work that organizes the bedlam that U.S. immigration policy produces on the border space of Arizona and Mexico into a compact, narrow corridor. Fueled by a desire to ensure a futurity, most migrants are indigenous men and young families leaving the dead ends delivered by their countries of origin, countries whose governments have sold off industries to the highest bidders as is what business as usual means in a post-NAFTA world. As Mexican artist Teresa Margolles or Rafa Esparza comment on the ways in which violence intervenes in the daily lives of the most vulnerable of both Mexican and U.S. society, Karlito's work too is a vehicle for a much-needed elegy for the migrant who comes north to labor. He brings land to art. And while the bricks themselves innovate on a page out of minimalism, to experience them in the seemingly antiseptic walls and floor of a gallery space allows for the Sonoran desert to leave its locale and trouble the viewer comfortably distanced from the deadly terrains. For me, Karlito's work troubles me through the reminder of the debt I owe the migrant, the uncomfortable intimacies that contour the histories between us, the circumstances that reinforce the tensions.

I am a passenger watching the scenery of the borderlands beyond the brink of madness. One sitting president called the Deporter-in-Chief helped set the rhythm in place for what would come with the new administration less than a year later. We all are—at least the lot of us in the vehicle making this trip, a mere tithe to the desert to spare the living crossing through it. Every day can be marked by a colorful crucifix.

Over the next nine hours, over nothing more than the stretch of six miles at 3 mph, we are all mad. Or obsessed. It is this affective drive that impelled volunteers like Guillermo and Stephen to make this trip every two to three weeks for the last two years. No one should go through this. Everyone should run thumb and forefingers into the bullet holes of signs around the water barrels. Everyone should come close to being trampled by the cattle roaming freely. No one should risk this. Everyone should notice the wake of buzzards flying too close for comfort. No one should be separated from their families. These imperatives shouldn't fall on the luck of the draw.

When we arrive at Elephant Head, I notice something that wasn't on the first blue container: La Virgen de Guadalupe. Or, rather, a glossy sticker with her likeness.

All of my twelve years' worth of nostalgic Catholic-school hackles go up at the sight of the feminine deity that made her debut on a hill in Tepeyac, Mexico. An apparition that, today, only an indigenous man re-christened Juan Diego under similarly violent conditions could witness. As chronicled in a tract written in the mid-seventeenth century, *Nican Mopohua*, Juan Diego Cuauhtlatoatzin was an indigenous man born in fifteenth-century Mexico when it was still Tenochtitlan, a subject of the Aztec empire who was basically caught in the crosshairs of colonization. Juan Diego was an early adopter of Catholicism, opting for baptism over complete subjugation. He was canonized in 2002 for being the holy witness to the apparition of the Virgin Mary, who appeared to Juan Diego on the hill of Tepeyac in 1531, and who exhorted him to tell the bishop to build a shrine to her there. Was it because praying to the Virgin in their image made it easier to believe? This of course is relevant because Tepeyac was the site of the recently destroyed shrine to Coatlicue, the mother deity in the Aztec polytheistic tradition. In 1531, just as autumn transitioned into winter, Juan Diego on his return from a fourth encounter with the Virgin opened his tunic, and luscious red roses fell to the floor. This gesture also revealed the imprint of the Virgin Mary's image on the cloth of his humble vestment. Roses would have been impossible to grow during that season.

Stephen notices me noticing her and says it's a way migrants hopefully can understand that the water station is there to help. I nod. He reminds me of the white solidarity folks back in Los Angeles. Stephen, a civil-rights attorney for the ACLU, reminds me of the kind of men who would teach me about parts of the Salvadoran Civil War my mother would omit. I nod, affirming that assumption and hoping non-Catholic migrants can decipher the tank as a site of relief. But behind my sunglasses and smile I bite my lip and pinch the muffin top peeking over my belt to keep the flood of emotions at bay. When will the colonial encounter finally pay its debt to the migrant, the descendant of those who under duress chose one god of Catholicism over the many gods and divinities of Aztec/Toltec/Mayan cosmological spirituality to call on for the variety of supplications that emerge in a life?

I pull the soft red bandana from my back pocket and rub it over tearstreaked cheeks and the sweat from my brow.

As the morning progresses and the sun's rays intensify, I feel the perspiration pool in and around my body's various concaves and then disappear. The desert is taking its rightful tax of moisture from me, collecting its debt as it does every day. We snack on sweet baby peppers and throw the ends out the window, to which Guillermo will say it will be a few hours tops before the desert consumes our biodegradable trash. We go on like this for hours. Our bodies flirting with being untraceable, all while traversing Arivaca's veins and arteries.

Time seems to be marked by how close or far we are to a curious mountain peak known as Baboquivari, a sacred place for the Tohono O'odham nation as the creator, I'itoi, resides in a cave at the base. Baboquivari represents a genesis, of sorts. Or where to return, for many. Throughout our ride-along, Guillermo will stop for all of us to take in the scenery, snap photos, and stretch our legs. It feels like Baboquivari is looking out for us as we do our best looking out for others. Back in the car, rolling at our near-glacial pace, Guillermo, an old punk like me, who lived a decade in a Northeast Los Angeles neighborhood (like me again) but now lives in Tucson (yep, me, too), regales us with a story about his dying grandmother. He traveled from California one spring break years ago so that he and the cousins could gather to go camp and pray for their Yaqui grandmother's health. They passed a joint around as they hiked up the mountain to Baboquivari's peak. Being young men on the precipice of adulthood themselves, they silently competed with one another—who could walk faster? Who could carry the most gear? Who could keep up?

I was not going to let those guys know I had a flu, Guillermo says, carefully guiding our vehicle over sharp, rocky terrain, *but I was dragging behind them when I felt something watching me. It was a mountain lion, and I turned around so quickly I scared it away.* The rest of us in the car sigh in relief collectively. But Guillermo isn't going to let us off the hook. *Did you know*, he begins, *that a mountain lion loves to eat a fresh kill? He'll sneak up behind you, take a swipe at the base of your neck, bite down on your cerebellum, and paralyze you.*

Wait. Wait. Are you basically watching yourself get eaten alive? I ask, looking out toward Baboquivari, hoping for the hundredth time that hour that we won't break down.

I touch my own ancestral amulet in my pocket, a piece of black kyanite mooncharged with protecting energies, or that is the metaphysical response to the circumstances currently beyond my control. I want to turn my energetic GPS on so my ancestors can find me, protect me somehow. Our guides are continually asked what happens if we encounter migrants on these trips; Stephen says simply they are to be given food, first aid, and water.

No one mentions felony.

No one mentions the way your right to vote or to secure gainful employment becomes jeopardized with the mere provision of water, food, and medical aid to a migrant found wandering in one of the few deadliest deserts in North America. We are wanderers with maps and GPS, Havarti cheese, and herb crackers. We travel with over a hundred gallons of water and a full tank of gas. We travel with the privilege of knowing our way back home.

BRENDA IIJIMA

Who We Are as Floral, Faunal, Mineral Beings

The conceptual basis of the "human" looms over the horizon of presence, dominating the conditions of being. My preoccupation has been to imagine this term dissolving, encouraging human persons to be drawn into the social, cultural, and material collective of floral, faunal, and mineral consciousness in ways that have been stymied and flatly denied. Once this taxonomic membrane has been collapsed, humans have a chance to meld with animacy and regain a connection with the world.

It can be startling to remind humans of our animal identity— as *Homo sapiens*, essentially apes. Humans share 98 percent of our DNA with chimpanzees. The genetic similarity between a cat and a human is 90 percent; humans and mice, 85 percent. In fact we are transpecies, our bodies are populated by microbiota, living floral entities, to the degree that autonomous life isn't possible without mutual cohabitation within and across bodies of each other.[1] According to a recent National Institute of Health (NIH) estimate, 90 percent of cells in the human body are bacterial, fungal, or otherwise non-human.[2] *The smallest organism changes the world infinitely.*[3]

Our bodies are composites of plant, animal, and mineral memory and impulse. Humans are continually fortified by plant, animal and mineral nourishment ingested and integrated into our bodies to form our cellular structures.[4] All living persons of the world share similar DNA. Genes that are unique to humans account for less than 1 percent of our genetic information.[5] A human individual is a holobiont: an assembly of life forms coexisting together as a multiple and as one—the person with a name that absorbs the unnamed members of their mutual body. A holobiont is an organism plus its persistent communities of symbionts.[6] A person is a multiple and is continually in flux, changing within environmental conditions that are also always transforming. The human body has numerous holes, apertures, and openings, where life flows within and through—the body is synthetic of its interaction and response with nature—

cell with cell, viscous, mineral. Organisms are porous, permeable. Everybody drags the world with them and the world drags everyone along. We touch something and it touches back—what we touch may be alive, electrically charged, replete with meanings. This exchange happens on the micro and macro levels. *She shook herself free, leaving several parts of herself behind in the branches and taking some bushes with her.*[7] Rethinking how it is that we are actually many beings moving through time and space together, collectively responding to our environment changes how we negotiate personhood altogether. "I" must be understood as polyphonous, dissonant, cooperative, multi-possessing. This means the voices in our head are real voices, and voices don't only emanate from the top of our body; our entire body is signaling and vocalizing via energy exchange. The voices are myriad. The interplay between living entities *within bodies* creates an embodied consciousness that animates pathways of intuition, mental telepathy, erotic connection, clairvoyance, the ability to navigate the unfamiliar and seemingly ordinary sensual and psychic territory. Our gestures of expression are thus polyvocal, polyvalent.

Personhoods that exude complex inter-organization are a norm, not an exception. Anne Pringle, a mycologist at Harvard University's Department of Organismic Evolutionary Biology studies the interdependence involving lichens and other beings. She writes that "What was once thought to be a mutualism involving two species may be an entangled symbiosis of thousands of species, interacting in every conceivable fashion. A lichen is not just a fungus and its photosynthetic algae. Lichens house hundreds, thousands, or perhaps tens of thousands of other species within the thallus, including other kinds of fungi and myriad bacteria."[8] Another example of the dynamic interplay of bodies is a slime mold (*Physarum polycephalum*). According to the Paris Zoological Park that is exhibiting them, *Physarum polycephalum* has 720 sexes and can heal itself. The mold is able to subdivide into different organisms and then fuse back together. A study published in the journal *Proceedings of the Royal Society* and co-authored by Audrey Dussutour, a biologist at France's National Center for Scientific Research, showed that *Physarum polycephalum* could learn to ignore noxious substances and remember that behavior up to a year later. This unicellular person, thought to be a million years old, is thus a mature member of Earthly life.[9] The microscopic members of society are busy correlating with macro members, and vice versa. An "I" is already a society of presences communing amongst and together, as one another, and also as divisible.

In an insular move, (predominantly western, i.e. European and North American) human floral mineral animals have designated "human" as an exclusive category, listing features such as opposable thumbs, complex language, emotion, and tool usage as distinguishing characteristics—but over time these claims of

difference have collapsed, proved to be incorrect. Every living being responds ho-
listically to the terms of their engagements with the world. Particular environmental niches require different skills and abilities, ways of moving in the world,
ways of expressing. We are shaped by the world as we shape the world. It is a dubious practice to measure intelligence on a sliding hierarchical scale in comparison with humans, as the supposed apex species.

Human existence is alienated from belonging contextually to earthly life.
The human sphere can feel like a self-contained bubble that refuses the embrace
of the intricacies of a shared world. Other beings are held at the periphery of human consciousness, on the outskirts, the margins—in a world which happens to
be within the same world cohabitated with humans. The majority of human policies and decisions don't consider other animal, plant, and mineral realities in
the decision-making process, except in their use value. The effects of this blind
spot, this ignorance, this lapse in collective negotiation has been a disaster for all
sentient life. Life is an interrelational interchange—a cacophonous experience of
sensory engagement. "The lived body, lived mind, and lived environment are all
[thus] a part of the same process, the process by which one enacts one's world.[10]
Earthly life is interwoven, co-constituted mutual repetition. A holistic phenom-
enology generates a fully saturated ontology. Materially, consequences reverber-
ate through the flesh and fiber of existence.

The species divide is punitive. To be deemed "human," understood historically (by western, white heteropatriarchy instilled and buttressed by capitalism),
is what has constituted personhood. To be "human" was understood on a scale
of more and less human: the subhuman, beastly; equated with wild animals, de-
generate life. The logic is racist, eugenic, and extractivist. The divisiveness of the
category human is the major feature and tool of a symbolic and cultural hege-
mony of power and control. The history of "Man" in tandem with a system of
exploitation: capitalism—a social invention of the European Enlightenment period that continues to haunt human, animal, floral, and mineral biological, social, and cultural relations. Enmeshed in the logic of hierarchical violence along
race, gender, class, and species divisions, whom we can refer to as "person" is restricted—dormant in possibility, punitively meted out, barely realized. The inability to regard others as persons is a direct result of this legacy of thinking that
qualified only hetero, white male, property-owning Christians as true individuals. The category (categories) "human" is thus a complicated invention of domination, subjection, and complicity.[11] Only humans qualify as persons and only a
small subset of the population were (are) considered human. Rinaldo Walcott, in
discussion around Sylvia Wynter's work, spells out the ways that this system has
created "the subgenres of humanness—in particular, non-white, queer and feminine modes of humans." The goal, then of Wynter's project, according to Walcott,

"attends to the ways in which we have come to and produced our contemporary conditions of being human—wherein Man is the measuring stick of normalcy and Man's human Others are excluded from this category of being—and how we might unsettle and undo this conception of humanness."[12] The human is a specious category that endows dubious status to an elite few and is linked to a delusional sense of grandeur and power that whiteness attempts to maintain. Within animist, indigenous cosmological and terrestrial understanding, humanity is extended to all beings. Mountains, rivers, rocks, turtles, trees, birds, bears, the sky: are persons.

The traces of this rationale in "today's western and globally Westernized secular (biocentric liberal/neoliberal and thereby bourgeois monohumanist) perspective" continually pervade relationality among humans and all other persons.[13] We need only to consider police brutality against people of color; the industrial-prison complex; colonial-settler violence and extraction from indigenous communities; or the divisions in wealth, education, and housing to understand how relegations concerning personhood influence daily life. Other than human animals, plants and minerals are systematically factory farmed, exploited, and violated. In this system, humans give animals, plants, and minerals cultural identity and "worth." The well-being and safety of the human is considered most important. Harnessing the energy and life of other life forms has been standard practice. Mountaintops are blasted, rivers are toxified, raw materials are monetized, the oceans become a dumping zone.

Despite the brutal systemic legacy of naming, "human" continues to be an aspirational term. Humans seek humanity— the track record predicts elusiveness, not equity. Why continue to espouse human exceptionalism? Why prioritize humanity? The category is defunct. The accretion of violence associated with the category "human" begs a correction. Looking to "humanity" to intervene on catastrophe is a faulty, mostly foreclosed premise. I submit that the qualification "human" has succeeded in its genocidal and ecocidal mission. The term "human" has splintered life into categories that fall on a sliding scale of importance and expendability. Humanity has created too many missing persons, too many bodies subject to colonization, slavery, commodification, and untimely death.

Donna Haraway has suggested approaching the animal other as a stranger, so better to acknowledge their integrity, recognize differences, engage with respect. Establishing a more intimate relation anticipates closeness and care. Thinking about flora, fauna, and mineral as familial brings recognition of the interrelatedness of telluric experience. Not all families and their family members get along or understand each other, but all family share an origin story. There is accepted mutuality, inheritance, and commonality within difference when a baseline origin is affirmed. In the very immediate present, origin opens up understandings of mineral, floral, and faunal symbiosis. Minerals transform the world that flora live in, flora transform the world of minerality, and fauna also manipulate the other. Flora is mineral, mineral is fauna. *Luminosity exudes from marrow moving, femur and shin—the calcium opens. Blue as an indication of temperature or touch of time passing.*[14] Possible liberation comes in moving toward a recognition of a weird cosmo-geomorphic familial connection unified insofar as contradiction and heterogeneous plurality sustain relation.

Interdependency and inseparability heighten the sensitivity necessary for the participation of myriad assertions of personhood (all other persons seem to get this; humans are stubborn to adjust). A solidarity of the incongruous, ritualized in ceremonial communion dissolves universal history (from the point of view of humans) and heightens a perspectival subjectivity in perpetual cosmopolitical tension with the other humankinds hidden under the corporeality of other species.[15]

In a radical sense everything is in the process of reincarnation—fragments of the body shed and are integrated into other forms. More dramatically, through death there is a reuptake into the active, living presence—matter becomes the fodder for emergent forms of life. Through death it is obvious how unstable form is, shapeshifting energies regroup, rewire, reformulate as other life. When this subtle, generative process of shared energy flow is disturbed (reappropriated, sped up, monetized, commoditized, weaponized) the necessity of holistic worlding becomes impaired.

Outside the United Nations, in New York City, where the Climate Action Summit took place on 23 September 2019, Kayapo Tribe Chief Raoni Metuktire, whose home is the Amazon rainforest, spoke with reporter Nermeen Shaikh:

> [translated] Today there are many things happening in Brazil. In the previous government it wasn't like this, it wasn't so bad. Now the Bolsonaro government is authorizing deforestation, he's authorizing the entrance of wild cat miners and loggers and mining companies into indigenous territories. This is bad because it will destroy everything. It will destroy the forest. Destroy the Amazon. It will be bad for us in the future. This is what I defend. I don't defend standing virgin forests just for me—no, I'm thinking of the future, our grandchildren, and great-grandchildren living in peace in this forest so what Bolsonaro is doing is very bad for me.[16]

Chief Raoni Metuktire's statement resounds with the fact that home isn't property-line demarcation and territory delineated into neatly defended dividing lines; rather, home is "being *with* a world" with myriad participant members depending on one another for sustenance and safety.[17] Destroy one member, one family, one species, and a chain reaction occurs.

"As human beings we inhabit an ineluctably material world. We live our everyday lives surrounded by and immersed in matter. We ourselves are composed of matter. We experience restlessness and intransigence even as we reconfigure and consume it."[18] Translation and mutation in reunion. "Worlds whose coexistence creates, experiences, invents, declines, sometimes as a composition, sometimes as simple copresence."[19] As the boundaries between self and the world loosen, resonances link nerve endings so it becomes difficult to understand where a body ends and where another body begins. This sequence from Will Alexander's poem "Concerning the Henbane Bird" gets at the spontaneous phase changes of experience, and honors shape-shifting identity:

> I am a storm obscured by vigorous wastes
> & acids
> descending
> to 'streams'
> & 'lakes'
> & 'seas'
>
> as 'compressible liquid'
> as 'solvent'
> as 'ionising agent'
> but, perhaps
> I am 'lavender'
> 'camphor'
> as flowing diamond through smoke
> unlike the cobalt traced as eclectic rigidity . . .[20]

Terminology is echoed. Representations are mirrored. Socially and culturally and also biologically, bodies harmonize with another. Each instantiation is mimicked, reproduced as collective flattery and also individualized as personal glamour. Life forms seem to enjoy becoming like and also flaunt difference. Social and cultural identity is active and ripples. Expressions remake the world with each utterance. As Francis Ponge has written, "Every word has many habits and powers; one must always conserve and employ them all."[21]

> Lucidity, everyone breathes
> everyone's breath fills the air
> the air is breath is breathing
>
> The personhood
> of the swamps and bowers,
> dales and steppes calls our attention

We want to bond with cockroaches, rats and hippopotami,
in the very least extend the invitation of mutual autonomy, mutual
     recognition

Mutual affection with musk oxen, water buffalo, ponies, donkeys,
mules, tapirs, gazelles, little horn, big horn, pronghorn, antelope
     antelope and their cultural traditions earth would be off with
the losses

Bison, blue wildebeest, dik-dik, eland, gerenuk, red deer, reindeer,
key deer, elk, moose deer, mule deer in ecotones across field and
forest your secrets are glowing is an understatement, written language may mute the qualities of being into symbols, we apologize
perpetually for the discrepancy[22]

The onset of the Anthropocene and the epic die-out of floral and fauna species is exacerbated by the resistance humans have in committing to a shared, collective sentient life on the planet. Solitary human life isn't possible—humans cannot survive the death of participatory sentience. Life is biodiverse. Entire species go extinct on a daily basis, and the death toll is accelerating. The knowledge of living on the planet is being lost with each death of a plant and its lineage, each animal and its deep knowledge of connection and place. Plants have fine-tuned social, cultural, and historical knowledge as do animals and minerals. "Conceiving matter as possessing its own mode of self-transformation, self-organization, and directedness, and thus no longer as simply passive or inert, disturbs the conventional sense that agents are exclusively humans who possess the cognitive abilities . . . to master nature.[23]

The flooding continued for another day
Polemical aversions *ecology favors anarchism*
Buckled bloodied history margin stratum deep Earth
A new stretch of the pipeline
Was constructed
It immediately failed
Spilling oil into aquifers
And damaging sacred lands
We collapse in a meadow
We gaze at Mars and other sparkling off-world regions
Five senses, the participatory public
Cognition, emotion, will, desire, purpose, intention, and belief
All conventional attributes of the traditional liberal humanist subject

The right to happiness

The right to food and shelter

For humans animals?

For other than human persons?

Flora and fauna?

Communicating

They we us pledge to be proactive

They we us pledge to attend to suffering[24]

The reckless disturbance of others, both living and dead, has led to this existential condition. I was thinking about how fossil fuels are ancestral remains of members of the earthly community who perished millions of years ago. In an effort to monopolize energy resources, drilling desecrates their graves, a violation. What is extracted is the bodily dead who absorbed the sun. Exactly at the time that the resting places of our dead relatives were procured as resource, emissions began to pollute the atmosphere. Communal memory is being burned.

NOTES

Thanks to Metta Sáma and the Center for Women Writers at Salem College, North Carolina, for giving me the space to vocalize these thoughts in an earlier iteration.

1. The human body, which contains about 10_{13} cells, routinely harbors about 10_{14} bacteria (Charles Patrick Davis, "Normal Flora," in *Medical Microbiology*, 4th ed., ed. Samuel Baron [Galveston: University of Texas Medical Branch at Galveston, 1996], https://www.ncbi.nlm.nih.gov/books/NBK7617/). There are also micro-animals that live symbiotically on and within human bodies.

2. Peter J. Turnbaugh, Ruth E. Ley, Micah Hamady, Claire M. Fraser-Liggett, Rob Knight, and Jeffrey I. Gordon, "The Human Microbiome Project," *Nature* 449 (18 October 2007): 804–10.

3. Brenda Iijima, "Sensitive Histories," unpublished manuscript.

4. Emanuele Coccia, *The Life of Plants: A Metaphysics of Mixture* (Meford, Mass.: Polity Press, 2019), 8. Coccia writes that "Autotrophy—the name given to this Midas-like power of nutrition, the one that allows plants to transform into nourishment everything they touch and everything there is—is not just a radical form of alimentary autonomy; it is above all the capacity that plants have to transform the solar energy dispersed into the universe into a living body, [to transform] the deformed, disparate matter of the world into a coherent, well-ordered, and unified reality."

5. "Thus, it was demonstrated in the Microbiome Project (National Institute of Health Research) that inside our body there are about 8,000,000 genes, out of which only 22,000 are those of the human genome. In other words, bonafide human genes account only for less than 1 percent of the whole genetic information we carry with us. The other more than 99 percent of the genetic information pertains to the microbes forming our microbiome," write Peter Greenlaw and Marco Ruggiero (*Your Third Brain: The Revolutionary New Discovery to Achieve Optimum Health* [Centennial, Colo.: Extraordinary Wellness Publication, 2015], 61).

6. Scott F. Gilbert, "Holobiont by Birth: Multilineage Individuals as the Concretion of Cooperative Processes," in *Arts of Living on a Damaged Planet: Ghosts and Monsters of the An-*

thropocene, ed. Anna Tsing, Heather Swanson, Elaine Gan, and Nils Bubandt (Minneapolis: University of Minnesota Press, 2017), 73. Lynn Margulis and René Fester are credited with the naming of this characteristic of symbiotic coexistence.

7. Armonía Somers, *The Naked Woman*, trans. Kit Maude (New York: Feminist Press, 2018), 87.

8. Anne Pringle, "Establishing New Worlds: The Lichens of Petersham," in *Arts of Living on a Damaged Planet: Ghosts and Monsters of the Anthropocene*, ed. Anna Tsing, Heather Swanson, Elaine Gan, and Nils Bubandt (Minneapolis: University of Minnesota Press, 2017), 157.

9. Romain P. Boisseau, David Vogel, and Audrey Dussutour, "Habitation in Non-Neural Organisms: Evidence from Slime Molds," *Proceedings of the Royal Society* 283, no. 1829 (27 April 2016), https://royalsocietypublishing.org/doi/10.1098/rspb.2016.0446.

10. Eleanor Rosch, introduction to *The Embodied Mind, Cognitive Science, and Human Experience*, revised edition, by Francisco J. Varela, Evan Thompson, and Eleanor Rosch (Cambridge, Mass.: MIT Press, 1991, 2016).

11. See Rinaldo Walcott's reading of Sylvia Wynter's "The Pope Must Have Been Drunk," in "Genres of Human: Multiculturalism, Cosmo-politics, and the Caribbean Basin" in *Sylvia Wynter on Being Human as Praxis*, ed. Katherine McKittrick (Durham, N.C.: Duke University, 2015), 190.

12. Walcott, "Genres of Human," 190.

13. Sylvia Winter, qtd. in Sylvia Winter and Katherine McKittrick, "Unparalled Catastrophe for Our Species? Or, to Give Humanness a Different Future: Conversations," in *Sylvia Wynter on Being Human as Praxis*, ed. Katherine McKittrick (Durham, N.C.: Duke University, 2015), 57.

14. Angel Dominguez, *Black Lavender Milk* (Timeless Infinite Light, 2015), 83.

15. Eduardo Viveiros de Castro and Déborah Danowski, "Humans and Terrans in the Gaia War," in *A World of Many Worlds*, ed. Marisol de la Cadena and Mario Blaser (Durham, N.C.: Duke University Press, 2018), 175.

16. "Meet Brazil's Indigenous Leader Attacked by Bolsonaro at U.N. over Efforts to Preserve the Amazon," *Democracy Now!* 24 September 2019, https://www.democracynow.org/2019/9/24/un_climate_summit_indigenous_leader_barred.

17. Vinciane Despret, *What Would Animals Say If We Asked the Right Questions?*, trans. Brett Buchanan (Minneapolis: University of Minnesota Press, 2016), 166.

18. Diana Coole and Samantha Frost, *New Materialisms: Ontology, Agency, and Politics* (Durham, N.C.: Duke University Press, 2010), 1.

19. Despret, *What Would Animals Say If We Asked the Right Questions?*, 166.

20. In Will Alexander, *The Combustion Cycle*, forthcoming from Roof Books.

21. Francis Ponge, *Pratiques d'ecriture, ou, L'inachevement perpetuel*, trans. François Rouan (Paris: Hermann, 1984).

22. Iijima, "Sensitive Histories."

23. Coole and Frost, introduction to *New Materialisms: Ontology, Agency, and Politics*, 10.

24. Iijima, "Sensitive Histories."

Acknowledgments
and Credits

This project was completed with generous assistance from Dorinda G. Dallmeyer, the Eugene P. Odum School of Ecology, the University of Georgia Office of Sustainability, and the Willson Center for Humanities and Arts.

Writing about the environment first appeared in *The Georgia Review*'s pages under editor Stanley Lindbergh and continues today with the support of editor Gerald Maa. It became a focus under Stephen Corey, who was editor in chief during the time most of these pieces appeared and who provided the original impetus for this collection. Corey's curatorial choices and editorial touch inform much of the work here. We're grateful for his service to the magazine and to the environment.

Contributors

DOUGLAS CARLSON is an assistant editor at *The Georgia Review* and the author of three nonfiction titles, most recently a biography of artist/naturalist Roger Tory Peterson. Prior to joining the *Review*'s staff in 2007, he was visiting writer-in-residence at Concordia College in Moorhead, Minnesota. He has served in editorial or advisory capacities for *Ascent* magazine, White Pine Press, New Rivers Press, and the UGA Press faculty editorial board.

SOHAM PATEL joined *The Georgia Review* in 2018 and works as an assistant editor while also managing the book review section. The author of four chapbooks of poetry and two full-length collections, Patel is a Kundiman fellow and a poetry editor at *Fence*.

SUSANNE PAOLA ANTONETTA's forthcoming books are *Entangled Objects: A Novel in Quantum Parts*, *The Terrible Unlikelihood of Our Being Here*, and *The Devil's Castle*. She is the author of *Make Me a Mother*, *Curious Atoms: A History with Physics*, *Body Toxic*, *A Mind Apart*, a novella, and four books of poetry. Her awards include a *New York Times* Notable Book, an American Book Award, a *Library Journal* Best Science book of the year, an Oprah Bookshelf listing, and a Pushcart Prize. She lives in Bellingham, Washington. For more, go to susantonetta.com.

JEROME BUMP, professor emeritus at the University of Texas at Austin, writes about the role of the humanities in the current pandemic and climate change crises on his website, jfabump.com, and in traditional print venues.

SUSAN CERULEAN is a writer, naturalist, and activist based in Tallahassee and Indian Pass, Florida. Her memoir *I Have Been Assigned the Single Bird*, a Wormslow Foundation Nature Book, was published in 2020 by the University of Georgia Press. Other books include *Coming To Pass: Coastal Islands in a Gulf of Change* and *Tracking Desire: A Journey after Swallow-tailed Kites*, both also from UGA Press.

ALISON HAWTHORNE DEMING is the author of five books of poetry and five books of nonfiction, with *A Woven World: On Fashion, Fishermen, and the Sardine Dress*, a project supported by a Guggenheim Fellowship, out in 2021 from Counterpoint Press. She is Regents Professor at the University of Arizona.

ELIZABETH DODD's most recent books are *Horizon's Lens* and *Dear America: Letters of Hope, Habitat, Defiance, and Democracy*, coedited with Simmons Buntin and Derek Sheffield. She is nonfiction editor at Terrain.org.

CAMILLE T. DUNGY is the author of four collections of poetry, most recently *Trophic Cascade*, winner of the Colorado Book Award, and the essay collection *Guidebook to Relative Strangers: Journeys into Race, Motherhood, and History*, a finalist for the National Book Critics Circle Award. She has edited three anthologies, including *Black Nature: Four Centuries of African American Nature Poetry*. Her honors include Guggenheim and NEW Fellowships and an American Book Award. She lives in Colorado with her husband and daughter, where she is a University Distinguished Professor at Colorado State University.

LOUISE ERDRICH is the author of seventeen novels as well as volumes of poetry, children's books, short stories, and a memoir of early motherhood. Her novel *The Round House* won the National Book Award for Fiction. *The Plague of Doves* won the Anisfeld-Wolf Book Award and was a finalist for the Pulitzer Prize, and her debut novel, *Love Medicine*, as well as her novel, *LaRose*, were winners of the National Book Critics Circle Award. Erdrich has received the Library of Congress Prize in American Fiction, the PEN/Saul Bellow Award for Achievement in American Fiction, and the Dayton Literary Peace Prize. She lives in Minnesota and is the owner of Birchbark Books, a small independent bookstore.

ROBERT FINCH is the author of eight collections of essays, coeditor of *The Norton Book of Nature Writing*, and recipient of a Guggenheim Fellowship. He lives on Cape Cod.

DAVID GESSNER is the author of eleven books that blend a love of nature, humor, memoir, and environmentalism, including *Leave It as It Is: A Journey through Theodore Roosevelt's American Wilderness*. Gessner teaches at the University of North Carolina Wilmington, where he is also the founder and editor in chief of the literary magazine *Ecotone*.

RAQUEL GUTIÉRREZ is an essayist, arts critic and writer, and poet. Raquel lives in Tucson, having just completed MFAs in poetry and nonfiction from the University of Arizona. A 2017 recipient of the Creative Capital Andy Warhol Foundation Arts Writers Grant, Raquel also runs the tiny press Econo Textual Objects (established 2014), which publishes intimate works by QTPOC poets. Raquel's first book of prose,

Brown Neon, will be published by Coffee House Press in 2021; and Gutiérrez's first book of poetry, *Southwest Reconstruction*, will be published by Noemi Press in 2022.

EMILY HIESTAND is a writer, designer, gardener, and the communications director for the MIT School of Humanities, Arts, and Social Sciences. She is the author of three books and a contributor to *Home Ground: Language for an American Landscape* and *The Norton Book of Nature Writing*. Her literary honors include a National Poetry Series Award, a Whiting Award, and a National Magazine Award for Essays and Criticism.

J. D. HO has an MFA from the Michener Center at the University of Texas at Austin. Ho's poems and essays have appeared in *North American Review*, *Ninth Letter*, *Crab Orchard Review*, and other journals. Other work can be found at jdho.weebly.com.

BARBARA HURD is the author of *Listening to the Savage: River Notes and Half-Heard Melodies*, *Tidal Rhythms* (with photographer Stephen Strom), *Walking the Wrack Line*, *Entering the Stone*, and *Stirring the Mud* (2001). The recipient of Guggenheim and NEA Fellowships, winner of the Sierra Club's National Nature Writing Award, four Pushcart Prizes, and five Maryland State Arts Council Awards, she teaches in the MFA in Writing Program at the Vermont College of Fine Arts. For more, go to www.barbara hurd.com.

BRENDA IIJIMA's involvements occur at the intersections and mutations of poetry, research movement, visual arts, floral and faunal consciousness, and ecological sociology. Her current work focuses on missing persons and submerged histories, extinction, and other-than-human modes of expression. A developing project involves choreography and vocalization centered on Fort Massachusetts, in North Adams, Massachusetts. She is the author of seven full-length collections of poetry and numerous chapbooks and artist's books. Her most recent book, *Remembering Animals*, was published by Nightboat Books in 2016. She is also the editor of *the eco language reader*. Iijima is the editor of Portable Press at Yo-Yo Labs (http://yoyolabs.com/).

JAMES KILGO (1941–2002) wrote extensively about nature and the landscape and our connections to them. His books include *Daughter of My People*, *Deep Enough for Ivorybills*, and *Colors of Africa*.

SYDNEY LEA, a former Pulitzer finalist, founded and for thirteen years edited *New England Review*. His twentieth book, and thirteenth collection of poems, *Here*, appeared from Four Way Books, NYC, in 2019. In spring of 2020, Vermont's Green Writers Press published *Seen from All Sides: Lyric and Everyday Life*, his collected newspaper columns from his years (2011–15) as Vermont poet laureate. With former Vermont cartoonist laureate James Kochalka, he produced a mock-epic graphic poem, *The Exquisite Triumph of Wormboy*.

BARRY LOPEZ (1945–2020) published more than a dozen works of fiction and nonfiction, including *Horizon* (2019). His *Of Wolves and Men* (1978) won the John Burroughs Medal for nature writing, and *Arctic Dreams* (1986) won the National Book Award. His short story collection, *Outside*, appeared in 2015. He was elected to the American Academy of Arts and Letters in 2020.

ANDREW MENARD is the author of *Learning from Thoreau* and *Sight Unseen: How Fremont's First Expedition Changed the American Landscape*. His most recent essays and articles have appeared in *Antioch Review*, *The Georgia Review*, and the *New England Quarterly*.

JASON MOLESKY is a PhD candidate in American literature and the environmental humanities at Princeton University. He has been a resident fellow at the Blue Mountain Center and a maintenance assistant in an underground coal mine. He holds an MFA from the University of Mississippi, where he was a John and Renee Grisham Fellow in creative writing. His work can be found at jasonmolesky.com.

GARY PAUL NABHAN is a Franciscan brother and political agro-ecologist who has been honored with a MacArthur Foundation "genius" fellowship and a Lannan Literary Fellowship. He lives and keeps an orchard in Patagonia, Arizona. Follow him at www.garynabhan.com.

NICK NEELY holds an MA in literature and the environment from the University of Nevada, Reno, and MFAs in nonfiction and poetry from Hunter College and Columbia University. His first book, *Coast Range*, was a finalist for the John Burroughs Medal for natural history writing. His new book, *Alta California*, details his twelve-week trek to retrace the first overland Spanish expedition through California. In the fall of 2020, he taught at Eastern Oregon University in La Grande and in EOU's low-residency MFA program with a concentration in Wilderness, Ecology, and Community.

AIMEE NEZHUKUMATATHIL is the author of a collection of illustrated nature essays, *World of Wonders: In Praise of Fireflies, Whale Sharks, and Other Astonishments*. She is also the author of four books of poetry, most recently, *Oceanic*, winner of the Mississippi Institute of Arts and Letters Award. She is professor of English and creative writing in the University of Mississippi's MFA program and was recently named a 2020 Guggenheim Fellow in poetry.

ANN PANCAKE is a native of West Virginia. She's published two short story collections, *Given Ground* and *Me and My Daddy Listen to Bob Marley*, and a novel, *Strange as This Weather Has Been*, which was one of *Kirkus Review*'s Top Ten Fiction Books of the year, won the Appalachian Book of the Year, and was a finalist for the Orion Book Award and the Washington State Book Award. She has also received a Whiting

Award, an NEA grant, Pushcart and Bakeless Prizes, and induction into the Fellowship of Southern Writers. She teaches at West Virginia University.

ROBIN PATTEN is a naturalist, writer, and teacher. Her work focuses on the natural world and the relationship between people and place, exploring where nature and culture meet. Her essays and articles have appeared in the UK *Guardian's* Country Diary column, *Camas: The Nature of the West, Montana Outdoors*, and the *Mindful Word*. Her "Carcass Chronicle" was the winner of the 2019 John Burroughs Nature Essay Award.

CRAIG SANTOS PEREZ is an indigenous Chamoru author from the Pacific Island of Guam. He is the author of five books of poetry and the coeditor of five anthologies. He is a professor of creative writing in the English department at the University of Hawai'i, Manoa.

CATHERINE REID is the author of several works of nonfiction—*The Landscapes of Anne of Green Gables, Falling into Place: An Intimate Geography of Home*, and *Coyote: Seeking the Hunter in Our Midst*. A creative writing fellow at such places as the American Antiquarian Society in Worcester, Massachusetts, and the Virginia Center for the Creative Arts, she is also a recipient of individual artist awards from the North Carolina Arts Council and the National Endowment for the Arts.

JULIE RIDDLE is the author of *The Solace of Stones: Finding a Way through Wilderness*. Her essay "Shadow Animals" appeared in *The Georgia Review* and received a Special Mention in *The Pushcart Prize XXXIX: Best of the Small Presses*. She is an editor for the journals *Brevity* and *Rock & Sling*.

SCOTT RUSSELL SANDERS is the author of more than twenty books of fiction and nonfiction, including *Hunting for Hope, A Conservationist Manifesto*, and *A Private History of Awe*. His most recent book is *The Way of Imagination*, a reflection on healing and renewal in a time of social and environmental upheaval. He is a Distinguished Professor Emeritus of English at Indiana University and a fellow of the American Academy of Arts and Sciences. He and his wife, Ruth, a biochemist, have reared two children in their hometown of Bloomington, Indiana.

REG SANER (1931–2021) was a longtime westerner and mountaineer whose writing centered on the terrain of the American West. His poetry collection *Climbing into the Roots* received the first Walt Whitman Award in 1975. Over his long career, his poetry and prose appeared in more than 150 journals and 60 anthologies.

LAURET EDITH SAVOY is a woman of African American, Euro-American, and Indigenous ancestry whose work explores how the nation's still-unfolding history has marked the land and this society. Her book *Trace: Memory, History, Race, and the*

American Landscape won the American Book Award from the Before Columbus Foundation and the ASLE Creative Writing Award; it was also a finalist for PEN American and other honors. Her books also include *The Colors of Nature: Culture, Identity, and the Natural World* and *Bedrock: Writers on the Wonders of Geology.* Savoy is the David B. Truman Professor of Environmental Studies at Mount Holyoke College and an Andrew Carnegie Fellow.

DAWNE SHAND grew up in Alabama's Black Belt and attended Selma's public schools during their first two decades of integration. Since then, she has lived and worked in Nice, London, and Boston. She sits on the board of the Massachusetts Women's Political Caucus and managed a congressional campaign in 2020. Her work has appeared in the *The Georgia Review, Kenyon Review, Scalawag,* and *Southern Cultures.*

SEAN P. SMITH is an academic interested in coloniality, tourism development, and the environment. His narrative nonfiction includes essays in *The Sun* and *Guernica* and "The Slow and Tender Death of Cockroaches" in *The Georgia Review,* which was awarded the 2017 John Burroughs Nature Essay Award.

TYRONE WILLIAMS teaches literature and theory at Xavier University in Cincinnati, Ohio. He is the author of several chapbooks and six books of poetry, most recently *As Iz, Howell,* and *Adventures of Pi.* A limited-edition art project, *Trump l'oeil,* was published by Hostile Books in 2017. In 2019, he coedited the anthology *Inciting Poetics* with Jeanne Heuving.